Italian Gardens

Georgina Masson

Italian Gardens

With an introduction by
Margherita Azzi Visentini

GARDEN • ART • PRESS

To Sue and Geoffrey Jellicoe, who first started me
on my exploration of Italian gardens, and to the owners of the gardens,
whose care has preserved this wonderful heritage.

Publisher's note: Factual statements about the gardens — such as their condition, their ownership or whether they are open to the public — were correct when first published in 1961, and may since have changed.

The publisher wishes to thank the American Academy in Rome for having graciously granted permission to reproduce those photographs taken by Georgina Masson and for supplying the scans.

© Antique Collectors' Club 2011
© American Academy in Rome for the photographs by Georgina Masson
© Margherita Azzi Visentini for the introduction
© The photographers for their images (see photo credits, p. 351)

The introduction by Professor Margherita Azzi Visentini has been translated by Catherine Bolton.

First published by Thames and Hudson Ltd. 1961
Revised edition Antique Collectors' Club 1987
Reprinted 1987
Reprinted 1989
New edition Garden Art Press (an imprint of ACC Publishing Group) 2011

ISBN 978-1-870673-57-0

British Library CIP Data

Masson, Georgina
Italian Gardens.
1. Gardens-Italy-History
2. Gardens-Italian-History
I. Title
712'.6'0945 SB466

Printed in Italy for the Antique Collectors' Club Ltd, Woodbridge
Suffolk IP12 4SD, UK
www.antiquecollectorsclub.com
This book is composed in Requiem.
Printed on Gardamat 150g by Cartiere del Garda
on the presses of Petruzzi Stampa, Città di Castello (Perugia)

FRONTISPIECE: A TUSCAN HILLSIDE NEAR FIESOLE

Contents

Foreword

To us today, who are accustomed to regard a garden as the normal adjunct of a country house or cottage, and as part and parcel of a town with any pretensions to civic pride, it is very difficult to understand what the rediscovery of the joys of country life and the pleasure in gardens represented for the Italians of the Renaissance.

Gardens had, of course, existed during the Middle Ages, probably in Italy on a far larger scale than is generally supposed, and both there and in France they provided the setting for romances of courtly love. Nevertheless, for the most part these medieval gardens were simply small enclosures, relegated by the exigencies of the times to the cloister and such sheltered space as was available within the walls of castles and cities.

Petrarch was the first man of modern times to envisage a garden as the proper setting for a poet or a man of learning, as it had been in the ancient world. He was the precursor of the humanist movement of the next century, of that band of ardent spirits whose study of the *humanae literae* – classical learning, literature and history – in fifteenth-century Florence gave the movement its name, and made their city the cradle of the Renaissance.

These humanists' aim was to recapture the spirit of the ancient world, with its ideals of beauty and knowledge perfected in the 'complete man' of the Renaissance, a balanced product of thought and action. This concept of balance and symmetry they also applied to architecture and to garden design, as their reading of the classical authors had revealed to them the part that gardens and the open air had played in the lives of the philosophers, poets and great men of antiquity. So Plato's teaching in the tree-planted gymnasium of the Academy in Athens inspired the members of Cosimo de' Medici's Platonic Academy to hold their gatherings in his villa at Careggi, just as the writings of Vitruvius, Varro and Pliny provided the sources for Early Renaissance villa and garden design.

By the sixteenth century the influence of the Renaissance had spread to the rest of Europe, and classical culture had come to be regarded as so universal a heritage that a French country gentleman like Michel de Montaigne could say that Roman history was more familiar to him than that of France, that he knew more about the plan of the Capitol than the Louvre, and the Tiber better than the Seine. For men of his stamp a journey to Italy was an essential part of their lives and a sight of the famous Renaissance villas and the gardens formed as integral a part of their itinerary as the classical monuments themselves. Italians and foreigners alike regarded these villas and gardens as contemporary re-creations of those of ancient Rome, indeed the architects who designed them had spent infinite pains in studying the monuments of antiquity, and this attitude was reflected in the drawings and prints of Rome that were then being executed in increasing numbers. Artists like Du Pérac and Lafrery, Van Heemskerk, Francisco d'Hollanda and Laurus included views of famous gardens like the Cortile del Belvedere, Villa Madama and Villa d'Este in their sketch-books and collections of prints portraying the ruins of classical Rome. It is significant that many of these artists were foreigners, whose work was designed to fulfil the demand for knowledge about the Roman monuments that the Renaissance had awakened in their patrons and compatriots, and the inclusion of views of the gardens in this context is an indication of the interest that they inspired as modern interpretations of the classical tradition. There is little doubt that these views also served as a means of diffusion for knowledge of Italian Renaissance garden design throughout Europe. In France at least we know that one of the artists had a direct personal influence on garden design – upon his return from Rome in 1582 Du Pérac was appointed 'Grand Architect du Roy' and gave instructions to the Royal gardener, Claude Mollet, for the layout of Saint-Germain-en-Laye for Henry IV and of Anet and other gardens belonging to the Duc d'Aumale. France had been the first country to respond to the fascination of the Italian garden; as early as 1495 Charles VIII had brought back a Neapolitan gardener – Pacello da Mercogliano – from his Italian campaign, and during the first half of the following century Primaticcio and Serlio had made notable contributions to the gardens of Fontainebleau.

A hundred years later the leadership in garden design passed from Italy to France, where the genius of Le Nôtre evolved the style that made the French garden supreme. But the ground had been prepared for Le Nôtre by the work of Du Cerceau and above all Jacques Mollet and his son Claude, whose gardens of the latter half of the sixteenth century and the first part of the seventeenth had drawn their inspiration from Italy. As Monsieur Fouquier pointed out in *L'Art des Jardins* it was only as the seventeenth century advanced that French gardens became 'an enlarged and amplified expression of the Roman garden, modified and interpreted by the French character' and, like so many other aspects of French culture during the reign of Louis XIV, a model for the rest of Europe.

It is to these two factors that the Italian garden owes its immense importance. Both by direct contact and later through the influence of the French gardens, it provided the basis of all modern European garden design, from the Renaissance to the advent of the English landscape style in the eighteenth century – though the inspiration of even this revolutionary movement can be traced to the Italian scene. In attempting to describe the Italian gardens of the Renaissance and in tracing their origins, it became increasingly clear to me that, in the eyes of their creators at least, they were the replicas of the gardens of classical times, and that it was not possible to understand their architects' intentions without some study of the gardens of ancient Rome. Therefore in the first chapter I have attempted a brief survey of various types of Roman gardens and the part they played in the life of the times.

What seem to have been strangely little studied are the classical architectural sources that were available to the Renaissance garden architects and were examined and measured by them as an essential basis for their own work. In a book of this kind these can be only cursorily dealt with, though there is a vast mass of material in existence in the form of contemporary drawings and letters that might well cast more light on this fascinating aspect of Italian Renaissance garden design. The same applies to the planting of Renaissance and Baroque gardens, where flowers played a far larger part than is generally supposed, as even the brief lists at the end of this book indicate.

Finally, it was with some surprise that I discovered, during the sixteen years of residence and travel in Italy that have gone towards the making of this book, that several notable gardens exist which appear to have escaped the notice at least of foreign students of Italian garden design. In actual fact this is really not so surprising as it first appears because Italy is at one and the same time perhaps the best and least known of European countries. When the beaten track is left behind one finds many unexpected treasures, and I am sure that my own 'discoveries' in the way of gardens have nowhere near exhausted Italy's riches in this respect. Further exploration of Northern Italy would almost certainly extend the number of gardens that I have, by good fortune, been able to add to the list of those which have already attracted the interest of garden enthusiasts. My thanks are due to the Italian friends who first introduced me to Il Bozzolo, Villa Sommi Picenardi, Castel Balduino and Villa Rizzardi. No guide exists to the gardens of the Marche, and it was a thirty-year-old article in the *Rassegna Marchigiana* that first led me to explore the gardens of this little-known province and to discover the enchanting Giardino Buonaccorsi and those of Pesaro and Ancona. I am sure that not only these remoter regions but even the environs of Rome may still have surprises in store – like that which I experienced when I first saw the superb parterres of Villa Ruspoli at Vignanello; I had often before passed its walls without suspecting what lay on the other side. No one has as yet made a really exhaustive catalogue of the gardens of Italy, and I hope that perhaps this book may provide the stimulus for its undertaking before it is too late, as gardens are more vulnerable than any other form of art to the twin menaces of vandalism and neglect.

I would like to express my gratitude to the owners, who so kindly allowed me to photograph their gardens and in many cases provided me with interesting information about them; also my admiration for the sense of duty and the personal sacrifice of many of them, who in a world of rising costs have preserved this precious heritage for their own country and the garden lovers of all nations.

For the kind permission to photograph gardens belonging to the Italian State I am particularly grateful to Commendatore de Tomasso, Inspector-General of the Antichità and Belle Arti of the Ministry of Public Instruction, and to the regional directors of the same department all over Italy. To Commendatore Melgiovanni, Director-General of the Demanio, I owe not only permission to photograph but a perfect spring day spent in the gardens of Caprarola. My warmest thanks go to the Ente Provinciale di Turismo of Pesaro for all the assistance I received while photographing the delightful gardens of the Marche, and to Count Fago Golfarelli, head of the Foreign Press Section of the Italian State Tourist Organization, whose help and advice have smoothed the path of so many foreign writers in Italy.

For many of the illustrations I am indebted to the authorities of the Vatican Library and Museums, the Gabinetto Fotografico Nazionale of the Ministry of Public Instruction, the National Museum of Naples, the Photographic Archive of the Uffizi, the National Library of Florence, the Galleria di Arte Moderna of Milan, the Pinacoteca of Treviso, the Museo Civico of Padua, the Photographic Archive of the American Academy in Rome, Mr H. Acton, Dr E. Richter, Signor V. Messina, the National Museum of Stockholm, the Wallace Collection, London, and particularly to Mademoiselle Cornillot, Conservateur of the Museums of Besançon.

I would like to thank the many public bodies and friends who have kindly allowed me to photograph drawings and prints in their collections, especially the Gabinetto Nazionale delle Stampe, the Civica Raccolta delle Stampe Achille Bertarelli of Milan, the Biblioteca Angelica, the American Academy of Rome and particularly Mrs Longobardi, as well as Count and Countess Borromeo d'Adda and everyone at Senago.

I am also indebted to the late Duke of Sermoneta, Prince Ruspoli and Mr Frank and Donna Orietta Doria for allowing me to consult documents in their archives, and to Marchesa Stiozzi Ridolfi for her advice on Florentine gardens, to Dr Paola Lanzara Locatelli for her assistance in preparing the lists of plants, to Mr and Mrs Ballance for their help and advice on classical gardens and plans, and to Vittorio Mazza for making the prints.

Among the many other friends whose help and advice has contributed to this book I would like to thank Mrs Stordy who typed the manuscript, Mrs Vraneck who corrected the proofs, and, especially, Mr H. F. Clark of Edinburgh University.

G. M.

Villa Pamphilj, Rome, 1961

Introduction

Georgina Masson's book *Italian Gardens*, now republished in its entirety nearly 50 years after it first came out (1961), is a significant work in the historiography of this field for a number of reasons. It was the first postwar monograph to examine the subject as a whole, from antiquity to the 18th century and from the northern reaches of the peninsula to the south, also investigating areas that had previously been overlooked. Furthermore, it tackled the subject from different and often pioneering angles, with a scope that was lacking in previous works about Italian gardens, yet also without any pedantry. Indeed, it is devoid of footnotes, written in a fluent and engaging style with passages that border on the colloquial, and has a large selection of beautiful illustrations, including many full-page photographs taken and printed by Masson herself. (Unfortunately, however, it did not include any plans or sections, which critics have long insisted are necessary and that were easily available at the time, a serious oversight that the publisher of this new edition has wisely strived to remedy.)

Thus, at first glance the book appears to be more of an elegant popular volume than an essay for experts, although its bibliography and documentary appendix attest to the author's extensive study of publications and the archival research on which the book is based. As a result, contemporary critics did not give the work the kind of consideration it deserved, although it gained a number of admirers, including David Coffin. Yet later studies have confirmed and investigated some of the ideas and the critical insight that the author offered quite nonchalantly, seemingly unconcerned with providing the appropriate coordinates.

Consequently, *Italian Gardens* emerges as a hybrid work that is halfway between tradition and innovation, a cross between an elegant coffee-table book and a scientific work, as it delightfully conveys a profound message that is topical even today. In short, it is a book that is hard to put down.

Unsurprisingly, the author herself is an intriguing transitional figure. A woman without specific educational qualifications, she was a well-read, curious and passionate autodidact, with a rare sense of enthusiasm and communicativeness, who started out as a journalist but turned to the history of architecture and the art of gardens. She eventually became so knowledgeable that by the 1970s she rivalled academicians and made an original contribution to her specific field of study – flowers in the Roman gardens of the 16th and 17th centuries – thanks to the experience she gained in the field, her patient and intelligent study of published sources, supplemented by groundbreaking archival research, and enormous determination.

The book, written in English (the Italian translation was published simultaneously), is the work of a foreigner. It thus joins the time-honoured literary genre – surprising and full of information – of the testimony of travellers, from the classic works of Michel de Montaigne, John Evelyn and Charles De Brosses (Masson constantly refers to these invaluable works) to later systematic ones by authors such as the Americans Charles Platt and Edith Wharton, and the Englishmen Inigo Triggs and Geoffrey Jellicoe. At the same time, however, it is also the work of an extraordinary insider, given that our author lived in

Italy uninterruptedly for 16 years and her great familiarity with the sites she describes here reveals aspects usually overlooked by the occasional or hasty visitor.

The interest of international historiography in Italian gardens, and particularly those of the late Renaissance and Baroque villas of Lazio and Tuscany, whose gardens constitute an essential element (it has long been said that a villa without a garden is not a villa), goes back to the early 19th century. This interest was dictated by the intention to reintroduce a logical bond between buildings and gardens that the landscape garden had broken, although some complexes – from Rome's Villa Madama to the Villa d'Este in Tivoli – continued to garner attention due to the fact that, over the years, they were always described in guidebooks and reproduced in collections of views, just like the monuments of antiquity, and were thus visited and appreciated.

For example, in their high-flown publication in folio, *Choix des plus célèbres maisons de campagne de Rome et de ses environs* (first printed in Paris in 1809 and reissued in a revised and expanded version in 1824), Napoleon's architects Charles Percier and Pierre-François Léonard Fontaine presented the surveys of an array of aristocratic residences around Rome. With respect to the villas' actual condition, however, the authors corrected and completed the illustrations for reasons that are unclear. In this work, they explained that "the large gardens of Italy present the variety and picturesqueness of modern gardens, but without any of their childish simplicity. They are arranged regularly around the residence and extend from it in an artistically devised progression, so that they blend into their rural surroundings".[1] The inspiration came from Ippolito Pindemonte and the work that, in 1792, opened the lively debate on the landscape garden promoted by Melchiorre Cesarotti at the Padua academy. Pindemonte warned against indiscriminate use of the landscape garden, which in his opinion did not lend itself to all settings but required particularly broad and naturally rolling terrains, unlike the ancient but equally valid traditional formal Italian garden, which could also be created on smaller and more level sites.[2]

The suggestions of Percier and Fontaine were promptly embraced by John Claudius Loudon. In his *Encyclopaedia of Gardening*, printed in London in 1834 (the first edition dates to 1822), he agreed that the "country seats of Italians . . . are arranged so as to produce the best effect; and advantage of the nature of the site has been taken with admirable skill. The regularity of the gardens is, as it were, an accompanying decoration and support to the architecture. The architecture, sculpture, and gardens of these villas are often designed by the same hand, and concur in the general effect to produce perfect harmony".[3]

A short time later, at country houses such as Trentham, Chatsworth and Bowood, to name only a few, formal flowerbeds replaced the rolling lawns designed by Capability Brown and extending right to the front door. Charles Barry and Joseph Paxton were among the main advocates of the return to form in Victorian gardens, and the sloping terraces of Shrubland Park, along with the architectural gardens of Sydenham, are significant examples. In order to justify these choices, several scholars studied the origins of the formal garden in the British Isles, discussed by Reginald Blomfield in *The Formal Garden in England* (1892) and Inigo Triggs

1. "[L] es jardins d'Italie présentent la variété et le pittoresque des jardins modernes, sans avoir rien de leur puérile simplicité. Ils sont plantés régulièrement autour de l'habitation, et c'est toujours par une progression artistement ménagée qu'en s'éloignant d'elle, ils se lient avec la nature agreste du pays." C. PERCIER, P. F. L. FONTAINE, *Choix des plus célèbres maisons de campagne de Rome et de ses environs*, Paris 1824, p. 3, and M. AZZI VISENTINI, "Considerazioni sulla fortuna del 'landscape garden' in Italia", in P. CAPONE, P. LANZARA and M. VENTURI FERRIOLO (eds.), *Pensare il giardino*, Milan 1992, pp. 83–88, pp. 85–87n.
2. I. PINDEMONTE, "Dissertazione su i giardini

inglesi e sul merito in ciò dell'Italia" (1792), in *Operette di varj autori intorno ai giardini inglesi ossia moderni*, Verona 1817, pp. 17–64, now in M. AZZI VISENTINI (ed.), *L'arte dei giardini. Scritti teorici e pratici dal XIV al XIX secolo*, 2 vols., Milan 1999, Vol. I, pp. 155–78. Regarding the Italian debate on the new garden, pp. 22 ff.
3. J.C. LOUDON, *An Encyclopaedia of Gardening*, London 1834 (4th ed., 1st ed. 1822), p. 48; A.A. TAIT, "Loudon and the return to formality", in E.B. MACDOUGALL (ed.), *John Claudius Loudon and the Early Nineteenth Century in Great Britain*, Washington, DC, 1980, pp. 59–76; M. AZZI VISENTINI, "Considerazioni sulla fortuna del 'landscape garden' in Italia", pp. 86, 88n.

in *Formal Gardens in England and Scotland* (1902), just as Colen Campbell had done in the early 18th century in his *Vitruvius Britannicus* (comprising several volumes, the first of which was published in 1715). Campbell reproduced classic English buildings, juxtaposing them – with nationalistic pride – against those depicted in the plates from Palladio's *I Quattro Libri dell'Architettura* (*The Four Books of Architecture*), for which Giacomo Leoni oversaw the first unabridged edition in Italian, French and English, published in instalments between 1716 and 1720 (although the first one is backdated to 1715).

The works cited so far, written mainly by architects and landscape architects, focused above all on underscoring the architectural structure and layout of the individual villas and their gardens, whose compositional principles were suggested as examples for modern landscape architects to follow. However, when art history was first established as a modern discipline in Germany in the mid-18th century, there also emerged growing interest in the history of the Italian garden per se, its development and its relationship with other artistic expressions, i.e. architecture, sculpture and painting.

One of the pioneers in this field was the Berlin scholar Wilhelm Petrus Tuckermann, whose *Die Gartenkunst der italienischen Renaissance-Zeit* (1884) developed the concepts that Jacob Burckhardt had set forth in *Der Cicerone* (1855; *The Cicerone*, 1873) and *Die Kultur der Renaissance in Italien* (1860; *The Civilization of the Renaissance in Italy*, 1878) and traced the history of the villa garden in Italy, examining the area around Rome, Tuscany, Genoa, the Lombard lakes (which were transformed into a botanical paradise following the introduction of exotic species in the 19th century) and Sicily. This work covers everything from ancient Rome to the revival of the Italian villa promoted by Karl Friedrich Schinkel in the early 19th century on the banks of the Havel in Potsdam and elsewhere. It also examines factors that influenced its evolution, from the orographic conformation of the land to climate, which varies widely from one end of Italy to the other. Tuckermann cited the Cortile del Belvedere and the Villa Madama, both in Rome, as the starting point for a new way of conceiving the relationship not only between interior and exterior and between buildings and gardens in the villa setting, but also between the villa and the landscape, positing an argument that, later taken up by James Pray in his article "The Italian Garden" published in 1900[4], was unanimously accepted. The book is illustrated with about 60 figures, views and plans taken from old prints or created specifically for the work, as well as several photographs.

It was soon followed by the works of German art historians Bernhard Patzak on the Imperial Villa in Pesaro (1908) and Walter Friedländer on the Casino of Pius IV at the Vatican (1912). Alongside the works of Domenico Gnoli (1905), Thomas Ashby (1908) and Christian Huelsen (1917) about the collections of ancient statues in the gardens of Rome, these publications immediately became key references.[5]

---

4. J.S. PRAY, "The Italian Garden", in *American Architect and Building News*, no. 67 (February and March), 1900; M. AZZI VISENTINI, "The Italian Garden in America, 1860s–1920s", in I.B. JAFFE (ed.), *The Italian Presence in American Art 1860–1920*, New York– Rome 1992, pp. 240–265; M. AZZI VISENTINI, "La fortuna del giardino italiano negli Stati Uniti tra Otto e Novecento", in *Notiziario dell'Associazione Amici dei Musei e dei Monumenti di Bassano del Grappa*", January 2001, pp. 21–46.
5. B. PATZAK, *Die Renaissance und Barock Villen in Italien*, vol. III, *Die Villa Imperiale in Pesaro*, Leipzig 1908; W. FRIEDLÄNDER, *Das Casino Pius des Vierten*, *Kunstgeschichtliche Forschungen*, III, Leipzig 1912; D. GNOLI, "Il giardino e l'antiquario del Cardinal Cesi", in *Mitteilungen des kaiserlich deutschen archaeologischen*

Instituts: Roemische Abteilung, 20, 1905, pp. 267–76; T. ASHBY, "The Villa d'Este at Tivoli and the Collection of Classical Sculptures which it Contained", in *Archaeologia*, 61, 1908, n. 1, pp. 219–255; C. HUELSEN, "Römische Antikengärten des XVI Jahrhunderts", in *Abhandlungen der Heidelberger Akademie der Wissenschaften: Philosophische-Historische Klasse*, 1917, n. 4. The Imperial Villa in Pesaro was the subject of in-depth critical examination starting with the publication of P. Mancini's monograph in 1843. Before Patzak, it was discussed by the Germans H. Thode (1888), F. Seitz (1905) and G. Gronau (1906); cf. M. AZZI VISENTINI, *La villa in Italia. Quattrocento e Cinquecento*, Milan 1995, with a current bibliography, pp. 342–358; see p. 349 for the Imperial Villa.

In the late 19th century, the appeal of the Italian villa garden also spread across the Atlantic, thanks to New York artist Charles A. Platt, who took his paintbrushes and camera with him when he accompanied his brother William to Italy in 1886, in the hopes of dissuading him from the landscaping style he had embraced at Frederick Law Olmsted's firm. Platt would return to Italy several times. In 1893 he wrote several articles on the subject that were collected in *Italian Gardens*, which was published the following year. This work examines the gardens of 19 villas (15 in Rome and the Roman countryside, the Neapolitan villa of Portici, Florence's Boboli Gardens and the garden of the Villa di Castello, and the Giusti Garden in Verona) and is illustrated with Platt's own sketches and photographs, accompanied by texts that are little more than long captions. Platt's goal was to demonstrate the "evident harmony of arrangement between the house and surrounding landscape". Platt noted that the most striking element was "the design as a whole, including gardens, terraces, groves, and their necessary surroundings and embellishments, it being clear that no one of these component parts was ever considered independently, the architect of the house being also the architect of the garden and the rest of the villa".[6]

Uninterested in the history and meaning of the works (he ignored both ancient and recent literature on the subject, citing only the book by Percier and Fontaine, albeit criticizing them for the disparity between the published plates and the actual condition of the buildings and gardens), he was instead fascinated by the current condition of the gardens, so full of plants and flowers that "[t]he impression . . . is one of great tangle, and of a profusion of growing things", and by their layout. Describing the Villa Aldobrandini in Frascati, he wrote that "[t]he arrangement of the terraces at the back and front of the house is very remarkable, and admirably adapted to the formation of the land", noting that "[t]he most interesting feature of this villa is the manner in which the hill at the back of the house has been cut out and formed into an architectural semi-circle with fountains", although "[t]he actual architecture of the moment is very bad, the niches and grottoes being filled with colossal and grotesque figures". Platt evidently did not understand the true historical and artistic significance of the extraordinary invention of the *teatro d'acqua*. Designed by Giacomo della Porta and completed after his death by Giovanni Fontana and Orazio Olivieri, the water theatre was a fundamental part of both the iconographic programme and the architectural project of the complex. Tuckermann was of a far different opinion, considering the water theatre a "fantastic Baroque architecture". With regard to the villas of Frascati, Tuckermann also noted that "there is a surprising number of new and previously unknown tasks that the architect and sculptor must handle in the architecture and sculptural decoration of these villas, whose most significant and distinctive element is the perfection achieved with waterworks, whose beauty consists of the contrast between the power of nature harnessed by art, and vegetation, trees, oaks and chestnuts, which are allowed to grow freely".[7]

The popularity of the Italian garden, which Platt helped introduce to the United States, sparked a more profound critical debate, for which his brief and unsatisfactory "notes" – as some of Platt's contemporaries disparagingly referred to his works – were inadequate, as they were effectively little more than long captions for the illustrations.

6. C. A. PLATT, "Formal Gardening in Italy, in *Harper's New Monthly Magazine*, 87, 1893, 518; C. A. PLATT, *Italian Gardens*, New York 1894, reprint, with an overview by Keith N. Morgan and additional plates by Charles A. Platt, London 1993, pp. 15–16. Regarding the critical success of the Italian garden in the United States at the turn of the 20th century, see M. AZZI VISENTINI, "The Italian Garden in America, 1890s–1920s", in I. JAFFE (ed.), *The Italian Presence in American Art 1860–1920*, New York–Rome 1992, pp. 240–265; M. AZZI VISENTINI, "La fortuna del giardino italiano negli Stati Uniti tra Otto e Novecento, in *Notiziario dell'Associazione Amici dei Musei e dei Monumenti di Bassano del Grappa*, January 2001, pp. 21–46.
7. C. A. PLATT, *Italian Gardens*, p. 59; W. P. TUCKERMANN, *Die Gartenkunst der italienischen Renaissance-Zeit*, Berlin 1884, pp. 121, 124.

It was at this point that the American writer Edith Wharton entered the scene. She was commissioned to write a series of articles on Italian gardens, illustrated with watercolours by the famous painter Maxfield Parrish, photographs and drawings (but no plans, which the publisher decided not to include, despite Wharton's opinion to the contrary), and collected in her famous *Italian Villas and their Gardens*, published in 1904. For Wharton, the essence of the Italian garden involved the combination of three elements: rocks, water and evergreens. Furthermore, she felt that the relationship with the landscape was fundamental, whereas she considered flowers – on which Platt, instead, greatly insisted – to be mere accessories. Wharton examined more than 80 villa gardens (as well as the garden of the Palazzo Giusti in Verona and the Padua Botanical Garden), ranging geographically from the Brenta Riviera to the Ligurian coast and from the Brianza district to the Roman countryside, chronologically from the early Renaissance to the late Baroque, and typologically from royal residences to modest country houses. The book's extensive bibliography and broad array of quotations denote direct knowledge of the main sources, from ancient descriptions and views to travel journals and the modern works of Burckhardt, Gurlitt and Tuckermann, the latter considered the main reference available on the subject at the time. Like Platt, Wharton felt that the Villa Lante at Bagnaia surpassed "in beauty, in preservation, and in the quality of garden-magic, all the other great pleasure-houses of Italy". She enthusiastically examined every detail to conclude that at the Villa Lante "one sees one of the earliest examples of the inclusion of the woodlands in the garden-scheme".[8]

Wharton also lavished great attention on the Villa Gamberaia, which "stands nobly on a ridge overlooking the village of Settignano and the wide-spread valley of the Arno", a "distinctly Tuscan" residence of the early 17th century that, "even in Italy, where small and irregular pieces of ground were so often utilized with marvellous skill, . . . was probably the most perfect example of the art of producing a great effect on a small scale".[9] The Villa Gamberaia became famous after it was purchased in 1896 by the Romanian Princess Jeanne Ghyka, who promptly commenced the period restoration of the gardens, with a *parterre d'eau* set in an architectural frame created with cypresses, composed of a series of arcades arranged in a semicircle with a view of the landscape (although Wharton was critical of the restoration work). Ghyka transformed it into a rendezvous for the large and prestigious British and American expatriate community that had settled around Florence in the early 20th century and had effectively brought the Italian garden back from England and the United States, where the art had been redeveloped, to revive it in its land of origin.

The British architect Cecil Pinsent was a sensitive interpreter of this return to form. Starting in 1907, he and Geoffrey Scott were involved in work to renovate the house and create the formal garden at I Tatti, in Settignano, the property that Bernard Berenson had purchased in 1905. In 1911 Pinsent and Scott were commissioned to build the villa and design the garden of Le Balze in Fiesole, owned by the American Charles Augustus Strong,

8. She noted, "It was undoubtedly from the Italian park of the Renaissance that Le Nôtre learned the use of the woodlands as an adjunct to the garden; but in France these parks had for the most part to be planted, whereas in Italy the garden-architect could use the natural woodland, which was usually hilly, and the effects thus produced were far more varied and interesting than those possible in the flat artificial parks of France". E. WHARTON, *Italian Villas and their Gardens*, New York 1904, reprint, with new introductory notes by Arthur Ross, Henry Hope Reed and Thomas S. Hayes, New York 1988, pp. 132,

139, 42 (in order of quotation). Wharton, who designed her own house and garden of The Mount in Lenox, Massachusetts, with her niece Beatrix Farrand Johnson, her travel companion in Italy and one of the first professional landscape architects in the United States, focused on Italian gardens after the return to form in America.
9. E. WHARTON, *Italian Villas and their Gardens*, p. 41. The Villa Gamberaia, which had just been restored by its new owner, had already been discussed by Gabriele D'Annunzio (*Taccuini*, ms., 1896 and 1898), C.W. EARLE (1899) and Janet Ross in *Florentine Villas* (1901).

and in 1915 they restored the garden of the Villa Medici, also in Fiesole, which was the residence of Lady Sybil Cutting.[10]

Wharton unsuccessfully tried to convince her publisher that the book should include plans and perspective views of the main villas and their gardens, as they were essential in order to understand their layout and, furthermore, were also available in part. The prints made between the 16th and 18th centuries by Dupérac, Falda, Venturini, Barrière and others had been supplemented in the 19th century not only by the plates published by Percier and Fontaine, but also by several important collections of surveys of monuments – including villas and gardens – in Rome and Genoa, drawn up respectively by Paul-Marie Letarouilly, a pupil of Percier and Fontaine, and Martin-Pierre Gauthier.[11] Thus, Triggs returned to this subject and in *The Art of Garden Design in Italy*, published in 1906, he examined about 30 villas, illustrating his descriptions with numerous lovely photographs, most taken by Aubrey Le Blond specifically for the book, period drawings and views, paintings and engravings. They were complemented by plans, some of which were specially drawn up by the author, while others were taken from previous works. Indeed, Triggs noted that "gardens can hardly be judged by pictures and photographs alone, and it is essential that these should be supplemented by a survey drawn to scale; it is hardly possible to form a correct judgment unless the two are consulted together, and without the information which a plan gives it is difficult to grasp the conditions under which the designer worked".[12]

Marie Louise Gothein made excellent use of this material and in her brilliant overview of the history of gardens, which took her ten years to write and whose first edition was published in 1914, she devoted a detailed chapter to the Italian garden of the Renaissance and Baroque periods in central Italy, particularly in Rome and Lazio. Reiterating Tuckermann, she acknowledged that it originated with the Cortile del Belvedere and the Villa Madama, whose style was anticipated in the Medici villas of the 15th century, from Careggi to Poggio a Caiano, and whose epigone was the Roman Villa Albani. However, she did not overlook examples from northern Italy, from the Palazzo Doria in Genoa to the Villa Brenzone at San Vigilio, on Lake Garda, whose garden had been described a short time earlier by Henry Thode.[13] She also cited Isola Bella on Lake Maggiore, the Padua Botanical Garden and the Palace of Te in Mantua, which had already been discussed extensively by critics. Gothein dealt adroitly with both ancient and contemporary publications as well as literary and iconographic sources, from the letter in which Giovanni Rucellai described the garden of the Villa Quaracchi to *Hypnerotomachia Poliphili*, and from the plans and views by Falda and Venturini to the surveys of Percier and Fontaine as well as those of Letarouilly, Triggs and others. As she noted in the preface to the first edition, she was well aware that, in order to understand a garden fully, one must commence with a critical study of the sources, because "what you actually see with your eyes has to be 'restored', like a corrupt text, into its original context, and then compared with traditions and ancient examples".[14]

10. Cutting and Scott were married a short time later. About Pinsent and the Villa Gamberaia, see M. FANTONI, H. FLORES and J. PFORDRECHER (eds.), *Cecil Pinsent and His Gardens in Tuscany*, Florence 1996; P. OSMOND (ed.), "Villa Gamberaia. Sources and Interpretations", in *Studies in the History of Gardens & Designed Landscapes*, vol. 22, 2002, n. 1.

11. P.M. LETAROUILLY, *Les Edifices de Rome Moderne*, Liège 1849; P.M. GAUTHIER, *Les plus beaux édifices de la ville de Gêne et de ses environs*, 2 vols., Paris, 1818–32. See also G. STERN, *Piante, elevazioni e spaccati degli edifici della Villa di Giulio III*, Rome 1784; *Recueil d'architecture dessiné et mesuré en Italie dans les années 1791, 92 et 93*, Paris 1821.

12. H. I. TRIGGS, *The Art of Garden Design in Italy*, London, New York and Bombay 1906 (reprinted by Schiffer Publishing, Atglen, PA, USA, 2007), Preface, p. v. The book on the gardens of Italian villas followed the work by this author on formal gardens in Great Britain: H. I. TRIGGS, *Formal Gardens in England and Scotland*, London 1902.

13. H. THODE, *Somnii Explanatio. Traumbilder vom Gardasee in S. Vigilio*, Berlin 1909.

14. M.L. GOTHEIN, *Geschichte der Gartenkunst*, 2 vols., Jena 1914; English edition: *A History of Garden Art*, New York 1928 and later editions.

The American Academy in Rome, founded in 1894, encourages its fellows who are aspiring landscape architects (a profession that acquired a specific profile in the United States when the American Society of Landscape Architects was founded in 1899)[15] to survey Italian villas and gardens, which critics have long praised for the perfect relationship of buildings, gardens and the landscape. One of the first works of this type is the series of plans, elevations and sections of Isola Bella, on Lake Maggiore, completed by Edgar Williams between 1910 and 1912, and published in the July 1914 issue of *Landscape Architecture*. Thus, over the years an extraordinary graphic corpus was compiled. Brought to the attention of critics only recently, it constitutes valuable documentation and, in some cases, provides the sole testimony of complexes that were later extensively reorganized or no longer exist.[16]

The Frenchman Georges Gromort, who taught at the Académie des Beaux-Arts in Paris, also drew up surveys of Italian gardens and published them in a pretentious folio work titled *Jardins d'Italie*. Originally put out in two volumes in 1922 and then reprinted, updated and supplemented by a third volume in 1931, this work has more than 200 plates with views of Roman, Tuscan and northern Italian villas, and over 30 plans, some made specifically for the publication and others taken from existing materials. They are accompanied by detailed descriptions.

The successful *Italian Gardens of the Renaissance* was published in London in 1925 and features surveys of the gardens of 26 Italian villas, mainly in Lazio and Tuscany (Siena, Lucca and Florence), but also around Genoa, Verona, Milan and the Lombard lakes; most of them were sketched on site. The book features drawings and photographs by John C. Shepherd and plans and texts by Geoffrey A. Jellicoe, students at the Architectural Association of London. They were executed during a study trip in 1923-24 in order to write a thesis on Italian villas and gardens, a subject suggested by their supervisor because, as Jellicoe recalled many years later, "no surveys had been made since the somewhat crude drawings of the French architects Percier and Fontaine a hundred years previously". The authors concur that the Villa Madama represents "the greatest conception of a country pleasure house of the Renaissance, and even though never completed, [it] exercised a wider influence than any other on garden design."[17] Masson dedicated *Italian Gardens* to Geoffrey Jellicoe and his wife Susan, as they were the ones who introduced her to the gardens of Italian villas.

The Italian contributions of this period lavished attention on the formal aspect of gardens, but they also offered historical and artistic considerations, documented by countless illustrations and literary documentation on the subject. Notable contributions include the articles by Luigi Dami that were published starting in 1914, followed by his book *Il giardino italiano* (1924), which has 351 illustrations, mainly views of plans from period engravings, drawings, paintings, woodcuts and photographs, slightly more than 20 pages of text and 508 entries under "bibliography and iconography", i.e. "itinerary guides, engravings from the 17th and 18th centuries, topographic plans, art and gardening treatises, travel memoirs and informative magazine articles" referenced in 42 footnotes or short thematic entries. Even today, this material is an invaluable source of information for understanding the architectural, symbolic and practical role of the garden as part of a villa or palace.

---

15. See W.H. TISHLER, *American Landscape Architecture. Designers and Places*, Washington, D.C. 1989.

16. Regarding these surveys, in some cases the only ones still existing for famous gardens, see V. CAZZATO, *Ville e giardini italiani. I disegni di architetti e paesaggisti dell'American Academy in Rome*, Rome 2004.

17. G. GROMORT, *Jardins d'Italie*, vols. I and II, Paris 1922, vol. III, Paris 1931; J.C. SHEPHERD and G.A. JELLICOE, *Italian Gardens of the Renaissance*, London 1925,

4th edition, London 1986 (the source of the quotations), Foreword and p. 12. The author would later discuss the events surrounding the preparation of the volume and the limitations of some of the surveys: G.A. JELLICOE, "An Italian Study, being an analysis of Italian Gardens of the Renaissance Published in 1925", in G.A. JELLICOE, *The Studies of a Landscape Designer over 80 Years*, 4 vols., vol. I, Woodbridge, Suffolk 1993, pp. 61–157.

Dami's introduction provides an overview of the development of the Italian garden, through which we can glean, "in their various appearances and examples, the forms that arose between Florence and Rome in the 15th and 16th centuries to constitute the Italian art of the garden." According to Dami, the moment of transition between the Middle Ages and the Renaissance can be found in the Florentine villas in which the house and garden are connected by a portico or loggia and, in turn, are linked to the land and thus the landscape. Likewise, the starting point can be found in Bramante's Belvedere – about which Dami noted that "it is not actually a garden, or principally a garden, but something purer and more abstract, a deftly executed essay in architectural perspective" – and the Villa Madama, where "just as Bramante had shown him, [Raphael] exploited the resources and obstacles of the terrain. In terms of overall concept, however, he took a step back", at least as far as gardens are concerned. "He went to the trouble of cutting a lovely throne for his construction on the slope of Monte Mario; and there he magnificently set his queen, with the Tiber facing it, in a dominating view with the mountains behind it as a framing background view. Those who came after could not ignore this environmental connection, the 'placement' of the building in a sensitive part of the landscape, which thus subjugated the landscape and led it to participate and collaborate with the invention." Grottos, islands, labyrinths, fountains, statues and other elements were part of the furnishings of the gardens, with the vegetation – mainly trees and shrubs – that was selected and thus "planted in 'rows'" to form vegetal architectures. Indeed, "gardening was forgotten in this garden". Moreover, the author noted that "flowers are still popular . . . but are unimportant in the general composition of the garden, as they are too delicate and too widely scattered to be significant in the sweeping play of large elements". They "are collected in special enclosures that were often called 'secret gardens', removed from view by walls and tall hedges". Dami did not like the gardens of the northern Italian plains, particularly those of the Veneto villas, "whose main elements were, at most, a loggia, a few fountains, lemon houses, a few niche grottoes, small series of square flowerbeds, hedges, pergolas, kiosks and mazes. Displayed simply to the observer in a lacklustre language without any of the compositional vigour of Florence and Rome", albeit with a few exceptions such as the Villa Barbarigo a Valsanzibio, they present a "more prosaic or unsophisticated character".[18]

In addition to Giulio Fasolo, who in *Le ville del Vicentino* (1929) also illustrated statuary and gardens, Adolfo Callegari and Bruno Brunelli helped people discover the gardens of the Veneto villas – unappreciated by Dami – with their *Ville del Brenta e degli Euganei* (1931). The book is richly illustrated with photographs, a few plans and numerous outstanding period views, some of which are no longer available. The introduction, discussing various aspects of the Veneto villa and its use, is followed by a detailed examination of 31 villas. Callegari also curated the Veneto section at the seminal "Italian Garden Exhibition" organized at the Palazzo Vecchio in Florence in 1931 and he edited the chapter on it in the catalogue. With nationalistic pride, the exhibition asserted and confirmed Italy's leadership in the art of gardens, "a leadership in chronology, number and quality", according to the exhibition curator, Ugo Ojetti, who also illustrated the initiative's three objectives. First of all, it strived to "show a vast audience . . . the history – spanning two millennia – of the Italian garden, i.e. the symmetrical and architectural garden that is always attuned to the architecture of the villa . . . and repeats its balance, restraint and dignified serenity. Extending far from the façade of the house, through its avenues and flowerbeds, its trees and shrubs, its terraces and porticoes of masonry or greenery, and its grottoes, nymphaea and fountains, it maintains man's continuous and orderly and visible domination of nature". Thus, the goal of the exhibition was to "assert Italy's claim to the origins and most beautiful examples of this type of garden that, from England to North America and the Riviera, has once again triumphed over the romantic English garden and the artificial wild park". Lastly, it aimed to inspire those who created gardens "to find in our past the recommendations and models that must be modernized with good taste in order to adapt them to new needs".[19]

The British-American colony residing around Rome and Tuscany, which had contributed enormously to the knowledge and revival of the Italian garden, disbanded during the long and dramatic war years. Nevertheless, several important scientific contributions appeared in the early 1940s, from Mario Bafile's *Il giardino di Villa Madama* (1942), based on a careful study of the drawings by Raphael and his assistants, to John Coolidge's article about the Villa Giulia, which examines the complex in light of previously untapped documents (1943).[20]

During the difficult but inspiring reconstruction period, there was renewed interest in Italy's enormously rich but little-known artistic heritage, which was in poor condition and in which the country proudly sought its identity, particularly through the villas and their gardens. The post-war rediscovery of Italian villas and the awareness of the need for appropriate policies to protect and conserve them have traditionally been traced back to the famous photographic exhibition on the Veneto villas that was organized in Treviso in 1952 by Giuseppe Mazzotti, who was the director of the provincial Tourist Board at the time. The exhibition then travelled to a number of European cities and was brought to the United States, and by presenting this incomparable historic and artistic legacy it also revealed its pitiable state of decay. As a result, efforts were made to establish an institution responsible for preserving these villas and making them known: the Ente per le Ville Venete, now the Istituto Regionale per le Ville Venete, which was officially founded in 1958, followed by the Ente Ville Vesuviane in 1971. The Centro Internazionale di Studi di Architettura Andrea Palladio was also founded in Vicenza in 1958. The latter has played a fundamental role in critical research into the architecture of the Veneto as well as other regions, and particularly the heritage represented by these villas. In the meantime, in 1955 Italia Nostra, an association whose goal is to protect the historic, artistic and natural heritage of the peninsula, was established in Rome.

At the same time, and despite the fact that academia continued to take a somewhat wary view of a field that many considered fatuous, the subject of gardens was scientifically examined in chapters written by foreign and Italian scholars, including James Ackerman. His essay and book (published respectively in 1951 and 1954) discussed the Cortile del Belvedere as part of Bramante's project for the new Vatican of Julius II. There was also renewed interest in the Monsters of Bomarzo, re-examined in 1953 by Mario Praz in an article published in *Illustrazione italiana*. An entire issue of *Quaderni dell'Istituto di Storia dell'Architettura* was devoted to Bomarzo in 1955, with essays by Arnaldo Bruschi, Leonardo Benevolo, Paolo Portoghesi and

---

18. L. DAMI, *Il giardino italiano*, Milan 1924, pp. 7, 14, 20, 15, 25, 21 (in order of quotation).

19. See the catalogue titled *Mostra del giardino italiano*, Florence 1931; U. OJETTI, "La mostra fiorentina del giardino italiano", in *Il giardino fiorito*, April 1931, pp. 29–30; V. CAZZATO, "Firenze 1931: la consacrazione del 'primato italiano' dell'arte dei giardini", in A. TAGLIOLINI and M. VENTURI FERRIOLO (eds.), *Giardino: idea, natura, realtà*, Milan 1987, pp. 77–108; M. AZZI VISENTINI, "Storia dei giardini: osservazioni in margine al recente sviluppo di questa disciplina in Italia", in L. PARACHINI and C.A. PISONI (eds.), *Storia e storie di giardini. Fortune e storia del giardino italiano e verbanese nel mondo*, Verbania 2003, pp. 45–86, on pp. 55–56.

20. M. BAFILE, *Il giardini di Villa Madama*, Roma 1942; J. COOLIDGE, "The Villa Giulia: A Study of Central Italian Architecture in the Mid-Sixteenth Century", in *The Art Bulletin*, XXV, 1943, pp. 177–225. In recent years archival research has made a vital contribution to our critical knowledge of Italy's heritage and, in particular, of its villas and their gardens. This is also confirmed by the discovery of a letter in which Raphael described his project for the Villa Madama, of which until the mid-1960s there was only indirect evidence, i.e. it was repeatedly cited by sixteenth-century sources. This letter has finally revealed the enormous attention that was paid to incorporating the complex into the site, becoming an essential part of it, and its intentional ties to classical models, underscored by the terminology that Raphael used. It has likewise corroborated the insight of scholars who had examined it previously, including Masson. P.H. FOSTER, "Raphael on the Villa Madama: The Text of a Lost Letter", in *Römisches Jahrbuch für Kunstgeschichte*, XI, 1967–68, pp. 307–12; R. LEFEVRE, "Su una lettera di Raffaello riguardante Villa Madama", in *Studi Romani*, XVII, 1969, pp. 425–37.

others; Maurizio Calvesi would return to this subject the following year. Bruschi discussed Bagnaia and the Villa Lante in the same magazine in 1956, the year that Carl Franck published his seminal work *Die Barockvillen in Frascati*, which for the first time considered the system of the 12 villas depicted in the view of ancient Tusculum and its environs drawn and engraved by Matthaeus Greuter in 1620.[21]

It was during these lively and stimulating years that Masson entered the scene, rather unobtrusively and virtually unnoticed at first. Information about the author before her thirty-year sojourn in Italy is sketchy and inaccurate. Georgina Masson was the pseudonym of Marion Johnson (although it is unclear if Johnson was her maiden or married name) and it was invented based on the name of one of her grandmothers. Known to her friends as Babs, she was a British citizen who was born in 1912 in Rawalpindi, Pakistan, the daughter of an officer in His Majesty's Army. Thanks to her father, she was able to attend the Royal School for the Daughters of Officers of the Army in Bath, of which she would long have fond memories and where she earned her only diploma. She lived in India, Egypt, Morocco, Algeria, China, Malaysia, Congo, France, Switzerland and the United States, evidently with her husband, a British officer from whom she later separated. After spending some time in Paris, where she had a job in public relations (or, more probably, military espionage, although information is vague), she moved to Rome around 1943. In the Italian capital, it seems that she was employed, either directly or through her husband or partner, by the Foreign Office of the Fifth Army until approximately 1947. Vivacious, sophisticated, extroverted and at ease with everyone, it seems that Masson was promptly accepted into the British intellectual circles in and around Rome (she also became a close friend of notable figures such as Hugh Honour, Iris Origo, Archibald Lyall, Elena Croce and, naturally, Sue and Geoffrey Jellicoe, to whom she dedicated this book) as well as those of the Roman aristocracy, developing a keen interest in the architecture of the residences in which she was received.

It was thanks to her contacts and her obvious passion for villas and gardens that, starting in the late 1940s and for more than 20 years, she was given the chance to live in a cottage that was originally built to be part of stables. The cottage was situated under the Palazzina Corsini, which was later incorporated into the park of the Villa Doria Pamphili on the Gianicolo in Rome. It was offered to her by its owners – also Masson's friends – for very low rent, and she transformed it into a cosy place to work and entertain friends. On the land bounded by a small rocky basin next to the house, Masson created an intriguing garden that boasted several rare botanical specimens she had found during her strolls through the park, including *Fritillaria obliqua* (one of the bulbous plants introduced to Europe from Turkey before 1581 and that, thanks to her, was also brought to the Royal Botanic Gardens, Kew, in London), alongside native species such as oleanders and plants grown from the seeds of fruit she ate, such as the lush avocado grove. The outcome was a one-of-a-kind ensemble that mirrored its creator's unique personality.[22]

In the late 1950s Masson began to study historic Italian villas and gardens on a professional level. However, her first article on the subject, "Four Palladian Villas", was actually published in *Country Life* in 1950 and two years later the magazine published another one, "Villa Barbaro, Maser". For *The Architectural Review*, to which she began to contribute regularly in 1951, she wrote an article entitled "Venetian Gardens" and reviewed the exhibition about Veneto villas curated by Mazzotti and later shown at the Royal Institute of British Architects in London; both articles were published in 1954. In 1955, she also published "Palladian Villas as Rural Centres" in the journal. This article marked the first investigation of a topic – that of the villa as the central complex of a farming estate – that Fausto Franco had merely mentioned in passing in 1936. Franco would return to this subject in 1956, and it would later be developed extensively, above all by agricultural and economic historians.[23] Furthermore, she also studied flowers in Italy's historic gardens, a subject in which, as already noted, she took a keen interest and to which she would return repeatedly, as we will see.

Her book *Italian Villas and Palaces* was published in 1959, followed two years later by *Italian Gardens*. Although these works are connected as far as their subjects are concerned, there are nevertheless significant differences between the two, as the latter reflects a far more complex and mature critical approach, based on a broad range of sources that the former — mainly descriptive — seems to ignore. *Italian Villas and Palaces* presents a selection of 95 palaces and villas built between the 15th and 18th centuries. They are classified by geographical location and are mainly in central and northern Italy, with a few examples from Naples and Sicily under Bourbon rule (the Royal Palaces in Naples and Caserta, the Palazzina Cinese in Palermo, and the Villa Valguarnera and the Villa Palagonia in Bagheria). Alongside the descriptions of these buildings and their interiors, the gardens are also mentioned briefly.

Italian Gardens is instead a work reflecting more mature critical interpretation. Masson roamed the peninsula inseparable from her Rolleiflex camera, which she first used in 1950 for her debut article. She managed to capture countless details that had never been reproduced before and showed great familiarity with the sites she described, ranging from the gardens of ancient Rome to the residences around Palermo during the Arab-Norman period, the Royal Palace at Caserta (in which she recognized French influence combined with Italy's great tradition) and on to the newly finished Villa San Remigio at Pallanza (which takes up the tradition of the Italian Renaissance and Baroque garden to a certain extent). She discovered entire areas and individual sites that were little known or had previously been completely overlooked, such as the gardens of the Marche and the parterres of the Ruspoli Castle in Vignanello, whose miraculous conservation she was the first to note.

21. Ackerman's article and book on the Cortile del Belvedere are more detailed examinations of the subject of his doctoral dissertation (New York University), which was one of the first in the United States on the construction of outdoor space. J. ACKERMAN, *The Cortile del Belvedere (1503–1585)*, Vatican City 1954; M. CALVESI, "Il Sacro Bosco di Bomarzo", in *Scritti di storia dell'arte in onore di Lionello Venturi*, vol. I, Rome 1956, pp. 369–402; D. COFFIN, *The Villa d'Este at Tivoli*, Princeton, N.J. 1960; A. CANTONI, *La Villa Lante di Bagnaia*, Milan 1961; C. LAMB, *Die Villa d'Este in Tivoli*, Munich 1966.
22. This eccentric and treasured garden, was immortalized in several photographs and was discussed by Marella Caracciolo (M. CARACCIOLO, "The Secret Garden of Marion Johnson / Il giardino segreto di Marion Johnson", in A. CAPODIFERRO and C. LAUF (eds.), *Georgina Masson 1912–1980. Selection from the Photographic Archive / Selezioni dall'Archivio Fotografico*, Milan 2003, pp. 70–75). Sadly, all trace of the garden was lost when the acquisition of the entire Villa Pamphili complex by the Italian government, a process commenced in 1958, went into effect in 1971. At that point, its management went to the State Property Office, which turned the area into a car park and depot. The most recent monograph about the villa does not even mention the English scholar and the 20 years she lived there (C. BENOCCI, *Villa Doria Pamphilj*, Rome 1996). Forced to leave her beloved cottage in 1971, Masson initially moved to Tuscany but then spent about eight years in the neighbourhood of the American Academy, back in "her" Gianicolo, one of her favourite haunts. In the area she would meet numerous friends who still

remember her fondly, from Paola Lanzara to John Van Sickle.
23. F. FRANCO, "Classicismo e funzionalità della villa palladiana, 'città piccola'", in *Atti del I° Congresso nazionale di storia dell'architettura* (1936), Rome 1938, pp. 6 ff.; F. FRANCO, "Piccola urbanistica della casa di villa palladiana", in *Venezia e l'Europa*, proceedings from the 18th International Congress of Art History, Venice 1956, pp. 595–98; see also the recent works by D. COLTRO, *La terra e l'uomo. Cultura materiale del mondo agricolo veneto*, Sommacampagna (Verona) 2006, and R. DEROSAS (ed.), *Villa. Siti e contesti*, Treviso 2006. Villas and gardens were unquestionably the main theme of Masson's works and she also discussed the gardens of Dumbarton Oaks, where she studied in 1966 (G. MASSON, *Dumbarton Oaks. A Guide to the Gardens*, Washington, D.C. 1968). Masson also wrote several successful biographies: *Frederick II of Hohenstaufen: A Life* (1957), *Queen Christina* (1968), *Courtesans of the Italian Renaissance* (1976) and *The Borgias* (1981). Some of her works were about the history of ancient Rome (*A Concise History of Republican Rome*, London 1973; *Ancient Rome: From Romulus to Augustus*, New York 1973). Her book titled *The Companion Guide to Rome* (London 1965 and later editions) was particularly successful. She also wrote *Fodor's Rome: A Companion Guide*, New York 1971. For a list of Masson's most important publications, their editions and translations into other languages, see A. CAPODIFERRO and C. LAUF, *Georgina Masson 1912–1980*, pp. 78–79, a catalogue for the exhibition held at the American Academy in Roma, to which Masson bequeathed her rich photo archives with thousands of photographs.

She had direct access to a myriad of sources – literary and iconographic, printed and manuscript, and well known, obscure or previously unpublished – and, in keeping with the slant she had chosen, she tossed off this information casually, as if carried away in a conversation.[24] By the same token, with a nonchalance verging towards snobbishness, she barely touched subjects that deserved far more in-depth treatment.

One example is her passing mention of the literary coteries in the gardens of Roman antiquities shortly before the tragic 1527 Sack, including that of Johannes Goritz (better known in Italy as Coricio), on the slopes of the Campidoglio, with a view of Trajan's Forum and a grotto dedicated to nymphs. His feasts were evoked in a nostalgic letter that Cardinal Jacopo Sadoleto wrote in 1529 from Carpentras, where he was posted at the time, and with whom Masson associated the amusing detail of a painting by Vincenzo Campi in the Galleria Doria. The topic, alluded to by Gnoli in the 1930s and mentioned in passing by Gustavo Giovannoni, whose monograph about Antonio da Sangallo the Younger reported a drawing depicting a portal of Goritz's garden, was later deservedly developed by David Coffin in his *Gardens and Gardening in Papal Rome* (1991). Likewise, in her essays from the 1970s, reprinted in *Fountains, Statues and Flowers. Studies in Italian Gardens of the Sixteenth and Seventeenth Centuries* (1993), Elisabeth B. MacDougall took an in-depth look at the reasons behind the artificial grotto dedicated to nymphs or other water gods.

To offer yet another example of Masson's approach, in discussing the transformations that had gradually taken place in the park of the Villa Doria Pamphili on the Gianicolo, Masson mentioned imaginative sketches of gardens, in both an Italian and "Anglo-Chinese" style, from an album in the Doria Pamphili Archives. They were attributed to a certain "Faragine di Bettini", the young protégé of a family member, the Apostolic Nuncio in Paris in the late 18th century, whom he then followed to Rome.[25] However, it would be pointless to look for this name – which was also misspelled – or many others, as there was no index of names in the *editio princeps* and the one in the 1966 edition is sorely incomplete. Twenty years later Minna Heimbürger Ravalli's monograph, *Disegni di giardini e opere minori di un artista del '700. Francesco Bettini* (1981), finally shed light on this highly eccentric figure who created a large collection of drawings, mainly of gardens, in three volumes entitled *Caos o Farragine* that are preserved in the Doria Pamphili Archives in Rome, along with other manuscripts, drawings and prints by Bettini. Fortunately, the thorough indices in this edition greatly facilitate consultation.

Indeed, Masson's book has a plethora of original insights that mention – or, rather, barely graze – unprecedented problems, which later studies would tackle with far greater scientific depth, applying the interdisciplinary approach that has characterized the astonishing development of garden history over the past several decades. These issues range from the relationship between art and nature, science and technique, to the meaning that the garden was intended to convey and thus its iconographic programme, entrusted chiefly to statuary; from the use of the garden to its transformations over time, including reconstruction and

---

24. As of the mid-19th century, photographs—often by the author of the work (as in the case of Platt and Masson) or under his or her supervision—became an essential part of writings about gardens. See CAPODIFERRO and LAUF, *Georgina Masson 1912–1980*. The literary and iconographic sources used by Masson include the woodcuts from *Hypnerotomachia Poliphili* (1499), the Roman drawings of Francisco de Hollanda and Pirro Ligorio's studies of Roman antiquities; prints of villas and gardens by G.B. FALDA, F. Venturini, M.A. Dal Re, V. Coronelli, G.F. Costa and others; paintings by Hubert Robert and Fragonard,

etc. For sources on Italian gardens, see M. AZZI VISENTINI, "Fonti per lo studio dei giardini", in M. CUNICO and D. LUCIANI (eds.), *Paradisi ritrovati. Esperienze e proposte per il governo del paesaggio e del giardino*, Milan 1991, pp. 15–22; M. AZZI VISENTINI, *La villa in Italia*, bibliography on pp. 342–58; *L'arte dei giardini. Scritti teorici e pratici dal XIV al XIX secolo*, M. Azzi Visentini (ed.), 2 vols., Milan 1999, and the cited bibliography.
25. G. GIOVANNONI, *Antonio da Sangallo il Giovane*, Rome undated (but documented as having been published in 1959), p. 26 (Uffizi drawing 989). For Bettini, see p. 223 of this book.

restoration, and the evolution of how it was perceived, which descriptions and views allow us to grasp; from the sources and documents that can be used for these studies to methodological problems,[26] and on to the use of vegetation over the centuries and the presence and role of flowers. In effect, in the latter area of research, about which Platt and Wharton had opposite opinions, Masson made an original contribution, paving the way for important works by MacDougall, Lucia Tongiorgi Tomasi, Claudia Lazzaro and Ada Segre.[27]

Furthermore, Masson was the first to note the novelty of the residences of some of the new papal families in Rome during the late Renaissance and Baroque periods, such as the Villa Borghese and the Villa Doria Pamphili in Rome, and the Villa Mondragone in Frascati, in which the leading role is actually played by the sprawling informal parks depicted in the contemporary paintings of Lorrain and Poussin. This notion has recently been developed by scholars such as Mirka Benes, Alberta Campitelli and Tracy Ehrlich. Similarly, she was the first to suggest the Roman models as a source of inspiration for the landscape garden, invented by William Kent (who studied in Rome), a topic that John Dixon Hunt would examine in his insightful *Gardens and Grove. The Italian Renaissance Garden in the English Imagination: 1600-1750* (1986).[28]

The culmination of work that took a full 16 years to complete, *Italian Gardens* was nevertheless also a springboard for its author, who was at the forefront in a moment of great vitality in the field of the historic garden, which was of interest not only in Italy but throughout the Western world. In fact, she was invited to the landmark conference titled "The Italian Garden", which David Coffin organized at Dumbarton Oaks in 1971 and through which this now mature discipline unquestionably achieved proper recognition. Masson was one of the four speakers, along with MacDougall, Eugenio Battisti and Lionello Puppi, but she was the only one who did not have an academic title. Nevertheless, she had already gained international acclaim as a scholar for all intents and purposes, thanks to the

---

26. Regarding the development of this discipline in recent decades, see J.D. HUNT (ed.), *Garden History. Issues, Approaches, Methods*, Washington, D.C. 1989; M. CONAN (ed.), *Perspectives on Garden Histories*, Washington D.C. 1999; M. BENES, "Italian and French Gardens. A Century of Historical Study (1900–2000)", in M. BENES and D. HARRIS (eds.), *Villas and Gardens in Early Modern Italy and France*, Cambridge, UK, 2001, pp. 1–16 (this treatment has a strong North American perspective); M. AZZI VISENTINI, *Storia dei giardini*.

27. Masson also attempted to reinstate the distribution of the plants in a flowerbed on the island of Citera described and illustrated in *Hypnero-tomachia Poliphili* (see pl. 33; discussed by W. HANSMANN, *Gartenkunst der Renais-sance und des Barock*, Cologne 1983, p. 19) and devoted a brief but detailed chapter of her book to "The Flowers of Italian Gardens" (pp. 279–92), a starting point for later studies of a topic investigated not only by Masson ("Italian Flower Connoisseurs", in *Apollo*, Sep-tember 1968, pp. 164–71; "Fiori quali pezzi da collezione nell'Italia del secolo XVII", in *Arte Illustrata*, III [1970], 30–33, pp. 100–109; see below note 33) but also by C. LAZZARO, *The Italian Renaissance Garden. From the Conventions of Planting, Design, and Ornament to the Grand Gardens of Sixteenth-Century Italy*, New Haven and London 1990; L. TONGIORGI TOMASI, "Il giardino, l'orto, il frutteto. Le scienze orticole in Toscana nei disegni, tempere e incisioni dal XVI al XVIII secolo", in

L. TONGIORGI TOMASI and A. TOSI, "*Flora e Pomona*". *L'orticoltura nei disegni e nelle incisioni dei secoli XVI-XIX*, exhibition catalogue, Florence 1990, pp. 5–29; E. B. MACDOUGALL; "A Cardinal's Bulb Garden: A "Giardino Segreto" at the Palazzo Barberini in Rome", in EAD., *Fountains, Statues, and Flowers. Studies in Italian Gardens of the Sixteenth and Seventeenth Centuries*, Wash-ington D.C. 1993, pp. 219–347; A. SEGRE, *Horticultural Traditions and the Emergence of the Flower Garden in Italy (1550–ca. 1650)*, D.Phil. thesis, University of York (UK), 1995; A. SEGRE, "Untan-gling the Knot: Garden Design in Francesco Colonna's 'Hypnerotoma-chia Poliphili'", in *World and Image*, 1998, pp. 82–107; L. TONGIORGI TOMASI and G.A. HIRSCHAUER, *The Flowering of Florence. Botanical Art for the Medici*, Washington, DC, 2002; M. ZALUM, *Passione e cultura dei fiori tra Firenze e Roma nel XVI e XVIII secolo*, Florence 2008. On this subject, see also the introductory essays by L. Tongiorgi Tomasi, A. Campitelli and M. Zalum in G.B. FERRARI, *Flora overo cultura di fiori*, facsimile of the 1638 edition, L. Tongiorgi Toma-si (ed.), Florence 2001, pp. IX–LV.

28. See M. BENES, "Pastoralism in the Roman Baroque Villa and in Claude Lorrain: Myth and Realities of the Roman Campagna", in BENES and HARRIS (eds.), *Villas*, pp. 88–113; T. EHRLICH, *Landscape and Identity in Early Modern Rome. Villa Culture at Frascati in the Borghese Era*, Cambridge (UK) 2002; A. CAMPITELLI, *Villa Borghese. Da Giardino del Principe a Parco del popolo*, Rome 2003.

fellowship she received in 1965 – one of the first fellows and the first woman to receive this award – at the newly established Department of the History of Landscape Architecture of the prestigious Washington Institute, which is part of Harvard University. Although some objections remained, they were not tied to her dignity as a scholar, but rather to the lingering preconception that while the study of the historic garden was important in the education of a landscape architect, it should nevertheless focus principally on the structural aspect of the work, which was best investigated by an architect, trained or in training.[29]

It was during the period between the publication of *Italian Villas and Palaces* (1959) and the Dumbarton Oaks conference that several book series, which would be fundamental for the knowledge of Italy's villas and gardens, were launched. These included the invaluable volumes of reproductions of ancient engraved views published in Milan by Edizioni Il Polifilo, the first of which was *Ville del Brenta nelle vedute di Vincenzo Coronelli e Gian Francesco Costa*, edited by Licisco Magagnato (1960). The "Ville d'Italia" series, published by the Milanese Edizioni SISAR (later transferred to Rusconi) and directed by Pier Fausto Bagatti Valsecchi, was launched in 1970 with *Le ville di Roma*, edited by Isa Belli Barsali. Coffin's pioneering monograph on the Villa d'Este in Tivoli was published in 1960, and Battisti's books *Rinascimento e barocco* and *L'antirinascimento* were published respectively in 1960 and 1962. Battisti overturned the traditional idealistic vision of a rational and "classic" cinquecento, revealing its irrational, troubling, esoteric and alchemical aspects – in other words, decidedly "anticlassic" elements – for which the garden proved to be an exceptional field of experimentation (e.g. Pratolino).[30]

Thus, the times were ripe to examine garden history from an appropriate pulpit, finally granting to a still vaguely outlined discipline its own identity and, above all, the scientific dignity that it had lacked until then. Nevertheless, few scholars were willing to contribute a report to the conference, given the widespread and ongoing prejudice towards this field. In the preface to the conference proceedings, Coffin noted that, after the long silence that had followed the 1931 exhibition, "the past decade, however, has seen a renewal of interest in the history of gardens, and recent efforts have been made to relate the Italian garden to other fields of scholarship. The literary historian of pastoral poetry, the scholar of landscape painting, and the architectural historian concerned with the villa realize that the garden is essential to their interests. Therefore, this may be the opportune moment to

---

29. Testimonials regarding the early history of scholarships in Landscape Studies at Dumbarton Oaks are interesting in this regard. They reveal and underscore the widespread dichotomy between the concept of the role of the garden architect, who looks to the past for his or her future works, and those who are instead involved in historical research per se. These considerations also extended to Masson, whom Michael Rapuano, Chair of the Garden Advisory Committee, considered "a very fine garden historian . . . but here again we are getting into the historical aspects in lieu of design. If Miss Masson could direct her studies somehow so that her work would generate an interest in design, then I think she would be worth considering". This passage is from a letter to Leon Zach dated 20 July 1965. Leon Zach File, Dumbarton Oaks, and E.B. MACDOUGALL; "Prelude: Landscape Studies, 1952–1972", in CONAN (ed.), *Perspectives*, pp. 17–26, and note 27 on p. 23. Regarding the wariness of architectural historians towards the history of landscape architecture in

America and elsewhere in the 1960s and early 1970s, see D. COFFIN, Preface, in D. COFFIN (ed.), *The Italian Garden*, First Dumbarton Oaks Colloquium on the History of Landscape Architecture, Washington, DC, 1972, pp. VII–VIII. See also COFFIN, *The Study*, p. 33; M. BENES, "Recent Developments and Perspectives in the Historiography of Italian Gardens", in CONAN, *Perspectives*, pp. 37–76; MACDOUGALL, "Prelude", pp. 23–24; M. AZZI VISENTINI, *Storia dei giardini*, pp. 61–62.

30. On the critical success of the Italian garden, see M. AZZI VISENTINI, *Storia dei giardini*. Battisti, a brilliant art historian with interdisciplinary interests, was the first to introduce writings on the history of the images of Warburg and work on Panofsky's iconographic studies to Italy. His above-mentioned works were republished in Milan in 1989 (Feltrinelli). See also E. BATTISTI, *Iconologia ed ecologia del giardino e del paesaggio*, G. Saccaro Del Buffa (ed.), Florence 2004.

reassess many of our previous assumptions and to reconsider the potentials of other methodologies for the history of the Italian garden".[31]

In short, the field was opening up to the interdisciplinary interests that Masson had heralded in *Italian Gardens*, whose "outstanding scholarship" Coffin would acknowledge years later, while noting that the work was "obscured by its popular presentation and lack of scholarly apparatus".[32] Each of the four speakers brought an original contribution in his or her specific field, opening up new perspectives for research. MacDougall, who had completed her doctoral dissertation, "The Villa Mattei and the Development of the Roman Garden Style", at Harvard two years earlier (1970), discussed the iconography of the sixteenth-century Roman garden, a topic that she would go on to develop in subsequent studies and at the meetings promoted by the Dumbarton Oaks programme in Garden and Landscape Studies, which she directed (1972-88).[33] Battisti investigated the relationship between art and nature, theory and practice, form and technique, and rationality and irrationality in the Renaissance garden, which he had discussed in the two works cited above. For the first time, Puppi probed the rich and complex problems tied to the gardens of the Veneto villas that Dami had summarily dismissed, and he would produce a significant series of studies[34]. Masson examined the role of flowers in the Italian garden, a subject in which she had long been interested and would subsequently continue to research, planning a monograph on the subject that was never published due to her death in 1980.[35]

The conference at Dumbarton Oaks, as we have already noted, inaugurated a new and astonishing stage in garden history, which over the following decades would emerge as an extraordinarily complex and intriguing discipline to which Masson made a decisive contribution.[36] Therefore, this new edition of her most important work is long overdue and, with the benefit of hindsight, it will allow everyone to appreciate the extraordinary insights that other scholars would go on to develop.

Margherita Azzi Visentini

---

31. D. COFFIN, *Preface*, p. VIII.

32. D. COFFIN, "The Study of the History of the Italian Garden until the First Dumbarton Oaks Colloquium", in CONAN, *Perspectives*, pp. 27—35, at p. 32.

33. E.B. MACDOUGALL, "'Ars Hor-tulorum': Sixteenth-Century Garden Iconography and Literary Theory in Italy", in COFFIN (ed.), *Italian Gardens*, pp. 37—57. By this scholar, see also other essays on the gardens of Rome in the 16th and 17th centuries, the fountains, the iconographic programme and more, published between 1972 and 1989 and later collected in MACDOUGALL, *Fountains*, with two important new contributions, one on the flowers from the Barberini garden cited above in note 27, and the seminal essay on the Venaria Reale outside Turin.

34. E. BATTISTI, "'Natura Artificiosa' to 'Natura Artificialis'", and L. PUPPI, "The Villa Garden of the Veneto from the Fifteenth to the Eighteenth Century", in COFFIN (ed.), *The Italian Garden*, pp. 37—59 and 81—114. Battisti's essay was republished in an Italian translation in BATTISTI, *Iconología*, pp. 3—50.

35. G. MASSON, "Italian Flower Collec-tors' Gardens in Seventeenth-Century Italy", in COFFIN (ed.), *The Italian Garden*, pp. 61—80. In the years that followed Masson continued her research on the subject at public and private archives and libraries in Rome (Vatican Archives and the Caetani Foundation) and Europe, particularly in Brussels and Prague. The results of her

work were to be collected in a monograph that the Architectural History Foundation had agreed to publish, but Masson passed away in 1980. The material she wrote, much of it complete, is now at the Caetani Foundation in Rome. Awarded the title of Official of the Order of Merit of the Italian Republic on 2 June 1967, Masson—who had cancer by this time—returned to England (which she referred to as "home") in 1978, following the death of her faithful and inseparable companion, the stray dog Willy. As a member of the Royal Society of Literature, she received a pension from the Royal Literary Fund. Assisted by the friend with whom she lived, the poet Kathleen Raine, she died there in 1980.

36. M. AZZI VISENTINI, "La fortuna cri-tica del giardino storico italiano negli Stati Uniti negli ultimi trentacinque anni", in *A 25 anni dalle Carte di Firenze: esperienze e prospettive*, proceedings from the conference (Villa Ghirlanda Silva, Cinisello Balsamo, 9—10 November 2006), L. Scazzosi and L. Pellissetti (eds.), Florence 2008, and EAD., "The gardens of the Veneto and Friul, thirty years of studies: state of the art, new critical perspectives and new methodological approaches", in M. CONAN (ed.), *Recent Issues in Italian Garden Studies: Sources, Methods and Theoretical Perspectives* (Washington, D.C., Dumbarton Oaks, 19—20 October 2007), in press.

Roman Gardens

I t was no mere chance that a crystal spring chattering in the shade of an oak tree provided the inspiration for what is probably the best-known and loved lyric in the Latin language. The music of Horace's *Fons Bandusiae* holds a special magic for the Mediterranean world whose scorching summer heat makes shade and water not only a favourite poetical theme, but also the necessary adjuncts of pleasure — especially of pleasure gardens, which since their earliest origins have in Italy always been associated with poetry and the arts.

When Horace wrote his poem this conception of a garden as a place of inspiration and repose was still quite new to the Roman world. Gardens in the practical sense of a *hortus* or enclosure for growing vegetables, pot herbs, fruit and probably a few flowers had, of course, existed for centuries and so had the concept of the sacred grove, dedicated to a god or goddess or surrounding a tomb, but the stern world of the early Republic with its cult of the ancient Roman virtues of austerity and frugality was little calculated to produce anything so ephemeral and non-utilitarian as pleasure gardens, and these only made their appearance towards the end of the second century B.C. when the influence of the Hellenistic world began to penetrate Roman society.

In Greece, as in Italy, springs and groves of trees had long been dedicated to the gods, and temples, especially of deities associated with nature or fertility, often had gardens attached to them. Most famous of these was the park dedicated to Artemis at Scillus, which Xenophon had laid out after his return from the Persian expedition; his military exploits had evidently not prevented him from admiring the fabulous gardens of the Oriental kings — the *pairidaeza* from which our own word paradise is derived. These great enclosures, filled with running water and planted with planes, aromatic shrubs and blossoming fruit trees — the haunt of animals and ornamental birds — were often divided into four to represent the regions of the earth — and used partly as pleasure gardens and partly for hunting. No doubt the memory of these Oriental parks inspired Xenophon's design for that of Artemis at Scillus, with its wooded game preserve and fruit trees symmetrically planted round the temple.

Through Xenophon's own writings and his friendship with Socrates the Persian gardens were, however, to exert a much further-reaching influence upon the future of gardens in Greece and indeed in all Europe in classical and modern times. Their place in the intellectual world was finally established when Plato began teaching in the tree-planted gymnasium of the Academy, thus creating the association between philosophy and gardens that was to outlive even the thousand years' existence of the School of Athens and to be revived by the humanists of the Italian Renaissance.

Where Plato led, successive generations of philosophers followed, and the gymnasia with their colonnaded palaestrae, that had originally been designed as shelters from the sun and rain where athletes could exercise, became the accepted places of philosophical instruction, surrounded by stately avenues and shady groves of trees. Like Plato himself, the later philosophers also owned gardens in which, as is evident even from the meagre accounts that have come down to us, there already existed some of the features which have been associated with classical gardens ever since. These were principally shrines dedicated to the Muses, which often took the form of a rocky grotto or nympheum watered by a fountain or spring; shady porticos, built in imitation of the palaestrae of the gymnasia but also used for the display of sculpture, and tree-lined walks where sages such as Aristotle paced to and fro while teaching their pupils, thus earning for themselves the name of peripatetics.

The curious plants that Alexander the Great's officers discovered on their Oriental campaigns had a great influence upon the study of botany. The result was the creation of the first botanical gardens, the most famous of which was in the Athenian Lyceum. Theophrastus, Aristotle's successor at the Lyceum, had one of his own, and from his treatise describing the plants that grew there we know that already in the third century B.C. Athenians grew many of the same flowers and herbs that were to continue as garden favourites right through Roman and medieval times and on into the gardens of the Italian Renaissance. Apart from exotics whose identification is sometimes a matter of debate, these included such old familiar friends as roses, violets, madonna and martagon lilies, gladioli, paeonies, anemonies, poppies and 'narcissi' and 'hyacinths' though the last two may not have been the flowers that we call by those names today. Popular among the herbs were thyme, marjoram, mints, and southernwood.

With Alexander's conquests, Greek culture in all its forms spread through the eastern Mediterranean and far beyond, bringing with it the Greek conception of gardens. Though their early religious associations had by now been practically submerged by artistic and social ones, nevertheless the component parts of gardens remained the same; the small temples, grottoes, and nympheums that had originally been shrines dedicated to the Muses and tutelary deities now served as architectural ornaments. One interesting innovation, however, appears to have originated about this time: reliefs and paintings, known as *topía* portraying this garden architecture in a picturesque setting of rugged mountains and seaside cliffs, or on the shores of lakes and rivers. *Topía* were used to decorate the walls of porticos, thus producing the effect of bringing the gardens themselves right inside buildings, a preliminary stage in the interpenetration of house and garden which was to become such a distinctive feature of Roman and Renaissance gardens.

These Hellenistic pleasure gardens of Asia Minor, Syria and Egypt now rivalled their Oriental prototypes in size and grandeur, and in Alexandria the gardens of the Ptolemies reached undreamed of heights of luxury. Their banqueting halls were hung with tapestries, patios were planted with flowers and aromatic shrubs, pergolas shaded the paths, and hanging terraces were built in emulation of the legendary gardens of Babylon. Fountains became marvels of hydraulic ingenuity, water power was employed to play organs and to provide the motive power for automatons taking the form of gods and nymphs that moved and played musical instruments. Although Aristotle had amused himself with the invention of similar toys, it was left to two Alexandrians, Ctesibius and Hero, to endow them with an almost incredible virtuosity. Hero's treatise on the subject even describes the design of a fountain adorned with mechanical singing birds, which were silenced by the appearance of an equally mechanical owl – a conceit whose lineal descendant delighted our own John Evelyn during his travels in Italy in the seventeenth century. Such were the marvels of the gardens of the sophisticated Hellenistic world which together with the influence of Greek philosophy and art slowly began to penetrate the severely patriarchal life of Republican Rome.

Like foreign fashions in any time and place these innovations aroused the bitter enmity of Roman conservatives of the old school. Foremost among them was Cato, who among other things was the author of the *De Re Rustica*, an agricultural treatise which although it was modelled upon the Greek translation of a Carthaginian work, had very little to say about such frivolous things as pleasure gardens though it dwells at some length upon the virtues, medicinal and otherwise, of cabbages.

But Cato's was a losing battle. When some hundred years later, about 36 B.C., Varro wrote his more famous *De Re Rustica*, although he obviously enjoyed himself tremendously poking fun at the new villas where every part of the house and garden was given high-falutin Greek names, it emerges very clearly that not only did he himself have several which contained luxuries such as aviaries and ornamental fish ponds, but that the greatest Romans of his day, men like Julius Caesar, Cicero, his rival Hortensius and, of course, Lucullus, were the enthusiastic owners of this new type of pleasure garden. The fashion for pleasure gardens had been spreading slowly for over fifty years, Campania with its Hellenistic heritage providing the link between Greece and Rome. Indeed it is remarkable that most of the early villas and pleasure gardens of Republican times of which records have come down to us were situated in the country between Rome and Naples – near the seaside resorts of Formia and Terracina, or inland in the same area like Varro's villa at Casinum (the modern Cassino) and Cicero's family estates near Arpinum (now Arpino) where his father had made a garden before him.

Casa dei Vettii

Although in the country they would have been larger, the gardens of these early villas of the Republic probably resembled those of the Pompeian houses we can still see today. These Pompeian gardens are usually of two kinds – either a courtyard garden in the colonnaded peristyle of the house, like those of the Casa dei Vettii (pl. 1) where plants grow in pots and vases or small beds surrounding a pool or *piscina*, or in houses where there is only a small central courtyard, a portico opens on to the garden or *xystus* behind the house. In some cases the portico is prolonged so as to enclose the garden on two or even three sides. Very large houses might have both a courtyard garden and a *xystus*.

Casa di Lorio Tiburtino

The particular interest of these Pompeian gardens lies in the fact that even in a small space they contained so many of the features of later Roman gardens from which those of the Renaissance drew their inspiration. Two of their most important features in this respect are the interpenetration of house and garden and the axial planning, particularly of the houses of the second type. Here the main living-room usually opened into the courtyard on one side and the centre of the garden portico on the other, linking the two and affording a view down the entire length of the garden from the centre of the house. The effect of prolonging this view even farther was sometimes achieved by painting a garden perspective, complete with trees, fountains and trellises upon the wall at the far end. A very well-preserved example of one of these frescoes is still to be seen in the Casa di Lorio Tiburtino. This type of *trompe l'oeil* painting, that according to Pliny was invented by Ludius, was also employed in porticos and peristyles to give a feeling of greater space and, like the Greek *topia*, seemed to bring the out-of-doors right into the house. Another feature that increased this impression were the miniature representations of whole landscapes, also known as *topia*, that were sometimes made in peristyles.

Casa di Mario Lucrezio

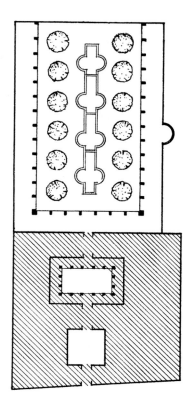

This type of *topia* may well have originated as an adaptation of the Hellenistic bas-reliefs of garden landscapes, ingeniously transformed to give the maximum effect in a limited space, even employing artificially dwarfed trees to this end, in the same way as in Japanese gardens of today. Some idea of what these toy landscapes were like may be imagined from the enchanting miniature garden in the courtyard of the Casa di Mario Lucrezio, with its tiny water staircase and pool adorned with Lilliputian herms and statues and representations of water birds.

Apart from paintings and miniature reproductions of landscapes, the Greek word *topia* was also used in a latinized form – *topiarius* – to designate the gardener who practised the art of topiary or the making of ornamental gardens, as opposed to the old Latin words *olitor*, *arborator* and *vinitor* which were applied to the cultivators of vegetables, trees and vines. The earliest mention of topiary in this sense comes in a letter from Cicero written in 54 B.C. to his brother, in which he says he had been to see his brother's villa, and praised his gardener's (*topiarius*) work in 'covering everything with ivy . . . even the spaces between the columns of the promenade, so that I declare the Greek statues seem to be in business as "topiarii" and to be advertising their ivy'.

The *xystus*, or garden proper of these Pompeian houses, whose whole design was axially planned in relation to the house (pl.2), almost invariably had as its central feature a watercourse that ran down its entire length, lined with marble or made of blue-painted cement and more or less elaborately adorned with fountains and statues according to the owner's means and taste. This central watercourse was flanked by paths and flower-beds that bordered symmetrical plantations of fruit and other trees (the famous quincunx), whose identity has been established by the ingenuity of archaeologists who, finding that the charred roots had left their impressions in the ground under layers of volcanic ash, proceeded to fill these with liquid plaster, thus producing recognisable casts of their structural formation for botanical examination. From this ingenious process and from frescoes we know that the favourite trees grown in Pompeian gardens were evergreens, planes and fruit trees. These included cypresses, bays, oleander, almonds and peaches, pomegranates, pears and quinces, apples and cherries. Ivy was extensively used for trellises and decorative purposes and shrubs like myrtle, box and Alexandrian laurel for bordering beds and later for topiary in the modern sense of clipped trees and bushes, which was invented by Augustus' friend Gaius Matius and called 'nemora tonsilia'.

The favourite flowers of Pompeian gardens were the same roses, lilies, violets and the simple domesticated indigenous field flowers that grew in early Greek gardens. In addition there were the pale mauve Florentine iris, the deep purple germanica, the yellow water iris, the narcissus we know as the narcissus poeticus, also daffodils, autumn crocus, yellow ox-eye daisies, monk's hood, anemones, marigolds, amaranth, cornflowers, cyclamen, pinks, foxgloves, gladioli, jasmine, lavender and melilot. Acanthus, periwinkles, and maidenhair were, we know from Pliny's *Natural History*, used in miniature landscape type of *topia* together with dwarf planes and cypress trees.

In spite of what seems to us a very limited selection of flowers, Pompeian gardens did not lack for colour. Mosaics and paintings decorated the fountains, nympheums and shrines of the protecting 'lares'; while many of the statues that adorned the gardens were probably painted as they were in Greece. Some relics of the religious associations of Greek gardens still survived in this garden sculpture. Statues and herms representing Priapus – the god of fertility – were common garden ornaments and so were Venus and Bacchus, whose cults were really much more closely associated with the gardens of a gay seaside

1 CASA DEI VETTII
The peristyle garden in the Casa dei Vettii at Pompeii, before A.D. 79. The Greek inspiration to which the colonnaded peristyle or courtyard bears witness was probably a legacy of the architectural influence of the Greek colonies in Southern Italy.

2 POMPEIAN HOUSE
Plan of a Pompeian house, showing the atrium, peristyle and xystus, with porticos and central watercourse.

resort like Pompeii. So many of them were quite evidently designed for convivial supper parties on summer evenings when host and guests reclined upon couches built under a vine-covered pergola beside a rippling water-staircase or wall fountain lit by gilded statues carrying clusters of small oil-lamps. Even the dining table might have a concave surface to hold water for cooling wine and fruit, for the gastronomic refinements of Hellenistic cooking had accompanied the introduction of pleasure gardens into Italy. Such was the gay world of the gardens of Pompeii that was overwhelmed on that fatal day in A.D. 79, to be preserved for us in all its fascinating detail.

Charming though they were, these Pompeian gardens bore much the same relation to the Roman villas as those of a small English country house to the vast layouts of Chatsworth or Blenheim. Of these great Roman villas – and in this sense the villa included not only a house and garden but an entire estate – Lucullus was the real pioneer and from the luxury of the entertainments he gave in them his name has become a legend. Lucullus began to lay out his Roman gardens and his country villas in the 'sixties' B.C., when as a man of fabulous wealth he retired from his conquests in Asia Minor to create a setting that he considered worthy of himself. The anecdotes related about him are legion but one will suffice to illustrate the grandeur of his ideas. Pompey criticised one of Lucullus' villas for being suitable only for the summer months and having no provision for winter. This provoked the retort: 'Do you think that I have not as much sense as cranes and storks who change their habitations with the seasons?' And indeed Lucullus owned gardens and villas in Rome, in the Alban Hills, at Monte Circeo and at Baiae near Naples.

The approach to the Roman gardens of Lucullus, which were sited where the Church of Trinita dei Monti now stands at the top of the Spanish Steps, was by a magnificent series of terraces and stairs whose remains were studied by the great Renaissance architect, Pirro Ligorio, in the sixteenth century. If the drawing that he made of them is substantially correct, the whole layout was evidently a superb example of what was to become a Renaissance forte – the architectural transformation of a rising site into a series of terraces, traversing the main axis which was constituted by a series of stairs and ramps that culminated in a colonnaded apse. Some modern authors have doubted the veracity of Ligorio's drawing, but it is significant that it bears a strong resemblance to the layout of the famous Temple of Fortune at Praeneste (the modern Palestrina), which was built some time beforehand.

In their choice of site as well as their design, these Roman gardens of Lucullus were to be the prototype of many others in Roman and Renaissance times. The hills in and around Rome, exposed to healthy breezes even in the summer heat and enjoying far-reaching views over the city and *campagna*, soon became the preferred sites for building villas; so much so that Varro complained that there was no more room left for market gardens and Rome was suffering from a vegetable shortage. In the city itself, the Pincian and Janiculum were the earliest favourites; outside, the Alban Hills where Lucullus, Varro, Cicero, Hortensius, and the younger Crassus had villas at Tusculum. Under Augustus, Tivoli and the Sabine Hills became very fashionable and Nero even went as far afield as the upper valley of the Aniene, creating artificial lakes and a villa where Subiaco now stands.

The choice of site for a villa was accorded the greatest importance by the Romans, not only for aesthetic considerations such as the view, but also for practical considerations of health and comfort, for which exposure to sun and wind were carefully studied. A hillside site facing south-east was the most highly recommended by the classical authors from Varro, writing about 36 B.C., to Palladius in the fourth century A.D. Palladius was much quoted in medieval times by Pietro de' Crescenzi, and the same precepts were to be repeated yet again by the great Renaissance architectural authors like Leon Battista Alberti and Andrea Palladio.

One of the main reasons for the choice of a south-eastern aspect was that the low winter sun would shine into the colonnaded porticos that formed such an important part of Roman villas and gardens – both Varro and Pliny the Younger are explicit on this point – while in summer with the sun high in the sky, they would provide shelter from it. These porticos, which were called gymnasia or palaestrae in imitation of Greek originals, were in Roman gardens really only sheltered walks of which two or even three might be built parallel to one another. Usually they were situated on terraces so that the owner could enjoy the view while pacing up and down. Cicero had two such porticos in his villa at Tusculum, which he called the Lyceum and the Academy. Varro scoffed at these 'citified gymnasia of the Greeks' but adds significantly that already in his day the Romans 'do not think that one such gymnasium is enough, and they do not think that they have a real villa unless it rings with many resounding Greek names, places severally called . . . *palestra, peristylon, ... peripateris*' and so on.

Collections both of paintings and of sculpture now formed an integral part of a villa, like that of Cicero's brother with its Greek sculptures. Hortensius made a shrine in his villa at Tusculum for Cydias' picture of the Argonauts, that had cost him 144,000 sesterces, and Varro poked fun at Lucullus for having better collections of pictures in his villas than fruit, which was a bit unfair to the man who first introduced peaches and cherries into Italy from Asia Minor.

For all Varro's jibes, the great Roman pleasure villa was in fact a self-supporting entity. The old Roman *hortus* or vegetable garden still existed, relegated usually to some obscure corner, and so did the ancient *leporarium*. But in Varro's day it was no longer limited to hares, but had become a large enclosure for herbivorous animals destined for the chase and the table such as deer, wild goats, and even boar. Ducks, pigeons, and thrushes were also bred for eating and so were snails and dormice – these last were eaten pickled in vinegar or stuffed with other dormice. Thickets of trees and berry-bearing bushes were specially planted to attract wild song birds for netting, which then as now were regarded as great delicacies; while fish ponds and aviaries also existed to supply the table.

But even a practical farmer like Varro had already ceased to regard animals and birds as purely utilitarian adjuncts of a villa. He also exploited their decorative qualities by entertaining his guests to the spectacle of animals being called by a man blowing a horn at feeding time, though he didn't go as far as Hortensius who dressed his keeper up as Orpheus. Peacocks strutted in Varro's gardens, and in writing about his villa at Casinum he proudly describes the aviary that was more magnificent than those of Marcus Laenius Strabo – who introduced the fashion to Italy – or even Lucullus. Certainly Varro's aviary (pl. 3) must have been a charming sight with its *tholos* or small circular pavilion reflected in the water of the fish ponds and its loggias and courtyards, where brightly-coloured birds flitted among flowers and miniature trees, as they do in the famous frescoes of the Empress Livia's villa (pl. 4) at Prima Porta which were probably painted just about the time when Varro was writing his book.

By now, what in modern diplomatic parlance is called the 'representational' aspect of Roman villas had assumed considerable importance. In his famous architectural treatise, probably written about 30 B.C., Vitruvius says 'for persons of high rank who hold office and magistracies and those whose duty it is to serve the State, we must provide princely vestibules, lofty halls and very spacious peristyles, plantations and broad avenues finished in a majestic manner'. Unfortunately, Vitruvius' specific references to villa and garden design are disappointingly sparse. He does, however, have quite a lot to say on the extensive use of *topia* as garden decoration. In the chapter on painting he describes how 'the ancients designed scenery on a large scale in tragic, comic, and satyric style. In covered promenades, because of the length of the walls, they used for ornament the varieties of topia finding subjects in the characteristics of particular places, for they

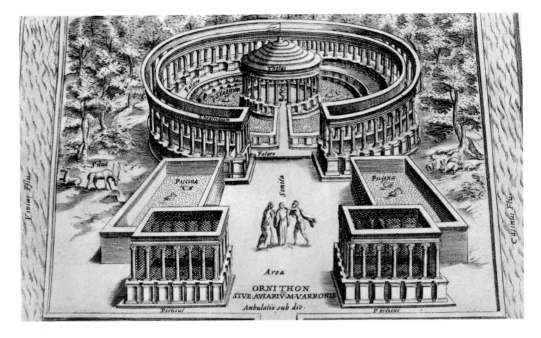

paint harbours, headlands, shores, rivers, springs, straits, temples, groves, hills, cattle and shepherds . . . and representations of legends, the battle of Troy and the wanderings of Ulysses' (pl. 5). Vitruvius then goes on to lament the fact that in his day this style of painting was being replaced by the decoration that Renaissance artists called *grotteschi*.

Vitruvius also explained the close relationship that existed between theatrical and garden design – apparently a recognised style of stage setting was a composition of 'trees, caves and mountains to imitate a landscape'. Subsequently, gardens in their turn borrowed from the theatre and, monumental fountains particularly, owed much of their inspiration to the *scaenae frons* of theatres. The ruins of two monuments of this type survived into modern times – the great fountain that terminated the Julian aqueduct (still standing in the Piazza Vittorio Emmanuele in Rome), and Septimus Severus' mysterious decorative building, the fountain-decked Septizonium, destroyed in 1588. Both of these also exercised a considerable influence upon Renaissance garden architecture.

3 VARRO'S AVIARY

A Renaissance reconstruction of Varro's elaborate aviary in his villa near Cassino, described in his agricultural treatise De Re Rustica, *from J. Laurus' *Roma Vetus et Nuova *published in Rome in 1614. The reconstruction was based on a description made by Pirro Ligorio who, apart from his survey of Hadrian's villa, in the sixteenth century compiled an enormous catalogue of the Roman ruins in Italy. Although these surveys are not a model of accuracy, the mere fact that such an important garden architect as Ligorio undertook them provides interesting corroborative evidence of his contemporaries' desire to model their gardens upon those of classical times. Thus we find that gardens as far removed from one another in time and place as the sixteenth-century Doria gardens in Genoa, and the eighteenth-century villas of the Marche contained aviaries and fish ponds inspired by those described by Varro, writing in about 35 B.C. The ornamental use of birds, animals and fish ponds was new to the Roman world in Varro's day, and he thoroughly enjoyed himself poking fun at his contemporaries' extravagances in this respect, but this did not prevent him from being very proud of his own. It was largely due to descriptions such as his that this custom, which survived even in medieval times, was adopted with such enthusiasm by the garden architects of the Italian Renaissance, and later spread throughout Europe.*

4 EMPRESS LIVIA'S VILLA

Fresco from the Empress Livia's garden room in her villa at Prima Porta, near Rome, and now in the Museo delle Terme in Rome. Dating from the latter half of the first century B.C., it gives a striking picture of the Roman love of trees, flowers and brightly coloured birds.

Vitruvius gives some insight into the Roman adaptation of Greek usage in villa and garden design. According to him 'in the country the peristyles of the mansions built town-fashion come first, then the atria surrounded by paved colonnades and overlooking the palestra and the promenades'. He was not, unfortunately, always the clearest of writers, and two passages in which he attempts to define the Roman use of the Greek word *xystus* are more than usually confused, but what does emerge clearly from his treatise is the immense importance that the Romans accorded to garden promenades. Even the composition of the soil with which these were made is described in detail, and we know from Pliny the Younger that in his Laurentian villa the promenades were so carefully kept as to be pleasant for walking barefoot. In some gardens the length of each promenade was actually inscribed on a marble tablet, so that walkers could calculate the ground covered in their constitutional, like any traveller pacing the deck of an ocean liner today.

The survival of his famous letters has made the gardens of Pliny the Younger the most familiar to posterity of all the Roman world. A love of nature must have run in the family, for he was the nephew and heir of the Pliny who was the author of the *Natural History*, and his letters are full of descriptions of other villas as well as his own. Of these he owned an inordinate number – in his letter to Romanus he said that he had several on the Lake of Como alone, of which his favourites were those called Comedy and Tragedy. Strangely enough the villa now known as the Villa Pliniana did not belong to him, though it owes its name to the celebrated descriptions in his letters.

By far the most famous of Pliny the Younger's villas were, of course, the one at Laurentum on the sea-coast near Rome and the Tuscan villa near the modern Città di Castello (now in the province of Umbria). The wealth of detail with which he described both villas in his letters to Gallus and Apollinarius have tempted many scholars to try to reconstruct their actual plans, but the very diversity of the resulting interpretations has proved that this is not really possible; though from the letters we can build up a very clear picture of what a luxurious villa of the first century A.D. was like – its siting, architectural layout, planting, and of the daily life of its owner.

One of the interesting things about Pliny's descriptions of the two villas is that although one, intended chiefly for winter, was on the sea so near to Rome that he could ride to it after a day's work, and the other, pre-eminently a summer villa, was in the remote mountains of Tuscany, the same basic principles held good for both. The most important of these were the loving care with which every individual room was situated in relation to the garden and landscape and its use during the different seasons of the year, and the spacious layout of the whole house. So extensive in both villas was the use of porticos, courtyards, terraces and outlying suites connected to the house by means of a covered gallery or *cryptoporticus*, that in reading the letters it is sometimes difficult to distinguish where the house left off and the garden began, while in the gardens themselves there were small pavilions or *diaetae*, a specifically Roman contribution to garden architecture and the prototype of the Renaissance 'casino'.

The ruins of what is believed to be Pliny's Laurentian villa are being excavated at the time of writing, but the coast near Rome has changed so much since classical times that the site – like the Roman sea-port of Ostia – is now some way from the sea. The remains of the villa are now planted with olives and stand among glades of great stone pines, out of sight and almost out of sound of the sea. But in Pliny's day, with a south-west wind blowing, the spent waves gently washed against the walls of the main dining-room that was built right out on to the beach, and had folding doors and windows that overlooked the sea on three sides. Even on its landward side this dining-room was not enclosed, but diners could look across the atrium and through the portico (glazed, probably with mica) to woods and hills in the far distance. The outline of what may well have been this same

5 ULYSSES LANDSCAPE
Landscape paintings known as topia and scenes from Greek and Roman mythology were a popular form of decoration for Roman garden architecture of which not a few examples have survived. Among the best preserved is this scene depicting Ulysses in the land of the Lestrygons. It was found in the Via Graziosa, Rome, in 1853. Photo Sansaini, by kind permission of the Vatican Library.

courtyard can still be traced, but the surrounding trees have now penetrated the house, completely blocking the view of the Alban Hills beyond. For stormy weather there was a secondary dining-room, out of sight and nearly out of sound of the sea, that overlooked a sheltered garden. This was surrounded by paths lined with clipped box and rosemary, and it was here that Pliny enjoyed walking barefoot under vine pergolas and among shady plantations of fig and mulberry trees. One of the main features of the villa was evidently a covered gallery or *cryptoporticus*, that Pliny says was so spacious as to be suitable for a public building. This was intended as a sheltered promenade, shaded in summer when the sun was overhead, but cooled by the sea-breezes blowing through its double rows of windows. In winter, on the other hand, it was warmed by the sun streaming in and perfumed with the scent of violets that were massed on the terrace in front.

Pliny's particular joy was evidently the little garden pavilion that he called his 'favourite', which stood on its own above the *cryptoporticus*. This had a *heliocaminus* – one of the few features of Roman villas that were not imitated by Renaissance architects, and has indeed only lately been revived since sun-bathing again came into fashion. Pliny's *heliocaminus*, unlike modern ones, had a central heating system to give greater warmth in addition to that provided by the sun's rays flooding down into an enclosed space; in it he could lie and sun-bathe in the brilliant sunshine, even on one of those brisk Italian winter days when the cold northern *tramontana* wind brings a crystal clearness to the air, with the scent of violets drifting up to him from the sunny terrace below.

This garden pavilion also contained a living-room, a bedroom, and a small secluded closet which Pliny obviously enjoyed more than anything else. In it was a couch, upon which he could lie and look out at beautiful views in every direction – the sea beyond his feet, the woods above his head, the neighbouring villas on the coast on one side, and on the other across the living-room and portico to the sea beyond. This was the place to which Pliny loved to retire for peace and quiet; and it was his refuge during the December festival of the Saturnalia – the one real holiday that Roman slaves enjoyed during the year, which he ruefully says was (like any Italian festival today) mainly celebrated by noise.

Although sport and the more violent forms of exercise did not play nearly such an important part in Roman life and gardens as they did in Greece, Pliny's villas were provided with enclosed courts for ball games and the Laurentian one had a positively sybaritic heated swimming-pool, where its owner could swim and look out over the sea. There were, of course, also the usual elaborate baths, and Pliny specially mentions the spacious cooling-room in the Laurentian villa. This might perhaps be identified with a ruined building whose *cryptoporticus*, still visible today, was cleverly designed to fill the room above with cooling draughts – a device that was imitated by Italian Renaissance architects.

Of the planting in the Laurentian villa, Pliny has disappointingly little to say, beyond his description of the dining-room garden and the famous violet-beds. He does, however, mention that box was difficult to grow so near the sea, and it seems likely that the site was not favourable for the elaborate garden layout of evergreens that the Romans admired so much and which was the main feature of his Tuscan villa.

In the Tuscan villa, the beauty of the site and the relation of the house to the surrounding landscape had also evidently been very carefully studied. Pliny says that it stood in a natural amphitheatre of hills and overlooked a vast plain bounded by mountains; that the winters were bitterly cold, but that in summer the house and garden were refreshed by healthy mountain breezes. The house itself faced south and its main façade was shaded by a long portico giving on to a terrace which was laid out as a formal parterre, with 'a great number of geometrical figures outlined in box' – the ancestor of how many thousands, from Renaissance times until today? A sloping bank ornamented with animals cut in box – again the predecessors of how many peacocks in country cottage gardens? – separated the terrace from a walk outlined by clipped evergreen hedges, that bordered a large expanse of acanthus. Beyond this was one of the famous promenades, laid out in the form of a prolonged oval like a Roman circus, whose central space was filled with box and other small shrubs clipped in a variety of shapes. The formal garden in front of the house ended at this point, bounded by a wall masked by a clipped box hedge, and beyond it were meadows, fields, and thickets which in Pliny's words 'owe as many beauties to nature as all I have described within [the garden] does to art'.

After describing the magnificent views over the surrounding country enjoyed from the large dining-room, Pliny tells how his own suite of quiet and secluded rooms opened on to a small courtyard with four planes planted round a fountain – trees that, according to his uncle's *Natural History*, had been introduced into Italy from Greece for their grateful shade. This suite included a garden room, whose walls were painted in the same *trompe l'oeil* style of birds flitting among trees and greenery as those of Livia's room at Prima Porta; in it was a fountain whose gentle flow produced a pleasing murmur. An abundant water-supply was one of the great joys of the Tuscan villa. A cascade fell into a marble basin below the windows of the main living-room, and near it were a whole series of hot and cold, warm and lukewarm, indoor and outdoor baths. But the house was not entirely surrounded by formal gardens, for Pliny describes a gallery and dining-room specially designed for use in the hottest summer days, where the vines of the surrounding vineyards almost seemed to grow in at the windows. This proximity of house and vineyards is still a characteristic of all but the most grand Tuscan villas.

But the chief glory of Pliny's Tuscan villa was the formal garden, which he called the 'hippodrome'. It owed its name to its elongated horse-shoe shape – the traditional form for a Greek hippodrome, which the Romans had adapted to garden architecture. The gardens of the historian Sallust on the Quirinal also had a famous 'hippodrome' and both it and Pliny's probably looked very like their lineal descendants – the Boboli amphitheatre and the Piazza di Siena of the Borghese gardens.

Pliny's hippodrome was surrounded by a raised path, shaded by planes whose trunks were covered with ivy which hung in garlands from tree to tree. Behind each plane were planted box and bay trees to afford an even deeper shade, and at the rounded end cypresses were grouped. Below this there was apparently a series of paths arranged in concentric circles which, as they emerged out of the cypresses' shade, were planted with roses. Box-lined paths led from here to small garden enclosures laid out in various styles. One had a little lawn, others contained clipped bushes with the names of Pliny and his gardener laid out in box, others were planted with fruit trees alternating with small obelisks. Beyond lay a small informal landscape garden planted with dwarf plane trees in what Pliny described as 'an imitation of the negligent beauties of rural nature'. Clumps of acanthus followed, then more bushes and names of clipped box laid out before a semicircular white marble seat shaded by a vine pergola. This must have been one of the most delightful places in the whole garden. Cooling fountains flowed beneath the marble seat, and their waters were collected in a polished marble basin, which was used as a supper table on hot summer evenings when Pliny and his guests listened to music after the meal was over. He even describes how the larger dishes rested on the rim of the basin while *hors d'oeuvres* in little bowls, made in the form of boats and water fowl, bobbed on the surface of the water. Near by there were more fountains, one of which ebbed and flowed like the famous spring near Lake Como that had intrigued him so much. In the midst of this shady spot, filled with the splash and gurgle of running water, there was a small pavilion with a dining-room and a quiet room where Pliny liked to take his *siesta*, resting in the cool green light that filtered through the pergola and trees and listening to the music of the fountains and little rills that filled the whole hippodrome.

If ever a garden was designed to provide the perfect setting for an Italian summer it was surely this. And considering Pliny's tastes, with his love of nature and his literary pursuits, it is not surprising that it was his favourite villa. How he spent his days there, and how much he enjoyed them we know from another of his letters written to a friend who wondered what he did with himself all the time in this isolated spot. Pliny, the famous orator, was Consul in A.D. 100, but his real interests in life were literary — he wrote a Greek tragedy when he was only fourteen years old — and one of the main reasons for his love of country life was the peace and quiet which it afforded him for writing.

Pliny got up with the sun, but kept the shutters of his bedroom closed so as not to be disturbed by outside sights and sounds while he worked out in his mind exactly what he wanted to dictate to his secretary — he was a very rich man and seems always to have done all his work by dictation. About eleven o'clock he would go out to take the air on the terrace, continuing his dictation, then he would call for his chariot or horse and ride or drive through the country, still turning over in his mind what he was writing. When he got home, although he doesn't mention it, he probably had a light lunch, followed by a *siesta*, after which he took a walk and then read aloud or rehearsed a speech, more to aid his digestion than to practise his elocution. Another walk followed before he was anointed with oil according to the Greek and Roman custom, did exercises, and took a bath. Supper, which was the main meal of the day, was served about sunset. If Pliny and his wife were alone with their household, they were read to during the meal and afterwards they listened to music or some other entertainment. Finally the whole household, which usually included writers and other literary men, took a last stroll in the garden and the day ended in conversation.

From this description of his average day in the country it emerges how admirably the Tuscan villa was planned for the requirements of a cultivated Roman of Pliny's tastes; also, with no less than three walks in the day, the importance given to the promenades in Roman gardens is more easily understood. The balance between physical and mental exercise and the cultivation of a healthy body as well as mind imitated the Greek ideal, and was to be revived in the 'complete man' of the Renaissance, whose days were consciously modelled along the same lines as these of Pliny.

Hadrian's Villa

Even more famous than the villas of Pliny, and destined to exercise an even greater influence upon Renaissance gardens, especially in Rome, was the supreme example of a princely Roman villa that the Emperor Hadrian built between A.D. 118 and 138 at the foot of the Tivoli Hills. In size and splendour Hadrian's villa resembled a small town rather than a palace — with its baths, theatres, swimming-pools, libraries and barracks, as well as the residential quarters of the Emperor and his household. Although most of medieval Tivoli was built with the stone and marble quarried from the villa, its ruins are of such gigantic size that they have withstood 1,400 years of decay and depredation.

Still in the sixteenth century many of Hadrian's buildings retained part at least of their original decoration, that today has almost vanished. According to a survey made by Pirro Ligorio at that time, extensive remains of mosaics, sculptures, paintings, marbles, stucchi and the rustic pumice-stone decoration of the garden grottoes were still visible, and the villa was a place of pilgrimage to artists and humanists alike. Already in the fifteenth century, Pope Pius II and Duke Frederick of Urbino had been there, and they were followed by Bramante, Sangallo, and Raphael — in April 1516 Raphael took Castiglione, Bembo and other eminent Venetian humanists there on a visit.

But for all their admiration, these cultured Italians of the Renaissance damaged the

6 HADRIAN'S VILLA
A model reconstruction of the Emperor Hadrian's villa near Tivoli which shows the scale upon which this imperial residence was conceived; its vast layout resembles a small town with its baths, swimming-pools, theatres, library and barracks. The model shows: A. The Marine Theatre, so called because of its island design; some believe it was intended as the Emperor's private study. B. The Canopus, named after the canal near Alexandria. C. The Pecile, really a large formal semi-public garden. D. The Piazza D'Oro, so called because of the great wealth of artistic treasures found there.
This model was made before excavations on the garden court of the Piazza D'Oro were completed, so the garden layout shown is approximate. Photo by kind permission of Dr E. Kichter.

villa more than the Goths, robbing its treasures in order to adorn their own villas and gardens with the plunder. It was only after the unification of Italy in 1870, and its purchase by the Italian State, that the sack of the villa was arrested and, especially in the last ten years, its systematic excavation and restoration was begun. Today, water is being reintroduced into its vast pools and basins, bringing new life to the romantic landscape of ruins, and enabling the ordinary visitor, not just the archaeologist, to appreciate something of its splendour in classical times.

For all its grandeur of scale and conception (pl. 6), and originally it covered an area of some 300 hectares, the first thing that strikes one about Hadrian's villa is the lack of a unified plan – this was no Versailles where every component part fitted into a comprehensive whole, radiating from the central block of a vast palace; nor indeed does it resemble in this respect the exquisitely balanced symmetry of the great Italian gardens of the Renaissance. It was only with the advent of the Baroque garden with its closer relation to nature that, in the vast seventeenth-century Roman park gardens, the influence of Hadrian's villa was to be felt to the full, though its architectural components had been a source of inspiration to garden architecture since the fifteenth century.

Each individual part of Hadrian's villa forms a complete unit in itself, axially planned, with the buildings and their garden courtyards and terraces more completely integrated even than in most Roman villas, and inevitably it was this aspect of the layout that held an irresistible appeal for the designers of the enclosed Renaissance gardens rather than the vast amorphous whole. The only coordinating elements in the general scheme of Hadrian's villa appear to have been the rough balance achieved between large masses of buildings and open spaces – construction becoming rarefied as it receded from the main built-up area until finally it was limited to individual pavilions scattered through the enormous park. The other unifying element was the profuse and masterly use of water in great pools, canals and cascades, whose distributaries bubbled up on a smaller scale in watercourses and fountains in countless courtyards and grottoes, so that there can scarcely have been a corner of the whole villa that was not penetrated by its glittering presence or musical sound.

Renaissance scholars seem to have been almost mesmerised by the classical authors' mention of the fact that Hadrian named different parts of his villa after the famous monuments of the Hellenic world which he had visited in the course of his travels. This, of course, was no innovation on his part; as we have already seen, it was a common practice followed by Cicero, Sallust and Pliny. Lucullus too called the waterways of his villa at Baiae after the Euripus and the Nile. But for centuries men who really should have known better spent their time trying to discover a resemblance between various parts of Hadrian's villa and the Greek Poikile, Academy, Lyceum and Prytaneiom and so on, with the result that different buildings are still called by these names, though whether they are the same ones as in Hadrian's day it is impossible to say. The only place where the original name can be applied with any certainty is the famous Canopus, called after the Alexandrian canal, where many of the Egyptian sculptures now in the Vatican Museum were originally found. But there any possible resemblance to the original ceases, for Hadrian's Canopus was in actual fact a large water garden designed in an original but completely Roman style, and this applies equally to the villa as a whole. So that although the buildings called the 'Poikile', or to give it its Italian derivative *Pecile*, the Academy and the rest may also originally have contained individual paintings or sculptures which were imitated from their namesakes, their actual construction was quite different.

Hadrian began to build his villa the year after he succeeded to the Empire and it seems likely that it was the fulfilment of a long-felt desire, as the highly personal and original design of the buildings has led archaeologists to the conclusion that the Emperor, who was a great connoisseur of the arts, was himself the architect. This personal element is nowhere more evident than in the fascinating building that Pirro Ligorio first called the 'Marine Theatre' – because of its 'island' construction in the midst of a circular pool. This held a great attraction for Renaissance architects and inspired the design of two of the most famous water gardens in Italy – the water parterre at Villa Lante and the island of the Boboli gardens.

The 'Marine Theatre' was really a small garden house within a house, and a far more effective precursor of the Petit Trianon for, by means of movable bridges, Hadrian could isolate himself completely from the outside world (pl. 7). A circular portico surrounds the pool, while the little pavilion in its midst has another portico leading to a small central garden where a fountain sparkled among flower-beds. Round this were arranged a dining-room, a library and a small Roman bath whose principal 'bathroom' had two staircases leading down to the waters of the pool, which could also be used as the Emperor's private swimming-bath.

The Canopus provides a complete contrast to this secluded spot and, judging from its size and splendour, it was intended for entertainment on a grand scale, as the focal point of the layout is the superb *triclinium* or dining-room. To make the Canopus Hadrian deepened a small existing valley, creating an open space some 119 metres long by 18 metres wide. Almost half this area is occupied by a great sheet of water known as the 'Canopus canal' which, like the watercourse of a Pompeian *xystus*, follows the main axis and occupies most of its length (pl. 8). The canal was flanked by colonnades, that on the left apparently being planted as a pergola, while the one on the right was interrupted half-way down by a

7 HADRIAN'S VILLA
The portico and circular canal surrounding the Emperor Hadrian's island retreat in the 'Marine Theatre' of his villa near Tivoli.

beautiful loggia, whose roof was supported by caryatids, four of which were copied from the famous Erechtheum of Athens (pl. 9). The climax of the whole design of the Canopus was reached in the dramatic semicircular *triclinium* at its far end, built in the form of an apse, whose rounded side was literally covered by a veil of water, falling in cascades, spreading like a glittering carpet over marble steps, and rushing in gurgling rivulets through small canals that surrounded the couches of the diners (pl. 10).

Since the recent excavations the great canal has again been filled with water, and the singularly beautiful marble arcade and facsimiles of the sculptures that were found in it

have been restored to their original sites. Swans given by the Queen of England float on the placid waters, and it no longer requires a great effort of imagination to picture the scene that the Canopus presented to the Emperor and his guests as they reclined on their cushions drinking snow-cooled draughts of the 'ardent Falernian', with statues from Greece and ancient Egypt mirrored in the water, and flowery pergolas and graceful colonnades stretching away into the green cypresses and ilex trees which surrounded the glittering marble pavilions of this fabulous villa.

To give a complete description of the garden courts, terraces and nympheums of Hadrian's villa would require a book itself, but there are three others which are of particular interest as exemplifying typical aspects of Roman garden design. The first is the huge enclosure with a pool in its centre, known as the Pecile, because for centuries it was believed to be Hadrian's copy of the famous Stoa Poikile — Polignotus' celebrated painted portico in Athens (pl. 11). In fact the Pecile is very much larger — it measures 232 by 97 metres — and quite a different shape, being an oblong with rounded ends. Actually, according to Pirro Ligorio's survey, the Pecile did indeed contain 'frescoes of Sea-monsters' which probably decorated its surrounding porticos, but these have since disappeared leaving only the bare walls. Ligorio also says that many statues and fountains were removed from it by the Governor of Tivoli, Cardinal Alessandro Farnese, to adorn his gardens — the famous Orti Farnesiani — on the Palatine in Rome. Evidently the Pecile was a large formal garden, and owing to its size some authorities believe that it also contained a racing track for use as a real hippodrome. One of its most characteristically Roman features were the porticos that surrounded it, especially the double one that flanked its free-standing northern wall on both sides, providing a continuous sheltered walk nearly five hundred

8 HADRIAN'S VILLA
The Canopus Canal in the Emperor Hadrian's villa near Tivoli, viewed from the triclinium end; stone-edged beds for creepers can be seen between the columns on the right, which probably supported a pergola. Across the water on the left are the caryatids copied from the Erechtheum of Athens (see plate 9) that formed part of a loggia; at the far end is the original marble colonnade and facsimiles of the statues found in the canal during excavation.

9 HADRIAN'S VILLA
The Canopus Canal in Hadrian's villa near Tivoli, showing the caryatids copied from the Erechtheum of Athens.

Overleaf:
10 HADRIAN'S VILLA
The Canopus Canal from the entrance, as it must have appeared to the Emperor Hadrian's guests arriving for a banquet in the triclinium at the far end..

metres long which would have afforded shade at any time of day. Probably the Pecile was intended as a more or less public garden for the Emperor's entourage, where they could swim and play games, take a daily constitutional and watch the chariot-racing.

Standing on the northern edge of the main built-up area of Hadrian's villa is a group of buildings enclosing a garden courtyard, which from their comparatively isolated site and self-contained design appear to have formed a separate unit. Owing to the number and richness of the artistic treasures discovered there in Renaissance times, the place is known as the Piazza D'Oro, and it seems likely that it was one of the *dietae* or pavilions designed for summer use and intimate entertainments, probably for the Emperor himself. According to Pirro Ligorio several of the buildings had 'apartments decorated with rustic stone work to look like artificial rocks' and although this decoration has long since disappeared, excavations now in progress are revealing an elaborate garden layout that lay concealed under the olive trees growing in the courtyard.

What is of particular interest about this garden is its strong resemblance to the *xystus* of a Pompeian house, surrounded by colonnades on all four sides. The central axis is marked by a straight watercourse, while two other watercourses of elaborate design, with semicircular niches for fountains, typical of many Roman gardens in Pompeii and Ostia, run parallel to it beside the flanking colonnades. The ample space between the

11 HADRIAN'S VILLA
The great swimming-pool in the middle of the Pecile of Hadrian's villa near Tivoli. The ruins on the left are believed to be the Emperor's own living-quarters; the ruined vault formed part of the heliocaminus or heated sun-bath of his private baths; those on the right, a magnificent suite of halls and courts which were probably part of the main entrance of the villa.

12 HADRIAN'S VILLA
The Temple of Venus in Hadrian's villa near Tivoli. The rushes and trees in the immediate background are growing in the Vale of Tempe, believed to have been so called after the famous valley in northern Thessaly in Greece. It is thought that this small artificial valley in Hadrian's villa was laid out as a landscape garden and would thus have provided a setting in the style of a 'sacred landscape' for the Temple of Venus, which is believed to be the only religious building in the whole of the vast villa.

three watercourses leaves plenty of room for a formal layout planted with flower-beds and fruit trees, to which clipped trees and the statues plundered during the Renaissance no doubt provided the vertical accents. But, as always in Hadrian's villa, the dominating theme would have been water, used with consummate art to provide the contrasting effects of placidity in the central watercourse and glistening movement in the two lateral ones. The exquisite pavilion at the far end of the garden has two suites of bedrooms grouped round small fountain courts, but the whole of the centre is occupied by a large hall and semicircular nympheum cooled by gushing fountains, which contains a semi-circle of raised seats or steps for use as the auditorium of a small theatre whose stage would have had as its back-drop a view through the columns of the hall down the entire length of the garden.

Very different in character from this enclosed and formal garden of the Piazza D'Oro are the ruins of a building near the Greek theatre, which for years appeared on plans of the villa under the somewhat generic name of nympheum. This is the part of the villa where excavators have most recently been at work, and they have discovered what is believed to be the only religious building in the whole place — a small temple dedicated to Venus. Columns found on the site have been restored to their original position, forming a small circular pavilion placed in the middle of what was once a semicircular

13 RELIEF OF AMALTHEA
The so-called relief of Amalthea in the Lateran Museum showing the use of rustic stonework typical of Roman and Renaissance gardens in Italy. The legend of the nymph Amalthea, who was supposed to have nursed the infant Zeus, was a familiar story in classical times, and Cicero's friend Atticus designed a garden in the style of a 'sacred landscape' known as the Amaltheum. Photo by kind permission of the Vatican Museum.

14 POMPEII FRESCO
A 'sacred landscape' painting from Pompeii in the National Museum in Naples; the wild rocky setting of the small temple is typical of landscapes of this type. Photo by kind permission of the National Museum of Naples.

portico, where a copy of Praxiteles' famous statue of the 'Cnidian Venus' was found (pl. 12). This building stands on a terrace at the edge of an abrupt drop into a small valley that borders the northern side of the main built-up area of the villa, with the outside edge of the terrace forming the chord of the arc described by the semicircular portico. Thus the statue of 'Venus', in her small open pavilion, appeared silhouetted against the landscape of the valley, with the rugged Tiburtine Hills forming a dramatic back-drop to the whole scene.

The close connexion that existed between Roman gardens and theatrical architecture at once leaps to one's mind when confronted by this sight, and Vitruvius' description of the recognised setting for satyric plays being 'made up of trees, caves and mountains to imitate a landscape'. Both in Greece and Rome just such a 'landscape' imitation of nature was regarded as an appropriate setting for religious buildings – we have seen how Xenophon's temple dedicated to Artemis stood in a natural park, and in one of his letters Pliny describes a similar park that surrounded the temple of the god Clitumnus, who presided over the springs of that name in Umbria. Thus it seems that Hadrian wished to provide his temple with the type of setting that is often called a 'sacred landscape', for the valley behind the temple is traditionally known as the Vale of Tempe, being identified with considerable likelihood with the 'imitation' of the Thessalian beauty-spot that the Emperor is known to have made in the villa. It is also known that Hadrian's 'Tempe' was laid out in the *ars toparia* style of an artificial landscape, not as a formal garden, and no doubt it recalled the poetic associations of its namesake. Steeped as he was in Greek culture, to Hadrian this evocation of the beautiful Grecian valley would probably have seemed the most appropriate setting for a temple of Venus.

The Vale of Tempe, like the Canopus, had been artificially deepened, much of the excavated stone being used for building the villa, and its rocky sides resemble a mountainous landscape in miniature. A small stream runs through it and even today, as a complete wilderness, it is an extraordinarily beautiful place. Huge cypresses, so old that they look almost as if they had been planted by Hadrian himself, soar up out of whispering beds of rushes, while the Tiburtine Hills in the distance change from blue to violet in the light of the setting sun.

The supposition that this valley was laid out as a landscape garden and formed an integral part of the park, is strengthened by the fact that its southern side is overlooked by a series of well-defined garden terraces that are associated with some of the most important buildings in the villa. Thus it would have served as a link between the ordered beauty of the formal gardens and the wild mountainous landscape of the Tiburtine Hills in the same way as the meadows and thickets that lay in front of the terrace of Pliny's Tuscan villa intervened between it and the view of distant mountains.

The Tuscan villa, as we have seen, had a landscape garden, but it was a mere toy laid out with miniature trees like the *topia* of a peristyle. The size of the Vale of Tempe would have required a layout on a very different scale. Landscape gardens in the grand manner are, however, known to have already existed in the Roman world in the first century B.C., but owing to their more amorphous character their sites are usually impossible to identify and, except in Monsieur Paul Grimal's book on Roman gardens, the subject has been little studied.

The earliest Roman references to a garden of this type are in the letters of Cicero to Atticus, in which he asks for a description of his friend's 'Amaltheum' (pl. 13). Amalthea was a nymph who, according to Greek mythology, brought up Zeus in a grotto, and Atticus in his villa in Epirus had apparently created a garden in the style of a sacred landscape inspired by the legend. All we know about Atticus' 'Amaltheum' is that it was laid out beside a stream shaded by plane trees, that led to a sanctuary which 'formed a landscape', and that Cicero imitated it in his villa at Arpinum.

Temple of the Sibyl

Some idea of what these sacred landscape gardens were like can be gathered from Roman paintings, particularly those of Pompeii, which show small temples in a landscape of gnarled trees and precipitous rocks, often adorned with statues and flower-garlanded herms (pl. 14). The only example of this type of Roman sacred landscape to have survived is the famous 'Temple of the Sibyl' above the waterfalls at Tivoli (pl. 15). Before the diversion of the river in the last century the little circular temple, whose real dedication is unknown, stood directly above the fall, which with its wild rocks and luxuriant greenery and the mysterious associations of the grotto of the Tiburtine Sibyl, possessed to a superlative degree the attributes of a sacred landscape. The temple was built some time about the beginning of Augustus' reign and its siting reflects the love of natural beauty that inspired Virgil, Ovid, Horace, and the other poets and writers of the Emperor's circle. Many of the scenes described in the *Metamorphoses* might have been modelled upon the Tivoli gorge, while Horace's 'echoing Albunea' and odes describing the sylvan setting of his near-by Sabine Farm, have immortalized the Tivoli landscape. No doubt, given the close association between Roman literature and gardens, these poems also influenced contemporary garden design; certainly in Horace's day the Tivoli gorge and its surrounding hills were a favourite place for villas.

Purely secular landscape gardens are also known to have existed in Roman times; the Pompeian frescoes show villas with porticos and gardens set in the same type of wild romantic scenery as the religious landscapes, usually beside the sea or a lake or river, where men are seen fishing and boats plying to and fro, with small garden pavilions perched on the dizzy heights

of wild outcrops of rock (pl. 16). The paintings bear an extraordinary similarity to the familiar Chinese landscapes of the willow pattern plate. All this is completely at variance with the classic type of Roman garden that we have examined up to now and it was not imitated by the earlier garden architects of the Italian Renaissance. The reasons for this are not far to seek – apart from the fact that these landscape gardens have left so few physical traces and the few literary texts describing them are more difficult to follow, their lack of man-made order and symmetry would not have appealed to the Renaissance mind which saw man as the central figure of a disciplined universe. It was only with the spiritual travail of the Reformation and Counter-Reformation that the Renaissance Italian began to see nature in a different light, resulting in the freer Baroque interpretation of natural forms that produced the great Roman park gardens of the seventeenth century and inspired the romantic admiration for natural scenery which ultimately created the English landscape garden.

The most celebrated and extensive landscape gardens of Rome were those of Nero's Golden House, of which both Suetonius and Tacitus have left descriptions (pl. 17). Suetonius says that the garden had 'an enormous pool, more like a sea than a pool, which was surrounded by buildings made to resemble cities, and a landscape garden consisting of ploughed fields, vineyards, pastures and woodlands, where every variety of domestic and wild animal roamed about'. Tacitus is more brief and more disapproving: 'its wonders were not so much customary and commonplace luxuries like gold and jewels, but lawns and lakes and faked rusticity – woods here, open spaces and views there. With their cunning and impudent artificialities Nero's architects and contractors outbid nature.' From this it is evident how little the fluidity of a landscape garden lends itself to precise description, beyond the fact that it 'outbids nature'. In any case such was the Roman hatred of Nero and all his works that within fifty years nearly all trace of his enormous palace and its gardens had disappeared under the Colosseum and the Baths of Titus and Trajan.

17 NERO'S GOLDEN HOUSE
A reconstruction by Signor V. Messina of the landscape gardens of Nero's Golden House, upon which Nero lavished enormous pains and expense. Much criticized by the Romans for the vast amount of space it occupied almost in the heart of the city, it did not long survive Nero's suicide during the revolution which put an end to his infamies in A.D. 68. The Colosseum now stands on the site of the lake; the raised terrace in front of it still exists and is now the garden of the Monastery attached to the Church of SS Giovanni e Paolo. Photo by kind permission of Signor V. Messina.

Villa Pliniana - Lake Como

18 POMPEII FRESCO
A seaside villa in a wall-painting from
Pompeii, showing porticos opening right on to
the water and a man fishing as in Pliny's
descriptions of his villas on Lake Como. In the
distance statues can be seen perched on craggy
rocks as they were in the garden of the
Sperlonga villa.

One result of this historical act of justice was that Pliny's descriptions of the romantic landscape settings of the sacred park of Clitumnus and the Villa Pliniana on Lake Como were in the end to have a much more enduring influence than the extravagant gardens of Nero. Seventeen hundred years after Pliny's death both became a place of pilgrimage to the English romantic poets. Byron's evocation of Clitumnus in *Childe Harold* is too famous to require repetition, but it is interesting to note that it could have applied equally well to an English landscape garden of his day. Shelley's letter describing the Villa Pliniana is less well known but in its way even more fascinating, because it portrays the scene in almost the same terms as Pliny's — 'what has become of the pleasant villa, the always verdant portico, the dense grove of plane trees, that rivulet so sparkling and green and the imprisoned lake below?' The Renaissance Villa Pliniana that Shelley saw was not only built on the same spot as its Roman predecessor, but evidently the inspiration for its design was also drawn from Pliny's letters, as the famous spring, issuing from a grotto supported by Roman columns, still refreshes a loggia used as a dining-room as it did in his time.

For all the romantic beauty and classical associations of the site of the Villa Pliniana, it is, nevertheless, an unusual one for a sixteenth-century villa, as the precipitous descent of the mountains into the lake make the creation of a formal garden as difficult as means of access from the land. But it was the provision of this last characteristic that attracted the Count Anguissola who built it – he went in fear of his life for having murdered a tyrannical member of the all-powerful Farnese family. The impregnable site of his retreat did not save him, however, for twenty years later he was also murdered and his body flung into Pliny's spring.

Though it was a rare choice for a Renaissance villa, this picturesque type of site evidently attracted the admiration of the Romans as much as it did the nineteenth-century romantics. For Pliny's descriptions of his Como villas, Comedy and Tragedy, show that his was no unique example of an eccentric taste, but that his lakeside villas and many others on the coasts of Italy must have looked remarkably like those portrayed in the Pompeian frescoes (pl. 18). Of the Como villas, he wrote: 'both are situated in the manner of those at Baiae; one of them stands upon a rock and overlooks the lake, the other touches it . . . the former enjoys a wide, the latter a near prospect of the lake. ... One follows the gentle curve of a single bay, the salient ridge upon which the other stands forms two. Here you have a single straight alley extending itself along the shore, there a spacious terrace that falls by a gentle descent towards it. From one you can fish yourself and throw your line . . . almost from your bed.'

Ahenobarbi Villa - Giannutri

The shores of Lake Como and the Bay of Naples have seen too many changes and have been too popular as pleasure resorts during the intervening centuries for more than the barest wreck of anonymous ruins of the Roman villas that once stood there to have survived, making even their theoretical reconstruction too hazardous to contemplate, though on the remote Tuscan Island of Giannutri there exist, practically unexplored, the remains of an extensive villa of the Ahenobarbi, that illustrate perfectly the wonderful Roman gift for dramatic siting. Up to now it has been difficult to imagine what these picturesque seaside Roman villas looked like, but a completely new light has been thrown on the subject by the discovery, within the last few years, of the very extensive remains of one of them near the remote village of Sperlonga on the Tyrrhenian coast (pl. 19).

Seaside Villa - Sperlonga

Sperlonga takes its name from the numerous caves or *spelonche* which exist in the rocky cliffs that alternate with sandy bays along the wild stretch of coast. In Roman times, the Via Flacca followed the coast between Terracina and Gaeta and the whole area was famous for its villas. The Via Flacca had long fallen into ruin and the coast beyond Sperlonga had become practically inaccessible except by sea but, owing to a tenacious local tradition, a large cave some distance to the south of the village was marked on all the maps as the Grotta di Tiberio. This was believed to have been the scene of an incident described by Tacitus and Suetonius that occurred when Tiberius was dining at a villa called the Cave – a fall of rock at the cavern's mouth killed several of the servants and created a panic among the guests, all except Sejanus who, with considerable presence of mind, protected the Emperor's body with his own, and as a result gained an increased influence over him.

Although there were traces of Roman stonework in and around the Sperlonga cave, owing to its remoteness no effective archaeological investigation had ever been made until a few years ago when a new road was being built on the site of the Via Flacca. Profiting from the opportunity, the Department of Antiquities obtained the loan of a working party and made an experimental excavation in the floor of the cave. This resulted almost immediately in the discovery of a number of fragments of antique sculpture. Thus encouraged, excavation on a larger scale was begun, revealing the existence of an immense quantity of broken sculpture – some 5000 fragments have been

19 AHENOBARBI VILLA
The loggia of the Ahenobarbi villa on the Island of Giannutri. The remains of garden terraces and steps leading down to a small cove with a blue and silver grotto like the famous one at Capri can still be traced. The site is dramatically beautiful, and although it is practically unexcavated the remains of the villa can be seen from miles out to sea.

discovered to date – and also a well-preserved circular basin and the remains of Roman walls that had evidently converted the cave into an ornamental grotto. Subsequent excavations have shown that the remains formed part of the extensive garden layout of a villa, only part of which has been explored at the time of writing, but even this has been sufficient to give an idea of the extraordinary interest of the discovery and its unique importance to the study of the garden architecture of Roman seaside villas.*

From a fragmentary inscription in Latin verse found in the cave, it appears that the villa was made by a certain Faustinus, who is known to have been a friend of the poet Martial, and a well-to-do landowner of the district. The inscription states that Faustinus had organized for the members of the Imperial family a 'felicitous work' – evidently the decoration of the cave and its surroundings. Martial was born six years after the death of Tiberius in A.D. 37, so that it is unlikely, to say the least, that his friend Faustinus carried out this work for the Emperor himself, although it is within the bounds of possibility that the cave was the scene of the fatal banquet, for the discovery of even prehistoric remains and fragments of Greek pottery show that it was in use long before the second half of the first century A.D.

The cave penetrates to a considerable depth into the rocky face of a headland that encloses the southern end of a bay, which is bounded to the north by the promontory upon which Sperlonga stands, and it would be difficult to imagine a more beautiful site for a seaside villa. The rocky slopes of the Auruncian Hills rise from the terraced fields of the small coastal plain which is fringed by a wide expanse of golden sand. In the middle distance the rugged headland of Terracina is reflected in the blue waters of the Tyrrhenian, and on the horizon Monte Circeo – the home of Circe – appears to float like some great cloudy galleon between sky and sea. It is indeed a fabled coast, alive with the legendary deeds of classical heroes – the stage of Ulysses' meeting with Circe and his encounter with the savage Lestrygons – in fact the scene of the 'wanderings of Ulysses' that we know from Vitruvius were a favourite subject for the painted *topia* that decorated Roman gardens.

In his inscribed verses Faustinus said that if Virgil could live again he would have to acknowledge himself defeated in his admiration for Faustinus' immense work representing events from the Homeric legend, which had never been portrayed in poetic description to such advantage as by the hand of the artificer, whose work was second only to that of nature. From this inscription and the number of fragments of sculpture that have been found of monsters and men in attitudes of violent action and terror, it seems evident that in the cave and its surroundings a scene or scenes from 'the wanderings of Ulysses' were portrayed in the manner of *topia* against the natural background of the coast where they were believed to have taken place.

The statues themselves are still in too fragmentary a state for any definite conclusion to be drawn as to what they represent, and there has been considerable debate upon the subject, to which further excavations may well provide the key. But already on the left-hand side of the cave entrance a large outcrop of rock has been discovered cut into the form of the prow of a ship, together with fragments of its original coloured mosaic covering and a name – that of the famous Argo. Some authorities believe that in this case the name Argo was simply employed as a generic one for a famous ship, as a mutilated passage in Faustinus' inscription and the sculptural fragments appear to indicate that the ship formed part of a representation of the monster Scylla's attack upon Ulysses and his crew.

Further excavations inside the cave have shown that not only was its interior skilfully adapted to form a grotto, whose walls were articulated with the semicircular niches typical of Roman nympheums, but that it, too, was evidently filled with sculpture. The base of a colossal group, possibly an example of the famous Laocoön, still stands in the middle of the circular pool that occupies most of the floor space. This pool is fed by natural freshwater springs and formed part of an elaborate series of fish ponds for the ornamental fish that the Romans admired almost to the point of mania and whose decorative qualities they exploited in the mosaic and fresco decoration of villas, baths, and even temples.

As might be expected, Varro had some very biting things to say in his *De Re Rustica* about the extravagances of his contemporaries in this respect. Making a play upon the words, he remarks that the fish ponds of ordinary men in their country villas are sweet, both as to water and because they produce fish for the table, whereas those of the nobles are bitter, not only because they contain salt water and fish that no cook would touch, but also for their enormous cost. *En passant* he adds that Lucullus' architect nearly ruined him by the enormous expense involved in the creation of his fish ponds at Baiae, where channels were tunnelled through the rocks to provide the correct admixture of sea and fresh water for his precious fish – an operation that made Pompey call him the Roman Xerxes. Apparently these pampered Roman pets, whose owners cherished them more than human beings, required a fresh supply of sea-water with every tide, as well as shelter from summer sun and winter cold and specially constructed breeding-places; all of which can be seen in the Sperlonga villa as well as seats designed for spectators to watch their movements. Extravagant though they seem to us, these Roman fish ponds must have presented an extraordinarily beautiful spectacle, with shoals of rainbow coloured fish darting to and fro in the crystal-clear water that mirrored the fabulous polychrome sculptured groups and the rugged cliffs towering above. It is precisely this contrast between artifice and nature that must have made the Sperlonga villa, and others like it, so extraordinarily fascinating though, with two exceptions, so unlike the Italian Renaissance conception of a classical garden.

At Sperlonga the lower levels of the cliff face on either side of the cave entrance were faced with walls and niches decorated with coloured mosaics and shells and probably fountains, which served as a setting for the sculptural group around the Argo. The ship itself had marble masts and was encrusted with blue, green, red, and yellow mosaic and appeared as if floating on the waters of an artificial pool. High on the cliff above are rough niches that could have held other sculptures; possibly one of them represented the rocky lair of the monster Scylla.

The sculptural group around the Argo was apparently only one of the many inspired by Greek mythology that decorated this fabulous garden. Though it is still too early even to guess at their actual siting in the general composition, it does not require much imagination to picture what a fantastic spectacle the whole scene must have presented, with the sparkling waters of its pools and fountains framed in brilliantly coloured mosaics, the marble galley floating in its pool, and statues, pavilions, and shell-encrusted grottoes embowered in the shade of cypresses and pines. While above them all the rocky cliffs and the amphitheatre of hills soared up to meet the blue Mediterranean sky. Nothing like it was to exist again for over a thousand years, from the time when the barbarian invasions plunged Italy and Western Europe into the long night of the Dark Ages, until with the Renaissance the human delight in gardens was again given full rein and two fabulous pleasure gardens peopled with classical heroes and monsters were made among the rocky outcrops and stony gorges of the Ciminian Hills.

---

* Since excavations started, in 1957, some 7,000 fragments of Greek statues have been unearthed. The nearby Museo Archeologica Nazionale di Sperlonga houses an excellent collection of the sculpture, including the "Ship of Odysseus". [2009]

Medieval and Early Humanist Gardens

The survival of anything but mere vegetable gardens in Italy through the Dark Ages probably owed more to an event that occurred in a remote African province of the Empire than to any other single cause, for it was in a garden given to him by his friend Valerius that St Augustine first assembled his followers in the little town of Hippo, and it was there that he carried on his teaching. Thus Plato's tradition was adopted by this great Father of the Church, and it is likely that the garden where he and his followers sought peace and isolation from the temptations of the world drew its original inspiration from those of the Greek philosophers, as it would almost inevitably have been a typically Roman garden attached to a villa whose enclosed courtyards and colonnades would have so admirably suited the Saint's purpose.

This example no doubt influenced the hermits who so often established themselves in the ruins of Roman villas in Italy, and it was from a grotto by the ruins of Nero's villa at Subiaco that the most famous of them emerged to lay down the rule of the first monastic Order in Western Europe at the end of the fifth century. Both at Subiaco, where he planted a rose garden, and later at Cassino, St Benedict established himself and his monks among the ruins of Roman buildings, and there can be little doubt that the monastery cloister evolved from the colonnaded peristyle of the Roman country house, nor that, without its shelter, classical culture and the art of gardens would never have survived the Early Middle Ages.

Though gardening was now practically reduced to the cultivation of medicinal and pot herbs and flowers for church decoration, it is interesting to note how the aura of the great classical tradition still survived and when, in 1070, the Abbey of Cassino was rebuilt, the garden was described as 'a paradise in the Roman fashion'.

From an early-tenth-century plan preserved in the Monastery of St Gall in Switzerland, we have a very good idea of what the gardens of these Benedictine monasteries were like. The plants were grown in rectangular beds, each one usually being preserved for a separate species, but in the garden of simples, roses, lilies and gladioli grew among scented herbs such as rue, rosemary, sage. The vegetable garden contained leeks, lettuces, garlic, parsley, chervil and poppies, grown no doubt for their seeds that were used for flavouring, and in the orchard, which was also the cemetery, the tombstones were shaded by pears, plums, mulberries and fig and nut trees. Surprisingly, the old Roman tradition of keeping wild and ornamental animals and birds still survived even in the enclosed space of a monastery garden, and fish ponds to provide food for fast days were, of course, an almost universal feature.

In Italy, where the cloister columns, especially in the south, were often decorated with sparkling mosaics, some other relics of Roman gardens survived. The well in the centre of the flower-beds might be replaced by a fountain as in St Paul's-Without-the-Walls and the Quattro Coronati in Rome (pls. 20, 21). Or a small garden pavilion with a fountain and seats would sometimes break the regularity of the colonnade, like the delightful one that projects into the cloister garden of the Cistercian Monastery of

Fossanova in the Pontine marshes, and the corner one, with its moresque fountain, in the vast cloisters of Monreale near Palermo.

It was in the Sicily of the Saracen emirs and Norman kings that the first purely secular pleasure gardens of medieval Italy made their appearance. What those of the emirs were like we can only guess, for in the Norman conquest of 1091 they were completely destroyed, but as Roger Hauteville and his descendants so identified themselves with the local way of life as to earn the title of 'baptised sultans', it is not surprising to find, judging from contemporary descriptions and such remains of their palaces as have survived, that the pleasure gardens of the Norman kings can have differed little from those of their Moslem predecessors. In the words of an Arab poet who visited Palermo during the reign of the last of them in the second half of the twelfth century, the king's palaces and gardens were 'disposed around the town like a necklace which ornaments the throat of a young girl' and indeed the countryside, to a depth of four or five miles around the city, as far afield as Monreale and Baida, was almost entirely given over to an enormous park dotted with pleasure pavilions.

Cuba

Roger the Great surrounded this park with a wall that enclosed hills and woods, water was brought in underground conduits to fill canals and artificial lakes, in the midst of which rose pleasure palaces like the Favara or Castello di Mare Dolce, and the Cuba (pl. 22). These and the Ziza and Menani were all built in the Oriental style, with stalactite vaults and water staircases like those of the Moghul gardens of Kashmir, but of them the Ziza is the only survivor in anything like its original state. Its gardens were still extant in 1526

20 ST PAUL'S-WITHOUT-THE-WALLS
The cloister of St Paul's-Without-the-Walls in Rome, whose coloured mosaics are so characteristic of Southern Italian cloisters. The monastic cloister was probably derived from the peristyle or colonnaded courtyard of Graeco-Roman houses.

21 SS QUATTRO CORONATI
The cloisters of the SS Quattro Coronati in Rome, where an antique fountain stands in the middle of the garden.

when Leandro Alberti saw it and described the small pavilion that stood before it in the midst of a pool, and the groves of oranges and lemons which filled the ruined garden enclosure. For it was to the Moslem emirs of Sicily that the Italian gardens of the Renaissance owed the sweetly-scented orange and lemon gardens that were one of their great charms, and although there is some argument as to whether the Romans cultivated citrons in their gardens – the *medica malus* of Pliny is thought to have been a citron – oranges and lemons were an Arab importation into southern Europe. From the chronicle of Hugo Falcandus it is evident that they were already well established in Sicily in the twelfth century, as were other exotics imported from North Africa, such as date palms and even blue water-lilies. Falcandus described the royal palaces and gardens as having pavilions, kiosks and courts surrounded with porticos – one with a central fountain decorated with lions as in the Alhambra – all of which were set in a delicious park planted with different trees, where wild animals and ornamental birds roamed free. In this connexion it is interesting to note that when Lorenzo de' Medici was making the garden of Poggio a Caiano four hundred years later he sent to Sicily for his peacocks.

While there is no doubt that these Sicilian pleasure parks, which were part garden, part hunting enclosure, were modelled on the Oriental paradises and that they afterwards disappeared almost without a trace so that their effect on subsequent garden development in Italy was small, they did serve to keep alive the tradition of pleasure gardens, and such was their fame that something of their influence did survive, and not only in Italy. From Leandro Alberti we know that still in the early sixteenth century Palermitan gardens continued the use of water on a grand scale – they boasted artificial islands in the midst of pools and one

22 THE CUBA
A reconstruction of the garden of the Cuba near Palermo in Sicily by R. Lentini. Though the dome has been destroyed the building itself still exists, also the small kiosks. Most of the vast landscape of the Conca d'Oro seen in the picture was used as a private park by the Norman kings and their descendants in the twelfth and thirteenth centuries. Photo by kind permission of the Gabinetto Fotografico Nazionale.

had a fountain in the shape of a boat placed in the centre of a dining table as a wine-cooler. It was after his visit to Palermo, when returning from the Crusades in 1270, that Robert of Artois created his garden at Hesdin which was filled with automatons and surprise fountains and was still famous in the fifteenth century when garden art revived in France. But the most widespread effect achieved by these Sicilian gardens was probably through the influence of the Hohenstaufen Emperor Frederick II, who on his mother's side was the grandson of Roger the Great and thus inherited the Kingdom of Sicily.

His epic struggle with the Papacy gave Frederick little time for the enjoyment of his remote Palermitan palaces; most of his life was lived in Southern and Central Italy, where from contemporary records it is known that he established gardens and hunting-enclosures beside his castles and hunting-boxes, that were themselves adorned with classical sculptures. As might be expected from a man whose tastes included an interest in archaeology (he excavated the tomb of Galla Placidia as well as collecting antique sculpture) and a passion for hunting, and whose great aim in life was to re-establish Rome as the capital of his Empire, Frederick's hunting-boxes and gardens were more Italian than Oriental. Like the villas of his Roman predecessors, they were sited with an acute perception for the natural beauty of the surrounding country and many had a pool or bath in the central courtyard. The gardens contained the familiar vine trellises, shady groves of sweet-smelling myrtles and meadows with fish ponds and, as we know from the poetry of the Court, the most prized flowers were the old Roman favourites – the violets and the rose. The garden proper, which was known as a *viridarium*, appears in most cases only to have been a small part of quite an extensive layout (almost reminiscent of the old Roman country villa), for the Court registers also mention model farms that were attached to the *loca solatiarum* or 'places of solace' as they were called. The hunting enclosures and menageries contained exotic beasts such as camels, hunting leopards, an elephant and even a giraffe, as well as white peacocks and other ornamental birds for which the Emperor's Court was famous throughout Europe.

Some measure of the renown of the Emperor Frederick's gardens is probably reflected in the great Italian agricultural treatise of the Middle Ages – the *Liber Ruralium Commodorum* written by the lawyer-agronomist, Pietro de' Crescenzi of Bologna; its standing as an agricultural authority remained unchallenged until the sixteenth century.

Pietro was born in 1230 of a Ghibelline family, whose political sympathies cost them many years of exile, and he only began his famous work when as an old man he returned to Bologna at the end of the thirteenth century. By this time Pietro must have made his peace with the Guelph faction for the book was dedicated to an eminent member of it, the Angevin King of Naples Charles II, who made the book public in 1305. Although largely based upon classical models such as Cato, Varro, and Palladius, the treatise was also evidently influenced by contemporary scientific works written in the Sicilian Realm, as the chapter dealing with the care of horses is very similar to the *De Medicina Equorum* of Giordano Ruffo who had been Frederick II's Grand Marshal of Horse, and indeed its author said that he had 'read and studied many ancient and modern books' before embarking upon his *magnum opus*. However, the book breaks new ground in an extensive section devoted to the design and cultivation of pleasure gardens, which is divided into three classes – small herb and flower gardens, gardens of from two to four acres for ordinary people, and gardens for kings and rich men of twenty acres or more. The first was of the familiar type portrayed in medieval miniature, of a grass plot with a fountain in the middle surrounded by herbs like rue, sage, basil, marjoram, and mint, and occasional lilies and roses. Turf seats were to be shaded by a vine pergola and sweet-scented and blossoming trees like cypress, bays, apples, pears, and pomegranates planted round the walls. The second garden had in addition a large orchard and a trellis arbour and was to be fenced

around with white briars and other prickly shrubs, with an outer hedge of pomegranates in hot countries and hazel trees and quinces in cold ones.

But it was in the section dealing with the gardens of kings and great men that the influence of the Royal gardens of the Sicilian Realm was most plainly evident, as Pietro apparently envisaged them as parks rather than gardens, with 'a fountain flowing through all its parts and places' and filled with hares, stags, roebucks, and rabbits. Aviaries made of nets enclosing the tops of trees growing near the King's palace were to be filled with ornamental and singing birds, a wood as a shelter for the animals was to be planted to the north of it, and an open meadow to be laid out in front, so that the animals could be seen disporting themselves in the open from the palace windows. The garden was to be planted with fruit trees and evergreens like pines, cypresses, and citrus trees and, if the climate was suitable, palms. This mention of exotics such as citrus and palm trees confirms the impression that Pietro had either seen or read about the Sicilian gardens. The strange fascination exercised by grafting one species upon another – which reached such extraordinary proportions during the Renaissance – is already evident; as the author says: 'much delight may be caused by various and wonderful graftings of trees on trees'.

Castello Sforzesco

Pietro also devoted a great deal of attention to the ways of growing and clipping trees to make battlemented walls of greenery round his garden enclosures and bowers of trees specially planted and trained so that their interlaced branches formed the entire walls and roof. An interesting example of what these tree houses looked like can still be seen in the Castello Sforzesco in Milan, in the Sala delle Asse, whose ceiling is entirely decorated with a *trompe l'oeil* painting of entwined branches interlaced with golden cords, believed to have been originally executed for Lodovico il Moro by Leonardo (pl. 23).

23 CASTELLO SFORZESCO
The painted ceiling of the Sala delle Asse in the Castello Sforzesco in Milan, originally commissioned by Lodovico il Moro and executed by Leonardo, but subsequently much restored. It shows the type of bower made by interlacing trees described by Pietro de' Crescenzi in his agricultural treatise. Anderson photograph.

24 CAMPO SANTO
The garden scene in Andrea Orcagna's 'Triumph of Death' in the Campo Santo at Pisa. Anderson photograph.

25 PALAZZO RUFOLO
The garden loggia of the Palazzo Rufolo at Ravello, overlooking the Gulf of Salerno, Naples, one of the very rare surviving examples of non-ecclesiastical garden architecture of the Middle Ages; the loggia was probably used for al fresco meals. Privately owned but open to the public.

For the most part, the medieval gardens of Italy live for us now only in the miniatures of medieval manuscripts and in rare early frescoes such as the 'Triumph of Death' and the 'Garden of Eden' in the Campo Santo at Pisa (pl. 24). But one relic of Italian pleasure-garden architecture of this period has survived in the thirteenth-century Palazzo Rufolo at Ravello (pl. 25). Built round a courtyard lined with exquisite double loggias in the moresque style, this palace also has a most unusual garden loggia that was probably designed as a cool *al fresco* dining-room, for its pointed arches are open to sea-breezes and command a wonderful view over the Gulf of Salerno. This garden is also particularly interesting for its historical associations, as the family of merchant princes to whom it belonged are known to have entertained the Angevin kings Charles II and Robert the Wise there, and it was this last King's illegitimate daughter Maria who was immortalized as Fiammetta in Boccaccio's *Visione Amorosa*.

In the *Visione Amorosa* Boccaccio paints a picture of the gay Neapolitan life at the beginning of the fourteenth century that includes a description of the Royal gardens laid out between the Castel Nuovo and the sea, which were evidently in certain respects far in advance of their contemporaries of the rest of Italy. The most remarkable thing about these gardens of the *Visione Amorosa* is that they were filled with sculpture at a time when this was unknown elsewhere; possibly the classical tradition had survived with greater force in the Naples area or had been given fresh impetus by the Emperor Frederick II, who often lived there and is known to have transported antique statues from the Castel dell'Ovo for the decoration of his Apulian castles. Apart from decorating a fountain, which was a common practice of the day, these statues were placed alternating with seats of red marble around a lawn; and it seems likely that some of them at least were Roman, as Boccaccio mentions fountains in the form of a wolf and an eagle from which little streams flowed that irrigated the flowers and grassy plots where beautiful ladies sang and danced or sat gossiping in the shade.

Villa Palmieri

Although the *Visione Amorosa* was probably begun in Naples it was completed in Florence about 1345, three years before Boccaccio began his masterpiece *The Decameron*, whose setting was the garden of the Villa Palmieri, which affords us the most vivid portrayal of *villeggiatura* life in a Tuscan villa that exists. The garden of the Villa Palmieri today dates only from the seventeenth century, but in Boccaccio's time it was evidently still predominantly medieval in character, with the familiar layout of a fountain standing in the midst of a flower-starred lawn and vine pergolas and shaded walks. In size, however, it seems to have been bigger than most medieval gardens and its planting more elaborate; the walks were bordered not only by roses but also by citrus trees and jasmine. In this sylvan setting, peopled also by rabbits and kids, the young protagonists of *The Decameron* crowned each other with flowers and sang and danced in the morning, dined by the fountain, rested in the shade playing chess and reading *Lives of the Romans* in the afternoon, and in the evening gathered in the meadow to tell their tales.

The picture is still almost the same as that of the medieval courts of love and the lays of the troubadours, but, significantly, a more serious note has already crept into their day of pleasure – their reading the *Lives of the Romans* was a portent of immense significance in the development of Italian gardens as it was typical of the author of *The Decameron*. Boccaccio was a passionate devotee of classical literature and so beggared himself by buying manuscripts of the Greek and Latin authors that he was obliged to ask his friend Petrarch to lend him money; knowing his habits, Petrarch left Boccaccio fifty golden florins in his will 'to buy a furred cloak to protect him from the cold of winter during his nocturnal studies'.

Boccaccio first met the poet, whose love of nature and classical studies single him out as the first humanist, in Petrarch's garden near the Church of San Valerio in Milan in March 1359. They talked of poetry and learning and Petrarch told Boccaccio about the Greek scholar Leon Pilatus, who afterwards became Boccaccio's friend and translator. But they also found time to plant a bay tree in memory of their meeting and Petrarch, who for all his humanistic enthusiasm for gardening was distressingly unsuccessful, hoped that Boccaccio would bring him luck and that the tree would take better than the others he had planted.

An autograph record of the gardening successes and failures of this first man of modern times to appreciate the beauty of scenery — Petrarch's ascent of Mont Ventoux just to see the view astonished his contemporaries — actually still exists in the Vatican Library. This takes the form of notes written in faded ink upon the margins of his own copy of Palladius' treatise on agriculture, in which Petrarch carefully stated the day, hour and phase of the moon at the time when he transplanted plants or sowed seeds. Although six hundred years have elapsed since these entries were made, one still shares his disappointment when at the end of a note he honestly admits that the spinach, beet, parsley and fennel seed in his Milanese garden had failed to come up.

In spite of his many travels, Petrarch seems to have made gardens in almost every place where he lived. The first was his famous one at Vaucluse that he modestly described as having been made with his own hands and being without equal in the world. But from the notes in his copy of Palladius, we know more about the garden that he laid out in Parma in 1348, where he added a pleasure garden to the existing vegetable plot, making a lawn and planting apple, pear and plum trees, rosemary and hyssop. Friends sent him cuttings of foreign vines, which he grafted on his own, training them up his fruit trees. Just how closely Petrarch's gardening was associated in his mind with his classical studies is shown by the fact that for this particular operation for some reason or other he was unable to follow the precepts of the *Georgics*; having gone against the authority of Virgil, he feared the worst and was very much surprised when his vines flourished.

Castle of Pavia

The fourteenth century was a period of transition, especially in Northern Italy. During the first half of it castles were still just fortresses, but later they began to evolve into pleasure palaces. First among the nobles of Northern Italy to lead this fashion was Petrarch's friend Galeazzo Visconti II of Milan, who was a keen botanist and wrote to the poet in verse asking him for plants from his garden. No doubt these were for the garden of the famous Castle of Pavia that Galeazzo began to build about 1360, where Petrarch stayed with him for five successive summers. His reception of the poet as an honoured guest whose presence shed lustre on his Court, the revolutionary design of Pavia Castle as a pleasure palace with an extensive garden and park, and his love of country life, show that Galeazzo was a precursor of the princely patrons of the arts who were such a feature of the humanist movement in the next century.

Thus, although it was walled and moated like a medieval castle and its main features were survivals from Roman times, such as fish ponds and a bath set in a central lawn surrounded by pergolas and fruit trees, Pavia Castle can fairly lay claim to have been the first Renaissance villa of Northern Italy. The life lived there and the amusements of the Visconti, and later the Sforza Court were, however, very different from the more studious pursuits of the owners of the later Tuscan and Roman villas.

Still today, the Lombards are distinguished from the rest of Italy by a certain expansiveness and love of out-of-door life. This characteristic was already evident in the fourteenth century when the chief diversions of Galeazzo's Court were picnic expeditions, hunting and horse-racing in the park of Pavia Castle, while the ladies amused themselves playing games and bathing in the carefully screened bath in the garden. Galeazzo also enjoyed taking his meals *al fresco*, and had a special balcony made outside the castle dining-room overlooking the garden, where he and his family ate, serenaded by the music of trombones, cornets and flutes.

Casa dei Borromei

26, 27, 28 CASA DEI BORROMEI
Garden frescoes from the old Casa dei Borromei in Milan showing life in a Lombard garden of the fifteenth century with a kind of rounders, cards, and other games in progress. In the background of plate 26 the Lake Maggiore and the Borromeo Islands can be seen; possibly the paintings represent the garden of the family castle of Angera, which dominates the lake. Photos Mario Perotti.

At Pavia also the out-of-doors began again to enter the house as it had done in Roman times. The ceilings of the principal rooms were painted blue and studded with stars and the walls were frescoed with landscapes and scenes of country life. These frescoes have long since disappeared, but in the old Casa dei Borromei in Milan and in an early-fifteenth-century hunting-box belonging to the same family near Oreno, there are two rooms frescoed in the same style. Although, of course, they are of a slightly later period, the paintings give an extraordinarily vivid impression of the gaiety and freedom of the life that was led in these Lombard gardens (pls. 26, 27, 28). In the Casa dei Borromei elegant ladies and their squires are portrayed playing cards, rounders and other games amongst flowers and fruit trees, and in the distance is a lake with a few rocky islets – the famous Borromeo Islands as they appeared in the fifteenth century. Possibly the frescoes represent scenes in the garden of the family Castle of Angera that overlooks Lake Maggiore.

Villa Borromeo · Oreno

The Oreno frescoes show even more clearly the connexion that existed between gardens and hunting-enclosures – evidently designed to provide suitable amusement for both sexes – in the Lombard life of the period. In the garden two ladies and a little dog are shown standing beside an arbour covered with pink roses, against a background of pomegranate trees laden with golden fruit. Unfortunately, the part of the fresco that is damaged is the central space between them, where the kneeling figure of a man in a red cloak is barely perceptible. A mounted huntsman with his hounds and falcon approaches the right-hand lady, while behind the other is the *lanca* or artificial pool that is still used today, as it was in the fifteenth century, to decoy wild fowl. Around the pool fly duck, snipe, and a heron battling with a falcon, while ducklings paddle tranquilly in the water (pl. 29). On the other walls are portrayed a bear hunt and two other ladies holding bear cubs in their arms.

Although he was familiar with courtly scenes such as these and had often played his part in them, Petrarch chose very different surroundings in which to live himself, and the site of the little country house that he built in which to end his days among the Euganean Hills is not only typical of his own taste, but also of the later Italian humanists' conception of a villa as the place of retirement for a cultured man of letters.

29 BORROMEO VILLA
Frescoes of a garden with a rose pergola and pomegranate trees and hunting scenes in the old hunting-box at the Borromeo villa near Oreno. During the fourteenth century gardens were closely associated with hunting-enclosures in Lombardy.

Petrarch's House - Arquà

Petrarch first went to Arquà in 1369, and fell so much in love with the smiling green landscape of the Euganean Hills that two years later he built the house whose captivating charm still holds something of his great personality. Here he wrote his *Lives of Famous Men*, corresponded with the great men of his day and gardened assiduously with his inseparable friend and literary executor Lombardo della Seta; and here at dawn on a summer day in 1374 he was found dead with his head lying on a book, in the study whose Gothic windows look out on the green valley that he loved so well (pl. IV). Of the garden upon which he lavished so many pains, unfortunately we know little, except that it contained shrubs — probably clipped as topiary ornaments — for poor Lombardo once spent three days in a boat travelling to and fro from Padua through the snow-covered marshes to fetch them. Needless to say, one was a bay, Petrarch's favourite *lauro*, that reminded him of his past triumphs — his coronation with the laurel crown on the Roman Capitol and the name of his beautiful Laura — and was beloved alike by the classical poets and the creators of Italian Renaissance gardens, between whose worlds Petrarch formed the link, bridging the gap between the Middle Ages and the humanist world to come.

Fifteen years after Petrarch's death was born the man to whom and to whose family Italian Renaissance gardens probably owed a greater debt than to anyone else. Cosimo de' Medici was born into one of the most fascinating periods of history in the city that for the next two hundred years was to play a part in European civilization comparable to that of Periclean Athens. When he was a small boy he may have played in the gardens that rich Florentines like Ser Durante Chiemontesi had made for themselves between the concentric series of walls that ringed the city, where in the Monastery of Santo Spirito scholarly enthusiasts like Coluccio Salutati and Luigi Marsigli met in the evenings to discuss classical literature and Salutati's discoveries of ancient codices. It was these two very different aspects of Florentine life that, when he was a man, Cosimo de' Medici was to bring together, by inviting his friends to discuss philosophy in the garden of his villa at Careggi in imitation of his 'divine' Plato.

Villa Medici - Careggi

In 1417 Cosimo's father, Giovanni di Bicci had bought the old castellated house at Careggi that in 1457 passed to him. Cosimo called in Michelozzo to transform it into a villa more in keeping with the changing spirit of the times, for he no longer regarded a country house simply as a semi-fortified dwelling to be used as a place in which he and his family could escape from the summer heat of the city and oversee the administration of his land. Michelozzo did little to change the main lines of the ponderous block of the old house with its battlemented walls, but he added a double loggia whose lightness and grace breathes the spirit of a new age. This loggia overlooked the garden, which was planted in conscious imitation of a classical garden with bays, box, cypress, myrtle, pomegranates, quinces, lavender and scented herbs and flowers. It was only among the flowers that there were any innovations, such as the carnations that had made their appearance in Europe during the Crusades; and oranges and lemons grown in pots were ranged along the paths and grouped round the fountains, one of which was adorned with Verrocchio's famous 'Boy with the Dolphin'. Today Careggi is a hospital in the suburbs of Florence, and of its former beauties little remains but the lemon trees, some of the pebble mosaics of the paths, and a gently trickling fountain. The surrounding vineyards, where Cosimo pruned his own vines, have also disappeared and with them much of the peace that he enjoyed as he sat under the loggia playing chess.

The Oecumenical Congress held in Florence in 1439, in an attempt to unify the Roman and Oriental Churches, which was attended by the Emperor John Paleologus, who brought such famous Greek scholars as Gemistos Plethon and Bishop Bessarion of Nicaea in his train, exercised an enormous influence upon Florentine intellectual circles. It was felt that these Greek scholars represented a living link with the classical past and their mere presence provided a tremendous impetus to the classical studies that had already begun to flourish in the city. So that when fourteen years later these same scholars fled to Italy after the fall of Constantinople, they were received with open arms and men's minds were already prepared for the spark that kindled the flame of the Italian Renaissance.

It is believed that it was to his conversations with Gemistos Plethon that Cosimo owed the idea of founding the Platonic Academy, whose studies did so much to free men's minds from the rigid Aristotelian philosophy of the past; and it was in the villa at Careggi that he gathered around him the friends who became its foundation members, making this Florentine villa the most famous intellectual centre of the world and the cradle of the humanist movement. It was there under the patronage of three generations of the Medici family – Cosimo, Piero, and Lorenzo – that the greatest men in the world of learning and the arts – Marsiglio Ficino, Niccolò Niccoli, Politian, Pico della Mirandola, Brunelleschi, Michelozzo, Donatello, and later Michelangelo – met and talked. Cosimo died there in the summer of 1464 and one of his last wishes was that Ficino should bring him his latest translation of one of the works of Plato.

It was from these gatherings aimed at the pursuit of ancient learning, literature, and history – the 'humanae literae' to which the movement owed its name – that Italian humanist studies trace their origin. The great aim of humanism was to recapture the spirit of the classical world with its ideals of beauty allied to knowledge and the perfection of the human personality – the 'complete man' of the Renaissance who was a balanced product of thought and action combined. In this we see a return to the Greek model that had inspired the Roman authors like Pliny the Younger, and it is not surprising to find that in their researches into their works these Florentines of the fifteenth century were fired anew by the classical love of nature and gardens as the setting for philosophical discussions, poetry, and music, nor that their conception of a garden conformed with the classical architectural concepts of symmetry and proportion. Contemporary architectural treatises, especially that of Leon Battista Alberti, show this clearly, though it is also plainly evident in the writings and letters of humanists in general. One written by Bartolomeo Pagello of Vicenza about 1460 provides a striking example. In it he says that although he does not want his villa to be as grand as those of Pliny the Younger, he wishes to have a library and a portico running down to the garden which should contain 'many apples, pears and pomegranates, damascene plums and generous vines; many plane trees near the house, clipped box and beautiful bays; and a fountain more clear than crystal, dedicated to the muses like the Castalian spring at the foot of Parnassus'.

Alberti, who in 1446 designed the epoch-making Florentine palace of Giovanni Rucellai with its *opus reticulatum* plinth and the earliest example of the use of the classical orders, also probably exercised a greater influence upon Early Renaissance garden design than any other architectural author of his time. Alberti presented his famous treatise, the *De Re Aedificatoria*, to Pope Nicholas V in 1452; it is generally considered that the work was written during the six or eight preceding years, much of which time the author spent in his native Florence, so that his theories were probably already well known to his friends there. As might be expected, in his directions for the siting of villas and the design of their gardens, Alberti continually quoted the practice of 'the ancients' and his instructions are in fact in many cases lifted straight from the works of classical authors, sometimes to a ridiculous degree, as when he repeats Pliny's warnings, culled from his letter describing the Laurentian villa, about the deleterious effect of sea winds and spray upon box, in an age when no one even thought of building seaside villas.

As with the classical writers, the siting of a villa was of primary importance to Alberti. A hillside site was recommended, both for the views 'that overlook the city, the owner's land, the sea or a great plain and familiar hills and mountains... in the foreground there should be the delicacy of gardens' and for its healthy exposure to sun and wind. He explained the useful practice of 'the ancients' in employing the site so that loggias should be filled with winter sun, but shaded in summer, recommending that some of them should, as in classical times, be semicircular in shape so as to provide shelter from winter winds, enabling the older members of the family to sit and gossip in the sunlight. Vitruvius' ideas of the representational functions of a villa were evidently uppermost in Alberti's mind when he wrote of the importance of 'spacious places' in which to receive guests, and the old Roman promenades live again in his 'places to walk and be carried [in a litter]'.

The intimate classical relation between house and garden was also revived in Alberti's directions for the design of a country house. Apart from the loggias linking it to the garden, the rooms were to be painted with garden subjects such as garlands and fountains, as the Floreria of the Vatican Palace was just about this time – though not one hopes with the sleep-inducing effects that Alberti attributed to this form of decoration, as it was subsequently used as the library!

Alberti's conception of gardens was also lifted straight out of classical works, especially his instructions for planting. Paths were to be bordered with symmetrically planted flowering trees, such as pomegranates and cornelian cherries, garlanded with roses, and box and scented evergreen herbs cut 'in the charming habit of the ancients' to write the name of the owner, and to make geometrical designs. Vine pergolas supported by marble columns, whose proportions correspond to the classical canons – their thickness being a tenth of their length – and labyrinths and shady groves planted with juniper, bays, myrtles, oaks, and cypresses garlanded with ivy. Fountains were to be everywhere, surrounded by pots and amphorae filled with flowers, that were also to be used for the adornment of the garden in general as they had been in the Hellenistic gardens of Alexandria and Agrigento.

Strangely lacking in Alberti's directions for the creation of gardens are any precise indications about layout and architectural elements, which played such a predominant role in Roman gardens, both of the Empire and Renaissance. His only reference to sculpture, that was such an important feature of Roman gardens of both periods, is a warning that although he does not disapprove of the use of statues 'that make one laugh', he considers that suggestive or downright indecent ones have no place in a garden which is 'a place for gravity more than a house in a city'. Alberti does, however, go into very considerable detail in describing how grottoes should be made as 'the ancients used to do, covering the surface with rough and rocky things, putting there little bits of pumice, spongy stone and travertine'. He quotes Ovid in this connexion and says that he had seen an artificial cave with a fountain made in this style whose decoration pleased him very much as, in addition to the rustic stone covering, there were designs of various sorts of cockle and oyster shells. Alberti does not specifically say that this grotto was an ancient one, but it is quite possible that this was so, as we know from Pirro Ligorio that similar decoration still existed in the ruins of Hadrian's villa in the sixteenth century, and very probably in other Roman ruins that were visible in Alberti's day which have since disappeared; other examples have since been excavated at Pompeii and Sperlonga.

It is remarkable, however, that this reference to grottoes is the only one in which Alberti says that he had himself actually *seen* anything of the kind – all his other references to classical gardens are purely literary. It is also the only passage in which he gives a detailed description of any architectural aspect of a garden – remaining instructions in this respect are purely generic – and for the rest he is mainly concerned with planting in the classical style. From this and certain other aspects of the treatise, it appears that for all his parade of classical knowledge, and it should be noted that this was culled from classical literary sources only, Alberti's conception of a garden, though aspiring to humanistic ideals, was still wedded to the past. The site and its relation to the surrounding landscape had regained the importance which it held in Roman times and so had the relationship of the house and garden as an integrated unit. The planting was faithfully copied from Pliny and small architectural accents such as pergolas with marble columns, some statues, urns, and amphorae and above all grottoes had returned to use, but the idea of axial planning and the employment of architectural adjuncts on a large scale were still absent. One of the features suggested by Alberti even seems to hark back to the Middle Ages – the large grassy space in front of the house for use as a *manège* and to practise archery, which recalls Pietro de' Crescenzi's meadow where tame animals were to be seen disporting themselves before the palace.

From contemporary descriptions of mid-fifteenth-century Florentine gardens that have survived, it is evident that they corresponded very closely to the instructions laid down by Alberti in his treatise, especially those of the suburban villas sited on the outskirts of Florence that he advocated as the ideal compromise between the seclusion of a country villa and the bustle of a town house, and particularly suitable as the retreat of a man of letters. A detailed description of just such a suburban villa occurs in the diaries of Giovanni Rucellai, who owned the famous villa of Quaracchi, built about 1459. The house stood on a slight eminence and was surrounded by a moat and fish ponds, but from the description of the tree-shaded and balustraded terrace that overlooked them it appears that here the water served a decorative rather than a defensive purpose. A simple axial plan already evidently existed in this garden, for its owner says that the chief pergola led from the front door that had a small loggia above it, down the centre of the garden, and that it was flanked by walks bordered by breast-high hedges of box, with the arms of the family suspended above as a festoon. The pergola terminated in the *giardino segreto*, which was a garden room, filled with sweet-smelling herbs and flowers such as marjoram, basil and sweet rocket, growing in terracotta pots placed round a small lawn. Topiary in the modern sense of clipped hedges and figures of box was one of the chief ornaments of this little private garden that must have been a truly delightful retreat, filled with the scent of flowers and the spicy aroma of herbs and also providing some much-needed privacy for the owner and his family, as it is evident that the garden lay open to the eyes and enjoyment of passers-by on the Pistoia road.

The main axis of the Quaracchi garden was continued on the far side of the *giardino segreto* by an avenue of trees that led to the banks of the Arno. Apart from this there appears to have been no attempt to achieve a symmetrical layout and a large part of the garden was given over to hedged orchards divided by seats shaded by evergreens. Except for a considerable amount of topiary, most of the main features of the garden were medieval – arbours of evergreen and honeysuckle, a mount planted with evergreens, and aviary and a rose garden. Already, however, it is evident that humanistic studies had revived an interest in horticulture and Giovanni Rucellai mentions with pride a sycamore and exotic fruit trees that he may well have brought back from his foreign travels.

Villa of Cafaggiolo

An interesting picture of what a Medici villa of this period looked like is to be seen in one of the fascinating lunettes of the Medici properties in the Topographical Museum of Florence. Although this painting representing the Villa of Cafaggiolo dates from the end of the sixteenth century, from the very simplicity of the layout it is probable that it had not been changed in the hundred and fifty years since it was first laid out (pl. 30). Cosimo had commissioned Michelozzo to build the villa in 1451, and at the time of his death in 1464 his grandsons Lorenzo and Giuliano were spending the summer there, and it was about this time that Lorenzo asked his father Piero's permission to lay out a garden. Lorenzo's love of flowers and the countryside is evident even from the boyish poems he wrote at Cafaggiolo, describing the 'beautiful fresh purple violets in the grass and the red and white rosebuds in the garden' and the song of the nightingales in the ilex woods. This appreciation of natural beauty was an endearing characteristic also of the later generations of the Medici, who as grand dukes of Tuscany still planted with their own hands and cared for the flowers in their gardens even in the more artificial world of the sixteenth and seventeenth centuries.

Lorenzo's Cafaggiolo garden has long since disappeared, but judging from the picture, with its topiary bower and circular fountain in front, and its simple square beds and small vine pergolas behind, it was typical of the period, resembling Quaracchi in its elementary axial plan and its tree-fringed walk by the river. Plans for similar layouts of country villas appear in Filarete's remarkable architectural treatise written probably about 1467 and dedicated to Lorenzo's father Piero de' Medici, of which manuscript copies exist in the Vatican and in the National Library in Florence. Filarete's gardens are grander, most of them being surrounded by porticos and having a central pool or fountain – one of them is even ambitiously entitled 'a gymnasium for princes'! Of even more strikingly classical inspiration were 'the labours of Hercules' painted in the loggias surrounding the garden of a villa which he designed for Francesco Sforza, but the garden itself was the old medieval type with walks surrounding a flowery mead.

A more ambitious type of layout was, however, at last coming into fashion, of which both plans and verbal accounts have survived. Among the drawings in the Uffizi there is a garden plan autographed in Peruzzi's own handwriting, that probably dates from the turn of the century. This already shows a simple adaptation of an irregular site to conform with Renaissance ideas of symmetry – an indication that it was probably definitely commissioned, not just a project. Simple though the layout is, the rectangular medieval beds have already been replaced by geometrically designed parterres, though the paths are still shaded by trellises in the traditional fashion. The central crossing is enlarged to form an octagonal space, with trellised bays at the angles, that project into the surrounding parterres; one of these bays contained a fountain and it seems likely that the whole space was covered by a trellised cupola. A small two-storied garden house completes the plan, where the greatest interest lies in the design of the parterres, with geometrical patterns that were in common use in Italian gardens for another two hundred years, until they were superseded by the elaborate French *broderies*.

Ducal Palace - Urbino

The description, in a letter written by Bernardino Baldi some years later, of the layout that Laurana designed for the *giardino pensile* of the Ducal Palace at Urbino at the end of the fifteenth century, shows that even in a small enclosed space the great architect had already employed some of the basic principles of Italian Renaissance garden design. The writer describes how Laurana imposed a geometrical plan on the whole garden by a series of paved paths that divided it up into squares and how he enlarged each crossing of the paths to form a circular space, the one in the centre of the garden having a circular fountain raised upon steps. The beds were also slightly raised above the levels of the paths and in the centre of each there stood a large amphora or vase of flowers on a raised circular base. Stone seats were placed round the walls which were covered with trellises of ivy and jasmine – an effective example of mixed planting for all seasons of the year that was used much later in Renaissance gardens.

So far, symmetrical planning appears only to have been applied to small gardens or to the *giardini segreti* that formed an isolated unit among the orchards, meadows and pergolas occupying by far the largest proportion of most gardens.

For the first time, in the architectural treatise written by Francesco di Giorgio Martini, towards the end of the fifteenth century, the revolutionary idea of a whole garden planned as a perfect geometrical figure makes its appearance. The author advocated the use of a circle, square, or triangle or even the more complicated forms of a pentagon or hexagon; and there is no doubt that Francesco di Giorgio had the layout of quite an extensive garden in mind, for he says that it should contain the old Roman 'deambulazione' and covered 'palestre', though he evidently envisages these as being made of clipped greens and not as architectural porticos. Alberti's maxim, corresponding to the humanist idea that a garden is a place for 'coveniete gravità' was evidently already well recognized, as Francesco di Giorgio insists that gardens should contain retired and 'secret places such as are desired by poets and philosophers'. But once having laid down these basic requirements, unlike Laurana, the author evidently still considered the details of garden design to be more a matter 'for the pleasure of those who build them', and that the owner should consult his own opinions as to the siting of individual features; an attitude which appears to have been very generally accepted until the sixteenth century when the foremost architects of the day were commissioned to design gardens in the same detail as houses.

The importance attributed to gardens in the minds of fifteenth-century humanists is illustrated by the curious allegorical romance that was written by Francesco Colonna about 1467, and was one of the earliest Italian works to be published by the Aldine Press thirty-two years later. The author of the *Hypnerotomachia*, who wrote under the pseudonym of Poliphilus, was – almost incredibly to the modern mind – a Dominican monk, for the romance is far from platonic and the setting frankly pagan. The title, a combination of three Greek words, was accurately rendered in the English version published in 1592 as *Love's Struggle in a Dream*; but it is in fact misleading, as the romance is really only a peg for the author's architectural theories, which are predominantly concerned with gardens. Much of the action of the story takes place in a succession of gardens, of which the 'place of heart's desire' – a whole island laid out as a garden – is the most important, but all are minutely described right down to the most insignificant details of planting, and the design of individual parterres is illustrated by woodcuts. It is generally considered that not only did Colonna describe many aspects of the gardens of his day as they actually existed, but also that, especially in the use of classical architectural motifs, his book must have exercised a profound influence upon garden design in humanistic circles throughout Europe, as it was soon published in French as well as English.

Colonna followed Francesco di Giorgio's tenets in laying out his imaginary garden of 'heart's desire' in the form of a circle of level ground, whose outer perimeter was bounded by a topiary hedge of clipped myrtle and cypresses. Inside it was laid out in concentric circles divided into segments, each of which was given over to a different type of planting. There were 'vegetable and botanical gardens, orchards, and a wonderful mixture of green trees, of gracious woods and delightful shrubs'. Each of these woods was of a different species – of bays and laurels, various kinds of oaks, or pines, or varieties of nut trees; there was a scented wood planted with cypress, juniper and rosemary, and an enclosure for animals hedged with myrtles and citrus trees. These wooded sections of the garden in turn gave way to a series of meadows divided regularly into sections by covered walks, shaded by trellises covered with honeysuckle, jasmine, convolvulus, clematis and other creepers. In the corners of the meadows were apple trees trained to form circles, whose trunks emerged from small ornamental platforms rising in steps, each one of which was planted with a different fragrant herb. Some of the meadows were enclosed by trellises and, in the medieval fashion, had a marble bath in the centre where the lovers of the romance disported themselves with nymphs (pls. 31, 32).

There was a rose garden planted, inevitably by a humanist, with the roses named by Pliny – the Damascene, Prenestine, Campanian, Milesian, Lychnian, and roses of Paestum of classical fame. This was surrounded by a peristyle garden whose Corinthian columns strike a new and truly Renaissance note in garden design, though the planting was very similar to the *giardino segreto* of Quaracchi – scented herbs and shrubs like marjoram, lavender cotton, box, juniper, and small myrtles clipped in varying shapes and grown in antique vases and pots. A flowery mead intervened between the peristyle and a river and in describing this Colonna displays a curiously mixed botanical knowledge, partly drawn from classical sources and partly from traditional medieval lore. But the result is definitely not just a list of names lifted from the works of the two Plinys, as were nearly all the other humanist descriptions of planting. It shows that this Dominican monk really knew and loved flowers and had studied their growth and habits. The flowers he described are very simple ones – the grassy space was planted with gladioli, blue, white, and purple hyacinths, helenium, lavender, and scented herbs like marjoram and mint; the river's edge with narcissus, orchis, gladioli, iris,

buttercups, mares-tails, pansies, balsam, and forget-me-nots. Even the list of names conjures up a charming picture and one that is unique in garden literature of the period, where few flowers other than roses and violets and an occasional carnation are ever mentioned, nor would the selection of plants be out of place in a wild garden of today.

The actual names Colonna uses provide further evidence of his curiously eclectic knowledge and make identification exceedingly difficult. Some of them are Greek, some Latin, and some the common names of the Italian countryside. One kind of orchid, for instance, he calls '*dilbulbo unomico*', evidently referring to the double tuber of the man orchid that, like the lady orchid, was, according to Italian country superstition, not only aphrodisiac but had magical properties and, like the mandrake, could actually produce men. Both varieties are mentioned as being cultivated in Italian gardening books of the seventeenth and eighteenth centuries.

The 'river' was evidently an ornamental piece of water enclosing a completely formal garden, laid out in a series of knotted parterres of highly complicated design (pl. 33). There is little doubt that elaborate parterres were a feature of contemporary gardens, for the author of an agricultural treatise, Giovanvittorio Soderini, who lived in Florence between 1501 and 1597, mentions with approval the new fashion of planting parterres in the form of coats of arms, clocks, and human figures in immortelles, thyme, and sweet-smelling herbs. This corresponds exactly to these described by Colonna, which a hundred years later were

31, 32 HYPNEROTOMACHIA
Illustrations from the 1499 Aldine edition of the Hypnerotomachia Poliphili, *a curious romance that really served as a peg upon which to hang the author's theories on architecture and gardens. It was translated into several languages and had a considerable influence upon garden design. Plate 31 shows a berceau or covered walk of the type used for roses, jasmine or other creepers, a common feature of medieval gardens that survived in Italian gardens of the fifteenth and sixteenth centuries. The introduction of what is apparently meant to represent a classical relief is of particular interest as it is one of the earliest illustrations portraying their use in Italian gardens.*

also advocated by the English garden authors Thomas Hill and Andrew Borde.

It is evident that already by 1467 the design and planting of parterres had become a highly developed art; the knots were carried out in a variety of scented herbs, whose contrasting tones of green would have been decorative even in winter, and in summer would have provided a charming setting for coloured flowers. The labour involved in their upkeep must, however, have been no light matter, as they had to be constantly clipped and replanted every three years if they were not to become shaggy and dominate the flowers instead of simply providing their setting. In view of this it is not surprising to find that both Italian and French gardening books of the seventeenth century recommend instead the use of box, and in Italy rounded bricks called '*pianelle*' were also used as a labour-saving substitute.

Marjoram, rue, southernwood, germander, lavender cotton, thyme, and cat thyme were the principal herbs listed by Colonna for the making of knots. The intervening spaces were planted with white and yellow pansies, primroses, love-in-the-mist, and purple and white violets. As a foil for these smaller flowers, clumps of hollyhocks and clipped balls of hyssop were symmetrically spaced among them, while the centre of alternate parterres was occupied, as in Laurana's garden at Urbino, by small Roman altars or large urns with a cypress tree surrounded by flowers or box clipped in such complicated forms as peacocks drinking from a bowl (pl. 35).

Another very charming flower garden is described in a later chapter of the *Hypnerotomachia*, situated in what appears to have been a Roman ruin resembling a small

version of the Colosseum. Though this at first sight may appear to be a fantasy, it should be borne in mind that Augustus' tomb in Rome was really converted into a garden, of which Bufalini's sixteenth-century prints are still extant, and that many Roman ruins like the Theatre of Marcellus had been converted into dwellings. The seats or steps inside this imaginary amphitheatre were laid out as beds planted with white and yellow narcissus, cyclamen, cornflowers, pinks and melilots, while the central area was divided by covered walks or galleries − *berceaux* as they are called in French − shaded by roses and clipped myrtle or cypresses and flanked by beds of yellow ranunculus, red anemones, carnations, primroses, yellow immortelles, love-lies-bleeding, wallflowers, lily-of-the-valley, white and orange lilies, hyacinths and columbines.

From the descriptions of these and other gardens that occur in the course of Colonna's narrative it is evident that flowers were cherished and many more varieties of them were grown in these early Italian Renaissance gardens than is usually supposed. The general assumption that flowers played a very minor role even in early gardens in Italy is probably due to the fact that, unlike the English and other northern peoples, Italians in general are not in the least interested in their names, and when describing gardens at almost any period in their history they only mention violets and roses, or an occasional lily and carnation. The rest are simply referred to generically − as Alberti does in his *De Vita Rustica* − as 'the thousand perfect colours of various flowers'. There are no 'ladies' smocks all silver white' or 'daffodils that come before the swallow dares' in Italian literature and very rarely even in art − the close examination of almost any Italian garden in a picture will generally only reveal the usual roses, violets, lilies and carnations and very little else that is definitely distinguishable as a botanical specimen. Nor do those usually inexhaustible mines of information − the account books of ancient family archives even of later centuries − help much more. The receipted bills generally only list the various kinds of citrus fruit trees, which were highly esteemed, possibly some bulbs; and the rest of the plants are dismissed as '*un buon cárico di fiori nóbili*'! D. H. Lawrence expressed the frustration of many an English traveller when he said that if you ask an Italian peasant the name of one flower he will simply say: 'It is a flower'; and of another: 'It is a flower that smells.' From this the rarity value and interest of Colonna's description of even a dream-garden of the fifteenth century in which lists of flower names are actually given will be readily appreciated.

Another very interesting aspect of the *Hypnerotomachia* gardens is their architectural setting, of which the amphitheatre and peristyle gardens are particularly striking examples, and the constant references to antique reliefs, statues and herms, altars and amphorae

33 FIFTEENTH-CENTURY PARTERRE
Woodcut from the Aldine edition of the Hypnerotomachia *of Poliphilus, Venice, 1499. The parterre was planted with fifteen kinds of flowers and herbs: 1 Marjoram, 2 Rue, 3 Hollyhocks, 4 Hyssop, 5 Tufted Columbine, 6 Germander, 7 Southernwood, 8 Primroses, 9 Lavender cotton, 10 Yellow pansies, 11 Love-in-a-mist, 12 Thyme, 13 Cyclamen, 14 Purple violets, 15 White violets.*

34 FIFTEENTH-CENTURY PARTERRE
Woodcut from the Hypnerotomachia, *1499.*

35 SMALL ANTIQUE ALTAR WITH A CYPRESS TREE
This was placed in the middle of the parterre (pl. 33). Woodcut from the Hypnerotomachia, *1499.*

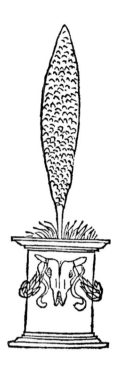

being used as garden ornaments, while at one stage in the narrative the hero and heroine wander through a landscape of classical ruins. In this, Colonna was very far in advance not only of the gardens of his time but even of the architectural treatises. We have already noted Alberti's deficiencies in this respect and even in Laurana's garden at Urbino there is no mention of sculpture, whereas a generation later the garden of Isabella d'Este's famous Grotta at Mantua, which was a good deal smaller, had statues ranged round the walls that were also covered with jasmine and ivy.

There is little doubt that the *Hypnerotomachia* must have played a considerable part in the gradually awakening humanist interest in classical art that had lagged considerably behind the rediscovery of learning and literature. As late as 1483 even Poggio Bracciolini, who was the first man really to examine the ruins of Rome with a lively visual sense, was mocked by his learned friends for placing Roman statues in his garden at Terra Nuova; they accused him of trying thereby to create for himself a gallery of noble ancestors, to which Poggio tartly replied that he had acquired nobility by the discovery of such marvels. Poggio's collection, together with that of Niccolò Niccoli, who even drank his wine out of antique vessels, was later bought by the Medici. For Lorenzo too had begun to collect and he laid out a garden in the Piazza San Marco with a casino, loggias and arbours where the statues were displayed for the benefit of artists and sculptors, and it was here that young Michelangelo came to study.

In one respect the gardens of the *Hypnerotomachia* are strangely anachronistic – the site was level and Colonna specifically mentions that there were no 'pools hidden in shadowy depths' – a feature that would have delighted the garden architects of the High Renaissance. In this, as in so many other things, it is evident that the gardens of the quattrocento humanists in general were – like those of Alberti and Francesco di Giorgio – for all their siting, regular plans, and what might almost be termed 'classical quotations', still strictly two-dimensional. The architectural exploitation of a sloping site, that was to add a third dimension, in a belated imitation of the current trends in painting, did not in fact make its appearance until the High Renaissance, when the leadership of the intellectual world had passed from Florence to Rome. It was only then that the Italian garden achieved full expression, after architects and artists such as Bramante, Raphael, Pirro Ligorio, and Vignola had studied and measured the ruins of antiquity before they embarked upon the design of their garden plans. Thus the Early Renaissance gardens of the quattrocento were really transitional in character; with their flat or slightly sloping enclosures divided up into square or rectangular divisions by covered galleries of greenery, and with their circular central fountains and their lawns before the house, they still hark back in many respects to the gardens of the Middle Ages. They are perhaps best described as garden rooms with a view that were an extension of the house itself, but not as yet definite architectural compositions that, timidly at first, but gradually with increasing boldness and confidence, linked the house to the landscape and finally in the Baroque period, merged into it.

This transitional type of garden reached its zenith in Florence, where it probably first originated, and because of this and its suitability for the intimate and civilized landscape of small hills and valleys it lingered long in Tuscany. Regional pride and conservatism that associated this particular style with the national heritage probably also played their part; financially too this type of garden was a great deal less expensive to carry out than the vast architectural layouts that characterized the sixteenth- and seventeenth-century gardens of Rome. Tuscan taste has always been more delicate and never equalled the Roman in its love of pomp and lavish display of wealth, nor was the Grand Duchy comparatively so wealthy as quattrocento Florence, that led the world in banking and trade, or sixteenth-century Rome. No doubt there were many contributory reasons, but the fact remains that with one or two notable exceptions, such as the semi-regal Boboli and Pratolino, Florentine and Tuscan gardens in general preserved this distinctive, slightly anachronistic, character right into the seventeenth century.

Tuscan Gardens

Of the early renaissance gardens of Tuscany, and even those of later periods, few have survived that have not been altered, sometimes almost out of recognition, by changing fashions and particularly by the nineteenth-century craze for the 'English' garden. In attempting the impossible by trying to create an English landscape even in the confined limits of the gardens of many small Tuscan villas, the formal parterres, which were an integral part of the original design, were destroyed and their place was taken by meandering paths and ugly irregular beds that bear no relation to the scale, character or site. It is usually only in very remote places, owing to the stout conservatism of past owners, or sometimes simply neglect, that part or all of the original layout has survived; and today, happily, it is usually recognized as a work of art to be cherished.

V VILLA GARZONI

36 IL TREBBIO
A lunette in the Museo Topografico in Florence, probably painted by Utens at the end of the sixteenth or the beginning of the seventeenth century, showing the house and garden of the Medici villa of Il Trebbio, near Cafaggiolo. This hunting lodge was restored by Michelozzo for Cosimo de' Medici probably about the year 1451. It is one of the very rare examples of an Early Renaissance villa which has survived more or less untouched since the fifteenth century. It now belongs to Signor Scaretti. Photo Alinari.

Il Trebbio · Cafaggiolo

The garden of Il Trebbio, the hunting-lodge *dépendance* of the famous Medici villa of Cafaggiolo, is one of these rare treasures — a garden of the quattrocento, that has retained its simple charm almost untouched through centuries of neglect to be preserved in excellent condition by its present owners. The house is a four-square castellated villa with a watch-tower, that was converted for Cosimo de' Medici by Michelozzo about 1451. It stands perched on a hill-top which commands some of the most beautiful views in Tuscany. The roads leading up to it are fringed with cypresses, and at every turn of the road one is confronted with a scene that brings to mind the view glimpsed through the window of some quattrocento 'Annunciation'. As might be expected in a castellated house of this kind, the garden is more medieval than Renaissance. It is a walled enclosure detached from the house, lying on a sloping site to the south. A lunette in the Museo Topografico in Florence (pl. 37), painted possibly by Utens or an unknown artist of the early seventeenth century, shows the layout of house, chapel, farm and walled garden, just as it probably looked in Cosimo's time and almost exactly as it is today. In the garden, the lower pergola is now missing and, in order to give a better view, the artist has represented it as lying at a slightly wider angle in relation to the house, but otherwise it is still the same.

The surviving vine pergola shades a grassy terrace, which runs the whole length of one side of the garden and is one of the very few in Italy to have retained its original columns (pl. 36). These are made of warm red semicircular bricks with grey stone plinths and simple foliage capitals. From it the view extends over the garden, laid out in square beds of flowers and vegetables, to the vast panorama of hills beyond. It is the typical Tuscan garden 'room with a view' in its simplest form, but a place of such enchantment that it is unforgettable. As one paces along, the scent of roses and the aromatic tang of cypresses, distilled by the hot Italian sun, rise up in waves to mingle with the sound of bees at work among the flowers and herbs of the beds below, and on an early autumn day golden-tinted vine leaves frame the never-ending vistas of blue mountains, broken only by the dark spires of the cypresses.

37 IL TREBBIO
The pergola in the garden of the Medici villa of Il Trebbio as it is today. It is one of the very few to have retained its original columns.

38 VILLA MEDICI FIESOLE
The giardino segreto of the Villa Medici at Fiesole. A corner that has preserved the layout and atmosphere of this earliest terraced garden of the Renaissance, which was built by Michelozzo for Cosimo de' Medici about 1458. The villa now belongs to Signor Mazzini.

Villa Medici · Fiesole

The Villa Medici at Fiesole is a complete contrast to the wild, almost medieval Trebbio, although it was designed by the same architect and built only a few years later – between 1458 and 1461. Both inside and out the Fiesole villa has suffered so many subsequent alterations that most of its original fifteenth-century character has disappeared. Superficially too, the garden has been much altered, but the fundamental lines of its terraces and, above all, its fabulous view have changed little since the day when it was built.

It is this view that fulfils more perfectly perhaps than any other Medici villa Alberti's maxim that the site should overlook a city or plain 'bounded by familiar mountains' and that in the foreground there should be the 'delicacy of gardens'. For this Fiesole villa has all of these in full measure, and even for that alone might well be considered the first true Renaissance villa of Italy.

According to Vasari, the building of the house and garden terraces cost an enormous sum of money, and even today their erection on the precipitous hillside would be a major undertaking, but the result achieved of a series of garden rooms projecting into space is truly superb. The main terrace upon which the villa stands is approached in typically Tuscan style by a long avenue of cypresses; on the hill above this is another cypress walk and a bowling-alley that probably formed part of the original layout. The terrace in front of the house is now an open grassy space, shaded by trees and bordered with lemon trees in pots, but this has probably undergone many changes since the fifteenth century (pl. VI). It is only on the prolongation of this terrace, in the little *giardino segreto* behind the house, that the Renaissance world lives still in the green shade of this garden room with its simple box parterres and gently trickling fountain. Perhaps it was here that Politian retired to write his *Rusticus* and his poems about flowers and beautiful ladies, or sat up late into the night talking to Lorenzo the Magnificent. Though only a few paces square and laid out in the simplest Renaissance style, with a circular opening and fountain at the crossing of the paths, this little garden was perfectly designed for talk or contemplation, with stone seats placed along the wall of the house for daytime shade and to catch the low evening sun, while at the corner

VI, VII VILLA MEDICI FIESOLE

the boundary wall is replaced by stone balusters so that the beautiful view over Florence and the valley of the Arno, that also inspired one of Politian's poems, can be glimpsed through them (pl. 38).

The lower terraces of the garden can only be reached from the cellars of the house or by a circuitous route leading from the entrance avenue, a somewhat clumsy arrangement that shows clearly the elementary stage of garden design at the time when the villa was built, which did not yet envisage the exploitation of a hillside site as an opportunity for the spectacular use of connecting stairs and ramps that was to become a *tour de force* of later Renaissance garden architects. The lower terrace is divided into two slightly different levels, the upper one being occupied as at Il Trebbio by a pergola, though here unfortunately the original supporting columns have disappeared. On this terrace, however, the timid beginnings of an axial plan are evident; a narrow flight of steps leads from the middle of the pergola down to the lower levels, where a modern reconstruction of simple rectangular parterres, grouped around a central fountain and punctuated by clipped box, has been laid out, though the only likely relic of the original garden scheme is the raised border that runs along the retaining wall of the pergola. The Villa Medici has lately been bought by a new owner who, as the phrase is so appropriate, would perhaps not mind being described as a 'Merchant of Prato'. Due to his very evident knowledge and appreciation, and the loving care of the old gardener, this beautiful villa is once again assuming the indefinable air that pervades a well-loved garden like the scent of the roses and lemon blossom which now fills it. And today, for all the changes wrought by the centuries, this Fiesole garden still recalls the days when Lorenzo the Magnificent gave suppers there to Pico della Mirandola, Marsilio Ficino and other members of the Platonic Academy, and together with Careggi it shared the honour of being the birthplace of the humanist movement.

Though geographically it is some distance away, there is another Tuscan garden of the mid fifteenth century that is closely related in spirit at any rate to these early gardens of the Medici. This is scarcely surprising as Aeneas Silvius Piccolomini, for whom it was made, was one of the most ardent humanists of his time. Shortly after he became Pope in 1485, as Pius II he visited his birthplace, the little village of Corsignano which stands on a hilltop overlooking the Val D'Orcia. During his short stay at Corsignano the Pope decided to rebuild the village as a model town and to rename it Pienza after himself. It was probably on the advice of his old friend Alberti that Pius chose Bernardo Gambarelli of Settignano, or Rossellino as he is usually called, to carry out his plan, which resulted in the creation of one of the most charming small towns in Italy.

Palazzo Piccolomini - Pienza

One of the principal buildings in Pienza is the Piccolomini Palace, whose design is based on Alberti's Palazzo Rucellai in Florence. Apart from his friendship with the architect, the introduction of the classical orders no doubt attracted the antiquarian Pope, who had himself visited most of the famous Roman ruins, including Hadrian's villa. Although the street façades of the Piccolomini Palace are modelled on those of Palazzo Rucellai, that facing the Val D'Orcia is completely original, for the whole of its length is occupied by a triple loggia of extraordinary grace which overlooks a small hanging garden and the vast sweep of mountain and valley beyond (pl. 39). There is little doubt that although Rossellino was the executor of this singularly beautiful plan, the Pope himself provided the inspiration for its design. Pius' appreciation of landscape and particularly of spectacular views is a recurrent theme in his famous *Commentaries*. In them he describes the beauties of the woods of Nerni and the Campagna seen from the Alban Hills, and he particularly loved the rocky promontory of Capodimonte on Lake Bolsena. Even when he became Pope he was accustomed to receiving ambassadors or holding a Consistory in the open air, seated beside a gurgling spring in the shade of the forest trees.

To a man of such tastes, Corsignano would have appealed not only because it was his birthplace, but also for its superb site. On entering the main door of Palazzo Piccolomini, even in the shadows of the narrow vestibule, one's attention is immediately drawn to the central doorway across the porticoed court, through which one catches a glimpse of green and an impression of vast sunlit space beyond. On entering the garden however, it appears as a small enclosed garden room, filled with the scent of the clipped box hedges that surround the raised parterres and provide a screen on the far side. This is pierced by three arches, and, it is only from there, and from the loggia of the *piano nobile* of the palace, that the subtlety of the garden design is fully appreciated, which in so small a space provides the amenities of a sheltered *giardino segreto* combined with one of the most spectacular views in Italy.

Here for once the original quattrocento garden design and furniture have survived almost untouched. The stone borders of the raised beds, which surround the garden on

39 PALAZZO PICCOLOMINI
The garden and loggias of the Palazzo Piccolomini at Pienza, built for Aeneas Silvius Piccolomini, who, as Pope Pius II, transformed his native village of Corsignano into a model town, renaming it Pienza. It has survived with relatively little alteration. The palace belongs to Count Piccolomini.

three sides and of the four central parterres, are still there, also the octagonal well-head with its exquisitely sculptured reliefs of garlanded urns and shells and the Piccolomini arms surrounded by twining acanthus (pl. 40). In one respect, however, the original layout has been altered. It was first laid out before Laurana created his epoch-making design for the *giardino pensile* at Urbino and, instead of the present circular space in the middle of the crossing of the paths made by the actual owner, there were simply four rectangular beds like those of medieval times; the charming little fountain is also a recent addition.

Villa Cigliano - San Casciano

Very little known to foreigners, but enchanting for its typically quattrocento Tuscan style, is the garden of Marchese Antinori's Villa Cigliano at San Casciano that survived almost untouched until the English garden craze of the nineteenth century. The house and chapel built by Cosimo de' Medici's friend, Alessandro Antinori, are perfect examples of quattrocento Tuscan architecture at its best. Unfortunately it is on the walled garden that the heavy hand of changing fashion has been laid. First in 1691, when a Baroque façade was added to the lovely quattrocento loggia that separates the courtyard of the house from the garden and a fountain built at its far end, and secondly – much more disastrously – about a hundred years ago, when all but vestiges of the formal layout were replaced by winding paths and irregular flower-beds.

The loss occasioned by this misjudged conversion is the greater because it is evident from what remains of the original garden that it must have been a perfect example of the Tuscan garden room, built as a direct extension of the house and planned as an integral part of its whole design. From the main courtyard entrance its whole length could be seen through the loggia at the far side, in the same way as in Palazzo Piccolomini. Its area was, however, far larger, for this is no longer the garden of a town palace but of a country house that is the administrative centre of a large estate. It is a typically country garden of the same homely type as Il Trebbio. In 1922 the walls were still covered with espaliered fruit trees, roses and jasmine, and the rose-beds edged with strawberries. In the old days its parterres were probably planted with medicinal and pot herbs as well as flowers. Sadly, all that remains of them now are the raised borders with fine stone mouldings that surround the walls, where lemon trees are ranged in pots, filling with their scent this sunny enclosed space that in spite of everything is still so reminiscent of old Tuscany.

Medici Villa - Castello

Very different in size and grandeur, though its basic principle is still that of a garden room built as an extension of the house, is the Medici villa at Castello that Tribolo laid out for Cosimo, the first Medici to become Grand Duke of Tuscany, about 1540. A house and garden had existed on the site since the previous century, when it had been bought by two Medici brothers. Giovanni was married to Caterina Sforza, Cosimo's redoubtable grandmother, who lived here from 1501 to 1509, after she had been released by the Borgias from the grim dungeons of Castel Sant' Angelo, where her experiences had quenched the beauty that before had 'glowed like the sun and rivalled lilies and roses'. The Grand Duke had never seen her and cannot either have remembered his gallant soldier father, Giovanni delle Bande Nere, who like himself had also paid visits to the old house during his boyhood, but these family associations seem to have endeared the place even to the cold heart of Cosimo, as he often came there in search of peace and quiet. In the end he retired there with Camilla Martelli, his beautiful young Cinderella of a wife, leaving his son by a previous marriage to

40 PALAZZO PICCOLOMINI
The well in the garden of Palazzo Piccolomini at Pienza.

attend to the affairs of State, and devoting himself to the cultivation of jasmine.

It is said that the original plan of the garden was suggested to Tribolo by Benedetto Varchi, Cosimo's historian friend who lived in the neighbouring Villa Topaja, and that it was so vast that neither Tribolo nor his successor Buontalenti were able to carry it out in its entirety. But even this partial execution aroused universal admiration among contemporaries – Vasari described it as the 'most rich, magnificent and ornamental garden in Europe'. While there is no doubt that, with its fountains and statuary, thrown into relief by evergreens and fruit trees, and its lovely view, Castello then presented a charming spectacle, its design was so conservative as to be positively anachronistic when compared with Bramante's Giardino del Belvedere in the Vatican which was begun nearly forty years earlier, and within the next ten years it was to be completely outstripped by the other new garden designs of Rome.

In many ways Castello is the perfect example of the classic Tuscan garden, which still drew its inspiration from the tenets of Alberti and whose main features were firmly rooted in the past. Like the famous Rucellai garden of Quaracchi, it was originally intended that an avenue of trees should lead from the Arno up to the house which, also like Quaracchi, stood on a terrace above ornamental fish ponds. In accordance with Alberti's ideas, this terrace was designed for jousting and used as a *manège*, as can be clearly seen in Giusto Utens' lunette in the Museo Topografico, which was probably painted about the turn of the sixteenth century.

41 CASTELLO
Utens' lunette of the Medici villa of Castello in the Museo Topografico in Florence, showing the garden layout at the end of the sixteenth or the beginning of the seventeenth century. The garden room of Castello is a typical Tuscan example, laid out by Tribolo for Cosimo I about 1540, its style is conservative in comparison with contemporary Roman gardens. The villa belongs to the State. Photo by kind permission of the Soprintendenza alle Gallerie of Florence.

CASTELLO

Although Utens' picture does not correspond exactly with earlier descriptions of the garden, this is only in small details, and broadly speaking its basic lines are the same as those that we see today, so that it may be taken as a fairly reliable guide (pl. 41). What at once leaps to one's mind when looking at the picture is the aptitude of Vasari's description when he said that the garden was a 'secret' one, for it is still basically the *hortus conclusus* of medieval times, in spite of its surrounding *boschi*, splendid adornments and symmetrical design. The nucleus of the whole garden layout was simply a square walled garden lying on a gentle slope behind the house, whose central feature was a circular fountain adorned with statues, surrounded, it is true, with a *bosco* or labyrinth instead of a flowery mead, but the series of simple rectangular beds that completed the layout would not have looked out of place in a medieval garden.

Both Vasari and Montaigne, who visited Castello in 1580, described another medieval feature that had evidently already disappeared by the end of the century, when Utens painted his picture. According to them, the paths of this central garden were shaded by pleached alleys that must have been one of its most attractive features, for in the words of Montaigne these '*bresseaux*' (*berceaux*) were '*de tous arbres odorans, comme cèdres, ciprès, orangers, citronniers et d'oliviers*', whose branches were completely interlaced. Vasari says that the garden walls were also all covered with espaliered pomegranates and bitter oranges. In Utens' picture, and according to Vasari's description, this main garden was separated by a wall, adorned with fountains, from what is today simply an upper terrace, which was originally designed as the lemon garden. Out of this leads the famous grotto, whose shell mosaics, surprise fountains, and animal sculptures aroused such enthusiasm in Montaigne and other travellers. Two flights of stairs lead from this lemon garden to an upper terrace with a marvellous view over the whole garden and the Arno valley. This terrace is sheltered from the north by woods, now threaded by meandering paths, in place of Utens' neat plantations, and a large pool with Ammanati's colossal statue representing the personification of the Apennines, hugging himself and shivering with cold.

Two smaller secret gardens were laid out on either side of the main one. That on the east contained a tree house, similar to one that survived until quite recently in the neighbouring Villa Petraia, with a room contrived among its branches, approached by a stair festooned with ivy. To Montaigne's delight this creeper also concealed the mechanism of surprise fountains and copper tubes filled with water that emitted musical sounds and strange noises. The secret garden on the opposite side, according to Vasari, was given over to the cultivation of 'strange and medicinal herbs', possibly the predecessors of the rather despondent clumps of rue and other old-fashioned herbs that still grow in odd corners of the garden.

Today, although no radical and far-reaching changes have been made, the garden of Castello is a sad place which has weathered the passage of the centuries worse than many Italian gardens that have been more manhandled. The reason lies in the fact that its beauty was not derived from its intrinsic design but from more ephemeral things such as the fountains and sculptures that ornamented it, and above all from its planting. When at the end of the eighteenth century Duke Leopoldo removed Giambologna's famous fountain of 'Venus' that, surrounded by its *bosco* or labyrinth of bays, cypress and myrtle, stood in the centre of the garden, the whole layout lost its focus. The subsequent replacement of the 'Venus' fountain by that of 'Hercules', which originally stood much nearer the house, did nothing to remedy the situation, for instead of replanting the circular *bosco* which provided both fountains with their proper setting of foliage and furnished the whole garden with a much-needed vertical accent of green, the 'Hercules' fountain now stands high and dry in the midst of a desert of geometrical parterres, shorn even of the fruit trees that fifty years ago brought some relief to this purely horizontal landscape, as they do in Utens' picture.

Flowers are annually planted in the beds and the orange and lemon trees, that include some of those wondrous grafts which would have delighted Pietro de' Crescenzi, are carefully tended; but for lack of proper planting the garden of Castello is now monotonous to a degree. The work and money required to bring it to life again would not be of astronomical proportions, nor with Utens' picture as a guide would it be very difficult. No large work of reconstruction is needed, but simply the replanting of the evergreen labyrinth, the espaliered pomegranates and oranges, the fruit trees, and perhaps some of Cosimo's favourite jasmine. It was these contrasting tones of foliage, as well as blossom and scent, that gave light and shade and life to the original scheme, which are now so sadly lacking. (This is clearly borne out by contrasting the effect produced by the 'Hercules' fountain in plates 42 and 43; in the latter, which was taken with this end in view, the fountain appears against its proper setting of contrasting greens.) The result would be an immeasurable gain to garden lovers, Tuscan and foreigner alike, for a garden of the Medici, and one moreover that is the epitome of its type, restored to its original beauty would be a unique sight. If that in itself would not be sufficient recompense for the responsible authorities in these materialistic days, surely its augmented value as a tourist attraction would redress the balance.

The re-creation of Castello would be all the more precious because so many of the other famous garden layouts of the Medici have disappeared through neglect or, owing to changing fashions, have been 'landscaped in the English style' out of existence. The greatest loss is undoubtedly Pratolino, whose magnificence aroused Montaigne to raptures though, as usual with the early travellers, it was the surprise fountains and grottoes filled with automatons that delighted him more than the beauties of the garden itself; but he does describe the superb central alley, fifty feet wide and flanked by fountains and watercourses, that led down the hill behind the house to Giambologna's colossal statue of the 'Apennines'. Judging from Utens' lunette of Pratolino in the Museo Topografico, the garden, which was roughly contemporary with that of Castello and the Boboli, was more closely akin to contemporary Roman gardens in its copious use of water and shade. But it lacked the comprehensive planning and monumental treatment of terrain that distinguishes Roman gardens of any period. This fault rendered Pratolino particularly vulnerable to landscaping so that, except for Giambologna's colossus, practically the whole of the original garden has now disappeared.

43 CASTELLO
The Hercules fountain in the Medici garden of Castello, photographed so as to give an impression of its original setting, a background of trees as shown in Utens' painting, which it sadly lacks today.

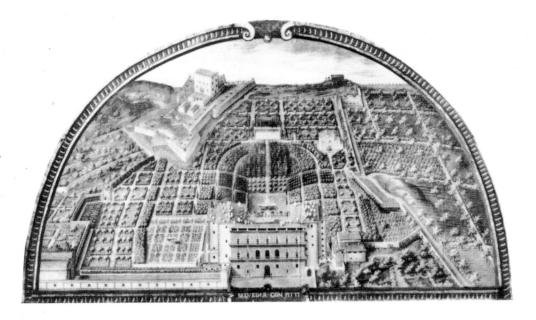

The Boboli Gardens

The most famous of all the Medicean gardens, the Boboli, on the other hand, probably owes the preservation of the main lines of its layout to the fact that they were determined by the natural lie of the land, and in consequence would have been exceedingly difficult and expensive to alter. The great amphitheatre behind the palace that forms the nucleus of the whole design was evidently a natural hollow, for in a letter written to the Grand Duke Cosimo I, in 1551, Baccio Bandinelli, who was commissioned to design a fountain for it, said: 'It seems to me that this field which I have seen has been so well placed by nature that I have seen no other like it.' This is confirmed by a fresco in the Palazzo Pitti representing Florence at the time of the siege of 1529 showing the valley.

From Baccio's other letters it is evident that he was mainly concerned with making fountains and other ornaments for the grand-ducal gardens, and we have it on the authority of Vasari that his friend Tribolo was the garden architect of Boboli as well as Castello. In his *Lives* Vasari says that Tribolo was responsible for the whole layout of the hill behind the palace, the siting of the fountains and small gardens and the planting of the *boschi*. He carried out this enormous design in one year, as well as continuing his work at Castello, for the Pitti Palace was only bought by Cosimo's first wife Eleanor of Toledo in 1549 and, worn out perhaps by such an effort, Tribolo died in the summer of 1550.

From Utens' lunette of the Boboli that hangs in the Museo Topografico (pl. 44), which was painted about the same time as those of Castello and Pratolino, it is evident that Tribolo's layout of this original part of the gardens, which was continued by Ammanati, was very different from the one we see today; also that although the site naturally lent itself to an architectural treatment in the grand manner, neither Tribolo nor Ammanati took full advantage of it. It is true that the contours of the small valley behind the palace were modified to form a definite horse-shoe shape, but more than half of this was filled with regular plantations, like those which surrounded the gardens of Castello, leaving a medium-sized square lawn, with a fountain in the middle as the central motif of the whole layout. From this a long alley, forming the main axis, led through the plantations to a rectangular tank on the hill above, where the fountain of Neptune now stands, and symmetrically-arranged walks delineated the outline of the horse-shoe

44 THE BOBOLI GARDENS
Utens' lunette in the Museo Topografico in Florence of the Boboli gardens behind the Pitti Palace in Florence as they were at the end of the sixteenth or the beginning of the seventeenth century. The palace and gardens belong to the State and are, of course, open to the public. Photo by kind permission of the Soprintendenza alle Gallerie of Florence.

VIII THE BOBOLI GARDENS

IX, X   THE BOBOLI GARDENS

shaped valley. But apart from this simple layout no attempt at a symmetrical plan was made, and the parterre garden was relegated to a site at one side of the palace, as it would have been in medieval times (pls. VIII, IX, X).

The extraordinary conservatism of Tuscan garden design of this period could not be better illustrated, when it is borne in mind that, apart from Bramante's Belvedere, Vignola had already started work on Caprarola three years before and Pirro Ligorio begun Villa d'Este at Tivoli in 1550, all of them gardens in which the treatment of the site was the primary consideration. This cleavage between the Roman High Renaissance conception of a garden and the Tuscan conservative one – that gave first importance to siting and planting, treating the architectural aspects as incidental ornaments – was underlined by the Roman-trained Baccio Bandinelli, when he wrote: '*Le cose che si murano debbono essere guidi e superiori a quelle che si piantono*' – (The things that are walled [or built] should dominate and be the guide of those which are planted). In this connexion it is very interesting to note that Baccio continues his letter to the Grand Duke Cosimo by saying that he would show him (evidently a drawing or a model of) 'the orders that Bramante used in the gardens and fountains that he did for Pope Giulio which Raffaello of Urbino later imitated for those he made for Popes Leone and Clemente, where I lived for many years' – a reference to the time when Baccio actually lived in Bramante's famous Belvedere court in the Vatican and evidently in Raphael's Villa Madama as well.

By the first half of the seventeenth century, the Boboli gardens had already undergone many changes in the direction indicated by Baccio – the great amphitheatre had been cleared of the plantations which filled its upper end and was surrounded by the wall with tiers of seats we know today, that give it the aspect of an ancient Roman hippodrome (pl. 45). This innovation provided a splendid setting for the lavish pageants and

45 THE BOBOLI GARDENS
The amphitheatre of the Boboli gardens, used in the seventeenth century for the lavish pageants and entertainments that were so much in vogue, as it is today.

46 THE BOBOLI GARDENS
Festivities in the amphitheatre of the Boboli gardens for the marriage of the Grand Duke Ferdinando II to Vittoria Della Rovere in 1637; a drawing by Stefano della Bella in the Museo Topografico. Similar magnificent festivities were held in 1608 for the marriage of Cosimo II and in 1661 for the marriage of Cosimo III. Photo by kind permission of the Soprintendenza alle Gallerie of Florence.

entertainments that were so much in vogue during the seventeenth century and formed an essential part of the celebrations for grand-ducal marriages and other great festivals. Those given for the marriages of Cosimo II, Ferdinando II and Cosimo III in 1608, 1637 and 1661, were really magnificent, if one may judge from the prints and drawings that are still preserved in the Uffizi and Museo Topografico (pl. 46). What is particularly interesting is the evidence that these provide of the revival of the old classical relationship between theatrical and garden design in Renaissance Italy. We know from Vasari that Tribolo had designed the settings for the masques and festivities that celebrated Cosimo I's marriage to Eleanor of Toledo, while Giulio Parigi – whose brother Alfonso laid out the famous Boboli *isolotto* – did the same for Cosimo II's wedding in 1608. A print of one of his settings, representing the Garden of Calipso, made for this occasion, is still preserved in the Uffizi, providing an excellent illustration of the similarity that existed between the two art forms. This is borne out by the dramatic effect of Alfonso's *isolotto* itself – with its prancing horses charging through the still waters of the surrounding pool and sea-monsters twining themselves round fountains and artificial rocks. Though the isolotto drew its basic inspiration from the Emperor Hadrian's severely classical 'Marine Theatre' at Tivoli, in Parigi's hands it had certainly undergone a dynamic Baroque transformation.

The same vitality is also evident in Stoldo Lorenzi's figure of 'Neptune' that Cosimo II placed as the centrepiece of the great fountain of that name on the site of Tribolo's rectangular tank on the upper terrace which commands a truly superb 'Albertian' view over the gardens and the whole of Florence (pls. 47, 48). It was probably about this time that Tribolo's original alley leading up to it was converted into a double series of *cordonate*, or shallow sloping steps. Ammanati and Buontalenti, as well as the Parigi brothers, were employed in carrying out these transformations of Tribolo's original scheme and in making additions to it. Buontalenti made the famous grotto with the stalactites, shell mosaics, and animal sculptures, like those of Castello; but the grotto setting for Giambologna's 'Venus', with its painted pergolas and little birds reminiscent of the Empress Livia's garden room, was the work of Pocetti. Another Boboli landmark, the colossal statue of 'Abundance', is really a monument to man's inconstancy – it was begun by Giambologna for Francesco I, as a portrait of his wife Giovanna of Austria, but the Grand Duke's interest waned and work on it was abandoned when he fell in love with

Bianca Cappello. For decades the unfinished statue lay neglected until Ferdinando II had the bright idea of commissioning Tacca's pupil Salvini to complete it as a memorial to his own good government. So now poor Giovanna, disguised as the abundance enjoyed by Tuscany during the reign of Ferdinando II, looks down over the gardens where she once lived as a neglected wife!

By the end of the seventeenth century the area covered by the Boboli gardens and the broad outlines of its layout were approximately the same as they are today. During the intervening one hundred and fifty years a succession of garden designers had welded Tribolo's original layout into a definite architectural form, in accordance with the Roman conception of garden design that now made its influence felt throughout Italy. The great extension to the Porta Romana, that included the *isolotto* and Cosimo II's maze and *ragnaie* – thickets designed for netting small song birds for the grand-ducal table – had already been made; so had Cosimo III's charming little Giardino del Cavaliere on Michelangelo's ramparts. The only subsequent addition was Pietro Leopoldo's *kaffeehaus* built in 1776. A plan of 1808 shows every intricate detail of the vast layout that impresses rather by its size than by its homogenity or charm. But it must be borne in mind that the functions of the Boboli as a garden were rather similar to those of St Peter's and the great Roman basilicas as churches – neither were designed for the retreat and spiritual refreshment of individuals, but to furnish a spacious and imposing setting for the pageantry of great functions.

Today the Boboli is basically unchanged, though some of Cosimo II's *ragnaie* have made way for the less severely practical but aesthetically more pleasing monumental cypress avenue that leads down to the *isolotto*. One aspect of the old Boboli gardens that has not survived, however, is the very extensive botanical section; for the grand dukes, especially Cosimo III, remained faithful to the old Medici family tradition of taking a profound interest in plants as well as garden design. Francesco I introduced the cultivation of mulberries into Tuscany by experimenting with them in the Boboli gardens, and Ferdinando II did the same with potatoes, while a whole garden was given over to the cultivation of pineapples. John Evelyn, when he visited the gardens in 1644, saw roses grafted on to orange trees and 'much topiarie'. Président de Brosses, some hundred years later, noticed many exotics, though for him already the great charm of the garden lay in the 'hills, valleys, woods, parterres and forests that are all without order, design or sequence' –

47 THE BOBOLI GARDENS
The isolotto of the Boboli gardens inspired by the 'Marine Theatre' of Hadrian's villa at Tivoli, as it was in the eighteenth century, from a print by G. Merz. Photo by kind permission of the National Library of Florence.

48 THE BOBOLI GARDENS
The isolotto of the Boboli gardens.

already the passion for the picturesque that was to sound the death knell of the Italian garden had begun to be felt in France.

But it is to William Beckford that we owe the most imaginative description of the Boboli gardens in the days of their splendour. In a letter dated the 14th of September, 1780, he wrote: 'I walked to one of the bridges across the Arno and thence to the Garden of Boboli, which lies behind the Grand Duke's palace stretched out on the side of a mountain. I ascended terrace after terrace robed by a thick underwood of bay and myrtle, above which rise several nodding towers and a long sweep of venerable wall almost entirely concealed by ivy. You would have been enraptured with the broad masses of shade and dusky alleys that opened as I advanced, with white statues of fauns and sylvans glimmering amongst them, some of which pour water into sarcofagi of the purest marble covered with antique relievos. The capitals of columns and ancient friezes are scattered about as seats. On these I reposed myself and looking up the cypress groves that spring above their thickets, then plunging into their retirements, I followed a winding path which led me by a series of ascents to a green platform overlooking the whole extent of the wood, with Florence deep beneath and the tops of the hills which encircle it jagged with pines, here and there a convent or a villa whitening in the sun. Still ascending, I attained the brow of the eminence, and had nothing but the Fortress of the Belvedere and two or three open porticos above me. On this elevated situation I found several walks of trellis work clothed with luxurious vines. A colossal statue of Ceres, her hands extended in the act of scattering fertility over the country, crowns the summit. Descending alley after alley and bank after bank, I came to the orangery in front of the palace, disposed as a great amphitheatre, with marble niches relieved by dark foliage, out of which spring cedars and dark aerial cypresses. This spot brought the scenery of an antique Roman garden so vividly to my mind that, lost in the train of recollections this idea excited, I expected every instant to be called to the table of Lucullus hard by, in one of the porticos, and to stretch myself upon his purple *triclinias*; but waiting in vain for a summons until the approach of night, I returned delighted with a ramble that had led my imagination so far into antiquity.'

Villa Bombicci - Colazzi

This atmosphere of classical grandeur that so fired William Beckford's imagination also permeates the whole site and garden of a villa that was built about 1560 in the countryside behind the Boboli. This is the Villa Bombicci at Colazzi, that for long was believed to have been designed by Michelangelo. As Agostino Dino, for whom it was built, was a friend of the great artist, it is possible that he had some influence upon its design, though it is now generally attributed to Santi di Tito (pl. 49).

The garden layout is in keeping with the severe grandeur of the house and its main features are the magnificent cypress avenue that provides a suitably dignified approach to the house and the spacious terrace, with its all-embracing view, that lies before it. At the back, facing due south, are two smaller terraces, affording sheltered walks for cold days. To these has lately been added (when the house was completed according to its original plan) a severely simple modern garden, whose use of stone, water and grass is an object-lesson in the art of proportion.

Though grand, one might say stately, gardens like the Boboli and Bombicci were inevitably influenced by the Roman monumental style of design, the owners of smaller ones remained faithful to the old Tuscan tradition so eminently suited to their scale and to the intimate, almost domestic, character of the surrounding landscape of the Arno valley. Here peasant cottages and small *podere*, with their fields divided into strips by olives and vine-garlanded trees, look just as they did in medieval times.

49 VILLA BOMBICCI
The terrace in front of the Villa Bombicci, built about 1560 at Colazzi in the countryside behind the Pitti Palace and the Boboli gardens to the south of Florence. It is often attributed to Michelangelo but was probably the work of Santi di Tito. The villa belongs to Signora Elena Marchi.

Villa Capponi · Arcetri

Two perfect examples of this smaller type of Tuscan garden still exist in the environs of Florence. The first – the Villa Capponi at Arcetri – is that rare jewel, a Tuscan garden of the second half of the sixteenth century preserved in all its original charm and cared for to perfection (pl. xi). When on the 7th of February, 1572, Gino Capponi bought a small house with a tower on the steep road leading up to the Pian de' Giullari, his choice may well have been influenced by the superb view which it enjoyed over the city of Florence to the 'familiar hills' of Fiesole in the distance. Certainly the site fulfilled all Alberti's requirements in this respect and the new owner promptly set about enlarging the house and providing the 'delicacy of gardens' and sheltered places for children and older members of his family to take the air on the days when the cold *tramontana* wind blows from the north.

It is likely that some kind of a garden existed on the terrace behind the house when Gino Capponi bought it, but we know that the enchanting little walled garden built at a lower level was his own creation and, owing to the similar style of its confining wall, it is

50 VILLA CAPPONI
The lemon garden leading to the grass terrace behind the Villa Capponi at Arcetri, near Florence, a Tuscan garden of the second half of the sixteenth century preserved in all its original charm. The villa belongs to Mr and Mrs Harry Clifford.

51 VILLA CAPPONI
A view over the garden room at the Villa Capponi at Arcetri. The cupola of the Duomo of Florence can be seen beside a cypress to the left of centre. The importance of the view to be enjoyed from a garden was stressed by Alberti in his famous fifteenth-century architectural treatise.

probable that he also laid out the lemon garden. The plan of the Villa Capponi garden is very simple and typically Tuscan in that it consists of three garden rooms; the first, and largest, is the open grassy terrace that runs the whole length of the back of the house, from whose north-western end Florence and the Arno valley are seen spread out as in a seventeenth-century bird's-eye view of the city. This part of the garden could, in accordance with Alberti's principles, be used for bowls and other games and for the family to enjoy the air on summer evenings. Leading out of its south-eastern end, and separated from it by a hedge and an important looking gateway surmounted by griffins, is the charmingly secluded little lemon garden, with lemon trees in pots punctuating the clipped box parterres (pl. 50). In spring these are planted with masses of blue forget-me-nots, the walls are festooned with wisteria and roses, while trees at the far end provide a welcome shade on summer mornings.

At the western end of the terrace, the little walled garden room – and it is a room complete with windows, lacking only a roof – was evidently very expressly designed for

XI VILLA CAPPONI

shelter on cold but sunny *tramontana* days, as its only entrance until this century was by an underground passage from the house. With its flower-filled box parterres, gurgling wall fountain and battlemented walls festooned with roses and wistaria, this little room is probably the most enchanting example of the Italian *giardino segreto* in existence. The hot sun beating down into this enclosed space distils a veritable bouquet of flower scents mingled with the spicy tang of the cypresses, whose dark spires frame the rolling panorama of the Tuscan landscape and the marvellous views over Florence, which complete the beauty of this lovely scene (pl. 51). Other terraced gardens with flower-filled box parterres and clipped yew hedges have been laid out below the original garden room; their design has been carried out with great sensitivity so that these twentieth-century additions to the original garden do not mar its character.

Villa Gamberaia · Settignano

Unlike the Villa Capponi, whose garden – until the recent additions – has remained as it was designed in the sixteenth century, the second of these typically Tuscan gardens, that of the Villa Gamberaia at Settignano, gradually evolved to its present perfection owing to the discriminating taste of a long succession of owners. In the fifteenth and sixteenth centuries the house and land belonged to the Gambarelli family, who were simple stone-masons until Giovanni and Bernardo became famous as architects under the name of Rossellino, Bernardo designing the Piccolomini Palace at Pienza. It is likely that at this time the house was a simple Tuscan farmhouse, but when Bernardo's son Giovanni sold it to Jacob Riccialbani in 1592, the new owner enlarged and embellished the existing building that was even dignified by the name of 'Palace'. The next proprietor, Zenobi Lapi, evidently carried the work even further, or possibly built an entirely new house, as an inscription bearing the date 1610, saying that he 'founded' it and created a splendid villa, was dug up in the garden in 1900.

After 1717 the Villa Gamberaia passed to the Capponi family, and it is likely that the garden then assumed its present form, for we know that Andrea Capponi laid out the bowling-green, placed statues in the garden and planted it with cypresses. In Zocchi's well-known print, executed some time between 1735 and 1750, the avenue is halfgrown while the bowling-green on the far side of the garden is flanked by mature trees that have since disappeared. As far as can be judged from the print, which was made during the ownership of Marchese Scipione Capponi, the main features of the layout already existed, as the avenue of cypresses leading to the *bosco* can also be seen already well grown, as well as the mosaic decorations of the wall behind the house, while the house itself stands on the raised terrace that is prolonged on the right to form what is now the water parterre.

Of the detailed layout of the garden Zocchi's print gives no clue, but a complete documentation of this is provided by a very interesting estate map of the whole property which is in the possession of the present owner. This map is evidently of a slightly later period than the print, as the drawing of the house at the top shows the addition of the stone animals and urns which still today ornament the terrace wall. This map, and its accompanying elevations of the house, grotto and monumental fountain in the *bosco* show the whole garden exactly as it is today, with two important exceptions – the pool at the end of what is now the water parterre garden is oval instead of its present semicircular shape, and the parterres themselves are laid out in the elaborate French style of *broderies* that had been gradually replacing the old Italian geometrical parterre in fashionable esteem since the second half of the seventeenth century. When Mrs Wharton saw the garden about 1900 this fish pond, as she described it, was still in existence, but the parterres were planted with roses and vegetables and the house was let out to summer lodgers. Even in this deserted state

the superb layout at once caught her experienced eye and she so rightly described it as 'probably the most perfect example even in Italy of great effect on a small scale' and with equal perception attributed its preservation to its 'obscure fate' – gardens that through the centuries had always belonged to rich owners were not usually so fortunate. Shortly afterwards Gamberaia was bought by Princess Ghyka, sister of Queen Natalia of Serbia, who restored it, and, with a stroke of genius, in the place of the vegetables filled the parterres with water, probably at the same time giving the old fish pond its present form.

Since then the Gamberaia has passed through the hands of several owners until it was bought after the last war by Signor Marchi, who has lavished on it even more thought and care than any of his predecessors. For when he took it over bombing had reduced the house to a burnt-out ruin and the garden to a pathetic relic, but today, thanks to his

XII, XIII VILLA GAMBERAIA

patient and perceptive work of restoration, its beauty is not only unimpaired but actually enhanced (pls. XII-XV).

    Today the garden is at once the loveliest and the most typically Tuscan one that the writer has seen. In it the light and air and breeze-swept site, advocated by all the garden authors from Varro to Alberti, is exploited to perfection. From the grassy terrace in front of the house, the domes and spires of Florence are seen in the distance across the olive groves and vineyards that, as in Pliny's Tuscan villa, come close up to the house (pl. 54). The sunlit bowling-green continues as a sheltered grassy walk the whole length of the

XIV XV   VILLA GAMBERAIA

XVI VILLA GAMBERAIA

52, 53 VILLA GAMBERAIA
*The monumental fountain and a detail of its
rustic stonework, in the bosco of the Villa
Gamberaia at Settignano.*

54 VILLA GAMBERAIA
The grassy terrace in front of the Villa Gamberaia at Settignano, a characteristic feature of Tuscan garden design advocated by Alberti; this terrace already existed at the beginning of the eighteenth century but the stone ornaments were added at a slightly later date. The villa belongs to Signor Marchi.

XVII VILLA GAMBERAIA

garden, merging gradually into the deep shade of the *bosco*, in whose cypress-scented depths it finally comes to an end in a little secret garden. This is cooled by the gushing waters of the monumental fountain and enlivened by gay stucco reliefs of nymphs and a huntsman and his dog set amongst a Baroque decoration of mosaics and rustic stonework (pls. 52, 53).

Half-way down the walk, just opposite the house, is a charming little grotto garden from which steps lead up on one side to a sunny lemon garden with box parterres and, laden with wisteria, on the other to the shade of yet another bosco (pl. 55). But the crowning glory of the whole place is the water parterre which lies spread out like some shimmering flower-strewn Persian carpet representing a 'paradise' garden, covering the floor of the beautiful garden room that extends from the house to the end of the terrace upon which it stands, terminating with one of the most breathtaking views in Tuscany. The layout is still the traditional Renaissance one of four parterres, divided by paths, with a circular open space containing a fountain at the crossing. The varying tones of green from clipped box, cypress and yew provide the setting for the shimmering sheets of water with their grey stone borders fringed with flowers. Here and there terracotta urns, filled with flowers and orange trees laden with golden fruit, provide vertical accents that are reflected in the pools. At all seasons of the year this garden is a place of surpassing loveliness, but perhaps it is at its most beautiful either when seen on a misty April day, when the fresh spring green provides a perfect foil for the brilliance of the tulips, or in the height of summer with the pink of the oleander blossom silhouetted against the brilliant blue sky, and the same colour scheme repeated in the great lotus blossoms mirrored in the waters of the semicircular pool.

55 VILLA GAMBERAIA
A bust of the goddess Flora rising from a sea of wisteria on the stairs leading from the grotto garden to the small bosco *in the Villa Gamberaia at Settignano.*

Villa Palmieri

Not far away from the old road to Fiesole, on the slope of the hill below San Domenico, stands the famous Villa Palmieri. Although its original garden was immortalized by Boccaccio in *The Decameron*, no part of the one that we see today dates from earlier than 1697. It was then that the charming little oval lemon garden was laid out by Palmerio Palmieri – the rich descendant of Marco Palmieri who bought the villa in 1454. The rest of the extensive gardens, whether in the English landscape or formal Italian style, were laid out by the Earl of Crawford and Balcarres during the last century and subsequent owners (pl. 56). Unlike the Gamberaia, Villa Palmieri has suffered from having been a 'show-place', and the alterations of many owners to suit the fashion of their day, so that little of its original character remains. How the delightfully Baroque design of the lemon garden escaped the nineteenth-century passion for landscaping is a mystery; the only solution must lie in the frivolous charm of this late example of a Tuscan garden room whose appeal was not lost even on the English romantics of the last century, when Queen Victoria was twice a guest at the villa.

Villa La Pietra

Florence has always held a greater attraction for the English than any other Italian city, and as imitation is the sincerest form of flattery it is not surprising to find that an English family which has been settled in the city for three generations has laid out its own interpretation of a Florentine garden. Although some of the gardens of the Villa La Pietra date from the seventeenth century, by far the largest part of the layout was created during this one by the late Arthur Acton and his Polish gardener (pls. 57, 58). Laid out on

56 VILLA PALMIERI
The lemon garden in the Villa Palmieri near Florence, dating from the late seventeenth century. The villa was bought by Marco Palmieri in 1454 and is famous as having been the setting of Boccaccio's Decameron in the previous century. The villa belongs to Signor Benelli.

XVIII VILLA LA PIETRA

57 VILLA LA PIETRA
One of the most beautiful corners of the gardens of the Villa La Pietra in Florence.

XIX, XX VILLA LA PIETRA

XXI VILLA LA PIETRA

58 VILLA LA PIETRA
The green theatre and one of the most beautiful corners of the gardens of the Villa La Pietra in Florence, laid out early in this century by the late Arthur Acton. It represents the foreigner's conception of the ideal Italian garden, and as such provides an interesting example of the influence of the Tuscan garden upon an English family that has lived in Florence for generations. The villa is the property of Harold Acton Esq.

a sloping site as a series of garden rooms, complete with green theatre, this aspect of the garden is typically Tuscan. But the extensive use of topiary and the introduction of motifs in the classical style and Venetian garden sculpture has given the garden a curiously individual character. It can perhaps best be described as a foreigner's conception of an ideal Italian garden, but as such it is not at all out of place in a city that is one of the meccas of the foreign traveller in Italy (pls. XVIII-XXI).

Villa Corsi Salviati - Sesto

The garden of the Villa Corsi Salviati at Sesto presents a complete contrast to all the Florentine gardens described so far, and indeed to most Tuscan gardens, as its site is a flat one in the middle of an extensive plain. But it is of particular interest for this very reason, as an example of how Tuscan garden art adapted itself to these limitations, also for the well-documented history of its evolution. The villa, then a simple country house, was bought by Jacobo Corsi in 1502, and some charming frescoes by Pocetti in one of the rooms show what it looked like during the sixteenth century. The garden façade of those days was that of a typical small Tuscan house, with rusticated stonework surrounding the door, a loggia on the top floor and a large tower dovecot. The garden was equally simple, a few squares of grass, where men are seen playing bowls, divided by paths, and a circular fountain ornamented by a statue, possibly the one by Baccio Bandinelli, referred to in later inventories. At the very end of the century, in 1593, some additions were made to the house and garden that included the building of an enclosed tennis' court.

The seventeenth century saw further additions made both to the house and garden – another tower, a gallery overlooking the garden and an aviary, which still exists though now it is used as a loggia, were added to the house. The garden was enlarged and laid out on such a grand scale that by 1644 it had almost reached its present extent and nearly all its main features already existed, at least in embryo. This seventeenth-century garden of Villa Corsi Salviati was typically Tuscan in character in that it consisted of four enclosed garden rooms. The central, and most important, was the parterre garden lying directly behind the house, as it still does today. Basically this was not so very different from the square grass plots of Pocetti's fresco, but these were now neatly hedged, probably with box. At the crossing of the central paths the familiar circular space with a fountain had been laid out, and two other small fountains had been added in the open space behind the house. One end of this rectangular room was now occupied by a neat plantation of trees, and the other by a large fish pond, whose oblong shape was broken by a semicircle on the far side. This was walled and decorated with a mask from which gushed a stream of water. Already it is evident that a more or less elaborate use had been made of water to give variety and life to the layout, for behind the fish pond was another garden room, arranged as a lemon garden, with yet another large pool. Describing an arc, this isolated the rabbit island that, in imitation both of the decorative effect and practical uses of the ancient Roman *leporarium*, was now becoming fashionable in Italian gardens. At the other end of the garden, behind the *bosco*, was a walled vegetable garden, divided by the winter orangery from a grass bowling-green.

For nearly a hundred years the house and garden remained untouched, until in 1738 Marchese Antonio Corsi modernized and enlarged them both in accordance with current taste, giving the house the graceful Baroque outline that we see today. In the garden the new owner swept away the boundaries that separated the three main 'rooms', and extended the semicircular pool of the rabbit island to form a large round pond, with fountains springing from the surface of the water in the French manner. In order to provide the space for this innovation, the fish pond was converted into an oblong canal, flanked by urns on pedestals with statues of the four seasons standing at the corners (pl. 59). The old aviary was converted into a loggia and its walls frescoed with classical ruins – a contemporary adaptation of the old Roman *topia*. It was probably about the same time that the old-fashioned square parterres behind the house were replaced by the existing diamond-shaped layout, to which further small parterres were added round the fountains near the house. The *bosco* was extended over the old kitchen garden, and somewhere in this area a maze, which has since disappeared, was also planted. The only feature of the garden that remained undisturbed was the grass bowling-green, for even the *ragnaia* planted outside the confines of the garden was given a symmetrical layout, with paths flanking a narrow canal,

59 VILLA CORSI SALVIATI
The garden of the Villa Corsi Salviati at Sesto, which is of particular interest as an example of the adaptation of a Tuscan garden to a flat site, and for the very fully documented history of its evolution. Bought by Jacobo Corsi in 1502, enlarged almost to its present extent in 1644, a hundred years later it was laid out much as it is today. The villa belongs to the Guicciardini Corsi Salviati family.

enlivened by small artificial cascades. There is no doubt that the garden gained greatly by these innovations, particularly by the heightened contrast of the large expanses of water and the deep shade of the *bosco* that give life and variety to the layout.

Early in the nineteenth century the *bosco* was further extended and converted into a landscape garden with a lake and artificial mound and mock castle in the romantic style. By the middle of the century Villa Corsi Salviati was famous for its flowers and semi-exotic plants, which included many varieties of citrus, lilies and cactus. To these were later added carnations, the double ranunculus known as the *Roselline di Firenze* (still a speciality of the garden), and the famous double jasmine, the *Mugherina del Granduca* (*Jasminium sambac* or *goenensis*) named after Cosimo III, that had hitherto been a speciality of the gardens of Castello. Subsequently the garden also became famous for a vast collection of stove plants introduced from Africa, South America and other tropical countries.

In 1907 the villa was inherited by its late owner, Marchese Giulio Guiccardini Corsi Salviati, who with great pains and admirable taste set about the restoration of as much as possible of its eighteenth-century character. Though, as he pointed out in his beautifully documented monograph on the villa, he 'took warning from the mania that possesses some people for re-doing our villas and gardens too much and, in their desire to bring them back to one period, depriving them of the traces left by the passage of time that give them a human and living character' – how well he succeeded in his object may be judged by anyone who visits the Villa Corsi Salviati today.

Although naturally, as the capital of the Grand Duchy, Florence became the great garden centre of Tuscany, as it was of the other arts, Siena and Lucca, who for so long maintained their independence, also developed garden traditions of their own. In the public library of Siena is preserved the manuscript of an agricultural treatise that contains some of the most charming descriptions of the art of gardening in sixteenth-century Italy. But it also gives a clear indication of why so few Sienese gardens of this period have survived for, as its author Girolamo Firenzuola says, these were 'not like the princely ones of Rome or designed for splendid festivities like those of the Venetians, but a place where the owner planted with love for his own use, peaches, cherries, pomegranates, pears and almonds in beds surrounded by rose bushes, and cultivated all kinds of herbs and vegetables – lavender,

XXII VILLA CORSI SALVIATI

sage, rue, wild thyme and marjoram, lettuce, asparagus, parsley, onions, salads, artichokes, cabbages and spring gourds'. In other words these early Sienese gardens resembled the *potagers* of old French chateaux and those of our own small manor houses, whose charm depends upon their planting alone, and for this reason few traces of them have survived.

Girolamo Firenzuola, who wrote his treatise while he was languishing in a Florentine prison as a result of the political struggle between his native city and Florence, was evidently a country squire in the Renaissance tradition; well read in Virgil's *Georgics*, but also a keen huntsman and an enthusiastic and practical gardener. His advice for ridding gardens of caterpillars is worth recording: 'Go into the garden at dawn on Sunday and on bare knees say three Ave Marias and three Paternosters in reverence to the Trinity, then take a cabbage or some other leaf eaten by caterpillars and put inside two or three of them, and say "Caterpillars come with me to Mass"; then take the whole thing along to church, and before listening to the Mass let it fall. After this the caterpillars will disappear from the garden – this is not a joke, it has been proved to work and its practice still in use!'

Apart from this and other useful advice on how to lay out a *ragnaia* for catching small birds for the table, Girolamo also described his ideal garden. This was a large walled garden room, whose principal decoration were trellises covered with a most intricate mixture of grafted fruit trees and creepers. For one of these he suggests festoons of ivy, with oranges, lemons, citrons and bitter oranges in pots at intervals along it, with jasmine plants concealed behind the ivy and trained to grow over balls of trellis work above, the ivy itself being trained to grow over wooden busts of men and women. For another trellis he advocates a hedge of pomegranates, with pears grafted alternately with quinces and medlars rising above it, and for the third, and most complicated, a hedge of clipped bays or other evergreens mixed with lentiscus or myrtle, with festoons above of jasmine and honeysuckle, and pots of broom set at intervals along it.

These three trellises were to be ranged around the garden walls, while the centre was to be partitioned into two parts – one with a lawn and the usual crossed paths and a marble table shaded by a creeper-grown cupola of trellis work. Behind this an ivy-clad screen framing a statue or painted landscape divided off the other half of the garden, part of which was to be laid out as a *bosco*, part as a herb and flower garden. Inside the *bosco* was to be concealed a kitchen for the preparation of *al fresco* meals; while the garden beds of the rest, surrounded by low-clipped hedges of lavender, rosemary, sage and myrtle, were to be planted with roses, violets, strawberries, capers and marjoram and other small herbs, these last to be clipped in the form of 'vases, boats and such things'. At each corner of the beds was to stand a stone column supporting a potted citron tree, and regularly ranged at intervals in between double and single damask roses and laurustinus bushes.

What an enchanting picture the whole description conjures up, and how closely the ideal garden of this Sienese landowner-author resembled the parterres of the *Hypnerotomachia* of Poliphilus. But gardens of this type were almost as ephemeral as Francesco Colonna's dream romance and nothing like them survives in Tuscany today, though in the remote province of the Marche one or two gardens still retain their elaborate wall-covering of espaliered lemons and beds edged with clipped scented herbs. It is interesting to learn from Girolamo Firenzuola's treatise that in Italian gardens of the sixteenth century herbs were still preferred to the more enduring box for this purpose, in spite of the latter's classical associations, for he writes: 'The ancients used box and bays for making hedges of greenery, now many kinds [of greenery] are used and these two little appreciated, because to tell the truth, oranges, lemons, ivy, pomegranates, myrtle, jasmine and honeysuckle are more beautiful, although some of these do not withstand the winter but for summer they are much more beautiful if not so lasting.' He goes on to say that he would make plentiful use of such greens but not of box as, like our own Queen Anne, he considered it a 'melancholy and smelly green' suitable only for use in courtyards or for bordering beds of seedlings or small vegetable plots, but even there he thought it was better mixed with myrtle 'which has a good smell of its own although it does not last so long and is inclined to dry up and has to be cut back every two years'. Poor Girolamo, how clearly he pictured his ideal garden in his prison cell! One can only hope that he was soon released and able to put his ideas into practice.

Vicobello & Celsa - Siena

The gardens of Baldassare Peruzzi, the famous Sienese architect who lived from 1481 to 1537, have proved to be almost as ephemeral as those described by Girolamo Firenzuola. Though two gardens near Siena – Vicobello and Celsa – are attributed to him, both have subsequently been so altered that today neither of them resembles his garden design preserved in the Uffizi except in the simplicity of their basic plans. The geometrical parterres and paths shaded by what the Italians call a '*bersò*' – the vaulted trellis or pleached alley known as a cradle or '*berceau*' in French – have disappeared.

Castle of Celsa

At Celsa, however, there is definite evidence that they once existed which, in view of Peruzzi's authorship of the nearby circular chapel, renders it likely that the garden was also originally designed by him. A drawing preserved in the Castle of Celsa shows the little garden, with the marvellous view, that lies in front of it, laid out with *bersò*-covered paths and a circular fountain placed in the curve of the wall on the far side. Probably about the middle of the seventeenth century, while still preserving its original ground-plan, this garden was transformed by the addition of imposing gateways and the creation of a semicircular pool on the site of the old fountain. These changes formed part of an ambitious project for the

conversion of the medieval castle into an elaborate villa, of which a drawing also exists in the castle. The only parts of the project that were put into effect, however, were the erection of the screen that links the two wings of the castle and the additions to the garden. The elaborate *broderies* shown in the project were apparently never planted in the parterres, as when Shepherd and Jellicoe drew a plan of the garden in 1925 these still retained their old geometrical layout which was very similar to those of Peruzzi's garden plan in the Uffizi.

Since the last war, Prince Aldobrandini, the present owner of Celsa, has restored the house and garden, introducing a formal design of the family arms in the parterres. He has also restored to good condition a charming seventeenth-century semicircular pool that lies to one side of and at some distance from the castle, at the entrance to the *bosco*. An interesting drawing of the original project for this pool and *bosco* also exists in the castle, showing the pool exactly as it is today, but with the bosco clipped and trimmed in the contemporary formal style (pl. 62). The avenues shown in the drawing as radiating out from the pool still exist, the central one is still clipped but the rest of the *bosco* is now wild woodland, carpeted with flowers, though still surrounded by a wall (pls. 60, 61, 63, 64). This wall and the situation of the *bosco*, so far from the castle, provide an interesting commentary upon life in seventeenth-century Tuscany, for they are features common to Cetinale and the other villas in the vicinity. The whole of this area was then so thickly infested by brigands that it was unsafe to allow trees to grow near the house for fear they might provide cover for attack, or even to walk in an open wood not surrounded by a wall.

60 VILLA CELSA
The pool and bosco at the Castle of Celsa near Siena as it is today. The path bordered by clipped hedges leading to it was not part of the original design.

61 VILLA CELSA
The bosco of the Castle of Celsa near Siena.

62 VILLA CELSA
The architect's design for the pool and bosco at the Castle of Celsa near Siena, belonging to Prince Aldobrandini, which was carried out in its entirety.

63 VILLA CELSA
A seventeenth-century plan for the conversion of the Castle of Celsa near Siena into a Baroque villa. Baldassare Peruzzi's (1481-1537) circular chapel is on the right. The only parts of the plan that were actually carried out were the alterations to the garden—they did not however include the broderie layout of the parterres and the erection of the central screen that links the two wings of the castle. The plan belongs to Prince Aldobrandini who is also the owner of the castle.

64 VILLA CELSA
The garden in front of the Villa Celsa near Siena as it is today.

Another plan of very considerable interest is kept in the Castle of Celsa, and is of a green theatre of elaborate design, adorned with sculptures, and on the back is written 'project for the theatre at La Marlia'. There are certain variations, notably the number of wings – shown here as three instead of four – and the number and placing of the statues, but the basic plan is undoubtedly the same as that of the most famous villa of the Lucca area. What is also interesting is that the writing on this project and on those for Celsa itself appear to be the same hand which, in view also of the similarity of the rustic stonework that surrounds both the semicircular pool at Celsa and the one behind the Villa Marlia, points to the possibility of both gardens having been designed by the same architect or his assistants. The close relationship existing between the seventeenth-century gardens of the Sienese and Lucca areas was commented upon by Monsieur Gromort in his *Jardins d'Italie* in which he attributes the green theatres of both the villas Marlia and Garzoni in the Lucca area and that of Villa Gori (to which might also be added Villa Sergardi) at Siena to the same period.

Villa Bernardini - Saltocchio

The Duchy of Lucca, which was the only Tuscan State to preserve its autonomy in defiance of Florence right up to the Unification of Italy, had a garden tradition at least as old as those of the capital and Siena, and when Montaigne visited the gardens of Lucca in 1581 he was filled with admiration. The earliest garden now existing in the Lucca area is that of the Villa Bernardini at Saltocchio. This dates from the end of the sixteenth century, but the only part of its extensive layout which is still kept in good order is the little *giardino segreto* beside the house (pl. 65). Like most of the gardens in the immediate vicinity of Lucca, the

65 VILLA BERNARDINI
The giardino segreto of the Villa Bernardini at Saltocchio near Lucca; this enclosed garden room set among trees is typical of gardens of the area. The villa dates from the end of the sixteenth century; it now belongs to Signor Querci.

garden of the Villa Bernardini was laid out as a series of garden rooms in the midst of boschi and not, as in the Florence area, built out into the infinity of space – though suitable hillside sites were not lacking for this purpose. The *giardino segreto* at Villa Bernardini affords a particularly beautiful example of this technique, with its curving pools and staircases providing an effect of surprising grandeur in so small an area.

Villa Marlia

Owing both to the large extent of its gardens and to its having been the summer residence of two ladies with imperial associations – Napoleon's sister Elisa Baciocchi, whom he created Princess of Lucca and Piombino and later Queen of Etruria, and the Spanish Bourbon princess Maria Louisa, who afterwards became Duchess of Lucca – the Villa Marlia is by far the most famous in the Lucca area (pls. XXIII-XXVI). For nearly six centuries the land, and probably originally a castle, had belonged to the Orsetti family before it was bought by Elisa Baciocchi, and a villa had existed since Renaissance times. The formal gardens, however, which are the great beauty of the villa, were laid out for the Orsetti family during the second half of the seventeenth century. True to the old Tuscan tradition, the architect created a great sweep of grass in front of the house for use as a *manège*, reserving the more ornamental aspects of the garden for the series of garden rooms that, in accordance with local taste, were concealed among the *boschi*. The only exception to this rule was the charming little parterre garden with its lovely semicircular pool, adorned with urns and flower-decked fountains that he placed directly behind the house.

The main garden, however, consists of a superb suite of garden rooms excavated – for that is really the word – from the thick mass of trees that lie to the east of the house and the *manège*. The entry is by a narrow passageway leading from the drive in front of the house, right into what is surely the most magnificent garden room in Italy, that calls to

XXIII, XXIV VILLA MARLIA

66 VILLA MARLIA
The great pool in the gardens of the Villa Marlia at Fraga near Lucca, set in the largest of a delightful series of garden rooms dating from the seventeenth century. The villa subsequently became the summer residence of Napoleon's sister Elisa Baciocchi, Queen of Etruria, and later of Maria Louisa Duchess of Lucca; it now belongs to Countess Pecci Blunt.

67 VILLA MARLIA
The 'ante-room' leading to the green theatre of the Villa Marlia at Fraga near Lucca.

68 VILLA MARLIA
The garden pavilion of the Villa Marlia.

mind some vast Baroque ballroom whose dancing floor is a great sheet of shimmering water. In this are reflected the dark clipped yews and lighter greens of the 'walls', the grey stone of the balustrades and presiding gods and goddesses, and like so many little lamps — the golden fruit of the potted orange and lemon trees (pl. 66). A spacious flight of steps sweeps down from the 'ball-room' to the 'drawing-room' of this enchanting garden palace, which is laid out with parterres of brilliant flowers, bordered by box hedges and potted citrus trees of every kind, while at the far end is a small alcove with a fountain.

XXV. XXVI   VILLA MARLIA

A gate at one side of the 'ball-room' opens into the deep shade of a green passage, through which can be glimpsed the sparkle of a circular fountain set in the midst of a small 'ante-room' that, in its turn, opens on to another passage and gateway leading to a sunny space beyond (pl. 67). This is the theatre, surely one of the most charming that was ever created to fill the passing hour with amusement for the gay world of seventeenth-century Italy. Frozen into stone, as if by the wave of some Baroque witch's spell, the figures of Columbine, Harlequin and Pulcinella stand enchanted on the stage, as they must so often have done in real life. It is a haunting scene and in the silence and brilliant sunlight of a summer afternoon it requires very little imagination to people it with the ghosts of those gay and frivolous figures that perhaps return there sometimes to recall past loves and intrigues, of which this little theatre must so often in real life have been the stage.

More seldom seen, but even more evocative is the little pavilion hidden away in the shadowy depths of the encircling woods, whose cool loggia was undoubtedly designed for gay *al fresco* meals on summer days, while its grotto, and the small room above, were just as surely the place of secret assignations (pl. 68). Unfortunately, Lucca does not seem to have produced a John Evelyn or a Mr Pepys who committed to paper a record of this long-lost world, though legends still cluster thick around another garden in the neighbourhood. This is the Villa Mansi at Segromogno whose garden was, unfortunately, landscaped during the last century. Here lived the very merry widow Lucida Mansi who in order to preserve her beauty is said to have made a pact with the devil. This provided, among other things, that she should bathe daily in the waters of the garden pool – needless to say her spirit is said to haunt it still.

Villa Torrigiani · Camigliano

Barely a mile away, near the little village of Camigliano, is the magnificent Villa Torrigiani, most of whose gardens suffered the same fate as those of Villa Mansi during the nineteenth century. But the Torrigiani have been more fortunate in the preservation of part at least of the delightful formal gardens laid out by the Santini family in the second half of the seventeenth century, before the villa came into their possession. Two beautiful irregularly-shaped pools in the lawn in front of the house survive from this period, also a large rectangular one laid out to one side. This is fringed by potted lemon trees and enclosed by yew hedges, in the same manner as the garden 'ball-room' of the Villa Marlia.

The outstanding feature of the Torrigiani garden is, however, the enchanting little sunken garden of Flora, one of the gayest and most delightful of Italian *giardini segreti*. This is connected to the lemon pool garden by double staircases which, although perfectly scaled to the diminutive size of the garden, are carried out in a very grand manner indeed that probably no other country or period could have equalled. But as the grand ladies and their *cicisbei*, clad in their seventeenth-century silks and satins, descended these stairs to walk among the flowers and scented herbs of the parterres, their host could imprison them in his secret garden by raising a veritable wall of spray from fountains concealed in the highest steps. As they ran forward, seeking some way of escape, by turning a tap he could pursue them down the whole length of the garden with surprise showers hidden among the pebble mosaics of the paths. When at last his guests thought they had found a refuge in the little temple of Flora at the far end, more deluges awaited them, forcing them to climb the stairs to the terrace above, only to receive a final soaking from a flower-garlanded statue of 'Flora' herself. Probably it was this elaborately executed practical joke – the most extensive and ingeniously conceived that the writer has seen in Italy – that saved this little garden from destruction, for *giochi d'acqua* have held an irresistible appeal to Italian humour from Roman times until today (pl. 69).

69 VILLA TORRIGIANI
The garden of Flora of the magnificent Villa Torrigiani at Camigliano near Siena. The formal gardens were originally laid out during the second half of the seventeenth century. This enchanting little sunken garden is one of the gayest and most delightful of the Italian secret gardens.

XXVII, XXVIII VILLA TORRIGIANI

Villa Garzoni

At Collodi, just outside the confines of the province of Lucca, stands the Villa Garzoni, whose garden, for all its geographical propinquity and similarity in detail, belongs to another world from those of Lucca. Here, instead of a series of garden rooms nestling among their *boschi* in the plain, is one of the most spectacular Baroque gardens of Italy, whose layout makes the fullest use of a precipitous hillside site in a manner that is usually associated with Rome. There is one difference, however, in that the house itself (originally an old castle), plays little part in the composition for reasons of necessity – it was too closely associated with the village to allow an extensive garden to be laid out around it. This difficulty was surmounted by the architect's siting the garden to one side and mainly at a lower level, making it serve as a link between the castle and the road. For this reason all the functional parts of the garden – its theatre, bath-house, seats and promenades are on the upper levels, while the rest is a magnificent spectacle that can be enjoyed both from above or below (pls. 70, 71). Equally ingenious is the designer's use of the superb yew hedges, clipped in fantastic form that enclose the lower garden to provide a shady passage, tunnelled in their depths, from there and the road to the upper terraces.

Collodi Castle originally belonged to the Republic of Lucca and was bought by the Garzoni family during the first half of the seventeenth century. In 1652 they began to alter the warlike character of their property by turning it into a villa and laying out the gardens. These were already famous and had probably reached their present state by the end of the century, though the water-works were improved and the bath-house added in the following one, when the castle was also remodelled into a palatial villa. One of the outstanding characteristics of the Garzoni gardens is the typically Roman Renaissance treatment of the hillside which has been reduced to an architectural layout of terraces linked by a series of staircases that provide the main axis of the whole composition. By the seventeenth century, however, this process has been carried one stage further, for the formal garden of parterres, stairs and open terraces gradually merges into walks shaded by clipped trees – the central axis is still marked, but now by a much less formal water staircase, whose rough stone surface repeats the natural effect of the glistening curves of the water. Finally the perspective disappears, with a last flamboyant flourish, personified by the statue of Fame, whose draperies flutter against a background of foliage and cypresses that gradually merges into the Tuscan landscape (pls. 72, 74). This skilful transformation from the formal to the wild, marks the Villa Garzoni as an essentially Baroque garden (pls. XXIX-XXXIII).

If its general layout is more Roman than Tuscan, the details of the Villa Garzoni are closely linked to those of other gardens in the area. The treatment of the stonework resembles that of the Villa Marlia and the seventeenth-century garden at Celsa, while the charming little green theatre is also related to those of Marlia and the Sienese villas (pl. 73). The Villa Garzoni has, however, one delightfully individual feature – its eighteenth-century bath-house – whose origins must be sought far further afield, in the *thermae* of the ancient Roman villas of Pliny and the Emperor Hadrian. For like these classical prototypes, the Villa Garzoni baths were for sociable gatherings and entertainment. There were separate bathing enclosures for the ladies and their cavaliers, but these were designed so that they could gossip together while remaining invisible and listening to an orchestra playing in a screened gallery.

Thus, with its classically-inspired bath-house, its Tuscan green theatre and its superb layout in which the Renaissance and Baroque styles are so skilfully blended, the Villa Garzoni provides a particularly appropriate postscript to the evolution of Tuscan gardens, linking them to the great Roman school whose influence had by now spread all over Italy.

70 VILLA GARZONI
The garden of the Villa Garzoni at Collodi seen from the top of the water staircase.

71 VILLA GARZONI
The garden of the Villa Garzoni at Collodi, just beyond the borders of the province of Lucca, seen from below. Dating largely from the second half of the seventeenth century, this is one of the most spectacular of the Baroque gardens of Italy. Though the terraced treatment of the hillside is reminiscent of Roman Renaissance gardens, the skill whereby this formal layout is made to merge into the forested slopes of the hill is typically Baroque. The garden and villa are open to the public. [p. 146]

XXIX VILLA GARZONI *[p. 147]*

72 VILLA GARZONI
The pool and statue of 'Fame' which is the culminating point of the garden of the Villa Garzoni at Collodi.

73 VILLA GARZONI
The green theatre in the garden of the Villa Garzoni at Collodi.

XXX, XXXI, XXXII VILLA GARZONI

74 VILLA GARZONI
The pool below the statue of 'Fame' in the garden of the Villa Garzoni at Collodi.

XXXIII VILLA GARZONI

Roman Renaissance Gardens

The Renaissance began in Rome, according to no less an authority than Gregorovius, on 30th September 1420, when the Colonna Pope Martin V made his State entry into a city ruined by centuries of neglect and destruction due to the Papal residence in Avignon and the wars of the Schism. At this time Rome was so devastated and deserted that according to Platina – the biographer of Martin V – it 'bore hardly any resemblance to a city', and more than twenty years were to pass before it began to emerge from this state of decadence.

The man to whom Rome of the fifteenth century owed in great part her remarkable cultural and architectural revival was Nicholas V, the first humanist Pope, who reigned from 1447 to 1455. As a member of the Curia, Cardinal Tommaso Parentucelli had often stayed in Florence during the years preceding his election to the Papacy and had made friends with many outstanding members of the humanist circle that dominated the cultural life of the city. It is not surprising, therefore, to find that shortly after his accession the Papal Court in Rome also became a centre of learning, which grew with his foundation of the famous Vatican Library.

By a fortunate coincidence the period of Nicholas' reign coincided with the culmination of a change in the humanist approach to antiquity – the ancient monuments of Rome were now no longer regarded as being of purely antiquarian and scholarly interest but as a source of inspiration to artists and architects. It was at this time that Poggio Bracciolini who, as we have seen, was probably one of the first men since ancient times to make use of classical sculpture to ornament his garden, wrote his famous catalogue of the Roman ruins in the *De varietate fortunae*, in which for the first time they were described from an aesthetic as well as an antiquarian standpoint. This new point of view was to herald a change in the evolution of architecture, and especially garden architecture, after the cultural leadership of the Renaissance had passed from Florence to Rome.

As became the first humanist and truly Renaissance Pope, Nicholas V was a great builder and among his many building projects was that of transforming the old Papal Palace in the Vatican into a palace in the Renaissance sense of the word. This plan included the creation of an extensive garden in which, apart from accommodation for the famous library, were to be built a theatre, a hall for ceremonial occasions and two *triclinia*, probably intended for banquets. This garden evidently formed an important part of the whole layout as aqueducts were to be built to provide water for the fountains and it was to be filled with many varieties of trees and flowers and even contained a botanical section. The death of Nicholas in 1455 put an end to these ambitious plans, but it is interesting to note that already the classical conception of a garden as a setting for a theatre and for great occasions had been revived in Rome. An interval of thirty years was to pass before another Pope displayed any interest in the Vatican gardens, then Innocent VIII contributed a villa built on the top of the Vatican Hill, to which commanding site and beautiful views it owed its name of Belvedere.

Palazzo Venezia - Rome

An earlier Pope, Paul II, was also a garden lover, though his was not in the Vatican but was built as an annex to the Palazzo Venezia, which had been his favourite residence since he was created Cardinal of San Marco. Now called the Palazzetto Venezia, this garden has been moved from its original site to make way for the modern Piazza Venezia and to a certain extent transformed, though its basic character is still the same as when it was built about 1466. The double porticos surrounding the garden are original but the rooms leading out of them are a modern addition and the level has been changed; in Paul II's day it was a '*giardino pensile*' connected to his own suite on the first floor of the adjoining palace. The main difference, however, is that originally the outer walls of the loggias were pierced by windows that commanded views down the Corso on one side and over more or less open country on the other.

In essence the design of the Palazzetto Venezia was simply that of a cloister, though with its windows opening on to the outside world it showed the timid beginnings of the influence of Alberti. It is astonishing to think that this enclosed garden is contemporary with the Villa Medici at Fiesole and that at this time Rome lagged so far behind Florence, and another twenty years were to pass before anything resembling a Renaissance garden was made in Rome. This was of great importance, however, not so much for its own layout as for the fact that it was the first essay of a Cardinal whose patronage, when he became Pope, resulted in a revolution in garden design that changed the whole conception of gardens in Italy and ultimately in Europe.

The man who was to be responsible for this far-reaching change was Giuliano Della Rovere, who at the age of twenty-eight was created Cardinal of San Pietro in Vincoli and thirty-two years later, in 1503, ascended the Papal Throne as Julius II. The personification of a Renaissance Maecenas and one of the greatest builders Rome has ever known, whose name will for ever be associated with that of Michelangelo and the creation of the new St Peter's, it was to Julius II that Rome chiefly owed her position as the cultural centre of the sixteenth-century world.

The first garden that Julius made was attached to the comparatively modest palace that he built about 1486 beside his titular church of San Pietro in Vincoli. Though all trace of it has been lost, an anonymous drawing of the sixteenth century shows the garden as a walled and wooded tract of land on the hill behind the church. Apparently it was quite large and celebrated in its day, especially for the Cardinal's already extensive collection of antique sculpture for which it provided the setting. This included the famous 'Apollo', later known as 'del Belvedere', the 'Venus Felix' and the 'Hercules and Anteus' now in the Vatican Museum.

Cortile del Belvedere - Vatican

Probably shortly after his election to the Papacy in 1503, Julius II transferred part at least of his collection of sculpture to the Vatican, and it seems likely that from the first he entertained the idea of using Innocent VIII's old Villa Belvedere for the display of works of art in the classical style. Though admirably sited, both according to the old Roman concepts and the tenets of Alberti, the Belvedere stood at some distance from the Papal palace and was separated from it by a rising stretch of open ground – a very definite disadvantage in the Roman climate, subject as it is to torrential rainstorms in winter and sultry heat in summer. It was probably this shortcoming that first inspired Julius with the idea of connecting the Belvedere to the palace and from that it was but a short step, given the grandeur of the Pope's ideas and the currents of thought of the time, to a project for creating a garden in the style of an ancient Roman villa.

Fortunately there was already living in Rome the architect who was best qualified to put Julius' ideas into effect. This was Donato Bramante, whose *tempietto* in the cloister of San Pietro in Montorio had already demonstrated that here was a man who could design a building in which 'the classic Renaissance has achieved its conscious aim to emulate classic Antiquity'. Before he went to Milan in 1474 at the age of thirty, Bramante had seen Laurana building the famous Ducal Palace of Urbino in his native province of the Marche, and his own work in Lombardy was infused with the same spirit of grandeur allied to simplicity, in which the influence of Alberti was also evident. In 1499 Bramante had settled in Rome with sufficient money upon which to live for some time without accepting commissions. According to Vasari, during the next few years he 'worked in solitude and contemplation, examining and measuring the Roman ruins in and around the city as far as Naples, studiously measuring the Villa Adriana' (Hadrian's villa near Tivoli). Vasari also says that he had been commissioned by the Borgia Pope, Alexander VI, to design some fountains, probably before he embarked upon the cloisters of Santa Maria della Pace and the *tempietto*.

Bramante thus came fully prepared to meet what was undoubtedly the greatest challenge of his career – a *carte blanche* commission from the newly-elected Pope to create the first great Roman pleasure garden since classical times for the personal use of this connoisseur of the arts. How he acquitted himself of his task may be judged from the fact that in 1506 Julius asked him to prepare the plans for the new Basilica of St Peter's. That Bramante's designs for what was called the '*atrio di piacere*', which we now call the Cortile del Belvedere, immediately created a sensation there can be little doubt. The number of descriptions, drawings and prints that have come down to us provide evidence of this, and even in its present dismembered state its revolutionary design can still be recognized. In the words of a modern critic: 'Bramante met the challenge with a design that brought into existence a new concept of space and dominated the future course of garden architecture.'

The general requirements of Bramante's commission were – first to provide a sheltered means of access from the Vatican Palace to the Villa Belvedere which was slightly out of line with the Papal apartments in the palace and separated from them by a wide stretch of rising ground; second, to create a setting worthy of the Pope's collection of sculpture; and third to design a garden that contained a theatre and provided a suitable stage for the pageantry of the Papal Court as well as a private retreat for a humanist pope of the Renaissance. This was no small order in a world whose conception of gardens was still little advanced from the *hortus conclusus* of medieval times. Bramante's solution shows not only the result of patient years of study of ancient monuments, but that here was a man who could interpret their spirit and infuse it with new life. The Belvedere court was no mere collection of antique motifs pieced together by a virtuoso, but a conception unique in its day, that related ancient art to the current trends in the study of perspective in painting, thereby introducing the vital third dimension into garden design. As a result, the level enclosed garden room of the Tuscan humanists gave way before the new-old Roman conception of moulding the terrain to an architectural form, axially related to the building of which it was an adjunct, linking this to the surrounding landscape (though not as yet merging into it) and opening the whole layout to the horizons of the outside world.

Briefly the synthesis of Bramante's plan was the enclosure of the area within the axis of the palace and the Belvedere by two vast loggias, triple at their lowest level, double and finally single as they coincided with the series of terraces by whose creation he gave a definite architectural form to the hill. A large area of ground before the palace was levelled to provide the stage of the 'theatre' in which jousts and pageants could be held. The auditorium took the form of a vast semicircle of steps at the foot of the palace, in emulation of an ancient Roman theatre. But the most revolutionary part of Bramante's design was his treatment of the terraces on the far side of the theatre – here was no timid series of enclosed garden rooms but a magnificent perspective achieved by the use of monumental stairs and ramps that linked the terraces and rose to a climax in a niche approached by a semicircular series of steps at the far end.

With this one plan Bramante dictated the basis of European garden design for more than two centuries to come. The Italian gardens that followed, and the French ones that drew their inspiration from them, were really variations on his original theme of the discipline of a propitious site to man-made forms in accordance with the Renaissance ideals of symmetry and proportion. These principles continued as the fundamental core of garden design, though the Italian Baroque gardens of the seventeenth century and their European counterparts increasingly reflected the changing attitude to nature produced by the spiritual travail of the Reformation and Counter-Reformation. Whereas to the Renaissance humanists even admired nature was subordinate to man, and their gardens were a purely man-made creation, subsequently the growing consciousness of man's insignificance was also reflected in garden designs where the formal layout gradually merged into the wild, and was progressively submerged by it. When the final break with the Renaissance tradition came in the eighteenth century, with the English garden that took the wild as its model, strangely enough even this owed its origins indirectly to Italy. Claude Lorrain's idealized classical landscapes of the Roman *campagna* were one of William Kent's sources of inspiration, while Burlington's architect Robert Castel maintained that the gardens of the old Roman villas showed a close imitation of nature and, judging from the Golden House, some of the Pompeian frescoes and Pliny's description of Clitumnus he had some grounds for his contention.

The outstanding feature of Bramante's design for the Cortile del Belvedere, that singled it out from all previous Italian Renaissance gardens and placed it far in advance even of the Villa Medici at Fiesole, was his use of the dominating central perspective that traversed the terraces at right angles, linking them by a series of stairs and ramps, and culminating in the final semicircular niche. The inspiration of this epoch-making design has long been attributed to some classical model or models, and many authorities have cited in this connexion the now vanished ruins of the gardens of Lucullus on the Pincian Hill, of which a drawing by Pirro Ligorio still exists. It is now generally believed, however, that the Temple of Fortune of Praeneste was a more likely source of Bramante's inspiration.

Like the site of the gardens of Lucullus, much of the hillside section of this vast structure had been built over and lay concealed beneath part of the modern town of Palestrina. Bombing during the last war and the subsequent clearance of rubble have now laid bare its elaborate layout of terraces connected by stairs and ramps, whose resemblance to the Cortile del Belvedere is striking. So too is the culmination of the temple design in a semicircular sanctuary approached by concave theatre-like steps. This part of the temple was incorporated into a palatial house by the Colonna at the end of the fifteenth century, but its main outlines were clearly evident even before recent restoration revealed its Roman core.

From a drawing of Pirro Ligorio's, in one of his sketch-books in the Vatican Library, it is evident that although, characteristically, he tried to portray the 'Forum of Praeneste' in an imaginary reconstruction, much of its original layout must still have been visible in his day (pl. 75). The drawing is also of interest because it shows the importance attributed to the ruins in the sixteenth century and, above all, by the man who was called in to complete Bramante's unfinished work in the Cortile del Belvedere.

There is no doubt, however, that the basic lines of the famous court were already well established by the time of Bramante's death in 1514; they were clearly shown in a drawing in the Uffizi, executed during the first half of the century before Ligorio started work. This drawing shows the Cortile with only the eastern porticos practically finished, while the

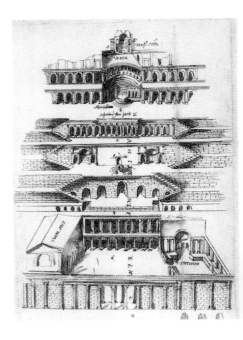

75 THE TEMPLE OF FORTUNE
Pirro Ligorio's (1500-1583) drawing of a reconstruction of the Temple of Fortune at Praeneste, the modern Palestrina, that he thought was the Forum of Praeneste. This drawing, which is in one of his sketch-books preserved in the Vatican Library, is of particular interest as showing that a good deal of the temple layout must have been visible in the sixteenth century, and it is generally considered that the building is a probable source for Bramante's revolutionary architectural design of the Cortile del Belvedere. Pirro Ligorio was called in to complete Bramante's unfinished work there some time after his death in 1514. Vatican Library photo.

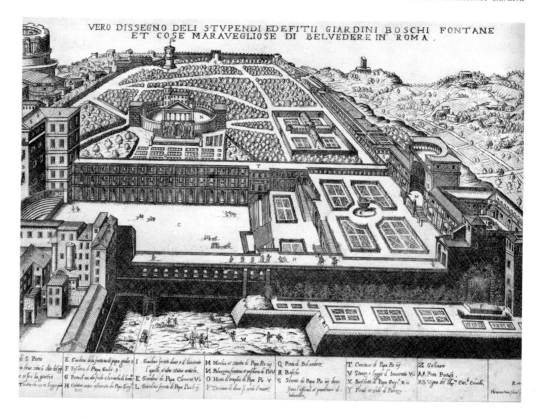

VERO DISSEGNO DELI STVPENDI EDEFITII GIARDINI BOSCHI FONTANE ET COSE MARAVEGLIOSE DI BELVEDERE IN ROMA.

terraces and stairs are well defined and the ramps and central alcove of the sustaining wall of the top terrace, that so resemble those of Palestrina, are practically complete. The drawing, however, also shows some variations upon what are believed to have been Bramante's original plans. A more commonplace double staircase has replaced the semicircular steps leading (like those of Palestrina) to the culminating niche. A sketch of these steps is still preserved among copies of Bramante's own drawings in the Soane Museum Collection and they are repeated in Francisco d'Hollanda's drawing of about 1540, now in the Escorial. In this connexion it is interesting to note that although Francisco d'Hollanda was apt to add a purely personal interpretation to the monuments he saw, when he was in Rome in 1539-1540 Bramante's own model of the Belvedere Court may well have still existed, and Baccio Bandinelli, who was actually living in the Belvedere about this time, mentioned plans or a model in a letter to the Grand Duke of Tuscany in 1551.

In the Uffizi drawing the culminating niche is already shown as being two stories high, though many authorities believe that Bramante originally intended it to be of one storey only, and this is borne out by Francisco d'Hollanda's drawing. Certainly this end of the court was much altered during the sixteenth century, and the characteristic aspects of a Roman villa garden modified by Julius III's new palace that was built behind it in 1551. Today the niche appears as an apse three stories high, that provides the setting for the famous bronze cone, while the whole layout of the court has been destroyed by the erection of the Braccio Nuovo of the Vatican Museum and the library building that occupy most of the central terrace.

Apart from its decorative function of forming the climax to the whole design, the culminating niche and its flanking walls or loggias served the purely practical one of providing a screen that concealed the asymmetrical position of the old Villa Belvedere in relation to the scheme. Hendrick van Schoel's print of 1579, which shows the layout of the Vatican gardens in his day, reveals this clearly (pl. 76). It also affords an interesting glimpse into the courtyard of the old villa. On a smaller scale Bramante's

76 CORTILE DEL BELVEDERE; THE VATICAN GARDENS
A print, dated 1579, of the Cortile del Belvedere and the Vatican gardens by Hendrick van Schoel, that, with the exception of the apse, M, on the right, corresponds to Bramante's original ideas. The court is now divided in two by the library and museum buildings erected on the central terrace. By kind permission of the Gabinetto Nazionale delle Stampe.

adaptation of the Villa Belvedere to comply with Julius II's requirements for a museum or art gallery and his personal *giardino segreto* was quite as epoch-making as his design for the whole cortile and, unlike the larger project, it appears to have been practically completed during the Pope's lifetime.

The importance attributed also to this part of Bramante's work by his contemporaries may be judged by the fact that the Venetian Ambassador to the Court of Hadrian VII included a detailed account of it in his official relation upon his return to Venice in 1523. This reads as follows: 'One enters a very beautiful garden of which half is filled with growing grass and bays, mulberries and cypresses, while the other half is paved with squares of bricks laid upright, and in every square a beautiful orange tree grows out of the pavement, of which there are a great many arranged in perfect order. In the centre of the garden are two enormous men of marble, one is the Tiber, the other the Nile, very ancient figures, and two fountains issue from them. At the main entrance to this garden on the left there is a sort of chapel built into the wall where, on a marble base, stands the Apollo . . . Somewhat further on, also on the same façade which runs along this side, and in a similar place on a similar base as high off the ground as an altar, opposite a most perfect well, is the Laocoön . . . not far from this, mounted in a similar fashion, is the Venus . . . On one side of this garden is a most beautiful loggia, at one end of which is a lovely fountain that irrigates the orange trees and the rest of the garden by a little canal in the centre of the loggia. At the other end, through a small door one passes out into two even more beautiful loggias, as high off the ground as half the Campanile of San Marco (because they stand on the peak of a hill). There is a marvellous view from here as charming as one could desire. At the entrance to the loggias on the left is a beautiful and devout chapel, perfectly ornamented . . . then a string of large and small rooms, gracious both for their decoration and their view, and this is the Pope's quarters.' Evidently there were two gardens. This is confirmed by Aldrovandi and by drawings; apparently they were separated by the loggia and the second garden overlooked the large walled stretch of woodland seen in Hendrick van Schoel's print in the midst of which stands Pirro Ligorio's Villa Pia.

The primary interest of the Venetian Ambassador's relation, however, lies in his description of the arrangement of the fountains and classical statues in the garden courtyard of the old villa, which was fully as revolutionary as the design of the Cortile del Belvedere itself. Fountains had been used as garden ornaments right through the Middle Ages but, with the exception of those in the moresque palaces of the Norman kings of Sicily, these were of the simple cup-shaped or basin type, usually placed in the centre of a garden. Even the magnificent ones of several tiers and adorned with sculpture that graced the Medici gardens of Castello in the middle of the sixteenth century were still only a grander edition of this primitive form. But here at the beginning of the century we have the Venetian Ambassador's description not only of the statues of the river gods of the Nile and the Tiber being used as fountains, but also of the arrangement of the 'Apollo', 'Laocoön', and other famous statues in what, for the lack of a better definition of so revolutionary an idea, he calls 'a sort of chapel built into the wall'. Several of Francisco d'Hollanda's drawings in the Escorial sketch-book portray the statues and fountains as described by the Ambassador and their arrangement is further confirmed by Johannes Fichard's description of 1536 and other sources, so that there can be little doubt that Francisco d'Hollanda's drawings represent the statues in their original Bramantesque settings. The 'Apollo' is shown standing in a niche where the vault is decorated with painted trellises and climbing plants and birds, in the familiar style of old Roman garden *trompe l'oeil*. The 'Tigris' and 'Cleopatra' were also placed in niches, but were transformed into wall fountains, while their niches were disguised with rustic stone and water plants to resemble natural grottoes (pl. 77).

Today we are so accustomed to this type of fountain and architectural setting for classical statues as being part and parcel of any Italian garden that we scarcely pause to think where it may have originated. The answer is – here in the garden courtyard of the Belvedere where, as a result of his patient years of study of the relics of the ancient world, Bramante revived in spirit and in fact the splendour of the classical gardens of antiquity. With the creation of the Belvedere court, water and sculpture again became an integral part of Italian garden architecture, not just incidents in a formal layout. The wall fountains of the Belvedere were both the descendants of the glistening flood that poured through the *triclinia* and nympheums of Hadrian's and the other great Roman villas and the progenitors of all the grottoes with their gurgling waterfalls, the great veils of water falling from monumental fountains and the glittering cascades that have made Italian gardens famous throughout the world, while they and the architectural use of sculpture – not just as an amusing conceit as in Alberti's day – have been imitated in every country where the classical garden tradition took root.

The sources from which Bramante drew his inspiration for this particular aspect of the Belvedere were, of course, the classical ruins, but after the destruction of centuries it is difficult even to guess which particular ones these might have been. Certainly Hadrian's villa, that in his day must have contained a great deal more of its original fountains, sculpture and decoration than when, after years of pillage, Pirro Ligorio examined it half a century later. Even then Ligorio found ample traces of paintings, *stucchi*, rustic stone decoration and even statues. No doubt there were many other ancient monuments that have since been stripped or destroyed so that even the resources of modern archaeology cannot evoke their former splendour. Nevertheless some existing monuments, and others of which we possess records, do cast some light upon the possible sources available to Bramante. One of these is a fragment of a relief on a Roman tomb in the Via Asinara, illustrated by Pietro Santi Bartoli in his famous book *Gli Antichi Sepolchri overo Mausolei Romani et Etruschi*, compiled in the seventeenth century (pl. 78). This figure of a river god or man portrayed against the natural rock, from which issues a cascade of water, might well have served as a model for the 'Tigris' and 'Cleopatra' wall fountains of the Belvedere. One of Francisco d'Hollanda's more than usually 'improved' drawings represents the grotto or nympheum of the Caffarella, of which Jean Morin's seventeenth-century print is certainly a truer rendering, as it shows the place much as it is today (pl. 80). This nympheum is of

77 FOUNTAIN IN THE CORTILE DEL BELVEDERE
Francisco d'Hollanda's drawing, made when he was in Rome in 1539-1540, of the 'Cleopatra' fountain in the Cortile del Belvedere. From his sketch-book in the Escorial. Vatican Library photo from a facsimile in the Library.

78 A ROMAN RELIEF
Fragment of a relief on a tomb in the Via Asinara two miles outside Rome, which was still in place in the seventeenth century and may have been one of the sources from which Bramante drew his inspiration for the 'Cleopatra' and other wall fountains of the Belvedere. Engraving from Pietro Santi Bartoli's Gli Antichi Sepolchri, *Rome, 1697.*

79   FOUNTAIN OF THE ACQUA
GIULIA
*Drawing by Paul Brill at the end of the
sixteenth century of the 'Trophies of Marius',
in actual fact the monumental fountain of the
Acqua Giulia of ancient Roman times, of
which ruins still exist; another possible source
of inspiration for Renaissance garden
architects. Fountains with triple arches
continued to be built in the seventeenth
century.* By kind permission of the
Gabinetto Nazio-nale delle Stampe.

80   NINFEO DELLA CAFFARELLA
*Jean Morin's print executed during the first
half of the seventeenth century, of the Ninfeo
della Caffarella, which, with the exception of
the table, is exactly as it is today. There is little
doubt that it inspired many nympheums in
Renaissance gardens.* By kind permission
of the Gabinetto Nazionale delle
Stampe.

particular interest as it once stood in the garden of the palatial villa of Herod Atticus – a contemporary of Marcus Aurelius. It achieved great fame in Renaissance times, as it was believed to have been the abode of the nymph Egeria, and became a place of pilgrimage to scholars and artists alike. Although it was probably tidied up, and the statue from a Roman sarcophagus seen at the far end was added about this time, there is little doubt that, with its niches and vaulted roof and a natural spring converted into a fountain, this nympheum was the prototype of countless others in Renaissance gardens, and possibly even a source of Bramante's use of niches for his wall fountains.

Paul Brill's drawing of the 'Trophies of Marius' and the ruins of the terminal fountain of the Julian aqueduct show another classical monument as it appeared at the end of the

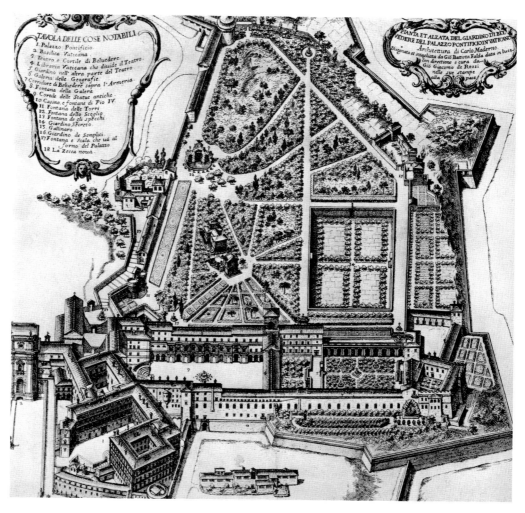

sixteenth century (pl. 79). This was also a fruitful source of inspiration to garden architects. The triple openings of the apse and flanking arches were repeated in innumerable monumental fountains in Italian gardens and cities. A somewhat free seventeenth-century interpretation of this theme, executed in rustic stone, appears in Falda's print of the Vatican gardens (pl. 81). This print also provides interesting evidence of the evolution of the gardens during the century that had elapsed since Hendrick van Schoel had made his study. (pl. 76).

The main structural difference is the division of the Cortile del Belvedere into two separate courtyards by the library building which had been erected at the base of the central terrace. But the real interest in comparing the two prints lies in its revelation of the different character of sixteenth- and seventeenth- century garden layouts. Today, when confronted with Italian gardens whose architectural form we know has been little changed during the centuries, we are all too apt to assume that the details of their layout are also much the same. But in actual fact a careful examination of the drawings and prints made of the gardens during the centuries reveals that their planting and layout were subject to continuous alterations according to the fashion of the various periods.

Thus in comparing these sixteenth- and seventeenth-century prints of the Vatican gardens it is evident that many changes had taken place in them. One of the most striking is that Paul III's walled garden behind the upper terrace of the Belvedere is shown in the first as a medieval type of garden, with the characteristic *berceaux* crossing in the centre and the simplest of flower-beds. A hundred years later it had been transformed into four rectangular plots edged, probably, with fruit trees. In the Cortile del Belvedere a similar process has taken place – the slightly more elaborate parterres, with their low trellised and creeper-covered surrounds, have also been replaced by tree-filled plots. By way of recompense, however, the rectangular flower-plots in front of the Villa Pia and the woodland that surrounded it in the sixteenth century have, in Falda's print, now been converted into an elaborate garden with complicated, though still basically geometrical parterres of flowers. Both these and some of the surrounding tree-bordered plots have been planted with palms and other exotics, while several fountains have been introduced into what has evidently become more disciplined *bosco*, whose star-like avenues radiating from the Villa Pia are of particular significance to the future of French garden design.

Villa Pia - Vatican Gardens

Pirro Ligorio built the Villa Pia for Pope Pius IV in 1560, ten years after he had begun work on the famous Villa d'Este at Tivoli, and its delicate and intimate character provide a striking contrast to the vast conception of the Tivoli gardens. This difference was no doubt largely dictated by the Pope's desire for a secluded retreat for his own use and not a grandiose garden for 'representational' purposes, as this already existed in the Cortile del Belvedere.

Percier and Fontaine maintained that Ligorio's design was executed 'after the manner of the ancient houses of which he had made a special study'. Perhaps it would be truer to say that the Villa Pia was a Renaissance Interpretation of the Roman *diaetae*, to which references abound in the classical literature that was so much studied at that time. As such it is of outstanding interest as one of the earliest examples of the Italian garden casino. The inspiration for the Villa Pia's design was undoubtedly classical, for there was no more assiduous student of ancient monuments than Ligorio, but the drawing of a *columbarium* near the Via Cassia in one of his sketch-books in the Vatican Library, with its porticoed entrance loggia and oval court, enlarged by an apse on the far side, appears to be a more likely model than a Roman house.

The *stucchi* of the interior court of the Villa Pia were derived from antique reliefs and coins, but one of the most interesting aspects of its decoration are the polychrome mosaics that adorn the exterior of the loggia, which are beautifully reflected in the waters of the surrounding fountain (pl. 82). The Roman use of such mosaics in conjunction with fountains is a well-attested fact; the best-known example is the famous marine mosaic in the lower sanctuary of the Temple of Fortune of Praeneste, which was covered by a softly flowing veil of water. But many others exist, notably in Pompeian gardens, one of the most attractive being the miniature fountain in the Casa di Mario Lucrezio. Although these ancient mosaics have only come to light as the result of modern excavations, no doubt others, which have since been destroyed, served Ligorio as a model, as they did for Giovanni da Udine's elephant fountain in the Villa Madama.

The great importance and the charm of the Villa Pia lay in its design as a secluded retreat set in the midst of a shady *bosco*, and in this its significance in Italian garden history cannot be overestimated, for it is the earliest of its kind, antedating even Vignola's Casino garden at Caprarola. Though modern landscaping has done much to deprive its surroundings of their original character, few would quarrel with Burckhardt's description of the Villa Pia as the 'most perfect retreat imaginable for a midsummer afternoon'. Still today, with its gently rippling fountains and shady porticos drowsing in the heat of a Roman *siesta* hour, it evokes an atmosphere of secluded peace that is the essence of the Italian *giardino segreto*.

82   VILLA PIA
The Villa Pia in the Vatican gardens. It was built by Pirro Ligorio for Pope Pius IV in 1560 as a secluded retreat for his private use, as distinct from the Cortile del Belvedere which was intended for public and State occasions.

The Farnesina - Rome

Contemporary with the creation of the Cortile del Belvedere was the first great Roman town villa built in accordance with Alberti's conception of a retreat that also enjoyed the amenities of a city. This was the pleasure house that the fabulously rich Sienese banker, Agostino Chigi, commissioned Peruzzi to design for him on the banks of the Tiber. Owing to its subsequent purchase by Cardinal Alessandro Farnese this villa has long been known as the Farnesina. Originally the layout included extensive gardens and a sumptuous dining loggia on the river bank. The loggia has been destroyed and only a portion of the gardens survive, though they still contain a fine pleached walk of bay trees. The great glory of the Farnesina today lies in the interior decoration of Peruzzi's characteristically dignified villa, whose lovely garden loggia was frescoed by Raphael. While the loggia walls are painted in simple architectural style, the great vaulted ceiling appears as a *trompe l'oeil* garden arbour, in which tapestries, representing the 'Marriage of Cupid and Psyche' and the 'Council of the Gods', are stretched in the central interstices of an airy framework covered with garlands. In the other open spaces between the garlands, Venus, nymphs and cupids are represented against a pale blue sky.

At first glance this style of decoration may appear to be a wholly imaginary creation, but in actual fact garlanded arbours such as this were really made in Renaissance Italy — Giovanni Boccati's picture of the Madonna, angels and saints at Perugia is shown in one closely resembling it. Exactly similar garlands, entwined with flowers and fruit, are still used for church and festive decorations today.

The figures in this singularly lovely decoration of the Farnesina loggia were the work of Raphael but the garlands were painted by Giovanni de Udine, who, we know from his friend Vasari, was a man of simple country tastes. Vasari says that Giovanni was a keen sportsman and liked nothing better than to take a day off in the country shooting with a bow or gun, and that he even made and painted an artificial cow as a hide for this purpose. This love of country life probably explains the unique character of the Farnesina garlands, for unlike so many of the flowers, apart from roses, jasmine and lilies, that appear in Italian paintings of the period, the flowers and vegetables that Giovanni painted are real ones, correct in every detail. Owing to this very unusual fact, these garlands of the Farnesina are immensely valuable for the light they throw upon what kinds of flowers were grown in gardens of the sixteenth century. Prominent among them are, of course, madonna lilies and great pink cabbage roses, violets and jasmine; but as well there are iris, poppies, convolvulus, periwinkles, clematis, daisies, golden-yellow day lilies or hemerocallis, dog roses, paeonies, cyclamen, narcissus, wallflowers, red anemones and chamomile. These can be clearly distinguished, but there are several others whose identification is rather difficult, though one looks like an acanthus flower and another like a rosy-pink squill. The flowers of blossoming trees are also depicted, such as elderflowers, hawthorn, pomegranates and some citrus blossoms, almost certainly orange or lemon.

Though the selection is rather limited, these are in fact the flowers that one would have expected to find growing in an early-fifteenth-century Italian garden, as many of them are old Roman favourites and others we have already found in the gardens of the *Hypnerotomachia* of Poliphilus. In any case they serve as a timely reminder of the fact that, although European garden flora was not extensive until the importation of the exotics in the next century, for all their predominantly architectural character flowers were not entirely banished from Italian Renaissance gardens and certainly played a part in the parterres of the Belvedere and Villa Pia in the sixteenth century.

Villa Madama · Rome

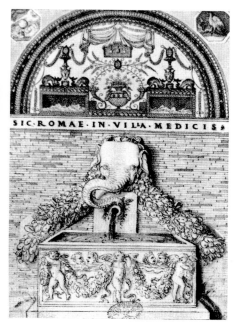

Characteristically enough it was a Tuscan, Cardinal Giulio de' Medici, who built the first Renaissance villa outside the walls of Rome. Its site on the slopes of Monte Mario overlooking the city may well have reminded a Medici of his family's famous Fiesole villa, while the splendour of the view and the countrified freshness of the surroundings would have held an instant appeal for a man reared in the Florentine humanist tradition. But here all resemblance with a Tuscan country house practically ceased as the Villa Madama, as it has been known for centuries owing to the subsequent ownership of Margaret of Austria, was entirely Roman in spirit and monumental grandeur. Begun about 1516, the principal authorship of the villa is traditionally associated with Raphael's name, but Vasari stated that the Cardinal entrusted the actual work of building to the famous artist's pupil and friend, Giulio Romano, who was also responsible for much of the decoration. However some drawings preserved in the Uffizi, by Antonio Sangallo the Younger, are regarded as strong evidence that he also had a part in its creation.

According to these drawings, the actual house was designed as a magnificent series of open courts and loggias intended for entertaining, the rooms serving merely as an enclosing framework, and there was to be little provision for living accommodation. The plan is one of the most perfect examples of the interpenetration of house and garden in existence, rivalling even the pavilions of Hadrian's villa in this respect, and its influence on Italian garden design was to be second only to that of Bramante. From all four points of the compass, passages led from the circular central court into loggias: that on the south opened on to the entrance court; the loggia to the east commanded a superb view over terraces and the Tiber valley; the northern one led into the *giardino segreto*; while that on the west opened into a great semicircular theatre, excavated in the hillside. But this magnificent layout was destined never to be completed. The premature death of Raphael, subsequent troubles with his successors and, probably, the insecure nature of the eastern end of the site, which was subject to landslides, retarded the work, so that less than half the projected building was completed at the time of the Sack of Rome in 1527. From contemporary descriptions and the number of entertainments held there, it seems that the gardens were well on the way towards completion by that date. Unfortunately, owing to centuries of neglect, few traces of them have survived except the *giardino segreto* and its adjoining fish pond or swimming-pool, though part of the rest of the garden has been restored during the twentieth century upon what are believed to have been its original lines.

From this and the Uffizi drawing it appears that the design of the gardens was retrograde in comparison with Bramante's Cortile del Belvedere. They seem simply to have consisted of a series of terraces lying along the side of the hill, and to have lacked the cohesive force of his central perspective and superb arrangement of connected levels. Their chief beauty lay in the two qualities that would pre-eminently have appealed to a Tuscan — the marvellous view and an attractive use of details; though the fountains and grottoes beside the swimming-pool are truly Roman in their grandeur, they form an isolated unit. Contemporary sources describe the use of sculpture on an extensive scale, but today no trace of this remains except Baccio Bandinelli's 'giants' that originally stood at the entrance to the *bosco*, and are now somewhat unsuitably placed in the *giardino segreto*.

The only notable piece of garden architecture to have survived in Villa Madama is Giovanni da Udine's elephant fountain, to which Francisco d'Hollanda devoted one of the few coloured sketches in his book (pl. 83). The elephant's head and the swags of fruit and flowers still exist, but the sarcophagus has been replaced by a plain stone tank; all trace of the mosaics immediately above the fountain has disappeared. Fortunately the rest have

83 VILLA MADAMA

The elephant fountain in the garden of the Villa Madama, a sketch by Francisco d'Hollanda. This is the only notable piece of garden architecture to survive in the garden of the Villa Madama, so called because it was once the residence of Margaret of Austria. It was begun about 1516, and associated with Raphael's name, although Vasari stated that the actual work was carried out by his pupil and friend Giulio Romano, and Antonio Sangallo the Younger probably also had a hand in its creation. Vatican Library photo from a fascimile in the Library.

survived and the vault is covered with sea-shells and a mosaic representing dolphins and sea creatures, surrounding Cardinal Giulio's curious device of a blazing sun whose rays pass through a crystal ball, setting fire to a tree-trunk, also his motto *Candor Illusus*.

Though this part of its decoration has been much restored, the fountain is of very considerable interest, for Vasari says that in making it the artist 'imitated it all in every detail from the temple of Neptune that had been discovered shortly beforehand among the ancient ruins of the Palazzo Maggiore which was all adorned with things natural to the sea'. The 'Palazzo Maggiore' was the name by which the Imperial palaces on the Palatine had been known since medieval times, and it seems that Giovanni da Udine's model was a semi-subterranean nympheum, probably part of Nero's Domus Transitoria.

Much of this can still be seen under the Flavian *triclinium*, though the mosaics of the floor and ceiling recorded in early excavations have disappeared, and there is no sign of an elephant's head.

Another fountain of Giovanni da Udine's, of which only the site is now recognizable, brought him even greater fame, and the reward of what Vasari describes as the '*cavalierato di San Pietro*'. This is also important in the history of Italian gardens as having been one of the earliest recorded examples of a fountain in a woodland setting, made to imitate nature, a type of garden scene that is much more generally associated with Baroque than Renaissance gardens. This fountain stood in a natural hollow, at some distance from the formal garden terraces, in which a small spring still rises in the midst of what was evidently then the *bosco*. In the words of Vasari, 'it was surrounded by a wood . . . and was made to fall with fine artifice over rough stones and stalactites dripping and gushing so that it really appeared to be natural, and above it among the grottoes and rough stones he composed a great lion's head garlanded with maidenhair and other water plants. It is impossible to imagine the grace of that wild fountain.' Indeed it must have presented a perfectly charming picture, with the water gurgling and sparkling beneath the trembling fronds of maidenhair in the dappled shade of the *bosco*, and it is not surprising that the Medici Pope, Leo X, rewarded the graceful compliment of the lion's head by making its designer a Cavaliere of the Order of St Peter.

Such was the beauty of the Villa Madama that, in the tragic days of the Sack of Rome, poor Giulio de Medici, who was by then Pope Clement VII, mourned as he watched it burning from the windows of Castel Sant' Angelo. Although Clement VII tried to restore the villa afterwards he must have realized that the brilliance and charm of life in Rome as she had been was gone for him. She might rise from her ashes, but the carefree suppers in the Villa Madama, eaten off golden plate, in the company of the greatest scholars and wits of the day could never be the same, as so many of the brilliant company had perished in the holocaust.

These evening gatherings of artists, writers, wits and scholars in Roman gardens had already become a great feature of the city's life during the reign of Leo X (1513-1521); appropriately enough, as he is the Pope to whom is attributed the phrase 'Let us enjoy the Papacy, since God has given it to us.' In his day the Roman '*vignate*' or vineyard-gardens were famous; there was scarcely a moderately prosperous family who did not own one. The city was then so small that most of the vast area within the Aurelian wall was given over to them. In this gay and prosperous period, these gardens that blossomed among the hoary ruins of ancient Rome were the setting for continual banquets and entertainments during the summer months. It was an enchanted world to which all who took part in it looked back in longing as a halcyon period in their own lives, as well as that of the city before the tempest of the Sack.

Such famous men as Bembo, Castiglione and Sadoleto recalled this period as one of the happiest in their lives; a letter of Sadoleto's, written in 1529, from Carpentras when he was bishop, recreates the atmosphere with nostalgic affection. He writes: 'Oh if I think again of times past, when so many of us used to gather together, and our age was much more readily disposed to hilarity than today. How many times those meetings and suppers that we held so often return to my mind. When in your gardens outside the walls, or in mine on the Quirinal, or at the Circus Massimus, or on the banks of the Tiber in the Temple of Hercules, or elsewhere, we held those reunions of gifted and respected men . . . where after our homely banquets, flavoured more with wit than gluttony, we recited poetry and declaimed orations, among our friends Fera, Beroaldo, Porzio, Capello, Donato and Coricio; now as I write all dead.'

The 'Coricio' that Sadoleto mentions at the end of his letter was one of the best loved of the group and the dinners in his gardens were famous in the literary world of the time. His real name was John Goritz; he was born in Luxembourg, but in accordance with the fashion of the day he preferred the latinized form. Goritz was a friend of Michelangelo and Raphael, and commissioned Sansovino's famous statue of the 'Madonna and Child' in the Church of S. Agostino. Raphael also painted a picture of 'Isaiah' for him that hung above the 'Madonna'. Goritz once complained to Michelangelo that Raphael had charged him too much for this, to which the great man replied with characteristic candour that 'Isaiah's knee alone' was worth what Goritz had paid for the whole picture.

In spite of this tiff, Raphael, as well as Sadoleto, Bembo and Castiglione, often used to dine in Goritz's garden on the slopes of the Capitol, overlooking the Forum of Trajan. The garden was a simple one, consisting mainly of a *boschetto* of lemon trees, in which stood statues, sarcophagi and fragments of ancient inscriptions. There was a cool and shady grotto and a fountain with an inscription above it, which read: 'The place of nymphs, drink, wash and keep silent.' It is doubtful if his convivial guests paid much attention to the last part of the inscription, except when they were writing verses in praise of the garden, that were afterwards hung on the statues and trees.

Just such a garden, though of a slightly later period, is glimpsed through the window of a curious sixteenth-century picture in the Doria Gallery in Rome. The artist, Vincenzo Campi, has portrayed a buxom cook at work in her kitchen, while outside one can see the dinner in progress, laid on a table in the open, just as it was in Goritz's garden (pl. 84). What strikes one at once is the number of ladies seated at the table, and (although Sadoleto prudently makes no mention of this in his letter) these dinners were mostly of mixed company of which the feminine part was made up of the witty courtesans of the period. This was an accepted custom and we know that Agostino Chigi did not hesitate to invite the most famous and brilliant of them all – the beautiful Imperia – to his dinners at the Farnesina, even when Leo X was present.

Once when he was looking for the site of John Goritz's garden, Domenico Gnoli – the famous Roman topographer – discovered a touching relic of one of the last of the gay parties that were probably ever held there. On a house in the (now destroyed) Via dei Carbonari on the slopes of the Capitol Gnoli found an inscription 'Coritius Trevir MDXVII'. One of the rooms and a portico on the ground floor of the house evidently dated from the sixteenth century, and he persuaded the tenants to allow him to dig up the ground of the yard behind. Here he found a sixteenth-century pottery plate with a design of a horse and a pottery candlestick with a painted inscription. At the top of this were written the words 'The sun must be dazzled when he looks at you' and on the base: 'Contessa of the beautiful demeanour'. 'Contessa' was in those days also used as a name – one of the Medici married a Contessina – and Gnoli attributed the inscription to the fact that each of the guests probably had his individual candle placed in front of him with a graceful compliment written on the candlestick.

From the very small amount of wax that still remained sticking to the holder, Gnoli assumed that it had probably been used once and that here was a relic of one of the very

last dinners that were ever held in John Goritz's garden before the Sack of Rome. Poor man, he probably buried his treasures there for safe-keeping when the armies of the Connétable de Bourbon were besieging the city. One hopes that he was more fortunate than Angelo Colocci, another famous garden owner, who was forced to dig up all of his in order to ransom himself twice over. Colocci had a fine library and a collection of medals in his garden house as well as a museum with antique sculptures; but he lost them all and fled to his native Jesi having saved only his life.

The most famous private collection of antique sculptures in a Roman garden about this period was that of Cardinal Andrea della Valle. Possibly these were saved by being hidden, or by the Cardinal having sufficient men at arms at his disposal to protect the palace and the garden he had built (about 1520) during the fearful days of the Sack. Certainly his collection was one of the artistic sights of Rome when Francisco d'Hollanda was there in 1540, for he did a drawing of it, and it had also been drawn by Martin Heemskirk some five years previously (pl. 85). This was, of course, the princely collection of a rich Cardinal connoisseur, but it was also noted for its arrangement, which was to lead a fashion that lasted right into the second half of the seventeenth century. In Cardinal della Valle's garden the statues and reliefs were more closely integrated in an elaborate architectural setting than in any other gardens of which we have previous records. This was in effect a logical development of the process begun in the Belvedere as well as a convenient way of arranging a large collection in a small town garden, where the planting appears to have been limited to some trellises and raised beds. But this type of arrangement became so fashionable that it was used to adorn whole palaces and villas. Sometimes it was added to the original structure as in the garden façade of the Villa Medici; it was even more lavishly employed in the seventeenth-century Villa Borghese and Palazzo Antici Mattei, while in Algardi's Villa Pamphilj the whole house seems to have been designed as a setting for the decoration.

It is interesting to note that when the Cardinal della Valle's collection was sold to Cardinal Medici in 1584 some of these same reliefs were used for the decoration of his Roman villa, but most of it was sent to Florence and placed in the Boboli gardens, where the 'white statues of fauns and sylvans . . . glimmering among the broad masses of shade and dusky alleys' so delighted William Beckford in the eighteenth century.

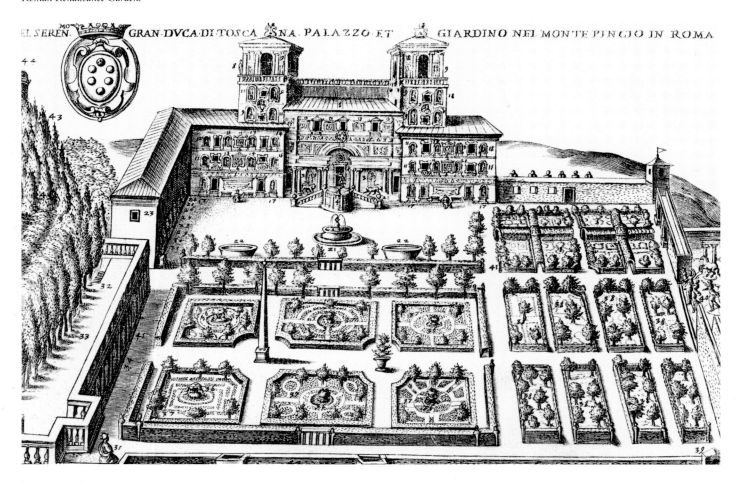

EL SEREN. GRAN·DVCA·DI·TOSCASNA·PALAZZO·ET GIARDINO·NEL·MONTE·PINCIO·IN·ROMA

Villa Medici · Rome

The Villa Medici on the Pincian Hill is the only great Roman villa of the sixteenth century whose garden layout has survived almost intact though natural growth and the evolution of a taste for less and less severely disciplined planting has increased its *bosco* character. The villa, which probably occupies part of the site of the famous gardens of Lucullus and was originally built in 1544 by Annibale Lippi for Cardinal Ricci, was only bought by Cardinal Ferdinando de Medici about 1580. With his purchase of Cardinal della Valle's collection of sculpture, this typical son of the great Florentine family set about the embellishment of the villa, and it is to him that it owes the rich decoration of the garden façade, which presents such a striking contrast to the austerity of the face that it turns to the outside world. This aspect of the villa is faithfully portrayed in an early print published in J. Laurus' *Roma Vetus et Nuova* in 1614, which also provides an interesting view of the garden at this date (pl. 86).

If the design of the garden is essentially that of a town villa, and far from revolutionary, it already displays certain characteristics of Italian garden design that continued in use through the centuries. The most striking of these is the clear space immediately adjacent to the house, behind which lies a well-drilled garden of floral parterres, while the shady walks and cypress-planted terrace stand at a respectable distance from it. This layout constitutes an inverted order of precedence in the planting which one might have expected in so hot and sunny a country as Italy, where it might reasonably have been supposed that the shady alleys would lead directly from the house.

86 VILLA MEDICI, ROME
The garden of Villa Medici on the Pincian Hill, built on what was probably the site of the gardens of Lucullus by Annibale Lippi in 1544 for Cardinal Ricci, and bought by Cardinal Ferdinando de' Medici in 1580. From J. Laurus' Roma Vetus et Nuova, Rome, 1614. The villa is now the French Academy but the garden is open regularly. By kind permission of the Gabinetto Nazionale delle Stampe.

87 VILLA MEDICI, ROME
The gardens of the Villa Medici today, one of the very few to have retained their original sixteenth-century layout.

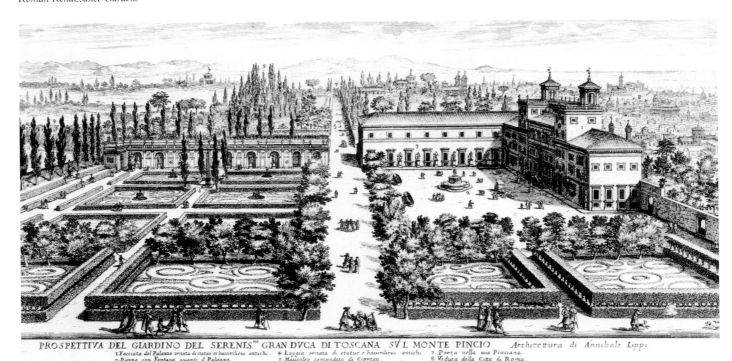

PROSPETTIVA DEL GIARDINO DEL SERENIS.^{MO} GRAN DVCA DI TOSCANA SVL MONTE PINCIO   *Architettura di Annibale Lippi.*

1 *Facciata del Palazzo ornata di statue et basirilievi antichi.*   4. *Loggia ornata di statue e basirilievi antichi.*   7. *Porta nella via Pinciana.*
2 *Piazza con Fontana avanti il Palazzo.*   5. *Mausoleo cercondato di Cipressi.*   8. *Veduta della Cità di Roma.*
3 *Galeria ornata dentro di statue antiche.*   6. *Obelisco di granito antico.*   9. *Mura della Cità di Roma che chiudono il Giardino.*

The answer lies in the Renaissance idea of symmetry, in which a built-up area was balanced by an open space; also the conception of the interpenetration of house and garden – the house opening up as it approaches the garden, in this case with a loggia, while the garden becomes more architectural as it nears the house. Or as Baccio Bandinelli phrased it: *'le cose che si murano debbono essere guidi e superiori a quelle che si piantono'*.

Another reason for placing the parterres behind the house was that they were meant to be seen from above, so that the full effect of their design would be appreciated. They were carried out in flowers and, probably, still bordered with variegated herbs, as in the *Hypnerotomachia*. They are referred to in the key as *'partimenti de semplici'*. It is interesting also to note that the main outline of the parterres is still the same as in Laurana's garden at Urbino, with a circular space at the crossing of the paths, while their geometrical layout is punctuated in the same manner by fountains and dwarf fruit trees in pots. This part of the garden remains practically unaltered today, though the obelisk has been replaced by a fountain, and all the corners of the beds have been modified to form curves corresponding with the new entries made in the surrounding hedge, even the original site of the fountains in the centre of each parterre being recalled by a circular bed (pl. 87). The long-lived popularity of the old *berceaux* is clearly attested in this early-seventeenth-century print, for two of them are still to be seen shading the walks among the hedged plantations of fruit trees on the right. This part of the garden is now incorporated in the extensive *bosco*, though the layout is exactly the same.

In order to give a picture of the whole garden, Laurus has not only diminished the size of the *bosco*, which is a great deal larger than the parterre garden, but also considerably foreshortened the distance that separates the cypress-covered mount from the house. The real position of this, and the extent of the upper *bosco* above the terrace, can be much more accurately gauged in Falda's prints, published about 1683 (pl. 88). In this the trellised gazebo, shown in the earlier print, is missing, but it is likely that the fountain which it sheltered may still have been there, as it was when John Evelyn visited the garden about 1644. The other outstanding feature of this part of the garden is the long walled walk that,

88   VILLA MEDICI, ROME
Print of the gardens of the Villa Medici, showing their evolution in the half century that had elapsed since Laurus' print was made, from G. B. Falda's Li Giardini di Roma, Rome, ?1683. Photo by Gabinetto Foto-grafico Nazionale.

like the old Roman promenades, catches the morning sun and still provides a sheltered place to saunter on a bright cold winter day when the *tramontana* is blowing.

Falda's print probably shows the garden largely as John Evelyn saw it, when already the simpler layout of Laurus' time had given way to more elaborate and extensive parterres, that are beginning to resemble the elaborate French *broderies*, while the kindly shade of the old *berceaux* has disappeared for ever. Like most of his contemporaries, Evelyn was principally attracted by the sculptures, of which few are now left, though sarcophagi and other fragments are effectively employed for displaying flowers. Already in Laurus' print Giambologna's 'Mercury', that the diarist admired so much, can be seen in the entrance to the loggia, and the famous 'Niobe and her Children' stand in a colonnade to the right of the *bosco*. By the time of Evelyn's visit, however, the 'Cleopatra' – like that of the Belvedere in reality a reclining Ariadne – would probably have been moved from the far corner to the lovely little loggia that Velázquez painted when he was staying in the villa about 1650 (pl. 89).

In this scene, which could well have been painted on the same spot today (pl. 90), and

in his other small canvas of the villa, Velázquez' genius has caught the secret not only of the intrinsic charm of all old Italian gardens but also of the Roman scene in general. This is not limited to the dappled shade of whispering trees in a sun-baked land, but the typically Roman characteristic of treating grandeur with insouciance. To a people who have grown up amongst the overwhelming monuments of antiquity, it seems perfectly natural to hang out the washing, as Velázquez has depicted it, in the princely surroundings of a Cardinal's garden terrace; and to leave one of its loggias casually boarded up. Evidently this surprising characteristic appealed as much to Velázquez as it did to the great French artists of the next century; to Fragonard, Hubert Robert, Pâris and the rest, who, as '*pensionnaires du Roi*' were the predecessors of the present Prix de Rome scholars of the French Academy that now owns the villa.

90 VILLA MEDICI, ROME

Villa di Papa Giulio - Rome

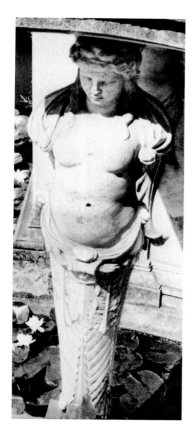

Much more characteristically Roman in design than the Villa Medici is the one upon which Pope Julius III expended vast sums in order to create a Renaissance pleasure house in the style of the classical suburban villa. Still known as the Villa di Papa Giulio, this is one of the few Roman villas of the period that perpetuates its founder's name. As Cardinal Ciocchi del Monte, Julius had already owned a villa on the Via Flaminia, about a mile outside the city walls, and upon his accession one of his fellow-cardinals paid him the compliment of presenting him with his own adjoining property. No gift could have pleased Julius better, for one of the most endearing aspects of his characteristically Renaissance enjoyment of the good things of life was his love of nature. Immediately after his election in 1550, the new Pope embarked upon the transformation and extension of his old villa, invoking a galaxy of talent for the purpose. Not only has Michelangelo's name been mentioned as having supervised the original plans, which Vasari attributed to himself, but Ammanati and Vignola also played what was probably the major part in its creation.

It is almost impossible today to picture the beauty of the villa as it originally was, for it has been shorn of its wonderful gardens that extended to the banks of the Tiber and over a large area in all directions. These were planted with elms, chestnuts, cypresses, bays, myrtles and pomegranates – no less than 36,000 trees and plants being used – and it was filled with fountains, fish ponds, grottoes, statues, aviaries and pavilions. Of this extensive layout only the villa itself and its adjoining nympheum and *giardini segreti* have survived; their design is so superb as to make one regret even more bitterly what has been lost.

The central focus of the whole layout is the magnificent horse-shoe-shaped court. This is divided by a porticoed screen from the nympheum that can be glimpsed lying behind it, while the central perspective continues through another loggia to the green of a small garden. The house, which from the outside appears as a solid mass, in reality simply provides the enclosing framework for this wonderful series of garden rooms, where the layout – except for the unfinished Villa Madama – is the most superb example of the interpenetration of house and garden in Italy. The graceful semicircular colonnades stretch out like arms to embrace the garden, and their close relationship with it is further emphasized by the frescoed vine and flower-covered trellises of the vault (pl. 92). Here birds and butterflies flit among the painted sprays of jasmine, the pink, white and crimson roses and the great bunches of grapes, that in reality once grew over the long arbour which shaded the path leading from the river to the house.

In the sixteenth century a fountain stood in the centre of the great court; its basin was the porphyry one from the Baths of Titus, now in the Vatican Museum. This was adorned with two shells of green veined marble, while the water flowed into it from the bill of a swan that stood beside a statue of Venus. In those days the whole court and its enclosing screens and loggias would have been adorned with the sculpture that filled one hundred and sixty boatloads when it was removed to the Vatican after the Pope's death.

An inscription with Ammanati's name indicates that he was the author of the screen separating the court from the nympheum (pl. 91). Though Vasari always claimed that he had made the original plans of the latter, and the caryatids have been attributed to Vignola, it is now generally considered that Ammanati's was the master hand. Whoever was its creator, this nympheum is one of the most perfect examples of garden architecture in Italy. In it the old classical relationship between theatrical and garden design lives again, allied to the Renaissance genius for the use of changing levels. A very rare sixteenth-century print by Du Pérac reveals this particular aspect from an unusual angle (pl. 93). It also shows the now-vanished landscapes, executed in imitation of the ancient

91   VILLA DI PAPA GIULIO
A corner of the nympheum of the Villa di Papa Giulio, designed as a cool retreat for hot Roman summer days.

topia, that decorated the walls. In this respect the villa played an important part in art history, for its rooms were among the first in any Renaissance building to have small landscapes depicted among their decoration of *grotteschi*. This fashion was introduced by Vignola into his villas at Caprarola and Bagnaia, and may be considered the precursor of the vogue for the Roman *vedute* and classical landscapes that became so popular in the eighteenth century.

Another aspect of ancient Roman villas and palaces was revived in this nympheum of Pope Julius' garden. Leading out of it are semi-subterranean rooms designed for coolness in summer, as they had been in the Imperial Palace on the Palatine and in Hadrian's villa. Surrounded by fern-decked fountains and lily-pools these rooms still provide a welcome

92   VILLA DI PAPA GIULIO
The garden of Villa di Papa Giulio, a Renaissance pleasure house in the style of a classical Roman suburban villa. Built for Pope Julius III shortly after his election in 1550, the villa was the work of a galaxy of talent. Michelangelo is said to have supervised the plans, while Ammanati, Vignola and, on his own evidence, Vasari took part in its construction. The villa houses the Etruscan museum and is open to the public.

refuge of cool tranquillity, even under the *solleone* of a Roman midsummer, as they did for their original owner when he snatched a brief day's repose in his much-loved villa.

Of the three small enclosed gardens that surround the central court and nympheum only one has retained a good deal of its original character and planting. This is the one on the left of the great court. Here a simple sixteenth-century arrangement of parterres, planted with clipped bay trees and shaded by pines, recalls the fact that the main function of these small enclosed gardens was to provide shade as well as the welcome relief of greenery in a predominantly architectural setting. Colour, however, was not absent, and the roses and oleanders growing in the garden today are probably planted in the same place as their Renaissance forebears. We know that the garden was filled with large vases containing plants and shrubs, probably many of them small citrus trees, specially imported from Naples. It seems likely that these and other highly prized plants would have been employed in the great central court, grouped around the Venus fountain, and in the more extensive and open gardens behind the nympheum, though now no trace remains here of the original layout.

Today the gardens of the Villa di Papa Giulio are floodlit on summer nights, and ballet performances are sometimes given there. The floodlighting is so skilfully arranged that it reveals the theatrical beauty of the nympheum to the full, while concealing the ravages of time and the daylight bareness of the courtyard robbed of its fountains and sculpture. This is undoubtedly the perfect occasion upon which to see the garden today, when it requires little imagination to people it with all the pageantry of a Papal Court of the Renaissance, and above all of the pleasure-loving Julius III. His banquets and entertainments were enlivened by French dancers attired in brilliant costumes and accompanied by the strains of the most skilled lute players of the time – one wonders what his reactions would have been to modern ballet.

Villa d'Este - Tivoli

Although situated some twenty miles away from the city, the gardens of the Villa d'Este at Tivoli may properly be considered as the most Roman as well as the most typically Renaissance gardens of all Italy. The Roman influence is easily accounted for, as a classical example of a hillside converted into garden terraces is close at hand. Pirro Ligorio, the designer of Villa d'Este, needed to look no further than the next spur of the Sabine foot-hills, where the remains of what was probably Quintilius Varus' villa can still easily be traced among the olive groves. But whereas, today at least, Varus' terraces appear as a succession of unrelated units, in Pirro Ligorio, Cardinal Ippolito d'Este had selected an architect who had studied the Temple of Fortune of Praeneste and had completed Bramante's unfinished work in the Cortile del Belvedere; the influence of both is clearly marked in the highly integrated design that he made for the Villa d'Este. This aspect of the layout becomes apparent at a glance in Du Pérac's print of 1575 and a seventeenth-century painting derived from it (pl. 94). Although both these show some projected features that were never actually carried out, notably the large semicircular fountain on the lower right-hand side, they reproduce the main lines of the garden exactly as it is today.

While its siting and marvellous view render Villa d'Este one of the most outstanding examples of the old Roman and of Alberti's precepts in this respect, in its layout it represents the quintessence of the Italian garden of the High Renaissance. Every inch of space within its boundaries was subject to manmade order and symmetry, and although scaled to draw the fullest effect from the vast spaces of the surrounding landscape, it is entirely separated from it. As Luigi Dami pointed out in his classic book on Italian gardens, the Renaissance garden architect treated his terrain as an artist who sets out to plan the composition of a picture within the limits of his canvas. He first reduced the ground to a simple regular figure and inside this everything was arranged in accordance with an overall

94 VILLA D'ESTE
A painting of the Villa d'Este at Tivoli some twenty miles from Rome, by an unknown artist of the seventeenth century, based on Du Pérac's sixteenth-century print. Designed by Pirro Ligorio, the garden is the most typically Roman and Renaissance garden of Italy. Not all the features were actually carried out. The villa belongs to the State and is open to the public. Painting in the collection of Harold Acton, Esq. By kind permission of the owner.

95 VILLA D'ESTE
The terrace of the hundred fountains in the gardens of the Villa d'Este at Tivoli. This superb promenade has always been regarded as one of the sights of Italy, visited by every traveller.

design. The main perspectives, whose effect was carefully calculated, began and ended at clearly defined fixed points. Usually, as in the Belvedere and Villa d'Este, they crossed the terraces of a hillside garden at right angles. These crossings, and even those of subsidiary paths, were marked by open spaces, and all of them were planned in relation to each other like the traffic centres of a city, and accentuated by fountains or stonework of some kind.

The Villa d'Este might well be cited as the textbook example of a garden of this type, for perhaps nowhere else have the details of such a layout been so carefully worked out and these basic principles of Italian garden design so clearly demonstrated. Unfortunately, we approach the garden today from the wrong end; it was never intended to be viewed first from the house but to be entered from the gate on the old Tivoli road at the bottom. From here, even with a much freer type of planting, it still appears as a magnificent series of vistas, rising one above the other and culminating in a grand climax where the great villa stands outlined against the clear blue sky.

Each pause in the ascent of this hillside garden, whether by the direct perspectives of the paths and steps or by the diagonals of the ramps or *cordonate* that recall Praeneste and the Belvedere, is marked by a new and varied use of water: by fish ponds at the lower level, glittering water staircases as the climb begins, then by great monumental fountains enclosed in garden rooms among the trees (pl. 95). The superb promenade of the 'hundred fountains' provides a breathing space before the steepest part of the journey, but even here, in the thickly planted *bosco*, the terminal and junction points of the ramps are marked by grottoes and fountains. Finally one last silver jet sprays upwards to the sky as the great open terrace before the villa is reached, and at last the climber turns to gaze at the vast panorama of the Roman *campagna*.

Where did Ligorio draw his inspiration for this dramatic and all-pervading use of water? The answer is almost certainly in Hadrian's villa that lies only a few miles away in the plain. In his somewhat muddled description of Hadrian's villa, of which he drew a plan

96 VILLA D'ESTE
Hubert Robert's bistre wash of the great fountain of the ovata in the gardens of the Villa d'Este at Tivoli, one of the most evocative representations of an Italian garden scene ever to have been made. The fountain has changed little since Hubert Robert spent the summer of 1760 at Villa d'Este with Fragonard and the Abbé de Saint-Non; then as now it was shaded by the great plane trees planted in the little forecourt that was designed as an al fresco dining-room. It was this picturesque aspect that appealed so strongly to the French artists of the day, and to travellers like Président de Brosses, who was there in 1739 and described it as one of the most beautiful fountains in the world. The design of the semicircular loggia, cut into the hillside beneath the great cascade, with its fountains, niches, and small water ways, was inspired by the triclinium of the Canopus in Hadrian's villa near by. The fountain is clearly represented in the print of the gardens made in 1575 by Du Pérac who was afterwards appointed architect to the King of France and designed for Henry IV, the gardens of Saint-Germain-en-Laye, that so resembled Villa d'Este, it is perhaps not stretching the point too far to say that Villa d'Este represents a link between the classical gardens of ancient times and those of sixteenth-century France. The drawing is in the Museum of Besançon. Photo Bulloz, by kind permission of the Musées de Besançon.

XXXV VILLA D'ESTE

for Ippolito d'Este, Ligorio even employed some of the same terms as were applied to the fountains in Villa d'Este. Thus he described the stretch of water in the Canopus as being made like the Euripus, and he imagined that the semicircular *triclinium* at the end had some connexion with the Tiburtine Sibyl, because it was designed, so he maintained, to echo the whispered (in Italian to whisper is *sibillare*) answers of the Gods. Some of the results of his examination of the Canopus *triclinium*, and his muddled thinking about it, are embodied in the great fountain of the *ovata* in the Villa d'Este, of which Hubert Robert made a bistre wash drawing which is one of the most beautiful and evocative representations of an Italian garden scene in existence (pl. 96). Here a great waterfall flows out from beneath the feet of a statue of the Tiburtine Sybil, beneath which a semicircular loggia is cut into the hill. This contains fountains, niches, and small waterways that were undoubtedly inspired by the similar arrangement, on a larger scale, in the *triclinium* of the Canopus. It is interesting to note that Antonio Del Re, who wrote a commentary upon Ligorio's work at Villa d'Este and Hadrian's villa in 1611 and published part of his descriptions of the latter, refers to both the waterways of the Canopus and the fountain of the *ovata* as being 'a guisa di euripo' – like an Euripus.

But even allowing for the inspiration that he drew from Hadrian's villa in the use of water, Ligorio's interpretation of it was personal: Hadrian's villa lies on a gently undulating site, while Villa d'Este stands on a precipitous hillside. Although Bramante had shown the way with his Belvedere wall fountains, to Ligorio must be given the full credit for having the vision that saw further than the small shining streams of a few fountains and instead filled the Villa d'Este with the dramatically rushing volume of light and sound that swirls over its grey stones and fills its green depths with music (pl. XXXV).

The fountains of Villa d'Este have for centuries been one of the sights of Italy, visited by every foreign traveller, and their reactions reflect the changing currents of taste as faithfully as the evolution of the garden itself, for it must not be imagined that it has remained stationary. When Michel de Montaigne was there in 1580, or 1581, both the house and garden were still unfinished but, with his perspicacious French eye for creature comforts, he noticed that an ingenious air-cooling system, modelled no doubt on that of the Romans, was already working in the rooms of the lower floor. What struck him most was the volume of water – specially in the fountains surrounding the fish ponds, whose spray made rainbows in the sunlight. Also the number of statues – plundered from Hadrian's unfortunate villa. Like all early travellers Montaigne was much entertained by the owl fountain, whose elaborate setting was designed as a background for the ingenious automatons invented long ago by Hero of Alexandria. The mechanical owl, whose appearance caused the singing birds to become silent, could be seen sitting on the right of the central fountain. Unlike most of his contemporaries Montaigne was not impressed by the water-organ, an understandable point of view, as he says it played continually upon one single note.

In John Evelyn's day the dragon fountain also made suitably horrid noises and he too was delighted with the owl fountain. He notes that the terracotta reliefs, representing the *Metamorphoses* of Ovid, that are now barely visible among the ferns of the hundred fountains, were to have been replaced by bronze and he was, characteristically, much taken by the garden of simples. But it is interesting to observe that Evelyn reserved his superlatives for his description of the typically Baroque gardens of the Villa Aldobrandini at Frascati, which corresponded much more closely to the taste of his own day than the purely Renaissance Villa d'Este.

The reactions of Président De Brosses, who visited Tivoli in 1739 and was in a position to compare Italian gardens with the great gardens of France, were completely the reverse. Even allowing for a national chauvinism, it is evident that he really was struck by the small size of Italian gardens in comparison with those of France, but, unlike Evelyn, he preferred

97 VILLA D'ESTE
'Roma Antica', a model of antique Rome as it was envisaged in Renaissance times, made in the style of classical topia in the gardens of the Villa d'Este at Tivoli; from Venturini's print in G. de Rossi's Le Fontane di Roma, *part 4, Rome, 1675. It was once considered to be one of the greatest attractions of the gardens. By kind permission of the American Academy.*

Villa d'Este to the Frascati gardens, describing the fountain of the *ovata* as one of the most beautiful in the world. Apart from the bad upkeep, the only thing De Brosses disapproved of in Tivoli was the Renaissance interpretation of Roman *topia* – the 'little Rome', which positively 'enraged' him. Perhaps if he could have seen it in the more romantic setting of today it might have appealed more to his eighteenth-century taste.

For, although the basic plan is still the same, the gardens of the Villa d'Este have changed greatly in appearance since they were first made. In his book Del Re gives a detailed description of how the gardens were laid out in 1611, which is borne out by Du Pérac's print. In those days the great shady stretches of *bosco* that we know were limited to a few carefully defined areas and most of the garden was far more sparsely planted in a strictly formal style. The only likely survivors of this period are the great plane trees that shade the enclosure of the *ovata* fountain, which, with its stone tables and cool grottoes, was evidently designed as an out-of-doors dining-room. Some relics of the colour that was introduced into the garden architecture and furniture also survive here; the tiles bordering the fountain bear the Este device of a silver eagle and the lilies of France, where Cardinal Ippolito had been Papal Nuncio. Many of the other fountains were painted with these devices, in gold and silver as well as being adorned with mosaics and wall-paintings in the old Roman style, while, in accordance with the classical custom, the garden streams and cascades were called after the great rivers of the world. In contrast to the open terrace in front of the villa, the steep slopes immediately below were apparently originally thickly planted as a *bosco*, with small evergreen trees such as bays, lentiscus, arbutus, myrtles, and holm-oaks, and the ground underneath was carpeted with soft green moss. Nearby was a walk bordered by high elms garlanded with ivy, like the trees in Pliny's Tuscan villa.

Del Re describes the 'little Rome' with tremendous gusto, and we know from other sources that it was considered one of the great attractions of the garden at this period (pl. 97). In a grotto underneath a rustic scene was arranged, with figures of peasants, hens, dogs, goatherds; one of these statues would have merited Alberti's censure – it represented a man caught with his trousers down in an 'act of nature'. There were also, of course, the inevitable surprise fountains and seats that wet the unwary when they sat on them. The fish ponds were apparently incomplete in 1611 when Del Re was writing; this probably accounts for their being still today simple rectangular pools, instead of having been divided up into the complicated series of water parterres with pagoda-like towers in the centre, shown in Du Pérac's print. But the part of garden which has changed most since the beginning of the seventeenth century is the level stretch of land that lies between the fish ponds and the garden wall. Du Pérac shows this, and even part of the adjoining slope, as being laid out with labyrinths and a flower garden. Either the labyrinths were never actually made or they had disappeared by Del Re's time, for he makes no mention of them, although he gives a description of the garden of flowers or simples that still existed in Evelyn's day. The existence of this garden is of particular interest as it shows that during the Renaissance period flowers were not necessarily hidden away in the seclusion of a *giardino segreto*, and even in the grandest and most monumental gardens, such as this, they might form a definite part of the main layout. A further point of interest is that here, as in the Vatican and Villa Medici, the old *berceaux* still survived and were evidently considered an essential part of this type of garden, even in a monumental setting. According to Del Re the central cupola of trellis work was surmounted by a gilded lily, and the small kiosks at the crossing of the paths sheltered fountains made of copper and stucco to resemble plants. These were nearly ten feet high and terminated in a large flower, providing a noteworthy example of the survival of this type of medieval and Early Renaissance fountain. The surrounding beds were planted with fruit trees and bordered with low clipped hedges of lavender, rosemary, sage, and box or myrtle. Within these boundaries they were laid out in patterns of marjoram, hyssop and what the author, unlike Colonna in the *Hypnerotomachia*, tantalizingly describes as 'other greens pleasing to the eye'.

Many changes had already occurred in this flower garden, and one feature that still exists had already appeared, when G. F. Venturini made a print of it for G. de Rossi's book on the fountains of Rome, Tivoli, and Frascati, that was published about 1675. Though the basic divisions formed by the paths were the same, the *berceaux* had disappeared, and in the place of the central cupola the famous cypresses, that still exist, had already been planted. The old flower-beds nearest the entrance are no longer visible and a tall hedge surrounds the area, but the others still retain their low clipped borders, though the simple herb designs had by now been replaced by *broderies* in the French style. The old copper floral fountains had been replaced by the stone ones that still stand in the grass of what is now called the 'parco'. But the greatest change of all is the replacement of the plantations of fruit trees by imposing fountains of rustic stone, shaped like pyramids.

Nearly a century later, in July 1760, the Abbé de Saint-Non decided to spend the summer in the Villa d'Este and, fortunately for posterity, he took with him two of the most brilliant *pensionnaires* who have ever studied at the French Academy in Rome — these were Fragonard and Hubert Robert. To this one season's *villegiatura* we owe the most beautiful sanguine drawings of Italian gardens that have ever been made, and to many who have never seen the Villa d'Este its cypresses and fountains, its *boschi* and terraces are endowed for ever with the romantic charm with which these two artists portrayed them. In one of these drawings, Fragonard drew the lower part of the garden as it was in his day. There are still some remains of the old flower-plots, but by now the salient feature of the planting is the typically eighteenth-century one of tree plantations enclosed by high clipped hedges, and already the luxuriant growth resembles much more closely that of our own day than the trim rows of trees and the neat garden parterres of two centuries before.

For all its romantic charm the Villa d'Este had sunk to a very low ebb when Saint-Non and his companions stayed there. It still belonged to the Este dukes of Modena, but for

XXXVI   VILLA D'ESTE

more than a century they had completely disinterested themselves in it. Long past were the days when the villa was the official Roman residence of the cardinals of the Este family, who kept high state, living there with a household of two hundred and fifty gentlemen and making it a centre of literary renown. Tasso is traditionally supposed to have written his *Aminta* while living in the villa, and the play is said to have been first read to a circle of intimates beside one of the garden fountains, before it was given its official *première* at the Este Court of Ferrara. Though of a later period, Fulvio Teste's letter, written to the Duke of Modena in 1620, gives a description of the daily life led in the villa when Cardinal Alessandro d'Este was in residence there. The letter's interest lies chiefly in the continuity of Italian villa life which it portrays, that had changed little since Pliny's day, though he had, of course, been taken as a model by the Renaissance humanists. A new note may, however, be observed in what was considered the proper setting for a prince of the Church at the beginning of the seventeenth century, which is greatly at variance with that of a hundred years before – 'frugality' was certainly not an adjective that would have appealed to Julius II in any context. However, Fulvio Teste writes: 'In the morning after they have heard Mass, some walk in the olive groves, others play tennis or other ball games or study or talk. At dinner all serve their master [the Cardinal] who usually honours some other prelate at his table, Monsignor Corsini and Monsignor Torelli are continually there, and there are always literary persons of most refined manners. The Cardinal's table is large, but not that of an ambitious prince, and there is a blend of gracious magnificence and frugality' – surely a difficult combination to achieve! The Cardinal was apparently very much attached to the 'little Rome' and often spent part of his afternoon looking at his evocation of the ancient city and comparing it with the Rome of his own day that could be seen on the far horizon of the *campagna* that stretches out behind it. A view that in the opinion of Fulvio – and many others – has no equal in the world. The rest of the day was passed in reading or conversation or the more frivolous pursuits of dice and cards.

In the nineteenth century Villa d'Este was rescued for a while from its increasing ruin by Cardinal Hohenlohe, who rented it for his lifetime from the Hapsburgs to whom it had passed by marriage with the last of the Este. Once again in his day the villa regained part of its former splendour and became something of an artistic centre. Franz Liszt lived and worked there for years, and the rippling sound of its fountains is reflected in the sparkling cadences of the music that he composed there.

Villa Farnese - Caprarola

Writing in 1580, Michel de Montaigne said of the Farnese Villa at Caprarola: '*lequel palais a très grand bruit en Italie*', and went on to add that he had seen nothing comparable with it in the whole country, though he considered its superb site, that we admire so much today, '*stérile et alpestre*'! When Montaigne saw it, Caprarola was at the height of its glory, and although some thirty-three years had passed since Cardinal Alessandro Farnese had commissioned Vignola to convert the foundations of an unfinished fortress into a palatial villa, so great had been the undertaking that the gardens were not yet entirely finished. But Montaigne did not err in his judgement. Caprarola was and has remained the most magnificent villa that was ever built in Italy. It owes this pre-eminence to many things – to the splendour of the site which, although it did not appeal to his eye accustomed to the gentler landscape of France, would have delighted Pliny and Alberti for the marvellous view that extends over open rolling country to the spectacular silhouette of Mount Soracte in the distance. Much also to the munificence of its owner, a man whose taste and patronage of the arts was remarkable even in Renaissance Italy. And last, but not least, to Vignola, whose most splendid work of garden architecture this is, though it is rivalled by the more delicate beauty of the neighbouring Villa Lante at Bagnaia.

98 CAPRAROLA
Watercolour sketch, based on G. Vasi's eighteenth-century prints, of the Farnese villa and garden layout at Caprarola, by P. Bonnet. Considered to be the most magnificent villa ever built in Italy, it was designed by Vignola (1507-1573) for Cardinal Alessandro Farnese, but the gardens were not completed until 1587. The villa belongs to the Demanio; open to the public; special permit for the gardens. Photo Gabinetto Fotografico Nazionale.

Bagnaia is pre-eminently a garden; at Caprarola the gardens are designed to fit a palace. From the foot of the hill upon which it stands, right up the steep and narrow street leading through the little town, the whole approach is dominated by the great pentagonal villa standing at the top, while the succession of stairs and terraces of the State entrance outdo any theatrical or operatic set for grandeur. To design a garden that would not be overwhelmed by such magnificence presented a problem indeed. Vignola solved it by calling to his aid an element that is greater than any man-made splendour – nature herself – and here for the first time we have an entire garden that exemplifies Stendhal's beautiful definition of garden art in Italy as a place 'where architecture is wedded to the trees'.

Instead of attempting the impossible task of creating an enormous garden layout that might equal the scale of the palace but would only have been dwarfed by that of the surrounding landscape of the Cimini Hills, Vignola decided to divide his garden into two, and placed these different components at some distance from each other, separating them by great plantations of trees. Although these last are actually enclosed by a wall, they give the impression of merging into the forested hillside, an effect that in a garden which is contemporary with Villa d'Este is startling indeed, and shows that its creator's ideas were very far in advance of those which Pirro

Ligorio applied at Tivoli, though his Villa Pia has something of the same setting. Villa Pia was begun in 1560 and the upper casino garden at Caprarola was only finished twenty-seven years later, so that Villa Pia was certainly the first to be built, but it would be interesting to know if Vignola's garden plans were complete when he began work on the palace; if they were, the idea of an isolated casino garden was his invention. But it is a question to which it is unlikely that a definite answer will ever be forthcoming.

Although the trees that surround Vignola's garden at Caprarola gave the appearance of merging into the landscape, the gardens themselves formed self-contained units whose boundaries were sharply defined in the Renaissance manner, and in them there can be no question of a gradual Baroque transition from the cultivated to the wild. The gardens that lie immediately behind the palace are separated from it by a deep fosse, which formed part of the originally planned defensive works. This and the curious pentagonal shape of the building, dictated by the fortress foundations, render the site an awkward one. Vignola's

100 CAPRAROLA
The great fountain in the giardino segreto
at Caprarola.

101 CAPRAROLA
The casino in the giardino segreto *at*
Caprarola.

solution was to make two separate rectangular gardens within the axis of the two façades of the palace that face directly on to the hill and to connect them to the *piano nobile* by bridges. These gardens were laid out with fountains and parterres, whose design could be enjoyed from the palace windows, while the space between them was planted as a *bosco*. The entire layout, including that of the upper casino garden and its surrounding woodland, is clearly shown in a watercolour sketch by Patrice Bonnet based on the eighteenth-century prints of Giuseppe Vasi (pl. 98).

The garden lying to the south-west of the house is approached by a small terrace with a grotto, where fountains were designed to produce the impression and sound of rain, a device that appealed to Montaigne. This was evidently the master-garden, as the layout which is shown in Vasi's print of 1746 and another of Bonnet's sketches, also in a rather faded fresco at Bagnaia, is more elaborate and included a narrow sheltered walk for cold weather, built half-way up the retaining wall backing on to the hill. This garden and grotto were the favourite retreat of Cardinal Alessandro's nephew, Odoardo Farnese, who lived most of the year at Caprarola, and in his day it was planted with roses. When Mrs Wharton saw the garden, probably at the end of the nineteenth century, the parterres had disappeared, but they have since been replanted in box according to the original design.

The other palace garden was originally divided up into small hedged plots planted with fruit trees, and had a fish pond with a gilded fountain in the form of the Farnese lily in the centre. Today in spring this is one of the loveliest places in the whole of Caprarola, for the grass is filled with the purple, white and yellow flowers of wild orchis and the old stone walls are covered with the varying shades of rose and pink blossoms of old camellia trees, while the whole place is alive with birdsong. From here a path leads into what is now a wood; climbing gently up the hill; it gives the impression of having left all sign of human habitation behind and one expects it to lead deeper and deeper into the forest. With some surprise, after a turn, one comes upon a wide grassy avenue bordered with pines, that leads up to an astonishing vista of fountains and cascades sparkling in the sunlight and framed in a setting of golden-hued sculptured stone (pl. 99).

No other garden in Italy, or probably in the world, contains a surprise as ravishing as this. The contrast is so striking between the shade and silence of the woodland and this sunlit open space filled with the ripple of water. In the astonishment of finding such a place, one recalls Vasari's phrase that this magical garden was 'born not built'. From the first moment of discovery it casts a spell that increases with each step, up the gently sloping *cordonata*, through a little fountain-filled court, surrounded by the dark spires of cypresses, and on up the graceful stairs leading to the garden of the casino itself. It seems impossible that anything so perfect may not end in an anti-climax, but the approach is indeed only a prelude to the infinite charm of this little garden, where whispering herms stand guard against the outer world, in this enchanted enclave of sunlit peace.

The casino and its garden were designed as a place of escape from the overwhelming pomp and circumstance that surrounded the life of a Renaissance prince of the Church, and this probably accounts for its extreme simplicity (pls. 100, 101). Its loveliness lies in no elaborate effects, but in the perfect grace of the golden coloured casino set in a sea of varied greens. There can be few places where architecture is so closely allied to nature, and where mythical creatures like the sea-horses of the fountains and the guardian herms seem so natural a part of the scene. Here the beauty of the pagan world lives again and looking at it Queen Christina of Sweden's strange comment upon the gardens of Caprarola: 'I dare not speak the name of Jesus lest I break the spell' can be understood. Nor would the pageant that Alessandro Farnese staged for Gregory XIII in 1585, with its procession of one hundred maidens dressed in white, bearing olive branches and clashing cymbals, have looked out of place in these surroundings.

The garden on the other side of the casino was evidently designed as an out-of-doors living-room, with clipped hedges and the forest trees for walls; it is carpeted with pebble mosaics, and was once gay with the music of countless fountains set among beds of flowers (pl. 102). This would have been the setting of the Cardinal's intimate entertainments, with a table laid out on the grass on summer evenings and an orchestra of nightingales in the surrounding woods. What a welcome escape it must have been after State banquets in the great halls of the palace, for all their splendour of painted ceilings and *topia* fountains. Alessandro must have been a man of ready wit who enjoyed relaxation in good company – otherwise he would not have built this Renaissance Petit Trianon or stood up to the austere San Carlo Borromeo as he did. When San Carlo rebuked him for the money he had spent on Caprarola, saying it would have been better spent on the poor of the district, Alessandro is said to have replied: 'I have let them have it all little by little, but I have made them earn it by the sweat of their brows'.

Caprarola has not always been the setting only of pageantry and grand receptions for popes and princes; once it was the scene of the happy ending of a romance. In 1647 Pope Innocent X was persuaded, much against his will, to allow his nephew Camillo Pamphilj to renounce his cardinal's hat. The young man had never taken higher orders, as was possible in those days, and he had fallen in love with Olimpia – the gay and vivacious widow of Prince Borghes – and she with him, for he was very handsome. The story goes that Camillo even dared to say to his august uncle that 'much as he admired the virtue of chastity he felt himself unable to practise it without a wife'. He and Olimpia were married

102 CAPRAROLA
The fountain in the flower garden behind the casino at Caprarola, designed as an out-of-doors living-room, the setting for the Cardinal's private parties.

secretly shortly afterwards and immediately set out for Caprarola. To the astonishment of the gay world of Rome, they lived there the whole summer through in the seclusion of the lovely villa. It was a happy marriage and Olimpia is said to have had 'all the gifts that can ensure domestic felicity'. They must have remembered the gardens of Caprarola with affection and talked about them to their children, for when one of their sons replanted the gardens of the Priory of the Order of Malta on the Aventine in Rome many of the flowers came from Caprarola.

Villa Lante · Bagnaia

Although no documentary evidence has been found to prove that Villa Lante at Bagnaia was designed by Vignola, his authorship of it has never been doubted, and it is believed that he started work on it about 1566 after he had already been engaged on Caprarola for many years. Nothing would have been more natural than for Cardinal Gambara to commission him to design his summer residence in the circumstances, as Bagnaia is only about twenty miles distant and Vignola's work at Caprarola must have been the talk of the district.

The forest-clad slopes of the Cimini Hills behind Bagnaia belonged to the city of Viterbo and here at the end of the fifteenth century, Cardinal Riario, one of its bishops, had built himself a hunting-box which still exists. The site is a beautiful one, and the city made over some of the land to the Episcopal See as a site for the summer residence of its bishops. It was here, shortly after his election to the bishopric in 1566, that Cardinal Gambara decided to build his villa.

What he required was not a magnificent palace for receptions, as at Caprarola, but a summer retreat suitable for a cultivated Renaissance Churchman. Some idea may be formed of the Cardinal's character from the fact that, while he bowed to San Carlo Borromeo's strictures with respect to the extravagance of making the villa, and spent the money reserved for the second casino on a hospital instead, he so loved the place that he resolutely resisted all efforts of the Holy See to get him to make it over to them, right up to his death in 1587. His successor, however, agreed to bequeath it to the See of Rome, who afterwards lent it to the bishops of Viterbo. It was only after the accession of Alexander VII in 1655 that the villa was granted to the Lante family for a peppercorn rent of six scudi a year, in compensation for the confiscation of their Roman villa. The grant was renewed in 1743, and the villa remained in the hands of the same family until well on into the twentieth century.

One cannot help feeling that in laying out the villa, Vignola had the tastes of his patron well in mind, and that the Cardinal's love of nature was greater even than that of most men of his kind, for if his garden is one of the most beautiful in existence the dwelling-house, or houses, play a very secondary part in the whole scheme. The villa was the joy of Cardinal Gambara's life, and its loveliness is such that no change in taste or fashion has been able to impair the admiration that it has aroused during the centuries: from Montaigne, who said that for the use of water 'certainly this place takes the prize by a long way', to Sacheverell Sitwell who wrote 'and were I to choose the most lovely place of the physical beauty of nature in all Italy or in all the world that I have seen with my own eyes, I would name the gardens of the Villa Lante'.

Like Queen Christina at Caprarola, Sitwell recognized the same pagan quality in the casino garden there and in the Villa Lante. It is apparent as soon as one enters the gate and sees Giambologna's 'Pegasus' prancing in his pool surrounded by water-nymphs. He is the guardian spirit of the *bosco*, and here, most appropriately, for the first time a Renaissance garden makes contact with the wild, where its paths and fountains penetrate the woods (pl. 103). It is only a tentative beginning, a slight change in an established custom, for the *barco* in the old Italian sense of an enclosed piece of wild ground used for hunting, and lying adjacent to the garden, had long existed, but now for the first time the two begin to intermingle and the *barco* is becoming a park (pl. 104). The gardens of the Villa Lante, in the strict sense of the word, are still separated from the park by a wall, and in the formal parterre garden round the lake there is no contact. But in Laurus' print of the villa, published in 1614, the kinship between the upper *bosco* garden and the park is evident (pl. 105).

Mercifully the Villa Lante has changed little since this print was made, and such differences as there are have added to its beauty. The vase-shaped fountain in the middle of the lake – in Montaigne's day a pyramid of water – was later replaced by the wonderful

103 VILLA LANTE
Fountain in the park of the Villa Lante at Bagnaia.

composition of four boys holding aloft Cardinal Montalto's arms of 'mounts' surmounted by a star of water (pl. XXXVII. The charming fountain of the 'little lamps' in the centre of the terrace behind the two casinos is still the same. The terrace above, scarcely visible in the print, is laid out as a garden dining-room, with a great stone table in the centre, down which runs a small water channel designed to serve as a wine cooler (pl. 106). One cannot help wondering if at the Cardinal's dinners dishes were made to float on it, as they did in Pliny's Tuscan villa.

From the terrace above there is a most perfect view of the parterre garden. From here its lovely lake, with the small stone boats in which Montaigne saw miniature

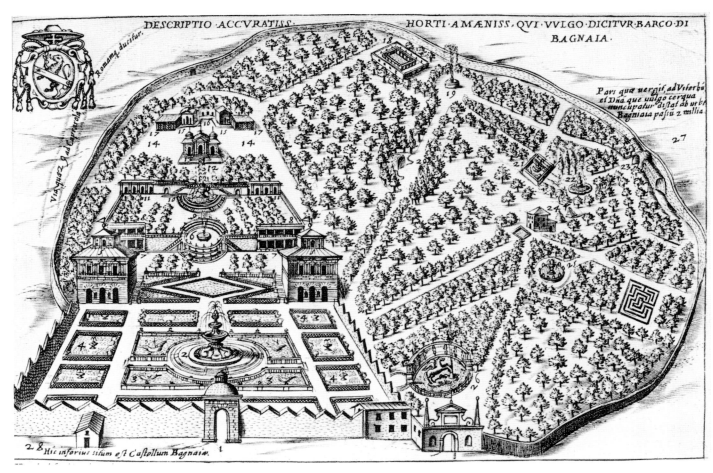

104 VILLA LANTE
The lower parterre garden and central fountain.

105 VILLA LANTE
The gardens of Villa Lante at Bagnaia, near Viterbo. They were begun for Cardinal Gambara in 1566 by Vignola; the second casino was built and the central fountain transformed for Cardinal Montalto. The villa passed into the hands of the Lante family in 1655. From J. Laurus' Roma Vetus et Nuova, Rome, 1614. The layout has changed little since this print was made, and its design is considered to be Vignola's masterpiece and probably the finest in Italy. The villa is privately owned but open to the public.

XXXVIII VILLA LANTE.

harquebusiers and trumpeters discharging streams of water at the central fountain, is seen framed in the foliage of the venerable plane trees. Higher up the trees and hedges draw closer together to shade the *cordonata*, down whose centre chatters and sparkles an enchanting cascade, made in the form of the elongated craw-fish or *gambero* of the Cardinal's arms (pl. 107). In the centre of the ultimate terrace Laurus' print shows a small casino, which was probably never built, but in any case its site is now much more suitably occupied by a particularly lovely fountain. Glistening jets of water issue from the mouths of dolphins, masks, and vases, cut in the same wonderfully textured stone as all the other fountains in the garden, to which water gives the colour of bronze, so that many people imagine that the boys of the lake fountain are actually made of metal.

This third terrace terminates the garden, not with the drama of some spectacular climax, as in the earlier Renaissance, but with two charming little pavilions, on either side of a fountain that gushes out from a tranquil background of forest trees. This is a significant factor for the future of Italian garden design, and the idea is the same as the open gates leading into the forest from the upper casino garden at Caprarola; both gardens draw their ultimate source from the wild nature surrounding them.

In Laurus' print, the two small adjoining *giardini segreti* are shown enclosed by trellises, as are also the parterres of the lake garden. This is an interesting reminder of the fact that even in the architectural gardens of the second half of the sixteenth century, both here and

in Villa d'Este, the simpler forms of earlier times still survived in flower gardens and parterres. Though it is possible that their use was sanctioned in Renaissance eyes by their appearance in Roman garden paintings, like those of Livia's garden room, these trellises were certainly used in medieval times as they are common in medieval miniatures. In any case, they were not destined to survive much longer, as we have seen in the Belvedere and Villa d'Este, and the old *berceaux* were soon to be swept away by the changing tide of fashion.

In Laurus' print the parterres of the lake garden are the simplest of squares, each with its own small fountain at the crossing of the paths. In Percier's and Fontaine's drawings of the early nineteenth century they are practically the same, but these authors are not always to be relied upon for exactitude in such details. Today the eight original beds on either side of the lake have been merged to form four parterres, and it seems likely that this change, which would have been in accordance with the taste of the period, took place late in the seventeenth, or possibly in the eighteenth century. Tradition has it that Le Nôtre, who was in Italy in 1678, had some hand in this transformation. Given the French associations of the Lante family at this time – the duchess of the day was the sister of Anne Marie de La

107 VILLA LANTE
The cascade in the garden of the Villa Lante at Bagnaia.

Trémouille, 'Princesse des Ursins' – the legend seems more likely to be true in this instance than for the other Italian gardens of which it is also related, though no documentary proof has yet been published to substantiate it. There may, however, have been some confusion with another French gardener who is said to have worked on the parterres of the villa and mysteriously drowned himself in the fountain.

Many writers have tried to define the haunting beauty of the Villa Lante; perhaps Sacheverell Sitwell came closest to it when he wrote: 'All you can say when considering a work of art (Villa Lante is as much a work of art as any poem, painting, piece of music), is that some portion of the weight of aesthetic comes from the other souls that have attached themselves to it in admiration.' Certainly the admiration had never been lacking, and Shepherd and Jellicoe in their classic *Renaissance Gardens of Italy* have reserved for it some of their rare superlatives, describing it as 'a perfect thing of the imagination . . . here rests the spirit that has wandered imperceptibly from the beauty of nature, the speckled mystery of the trees and the wonderful view, to the highest beauty that man can obtain, the calm formality of architecture'.

Villa Orsini · Bomarzo

One of the monsters in the garden of the Villa Orsini at Bomarzo, that dates from the second half of the sixteenth century. As was the case with other villas in the Cimini area, at Bomarzo a medieval stronghold was converted into a Renaissance villa. Owing to the site the gardens were laid out in the valley below, where natural stone outcrops were sculpted into every kind of gigantic figure, and surrounded by a wood which has long since vanished. Something of the mysterious atmosphere of the wood can be recaptured by seeing Bomarzo on a misty day. The gardens are owned by Signor Bettini and are open to the public.

109 BOMARZO
The giantess at Bomarzo.

Much has also been written in the last few years about the Renaissance garden that is geographically closest to Villa Lante – it is only about eight miles away – but is far removed from it in spirit. This is the strange Villa Orsini at Bomarzo, whose stone monsters have been the subject of local legend for centuries but until lately were quite unknown to the outside world. Typically in Italy, it was a Russian and a Swiss who 'discovered' them and made them known, though it would have been more natural to suppose that these fantastic creations, which probably have no counterparts except in the Orient, would have featured in every guide-book.

In spite of all that has recently been written about it, very little is really known about this villa, and the key to the mystery probably lies in the personality of the man who created it about the same time as Villa Lante. His baptismal name was Pierfrancesco, though he preferred to call himself Vicino Orsini, and he belonged to the extinct Mugnano branch of the historic family. The fact that no survivors of this part of the family exist has rendered research into the origins of the Bomarzo villa even more difficult than usual, as so far no mention of it has been found in the Orsini archive in the custody of the municipality of Rome, though it is possible that some documentary reference might be found in the rest of

the archive which is still in the possession of the family. The only established facts relating to the villa have been gleaned from scanty references in contemporary letters, notably one from Annibale Caro to Vicino written in 1564, in which he mentions the '*teatri e mausolei*' of Bomarzo, and from the place itself. What is interesting about this letter, apart from the fact that it dates the existence of the garden, is that Vicino had evidently asked his friend's advice for the frescoes of the fall of the giants or titans which were afterwards executed in one of the castle rooms. Though this theme was not uncommon at the time – the Palazzo del Te at Mantua and Palladio's Malcontenta in the Veneto both have rooms decorated with it – giants very evidently held a particular appeal for Vicino and at least one other member of his family, for they both created gardens in which rocks were hewn into this form.

Like other villages of the area Bomarzo is dominated by its castle and, in accordance with the changing spirit of the times, Vicino and his neighbours at Soriano, Bassano di Sutri and elsewhere set about converting the medieval strongholds into villas or palaces in the Renaissance style. One of the main adjuncts of an Italian villa of the period was a garden so, no matter what the difficulties of the site, a garden had to be created. At Bomarzo the difficulties were quite considerable as the castle is perched on a precipitous hill at the highest point of the village, and the only possible place was outside the village walls, on a fairly steeply sloping piece of ground to the west. This actually presented a promising site for the

110 BOMARZO
The tortoise with the statue of Fame on his back.

usual Renaissance terraced garden, and something of the kind was laid out there. But for some extraordinary reason, and for this the singular personality of the man himself can be the only possible explanation, Vicino Orsini principally concentrated his energies upon making the irregular valley below, strewn with great rocky outcrops, into the centre of attraction. And on this he must have lavished very considerable care and expense.

Running entirely contrary to the current ideas of symmetry and proportion, Vicino Orsini designed the whole of this part of his garden around the irregularly placed natural outcrops of stone, having them sculpted into every inconceivable type of gigantic figure, human, part-human, animal and purely fantastic. As a setting for them he apparently planted a wood, as the frequent inscriptions in the garden make reference to it as a '*sacro bosco*'. Evidently Vicino was highly conscious of the originality of his conception, as the same inscription continues: 'which resembles itself and nothing else'. Other inscriptions anticipate the astonishment of the visitor who finds himself in such a place and, comparing it to the marvels of the ancient world, claim that it surpasses them. The whole thing is strangely reminiscent of the Roman garden of Sperlonga, where sculpture was placed to form *topia* among the precipitous rocks of the seashore. Its creator, Faustinus, also cut inscriptions lauding his own work in eloquent terms, saying that it would have caused even Virgil to acknowledge his defeat, as no poet had ever represented the Homeric legends to such advantage. Vicino could not possibly have seen these

remains of the Roman villa at Sperlonga, but one cannot help wondering if the idea for his '*sacro bosco*' was not suggested to him by some reference in the classical authors. All the more so because a kinsman of his, Fulvio Orsini, was a noted antiquarian, who had assisted Alessandro Farnese in making his famous collection of classical sculpture, and the owner of an extensive library which included one at least of Pirro Ligorio's sketch-books of antiquities.

Today it is very difficult to imagine what this '*sacro bosco*' would have looked like, though the laudable efforts of the present owner in clearing the site and piecing together the fragments have made its original layout much clearer. What is lacking is the atmosphere of mystery provided by the deep shade of the surrounding trees, and the surprise of encountering the strange creatures with which the wood was populated, in the dim light. Today, anyone who wants to see Bomarzo 'aright' should visit it for the first time, either as Scott advised with Melrose 'by the pale moonlight' or better still on one of those strange winter days when the whole valley is shrouded in mist, though the bright Italian sun is shining only a mile away. Seen like this the monsters of Bomarzo regain that strange almost sinister atmosphere of mystery that is essential to them, which is entirely lacking in the sunlight. Even more impressive in this strange half-light are the monsters that are still surrounded by the remains of the wood – especially the great figure of the giant rending his prostrate foe, but above all the huge tortoise lurking like some primeval monster in the depths of the valley beside the stream (pls. 108-111, XXXIX).

Several writers have attributed the authorship of the Bomarzo villa to Vignola, without there being any documentary evidence upon which to base the assertion. Pirro Ligorio might have seemed a safer bet, given his association with an illegitimate but artistically influential member of the Orsini family – Fulvio Orsini knew him well enough to try and get him appointed as Michelangelo's successor at St Peter's. But so far, like so many other things connected with it, the identity of Bomarzo's architect has also remained a mystery.

XXXIX   VILLA ORSINI - BOMARZO

Villa Odescalchi - Bassano di Sutri / Villa Chigi - Soriano / Villa Orsini - Pitigliano

There is one fact about it, however, that has been passed over practically unnoticed by many people who have written about it, and this is that many sculptural and architectural details of Bomarzo are related to those of the gardens of other villas in the area. Very similar monumental vases and some smaller monsters occur for instance in the Villa Odescalchi at Bassano di Sutri, while the balusters there and in the Villa Chigi at Soriano resemble in style the urns and vases of Bomarzo. At Soriano there is also a gigantic figure, half-goat half-woman, cut out of the living rock of the natural fountain, while the mammoth pine-cones of Bomarzo also adorn the lake of Villa Lante, and the water-nymphs of the Pegasus fountain there have the same butterfly wings as a group of similar figures carved on a fountain at the back of the Bomarzo giantess. Strangest and most interesting of them all, and among the least known, are the relics of gigantic figures and small gazebos carved out of the living rock of a gorge near Pitigliano, some distance away from Bomarzo but formerly a possession of another branch of the Orsini family. The place is precipitous and utterly unlike the site of any other Italian Renaissance villa garden except Bomarzo. Here too a garden was laid out at some distance from the Orsini castle in the town, on a stretch of flat land above the gorge; one of its cypress avenues survived until the last war. The rocky outcrops of the gorge itself were hewn into gigantic figures, gazebos, seats and a connecting network of steps and paths, barely distinguishable among the brushwood. Pitigliano, in fact, presents an even greater mystery to the art historian than Bomarzo.

The passion for gardens which swept Italy as a result of the Renaissance evidently found a particularly assiduous group of devotees among the landowners of the Cimini Hills. It is a pity that this interesting group of gardens has never been made the subject of detailed study like the better known ones of Tivoli and Frascati, for they contain much that is of interest to the specialist, though the present condition of many of them excludes them from a general survey.

Villa Ruspoli - Vignanello

One happy exception to this rule is the little-known garden of the Ruspoli castle-villa at Vignanello, which contains the most magnificent box parterre in Italy (pl. 112). Vignanello originally came into the possession of the family in 1536 by the gift of Paul III to his kinswoman Ortensia Farnese, who was the wife of Count Sforza Marescotti (the family changed its name to Ruspoli through the inheritance of a Ruspoli heiress in the eighteenth century). This Sforza's grandson married an Ottavia Orsini in 1574, and it is a fact worthy of note that she was the daughter of Vicino Orsini of Bomarzo.

According to family tradition it was Ottavia Orsini who laid out the parterre at Vignanello, originally in rosemary. This is confirmed by certain details of its design, and it would have been natural for the daughter of Bomarzo's creator to take a lively interest in gardens. Although the site is a much less difficult one, as the castle stands on the outskirts of the village of Vignanello, the same problem presented itself of converting an old fortress into a Renaissance villa. No structural alterations were made, but the castle was linked to the garden by a bridge across the fosse, and immediately behind it the beautiful parterre garden was laid out. It is not known if Ottavia was the moving spirit in the creation of the whole garden which includes a *giardino segreto* and terrace leading to a *barco*, though this seems likely. But the parterre design was certainly inspired by her, as the central bed nearest the castle contains her initials O.O. arranged in a cypher to encircle those of her two sons

Sforza and Galeazzo. The particular interest of this motif lies in the fact that it enables the parterre to be dated with much greater exactitude than is usually possible. Marc Antonio died young, and after his death Ottavia managed the family estates for her sons who were still minors. His initials do not appear in the design, and as hers have the pride of place, it seems unlikely that the parterre was laid out during his lifetime. Marc Antonio was still alive in 1600, and by 1618 Sforza had assumed charge of the estates, so the parterre was probably laid out during the intervening years, possibly around 1612 when, judging from documents in the Ruspoli archive, bearing her signature, Ottavia was particularly active in the administrative affairs of Vignanello.

Thus the garden of Vignanello provides definite evidence of the type of parterres laid out in Italian gardens at the beginning of the seventeenth century. They constitute the main feature of a garden belonging to a rich and powerful Roman family of the period and, as such, one would expect them to reflect the latest fashions in layout. But it should be noted that for all their extent and complicated design, they are still purely geometrical and show no signs of the influence of the curls and arabesques typical of the French *broderies*, which became popular in Italy later in the seventeenth century. There is no doubt that the Italian parterre was originally, and long continued to be, simply geometrical, whereas in France *broderies* already existed in the sixteenth century. Henry IV's gardener Claude Mollet describes those he laid out in box in his *Théâtre des plans et jardinages* published posthumously in 1652. In the same way the somewhat sterile custom of filling in the background of parterres with earths coloured with smith's dust and filings was a French one, the *broderies* themselves becoming so elaborate that they did not require the additional patterns of flowers. It seems that this fashion took a very considerable time to reach Italy, as no mention of it is made in Italian seventeenth- and even early-eighteenth-century books on gardening, though these are practical handbooks dealing with every aspect of garden layout even down to the details of the composition of earth, etc., to be used for making paths. On the other hand, there is every evidence, here and in other sources of the extensive use of flowers in parterres, where specially prepared bricks, called *pianelle*, and later box began to oust the old use of clipped herbs by the first quarter of the seventeenth century.

At this time Italy, like almost every other European country, evidently succumbed to the current craze for imported exotics, especially bulbs. One can well imagine the feelings of an enthusiastic gardener when for the first time in the world's history his repertoire of flowers was suddenly enormously extended by all kinds of wonderful and colourful flowers coming from not only the Near East, from where a steady trickle had been arriving for the past fifty years, but from those mysterious 'Indies' which in Italy was a generic word covering India, the Cape of Good Hope, South and Central America and the Caribbean Islands, and North America as well. Later, some concessions were made to geographical exactitude, and the North American flowers were usually referred to in Italian horticultural books as coming from the 'Virginian Islands'. All these flowers were expensive and only available to the rich with powerful connexions, and it is plainly evident that it was very much the done thing for Roman cardinals and princes of the day to make a speciality of cultivating them, while learned members of the Accademia dei Lincei, like Fabio Colonna, wrote books about them and Mario de Fiori led the vogue for painting these luxurious flowers. This aspect of horticulture in Italy has been very little studied, and although most people are familiar with the part that Spain, as one of the great colonial powers in the New World, played in the introduction of new plants into Europe, and the contributions of our own explorers in this direction, they seem to forget that Rome, as the centre of the Catholic world, was a place to which many missionaries returned sometimes bringing seeds and bulbs with them.

112 VILLA RUSPOLI

The garden of the Villa Ruspoli at Vignanello, laid out probably at the end of the sixteenth or the beginning of the seventeenth century, by the daughter of Vicino Orsini who created the garden of the Villa Orsini at Bomarzo. The parterre is the finest of its kind in Italy, and a very rare survival of an early-seventeenth-century parterre whose geometrical design closely resembles those of Serlio's architectural treatise. The villa belongs to Prince Ruspoli.

Orti Farnesiani · Rome

Among the earliest gardens of this kind were the Orti Farnesiani on the Palatine, designed by Vignola for the Farnese Pope Paul III in the first half of the sixteenth century. These gardens have been practically destroyed by the archaeological excavation of the Palatine, and Vignola's design for the approach from the Forum, which was a development of the Cortile del Belvedere theme, has received much more attention than their horticultural aspect. But a glance at Falda's print of the second half of the seventeenth century reveals that by then, and actually much earlier, practically the whole of the large area on top of the hill was given over to parterres.

By the beginning of the seventeenth century these gardens were a famous botanical centre, and in 1625 their Prefect, Tobia Aldino, published his *Horti Farnesiani Rariores Plantae Exactissime Descriptae*, an interesting list of the rare plants cultivated there. The Orti Farnesiani appear to have made a speciality of flowering creepers, trees and shrubs which included passion flowers, morning glory, yuccas, acacia farnesina introduced in 1611, agaves, castor oil plants, aloes, and what were apparently Jerusalem artichokes which Aldino called *solis fiore tuberoso*. He mentions that their roots are edible and describes various ways of preparing them, either eaten raw with pepper, cooked like carrots with salt and pepper, or eaten with oil and vinegar or fried in oil or butter. There were also plenty of flowers. Aldino describes new varieties of carnations, the 'Byzantine lychnis' or rose of heaven, freak narcissus, and what at the time were called lilionarcissus – narcissus-type bulbs with lily-like flowers, especially the jacobean lily or sprekelia.

The book is also interesting for the information which it gives about what was evidently quite an extensive circle of Roman botanists and garden enthusiasts; prominent among them was Tranquillo Romauli, in whose garden the ferraria or Cape starry iris and American sumach first grew in Rome, and members of such great families as the Barberini, Caetani, Cesi and Cesarini, all of whom evidently had important collections of exotics. One of the most assiduous Roman gardeners of the period was Francesco Caetani, Duke of Sermoneta and Prince of Caserta, who was the first Italian to cultivate amaryllis. The Caetani archive still contains a unique treasure – two little manuscript books in which are listed the entire planting in the year 1625 of the parterres of his famous garden at the Tre Taverne near Cisterna. It is interesting to note that nearly all these plants were bulbous or tuberous, reflecting the current European craze for this type of flower. Other kinds only seem to have excited general interest and to have become fashionable in the following century, probably because communication and transport were then easier.

Although the Caetani list is a long and detailed one, the actual identification of the flowers is very difficult, because at the time nearly all bulbs were described as narcissi, hyacinths, or colchicum; though tulips, a few lilies, iris and many kinds of fritillaries are mentioned. The tuberose, for instance, was listed among the hyacinths as *jacinto indiano tuberoso*, all varieties of amaryllidaceae were classed with the narcissi, usually under the name lilionarcisso, the South African red Cape tulip or haemanthus was listed as a colchicum, and so on. From this it appears likely that a detailed study of the Caetani manuscripts might produce some surprises in Italian botanical history.

Apart from large numbers of what were evidently really tulips, hyacinths, anemones, ranunculus, cyclamen, colchicum, fritillaries, crocus, daffodils, narcissi, iris and lilies, this Caetani garden also contained sprekelia, amaryllis belladonna, and crowns imperial, tuberose, red and white paeonies, morning iris, lion's leaf, and crimson Turk's cap lily. Although the Caetani manuscripts do not give any general information about the layout of these parterres, fortunately they are described in Padre G. B. Ferrari's *De Florum Cultura*, first published in

113, 114   PARTERRES
Parterres from C. B. Ferrari's book on gardening published in 1638, which would represent the gardening fashions of the day and show that Italian parterres were still of geometrical design.

115   PARTERRES
Parterres from Serlio's architectural treatise, published in Venice in 1537. Italian parterres retained this type of geometrical design well into the middle of the seventeenth century, after which they were superseded by the more elaborate French broderies.

Latin in 1633 and in Italian in 1638. This book, which is a mine of information about gardens, gardeners and flower decorations of the period, says that the design of Francesco Caetani's parterres was laid out in *pianelle* and the different varieties of flowers arranged so as to give the effect of a coloured carpet at different seasons of the year. In order to separate the kinds of flowers that require more water from others, the Duke planted his tuberose, for instance, in pots sunk in the earth, and separated them from the rest by bricks covered with earth. Ferrari advised keeping a carefully drawn-up list of all the bulbs and other plants growing in parterres, exactly like those of the Caetani archive. He also gives specimen designs for parterres (pls. 113, 114). Although these may be taken as representing the latest fashions in the year 1633, they do not differ noticeably from the patterns published in Serlio's architectural treatise of a century earlier (pl. 115) nor even from one of the *Hypnerotomachia* parterres.

Padre Ferrari was in charge of the Barberini gardens, which were also noted for their exotics, and in his book he gives a list of the most famous ones growing there, together with illustrations. These include Egyptian papyrus, the hibiscus mutabilis, Judas trees, tamarind, sumach, yucca, begonias, passion flowers, exotic jasmines, large 'Canadian' strawberries – the parents of our garden strawberries – tuberose, amaryllis belladonna, sprekelia or jacobean lilies, and the scarlet lobelia or cardinal flower, so called because the flowers were the same colour as his eminent master Cardinal Barberini's robes.

One of the most charming chapters of Padre Ferrari's book is that which is devoted to flower arrangements in seventeenth-century Rome. As might be expected these were rather formal, as witness his bouquet of spring flowers, made up of anemones, narcissi and hyacinths (Plate 116). Ferrari compliments Tranquillo Romauli on the ingenious invention of basket-work frames, covering canisters of water, through which the flower-stalks could be pushed to form a regular mass of flowers in many shapes and forms. These later became so elaborate that whole basket-work models of figures or boats were covered in this fashion. Columns of flowers were also arranged in terracotta or metal stands, which were a succession of vases pierced with holes and designed so that the entire column was covered with flowers. Even sculptors and artists took a hand in designing these elaborate floral decorations, one of Bernini's pupils modelling the heraldic Barberini bees in wax and covering them with flowers. One of the most interesting passages in this chapter is the one in which Padre Ferrari dates and describes the origin of the Roman custom, which still survives, of making mosaics of flowers for Church festivals. Apparently this charming custom was originated in 1620 by Benedetto Drusi and his son Pietro Paolo to cover up masses of building rubble for a festival held in some part of the Vatican where building was still in progress. The result was received with such enthusiasm that it became the custom to make these flower mosaics on the feast days of the patron saints in the great Roman basilicas and churches – in St Peter's itself and St Paul's-Without-the-Walls. The tradition still survives in the church of SS John and Paul, when on 26th June – the feast day of these courtiers and martyrs of Julian the Apostate – a carpet of flowers is laid out in the church; but the best-known example occurs on the feast of Corpus Domini, when a whole street of the little town of Genzano is covered with flower mosaics.

The practical uses to which flowers were put in seventeenth-century Italy also emerge very clearly from Padre Ferrari's book; he mentions the new fashion for crystallizing flowers in sugar. Strangely enough he does not talk of roses and violets, but of broom, larkspur and pomegranate blossom and he also has a good deal to say about the distillation of essences. A still-room was, of course, a feature of any large private house in Europe by the seventeenth century, but in Italy its activities often seem to have included not only the making of conserves of fruit and flowers but also a distillery for the extraction of essences. Apart from their use as scents, these were also much employed in flavouring food and drink; the famous *sorbets* or water-ices were flavoured with orange and lemon water and soft drinks with essences of lemon, bitter orange and citron flowers. Together with crystallized flowers, these perfumed

116 Posy of spring flowers, hyacinths, Hyacinthus orientalis, *daffodils and jonquils,* Narcissus pseudo-narcissus *and* Narcissus jonquilla, *and double anemones,* Anemone coronaria pleno.

delicacies formed an important part of the refreshments at any fashionable entertainment.

In seventeenth-century Rome there appears to have been a perfect passion for perfumes of all kinds. This is probably partly explained by the very elementary conditions of hygiene reigning at that period, for in the next century, when general and personal hygiene had greatly improved, scents and even scented flowers were considered vulgar. But in the seventeenth century gloves were always perfumed, usually with jasmine, rose or ambergris, while scented balls and scent sachets were as fashionable a gift to send a lady as flowers today.

In her fascinating book *Un Mecenate in Roma Barocca*, Lina Montalto provides an enormous fund of documentary information about these fashionable foibles, and points out that the extensive cultivation of jasmine and citrus trees in Roman gardens of the period was partly due to this extensive use of perfumes. The Maecenas of her book was a Cardinal Pamphilj, the son of Olimpia and Camillo Pamphilj who spent their prolonged honeymoon at Caprarola. This Benedetto Pamphilj was an ardent garden lover, owning several villas, and he had a special perfume distillery attached to his suite in the Palazzo Doria in the Corso. Cardinal Pamphilj's favourite garden appears to have been that of the Priory of the Order of Malta on the Aventine (he was Grand Master of the Order), which was famous for its espaliers of oranges and lemons, its *bosco* of citron trees which was carpeted with fragrant wood strawberries, and for its flower garden. Here were arranged not only the usual parterres, but espaliers or palisades, like those Madame de Sévigné described in 1678 in the garden laid out by Le Nôtre at Clagny, where roses, jasmine, carnations and tuberose were ranged in pots in a succession of tiers to make low walls of flowers. Unfortunately we do not know exactly what flowers were used in the Aventine gardens for this purpose, as apart from jasmine and citrus trees the records only name stocks and the usual anemones, jonquils, narcissus, other 'fiori nobili' and water-lilies for the fountains. There were also aviaries and bowling-greens, but Cardinal Pamphilj's passion was music and his lovely gardens were frequently the setting for operas by Scarlatti and concerts by the most famous Italian musicians of the day.

In all her long history Rome can have witnessed few scenes more charming than these presentations of opera and concerts in villa gardens, with the protagonists attired in fantastic Baroque costumes and wonderful jewels specially designed for the occasion, set against a background of blossoming orange and lemon trees and banked espaliers of scented flowers. The tragedy is that no relic of them survives today, and it is only from the pages of the old gardening books and the entries among the yellowing papers of family archives that we can evoke some shadow of what they must have been. These Baroque flower gardens of the seventeenth century lasted for the most part less than a hundred years before the changing tide of fashion swept them away. Box parterres planted in arabesques – the *broderies* adopted by the Italians as *ricami* – were the first change, followed by early attempts at landscapes; at first limited to one part of the garden, but later often submerging all that had gone before. Many of these later box parterres and the early landscapes are charming, but one cannot help regretting that so very few of the typically Italian flower gardens with their geometrical parterres still exist.

Villa Muti · Frascati

Nearly all the famous Frascati villas had flower gardens, but few survived the eighteenth and nineteenth centuries. Only one now remains, the Villa Muti in Frascati which, as Mrs Wharton observed, is one of the most charming small gardens in Italy. Probably this survival is due to the fact that it was always a green garden, relying from the very first upon the charm of its simple box parterres set in a frame of clipped hedges and trees. It was the earliest of the Frascati villas, already existing in 1579, but the nucleus of the garden as we see it today was probably laid out by Cardinal Arrigoni in 1595. This consisted of the terrace upon which the house stands, whose layout has since been altered, and the

117 VILLA MUTI
The garden of the Villa Muti at Frascati, one of the most charming of the smaller gardens of Italy, the nucleus of which was probably laid out by Cardinal Arrigoni in 1595. The garden was extended in 1620 when this terrace was created, but the design of the parterre probably dates from the middle of the century, as the influence of the curving lines of the French style of broderies is already evident. The villa belongs to the Società Immobiliare.

charming small enclosed garden terrace that lies to one side of it. Here all but one of the original geometrical box parterres still exist, and one really cannot regret the disappearance of only a part of this layout as its place has been taken by a small early-eighteenth-century landscape which, although the water is now lacking from the pool, comes straight out of a Claude painting and is one of the most charming of its kind in Italy.

Already in 1620 a large terrace had been created, running the whole length of the house and the small enclosed garden. This was originally laid out in geometrical parterres but, probably about the middle of the century, these were replaced by an early and simplified form of *ricami* which are still there today (pl. 117). This is one of the most splendid box parterres in Italy; the enormous space it occupies has enabled the designer to give a robust character to his curves which is often lacking in later parterres of this type. Seen from the windows of the house, and when pacing along the terrace above, it provides an outstanding example of a green garden in all its varying tones of grass, box ilex and distant pines. The third stage in the evolution of this enchanting garden was reached when a *bosco* with pleached alleys of ilex was laid out below this terrace, and a further terrace and *bosco* made above the enclosed garden. This was partly converted into a landscape layout in the nineteenth century, but several of the old straight alleys remain.

Thus Villa Muti provides a unique example of the evolution of a green garden in Italy, from the end of the sixteenth century right through to the nineteenth, in which the various transformations have been executed with such skill as to contribute something from each period without in any way damaging the whole. Like all the Frascati gardens Villa Muti suffered severely from bombing during the war. Shortly afterwards it was bought by a building company and the house is still uninhabited. Unlike many who should have known better, this purely commercial concern has kept this singularly lovely garden in running order; it is to be devoutly hoped that they will continue to display this all too rare sense of responsibility and one day revive its original charm by reintroducing water to its fountains and pools that would give it the life it now lacks.

Villa Falconieri · Frascati / Villa Torlonia · Frascati

Two of the other Frascati gardens have changed hands since the war. Both had suffered grievously from bombing – Frascati was a German communications centre and the Alban Hills on which it stands commanded the Anzio beach-head – but have suffered possibly even more from subsequent 'restorations'. One of these is the Villa Falconieri, whose once-lovely gardens now contain such municipal abominations as floral calendars. The other is the Villa Torlonia which is now a public park. In 1925 Shepherd and Jellicoe described this garden as being 'the grandest of its age, laid out with true appreciation of scale'. A public park is presumably a place of rest, therefore making a wide car road through it might be supposed to rob it of its greatest amenities, by destroying that atmosphere of shade and tranquillity which has always been one of the great features of Italian gardens. Not content with this, however, mushroom lamps and hideous lamp standards have been erected all along this road, ruining the wonderful view over the Roman *campagna* from the stairs and terrace that was one of the garden's chief glories and for the enjoyment of which it was expressly designed. Even further horrors have been perpetrated in order to install *son et lumière*, the branches of the ancient ilexes of the *bosco* being mercilessly hacked away, leaving bare stumps, over which peer the tall metal standards of the floodlights. The former beauty of the Villa Torlonia can now really only be appreciated in old prints such as Falda's, which shows Carlo Maderno's masterpiece, the lovely fountain terrace and cascade – the most beautiful in Frascati – in their typically Baroque setting of woodland trees, while the spirit of the old *bosco*, on the terrace above, still dwells in Hubert Robert's drawing of the fountain spouting its clear waters in the shade (pl. 118).

118 VILLA TORLONIA
An eighteenth-century French artist's impression of a fountain in the Villa Torlonia at Frascati, a painting by Hubert Robert in Besançon Museum. Today the whole atmosphere of this singularly lovely seventeenth-century garden has been ruined by its inept conversion into a public park. Photo by Mensy by kind permission of the Musées de Besançon.

Villa Aldobrandini · Frascati

It is a relief to turn to the gardens of the Villa Aldobrandini, which suffered as seriously from bombing as any in Frascati, but whose owner, Prince Aldobrandini, has repaired the damage without diminishing one whit of their charm. Designed by Giacomo della Porta and executed by Maderna, the house was built and the garden laid out for the nephew of Clement VIII in the short space of five years. The garden is a classic example of the Baroque style at its most effective, laid out on a site which is peculiarly adapted to this type of garden. The steeply sloping piece of land before the house must always have had the character, more or less, of a town garden, as it lies between two roads leading into the town of Frascati. Here, as one would expect, there is an arrangement of terraces laid out to derive the maximum enjoyment from the magnificent view. The main perspective, in this case a trimly pleached alley, leads from the main gate to the terraces, focusing all attention on the house. This, for all its great height, is only two rooms deep, and the central hall, which runs the full width of the building, is open to the garden on both sides, thus continuing the traditional Italian interpenetration of house and garden. Originally the garden before the house was probably laid out in parterres, whose design could be enjoyed from its windows and whose formality would have

119 VILLA ALDOBRANDINI
The hemisphere of Villa Aldobrandini at Frascati. The villa was begun in 1598 for a nephew of Pope Clement VIII, Cardinal Aldobrandini. It is one of the most splendid Baroque gardens in Italy. The villa belongs to Prince Aldobrandini.

been in keeping with the semi-urban site. This may also have been used as a flower garden, as the terraces on either side of the house, which would normally have been used for this purpose, were planted with magnificent plane trees that still exist.

The main feature of the Villa Aldobrandini garden is, however, the great semicircular nympheum that stands behind the house (pl. 119). Splendid as it is, this also has a functional aspect, as the main reason for the existence of the Frascati villas was to provide a cool retreat from the burning Roman summers. This nympheum contains semi-underground rooms and is carefully sited so as to enjoy the maximum amount of shade from the house and the surrounding trees. Its rushing fountains cool the air as well as providing a magnificent spectacle, culminating in a soaring perspective of water-stairs and columns rising upon the precipitous wooded hillside.

The nympheum embodies all that is most formal in Baroque gardens – the ilex trees that frame it and the water-staircase are clipped and the scene equals that of a Renaissance garden for symmetry and grandeur. There is one great difference, however: whereas in a Renaissance garden the composition would certainly have been continued in a series of terraces, here the central perspective leads straight into a great fiasco; the terrace above the water-staircase is quite small and its only adornment is a rustic stone fountain. Nor has this scene greatly changed since Falda made a print of it about 1683 (pl. 120). Much of the stone setting of the fountain has disappeared, the open space is no longer surrounded by clipped hedges and a vista of green parterres, but even in the seventeenth century there were already free-standing trees around the fountain, while the hedges provided the merest screen between this semi-formal layout and the wild woods that pressed in on either side.

In Falda's print the perspective can be seen continuing to another fountain, where the background appears to be almost entirely trees. In actual fact the perspective continues to a higher level, but there it terminates in a great rustic fountain gushing forth from the forested hillside. Thus in three brief stages the garden has passed from the monumental formality of the nympheum to the wild of the forest, whose trees have been pressing in closer and ever closer on the perspective as it recedes from view. This layout is typical of the change that came over Italian gardens with the advent of the Baroque and its different

121 VILLA ALDOBRANDINI
The 'room of the winds' in Villa Aldobrandini
described by Evelyn, print by Falda from Le
Fontane di Roma, *part 2, edited by G. de*
Rossi, 1675. By kind permission of the
American Academy.

122 VILLA MONDRAGONE
The 'theatre' of the fountains in the Borghese
Villa of Mondragone, at Frascati, with the
water game as described by Evelyn. Engraved
by Falda, in Le Fontane di Roma, 1675.
The villa is now a Jesuit college. By
kind permission of the American
Academy.

conception of man and his creations' place in the natural scheme of things. There are also terraces and walks on the hillside, but, unlike a Renaissance garden, these are simply grassy alleys lined at first by clipped trees and hedges and gradually merging into woodland paths.

The evolution of the Baroque Italian garden from that of the Renaissance can best be described as a gradual blurring of the outlines or – as Lugi Dami did – a softening of the edges. The basic principles are still the same and near the house man's order still reigns, but as the garden recedes from it the architectural features gradually disappear, giving way to less violent contrasts of light and shade as the clipped alleys merge into the natural growth of the woods and the surrounding landscape. It is the logical development of the process that began at Villa Lante and in it one can perceive the beginnings of the taste for the picturesque.

By the second half of the seventeenth century, natural growth and the beginnings of the decay that was later to submerge many villas had already changed the aspect of these Roman gardens, increasing precisely this picturesque aspect that appealed so strongly to the French taste and artists of the time Hubert Robert had stayed at Villa Aldobrandini with the French Ambassador the Duc de Choiseul, as well as at the Villa d'Este. Pierre de Nolhac, in his book on the French painters in Italy, quotes a passage that not only sums up the fascination which these gardens exercised upon his compatriots of the period, and later generations, but could well serve as a warning to many would-be 'restorers' of Italian gardens. It reads as follows: 'What increases the charm of the Roman gardens is that venerable impression of the hand of time. Created during the centuries of opulence, with a disposition according to the regular forms of art, the change of fortune and other natural causes have caused their upkeep to be neglected, and nature has in part resumed her rights. Her conquests over art and the intermingling of their effects produces the most picturesque scenes. This negligence, this antiquity, and this impetuous vegetation compose the most wonderful pictures' and, it might be added, in them resides the magical charm of the old gardens of Italy.

John Evelyn and Président de Brosses, who saw Villa Aldobrandini at about a century's interval from each other, reflect not only the differences in taste of their day but also the changes which have since come over the gardens. To the English seventeenth-century diarist the Aldobrandini garden was 'full of elegance, groves, ascents and prospects surpassing in my opinion the most delicious places that my eyes ever beheld'. Although the water-staircase and nympheum pleased him, characteristically he reserves his most detailed description for the 'artificial grotto, wherein are curious rocks, hydraulic organs and all sorts of singing birds, moving and chirping by the force of the water, with several pageants and surprising inventions. In the centre of one of these rooms rises a copper ball that continually dances about three foot above the pavement by virtue of a winde conveyed secretly to a hole beneath it, with many devices to wet the unwary spectators.' One of Falda's prints shows this room exactly as Evelyn must have seen it, and a painting in the house confirms this representation in every detail (pl. 121). The room still exists on the right-hand side of the nympheum, and is a wonderfully cool place of refuge on a hot summer day, but the polychrome figures of the Olympian Gods and the Pegasus of this Baroque *topia* have long since disappeared, together with cooling draughts that supported the ball, and the 'pageants'.

Evelyn was so taken up with his admiration of these conceits that his description of the rest of the garden is summary, but he spared the time to note that the centaur on the right of the nympheum made 'a terrible roaring with a horn' and that the other fountains could reproduce a storm whose effect was 'most naturall, with fury of raine, wind and thunder'. Président de Brosses despised all of this, describing the music played by the automatons as frightful, adding that the whole invention seemed to him 'puerile and totally lacking in attraction'. He preferred the Pegasus and commended the coolness of the Olympus room, but his only real enthusiasm was reserved for the shaded walks and the garden in front of the house, which was charmingly laid out with espaliers of oranges and lemons, clipped hedges of bays, and great vases of myrtles and pomegranates. All of these have now vanished and the only formal garden that remains is the charming little *giardino segreto* laid out around the *barchetta* fountain.

Villa Mondragone - Frascati

Président de Brosses was certainly tired, and probably inclined to view things with a jaundiced eye when he visited Villa Aldobrandini, as his whole morning had been spent in looking at the other Frascati villas. He had been soaked to the skin at Mondragone; nevertheless he recognized that this and the Aldobrandini and Torlonia villas were the finest in Frascati. His party had been drenched, not by an unexpected storm, but because they had been unable to resist the temptation of playing the water game in the *giardino segreto* of Mondragone (pl. 122). This distraction seems to have appealed even to serious travellers like him, more than the marvellous view and the vast pile of the villa itself, where three hundred and sixty-five rooms commemorate Gregory XIII's signature of the Bull promulgating the Gregorian calendar there in 1582. Falda's print shows the game in progress, with the combatants manipulating the leather tubes which, according to De Brosses, with the taps turned on, were 'thicker than a man's leg'. These must, one imagines, have been rather slippery, and wetting oneself rather than one's opponent was probably an incidental hazard of the game. After this diversion, and having changed into clean clothes, it is not surprising to find that De Brosses was a bit bored with the fountains and *giochi d'acqua* of Villa Aldobrandini, though he thoroughly approved of one where the would-be joker was drenched himself by turning on a tap that looked as if it would soak others.

A few years after the Villa Aldobrandini at Frascati was completed, another Pope's nephew, Scipione Borghese, whose uncle had become Paul V in 1605, began to buy land to make himself a villa outside the Roman walls near the Porta Pinciana. It soon became obvious, from his continued purchases, that this Borghese Cardinal had something very magnificent in mind, but it was only after some time that the full scope of his plans became evident. This was to create a new type of Roman villa, or at least the first of its kind that had been made for fifteen hundred years, for there is little doubt that Hadrian's villa was the source of his inspiration.

Villa Borghese · Rome

Villa Borghese in Rome was the earliest of the great Roman park villas of modern times, in which the gardens and park dominated and the house and other buildings were mere incidents in the vast layout. The house itself, which was begun shortly afterwards by the Flemish architect Ivan van Santen, or Giovanni Vasanzio, was in fact never even intended to be lived in, but in the manner of the old Roman villas to house an art gallery and a library and to be used for entertaining. The luxury and grandeur of a society in which a man could create a park some three miles in circumference (already by 1650 the circuit of the villa was four kilometers) simply as a place of entertainment seems almost incredible today, but Scipione Borghese set a fashion that was later followed by several of his peers, and his own family continued to add to his villa right into the nineteenth century.

A book by D. Montelatici published in Rome in 1700 gives a detailed description of the Villa Borghese at that time, when Cardinal Scipione's plantation — there were four hundred pines as well as countless numbers of other trees — had come to maturity. The villa was divided into four sections in which the Baroque transition from the garden proper to more or less natural park land is evident. It is interesting to note, however, that, like Hadrian's villa, this Roman park villa had no overall symmetrical plan of the type that Le Nôtre was to design for the King and nobles of France. Isolated nuclei of formal layouts existed here and there throughout the vast expanse of the Villa Borghese — the largest naturally surrounding the house itself — but there was little or no relationship between them, as is evident from the prints of the period (pl. 123).

Although the villa was laid out as a park it should not be imagined that it was a park in the English landscape sense. The first great enclosure, that stretched from the gate near the Porta Pinciana to the house, was thickly planted with trees of many kinds, intersected by straight alleys lined with tall clipped hedges and punctuated by herms. In

the old Italian style many of the crossings of these alleys were widened out to form a circular space, usually containing a fountain, stone seats and sculpture (pl. 124). This particular type of park was peculiarly suited to the Italian climate where grass does not thrive and shade is one of the most welcome aspects of a garden. Some idea of the charm of the park as it was originally laid out can be gathered from old prints such as these, published in de Rossi's book and from Odewart's drawing of the fountain of the sea-horses, though this is of a later date.

This type of layout, where trees predominated and the architectural aspects were simply incidents in the larger part of the general scheme, which characterized these later Italian park villas, evidently held a great appeal for the French. For it was predominantly this type of garden that Le Nôtre and his successors later brought to perfection on a vast scale and was immortalized by Fragonard and painters of the eighteenth century like Boucher, Watteau and Lancret. The French so loved this type of garden that it came to be regarded as peculiarly their own, but it should be borne in mind that Villa Borghese began to be laid out in the first years of the seventeenth century, prior to Le Nôtre's birth in 1613, and that its origins date even further back, to the park of Villa Lante and Pratolino.

In the gardens of Villa Borghese immediately surrounding the house the Renaissance rules of symmetry were applied still – a large open court was laid out in front, and at the back and sides were parterres and *giardini segreti*. The *cour d'honneur*, with its lovely balustrades and fountains (though these are modern copies), is one of the few parts of the villa that has changed little since the seventeenth century (pl. 125). Its charm is such that it was appreciated even in the midst of the craze for landscaping, as is shown by a somewhat fantastic early-nineteenth-century picture in the Uffizi. The area immediately behind the villa, which formed part of the second enclosure, was also laid out as an open space. This is now a rather weak parterre garden surrounded by urns and sculptures but Montelatici describes it as being much more thickly planted and containing small circular summer-houses, whose creeper-grown cupolas were supported by columns. A 'theatre' – really a decorative hemisphere of columns and statues – an enclosure for rabbits and a flower garden were laid out among the disciplined groves that completed this part of the park.

The area on both sides of the house was occupied by a succession of *giardini segreti* with

124 VILLA BORGHESE
A fountain in the Villa Borghese in Rome. Engraved by Venturini, in Le Fontane di Roma, *part 3. By kind permission of the American Academy.*

125 VILLA BORGHESE
Fountains in the entrance court.

beds of anemones, Dutch tulips, and the usual generic 'jonquils' and 'hyacinths', which probably included many of the new exotic bulbs. These small enclosed gardens were divided up by an aviary and charming little garden pavilions that still exist, but the only place where some of the original planting has survived is in the *giardino segreto* farthest from the house, where relics of the old espaliered orange trees still cling to the wall (pl. 126).

The planting and arrangement of these two enclosures of the villa must have already

126 VILLA BORGHESE
One of the giardini segreti *of the Villa Borghese.*

been well advanced by 1614, for Cardinal Borghese entertained the Spanish Ambassador to lunch in the July of that year in the *al fresco* dining-room near the outer wall of the first enclosure. This was designed as a temple, set among the groves of the *giardino boscareccio*, which had been planted by Domenico Savini with bays, cypresses, planes, pines and oaks. The architect Girolamo Rinaldi also had a hand in the design of this garden, probably overseeing the general arrangement of the fountains and sculpture, some of which was the work of the famous Bernini's father, Pietro, who died in 1629.

The third enclosure of the villa – which was two miles round, and larger than the whole area of the two preceding ones – was laid out as a park. It is interesting to note that Montelatici, in his description of 1700, attributes its origin to classical sources and says that it 'seems irregular but art and industry have so well regulated it that it alternates from hill to plain and from wild to domesticated valleys'. One cannot help wondering if William Kent, who was already in Rome in 1713, read his book and studied the Villa Borghese. Montelatici continues by saying that the park contained open country with wild trees, *boschi*, a thicket, a pine grove, a *ragnaia* for netting birds, a lake, fish ponds, and enclosures for ornamental animals and birds such as deer, roe-buck, Indian sheep, hares, and even lions, also ostriches, peacocks, swans and ducks – quite evidently imitated from the ancient Roman *leporarium*. There were also several small houses and pavilions, some of which had already existed before the great park was made and had simply been enclosed in it.

The fourth enclosure, which was situated towards the Piazza del Popolo end of the villa, was smaller and principally laid out as flower and vegetable gardens. It contained the head gardener's house, and the expense-regardless aspect of these princely Roman villas is well illustrated by the fact that even a gardener's cottage was decorated with frescoes and had a *giardino segreto* adorned with fountains. This corner must have been one of the most charming parts of the whole villa; even its strawberry-beds were edged with low hedges of jasmine, while countless little fountains and irrigation channels gurgled among the espaliers of citrons and lemons, the blossoming pear and pomegranate trees and flower-beds. There was a tulip garden hedged with Dutch roses, vine and jasmine pergolas, and the flower parterres were laid out, some with *pianelle* and some with box edgings. These were planted with tuberose, amaranth, anemones, carnations, 'hyacinths' and 'jonquils'. Montelatici describes them as 'the rarest found' so evidently they included many exotics. Even in the midst of his very factual description Montelatici cannot resist dwelling for one moment upon the scent of this sheltered and lovely garden, with its painted aviary, paths of pebble mosaics and fountains whose jets could be changed to form a 'mist', 'stars', 'hail' or 'fireworks' of water.

Alas, all this has long since disappeared, and tarmac roads thronged with cars now pass over the site. Probably much of it had already gone by the end of the eighteenth century, and sad to say a Scottish artist – Jacob Moore who was in Rome in 1773 – probably played a hand in its ultimate destruction, as he was called in by the Prince Borghese of the day to redesign the layout of the villa in the English landscape style. The work was carried out by Camporesi and, though the result is pleasing and affords a welcome oasis of greenery and shade in the midst of the glare and noise of modern Rome, the Villa Borghese can no longer be described as a truly Italian garden.

Scipione Borghese had set a fashion in the grand style for the villas of Papal nephews, and two others were soon to imitate him. The first was Alessandro Ludovisi, the nephew of Gregory XV. But the villa which bore his name, whose lovely park still existed in Augustus Hare's day, was destroyed in 1887 to make way for the Via Veneto and the tourist hotels of today. The next was Innocent X's nephew, Camillo Pamphilj, whose romantic honeymoon was spent at Caprarola. Evidently he and his wife's love for gardens did not end there, for they made what was, and happily still is, the largest park villa in Rome.

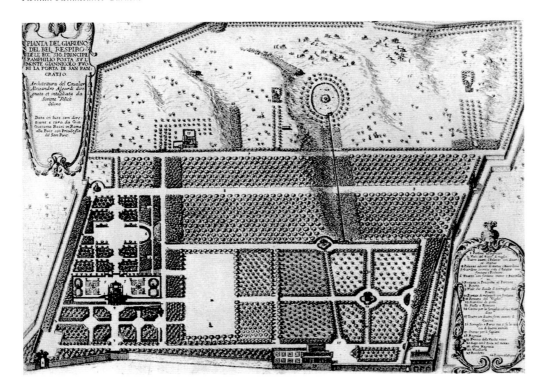

Villa Pamphilj · Rome

The creation of Villa Pamphilj in Rome whose circumference is close on six miles, began with the purchase in 1630 of quite a modest 'vigna', some way outside the Porta San Pancrazio on what is now the Via Aurelia Antica. This already possessed a dwelling-house, which was later extended and redecorated by Algardi, who also designed the *giardino segreto* and fountains that were laid out around it. The family must have continued to buy land in the area, as some time shortly after the accession of Innocent X in 1644 the building of the casino and the layout of extensive gardens that surround it was begun. Their vast extent and splendour are recorded in Barrière's prints executed between 1653 and 1659. As in the Villa Borghese, this casino was built entirely for pleasure and entertaining, and to house part of the family collection of sculptures and pictures, the old villa on the Via Aurelia being reserved for living-quarters.

Barrière's prints show Algardi's casino as it was originally projected, but never entirely built. The two lateral wings only existed on paper, and from the first it looked just as it does today, a large block surmounted by a belvedere, relying for its effect upon the most extensive use in any Roman villa of decoration of ancient bas-reliefs framed in contemporary *stucchi*. By the beginning of 1648, the casino and the *giardino segreto* behind it were practically finished; four years later the layout must have been complete, as the workmen were paid off and the account-books for the building of the villa closed.

As in the Villa Borghese, the old villa and Algardi's '*casino d'allegrezze*' were only incidents, and widely separated ones at that, in the enormous gardens and park that surrounded them. The formal gardens laid out on either side of the old villa were small; not so those of the casino, but even their size is dwarfed when compared with the extent of the park, as is clearly shown in Falda's print (pl. 127). This print probably shows the villa exactly as it was in Falda's time, as it faithfully reproduces most of the details shown in Barrière's earliest ones of Algardi's project. Such slight modifications as exist are a probable proof of its veracity, for the broad outlines of the whole plan are still the same today.

127 VILLA PAMPHILJ
Plan of the gardens of Villa Pamphilj, begun in 1644 by Algardi for Camillo Pamphilj, a nephew of Innocent X, from G. B. Falda's Li Giardini di Roma, ?1683. The largest of the Roman park villas, the circumference of the villa is today nearly six miles. It is still owned by the Doria Pamphilj family. Photo by kind permission of the Gabinetto Fotografico Nazionale.

The formal gardens surrounding Algardi's casino were laid out on three levels, the first in formal hedged plots of trees before the main entrance. The casino stands on the edge of this terrace, and on its far side extends to the level of the lower one, which is the *giardino segreto*. As Armando Schiavo has pointed out in his excellent book on the villa, the traditional attribution to Le Nôtre of the layout of this parterre garden can be disregarded. The vast Pamphilj archive contains no mention of it, but stronger proof is forthcoming from a study of the prints and plans of various periods. Barrière's show the layout as a severely simple one, with two groups of geometrical parterres and two pools. This is confirmed by Falda's print executed some ten years or more after the garden was laid out. It is only in a Piranesi print at the end of the eighteenth century that the parterres appear laid out in the style of the French *broderies* in which heraldic devices are apparent. The whole villa was surveyed, and this parterre drawn in detail in 1899, and the layout shows that the *broderies* included not only the Pamphilj lilies, but also the Doria device of a crowned eagle. The Pamphiljs became extinct in the male line in 1760, after which the villa passed through the female line to the historic Doria family of Genoa, who some time between then and 1768 assumed also the name and arms of the Pamphilj, quartering them with their own and those of the Landi. Some time after 1899, the parterre of the *giardino segreto* was brought up to date by the inclusion of the Pamphilj dove and the Landi arms.

The above somewhat detailed history of a single parterre garden serves not only as a warning against unconfirmed tradition, but as a further illustration of the conservative character of Italian parterre design. Still in the middle of the seventeenth century, in the grandest Roman garden of the day, the principal parterres were laid out in the old geometrical Italian style. It was only in the lower 'garden of the theatre' that the curves of the heraldic Pamphilj lilies lent themselves to a less rigid style in some of the parterres; though these still retained the same robust quality as the parterres of the Villa Muti and were enclosed by low-clipped hedges forming rectangles or the familiar Italian squares with a circular space at the crossing. These parterres were completely different in style from the elaborate eighteenth-century *ricami* that were subsequently laid out in the *giardino segreto* in imitation of the French *broderies* whose fine curves and arabesques stand out independently from a background of gravel, without any enclosing hedge. Where this type of layout is found in Italy, especially in the centre and south, it usually dates from late in the seventeenth century, and probably from the eighteenth.

Both the Villa Pamphilj and the adjoining Villa Corsini, which was subsequently incorporated into it, suffered severely from the fighting which took place in the area during Garibaldi's defence of the Roman Republic in 1849. The Prince Doria Pamphilj of the day was married to an Englishwoman – Lady Mary Talbot – and it was probably owing to her influence, as well as to the prevalent taste, that when it was restored, the '*giardino del teatro*' was laid out in the English style. The large hemisphere that gave it its name, however, still survives and so do some of the original grotto fountains and statues, and the stairs that connect it with the *giardino segreto* on the terrace above.

These changes in the original layout of the gardens of the Villa Pamphilj are not such a serious loss as in other gardens, as the chief glory of the villa is, and has always been, its park. In Falda's print this is shown as being laid out in much the same style as the Villa Borghese, with straight avenues dividing up the great plantation of trees. But already the design is freer, and fewer avenues and walks cut into the mass of green, though it is interesting to note that a large open grassy space was still reserved for use as a *manège*, while almost half the enclosure was open land where a hunt is seen in progress. Some time at the end of the eighteenth century part of the formal park and the hunting-enclosure underwent a change, which was almost certainly the result of the French influence that was

beginning to make itself felt even in conservative Rome. The 'fountain of the lily' – No. 11 on Falda's print – was moved to the top of the small valley on the right; and the stream below it, that fed the fish pond in the hunting-enclosure, was converted into a superb series of cascades terminating in an ornamental pool. These cascades were made in rustic stone and, apart from a few urns placed on pedestals, the watercourse had no formal setting but stood free amongst the natural woodland trees. Thus its character was much more closely linked to current trends in French gardens than to the classical Italian tradition. It is probable that its layout, which is unique in Roman gardens, owed its origins to the fact that a member of the Doria Pamphilj family was Papal Nuncio in Paris about this time. This Doria Pamphilj Cardinal was evidently interested in garden design, as he took with him on his mission a young protégé – Faragine di Bettini – whose sketch-books are still preserved in the family library. These are full of drawings of famous French gardens of the day, both formal and 'Anglo-Chinese', of which the rustic style seems to have appealed to the artist most. The books also contain many projects for the Villa Pamphilj; these include entertaining designs for a ferry across the *new* cascade. This drawing is dated

128 VILLA PAMPHILJ
A view of the lake in the Villa Pamphilj, a painting by De Camps now in the Wallace Collection. Since the war the lake has been drained. Photo by kind permission of the Wallace Collection.

1793, so it is likely that the cascades had been made not long beforehand. During the nineteenth century the ornamental pool was converted into a lake. As a result of the vicissitudes of the last war the cascades became overgrown and the lake has been drained but the charm of this singularly lovely corner of a late Italian garden is portrayed in De Camps' picture of it in the Wallace Collection in London (pl. 128).

Owing to its vast size, the Villa Pamphilj is one of the few Italian gardens where the English landscape style has been introduced successfully. Few would be prepared to quarrel with the charming setting it now provides for Bernini's 'fountain of the queen' or the 'lumaca' as it is more usually called, when comparing it with seventeenth-century prints of the original layout. Although de Rossi gives this fountain to Algardi, actually it was really designed by Bernini for the Piazza Navona (pl. 129). Some accounts say that Innocent X considered it too small for the piazza, others that his all-powerful sister-in-law coveted it for the villa. Either story may be true, but in any case the fountain has stood on its present site since the middle of the seventeenth century, as it is clearly shown in Falda's print.

The romantic beauty of the Villa Pamphilj held a special appeal for artists of the nineteenth century; one of the greatest – Camille Corot – made it the subject of one of his lovely Roman paintings. Here the casino is seen from the terrace above the 'theatre', painted in the afternoon light when its mellow tones showed to best advantage, surrounded by a sea of foliage. The enduring charm that, through all their vicissitudes, the great gardens of Italy have held for the people of every nationality, is perhaps best illustrated by this picture, as in what other place or circumstances would one have expected to find a typically Baroque subject providing the inspiration for an artist of the romantic school?

129 VILLA PAMPHILJ
Bernini's 'fountain of the queen' more commonly called the 'snail'. Engraving by Venturini in Le Fontane di Roma, *part 3. One of the original drawings for this fountain is in the Royal Collection at Windsor. By kind permission of the American Academy.*

Arcadian Academy - Rome

By the beginning of the eighteenth century France rather than Italy had become the acknowledged centre of garden design, and already in the north French gardens had become the fashion. Rome was more conservative, and could still produce at least one garden that was linked to the old Italian tradition. This last Roman garden, where the design represented the final flourish of Baroque originality before it was engulfed by cold neo-classicism apparent in the Villa Albani, was that of the Arcadian Academy. It was appropriate that this should be so, as the volatile proceedings of the Academy had resulted in its being excluded from its former seat in the Orti Farnesiani in 1699, by the strict orders of the Duke of Parma. In dudgeon, its members returned to their original home on the slopes of the Janiculum, commissioning an architect to build them new premises whose vivacious style was well suited to their temper. This is said to have been Francesco De Sanctis, co-designer of the famous Spanish Steps. Certainly the small casino, and especially the garden designed to accommodate the Academy during the early years of the eighteenth century, bear a strong stylistic resemblance to the delightful late Baroque stairs (pl. 130).

Perhaps it was the steeply sloping site that gave the architect his inspiration, for the design of the garden is basically that of a Baroque staircase that threads its way through green groves of bays, with occasional stone pines and cypresses providing punctuation marks. The main function of the garden was to provide an open-air meeting-place for the Arcadians, whose aim was to re-create the sylvan simplicity of their namesakes; in pursuit of this they adopted the pipes of Pan as their device and took for themselves the names of Arcadian shepherds. The charming little amphitheatre that was designed for their reunions still exists and in spring it is filled with the heady scent of a huge wisteria that covers the casino. The rest of the garden is a *bosco*, where occasional fountains gurgle in the shade. The scene is a delightful one for all its artificiality, and it is not difficult to people it with eighteenth-century pseudo-shepherds and shepherdesses, dressed in satin and engaged in literary conversations, as they descend its curving steps to the Baroque gates, where their carriages are waiting to drive them off to the next modish rout.

Thus in the fashionable flurry of the eighteenth century the long history of Roman Renaissance gardens comes to an end. In the Arcadia it has travelled a long way from Bramante's Cortile del Belvedere; but still in this last postscript to the garden art of Rome its architect showed that he had not entirely lost touch with the original conception that converted a rough hillside into a work of art, whose influence had spread throughout Italy and the whole of Europe.

130 ARCADIAN ACADEMY
The garden of the Arcadian Academy on the Janiculum. Dating from the beginning of the eighteenth century, it is attributed to Francesco De Sanctis, one of the architects of the famous Spanish Steps. The small amphitheatre was designed for the meetings during which the members read their literary compositions.

Gardens of the Marche and Veneto

The remote adriatic province of the Marche had contributed two of its greatest names to Renaissance Rome – Bramante and Raphael, both of whom were born within a few miles of the Ducal Palace of Urbino where Laurana had laid out one of the earliest Renaissance gardens. Though both of their working lives were spent far from Urbino, which had been one of the greatest cultural and artistic centres of the fifteenth century in the glorious days of Federico di Montefeltro, they must have seen this garden in their youth and perhaps some memory of it lingered when they were designing the Cortile del Belvedere and Villa Madama.

By the beginning of the sixteenth century the Montefeltro dynasty had become extinct in the male line, and through marriage the duchy had passed to Pope Julius II's great-nephew Francesco Maria Della Rovere who, in keeping with the family tradition, was to revive the cult of gardens in the Marche. In this he was aided by his wife, Leonora Gonzaga, the daughter of another family of garden lovers – the Gonzaga ones in and around Mantua were famous – and together they created two remarkable gardens. One of these, near Fossombrone, was still a tourist sight for foreign travellers in the seventeenth century but has since disappeared; the other at Villa Imperiale near Pesaro happily still exists.

Villa Imperiale - Pesaro

According to tradition, Imperiale owes its name to the Emperor Frederick III having been entertained there, on the way to or from his coronation in Rome, in 1452, by Alessandro Sforza, who was then Governor of Pesaro. Certainly when about 1522 Francesco Maria and Leonora decided to convert the place into a villa in the Renaissance style the old fifteenth-century house still existed. Although Laurana's garden at Urbino had been remarkable in its day, by the first quarter of the sixteenth century Rome had far surpassed the Italian provincial capitals in villa and garden design and it was to the Eternal City that all eyes now turned for inspiration. Corroborative evidence of this is shown by the fact that in 1522 Francesco Maria wrote to Castiglione, his Ambassador in Rome, asking him to try to procure a letter which Raphael had written shortly before his death describing the Villa Madama. Castiglione got a copy from Raphael's cousin, and this the Duke handed over to his Court architect, Girolamo Genga, who had the additional advantage of having seen Raphael's work at the Farnesina and Villa Madama when he was studying painting in Rome. In view of this it is not surprising to find that the work of Genga and his assistants on the Villa Imperiale owes much, both in the interior decoration of the old villa and in the new building and gardens that were made beside it, to the Farnesina and Villa Madama.

The original Villa Imperiale had consisted of a semi-fortified country house with a tower, built round a courtyard. Its rooms were now entirely redecorated with frescoes in

accordance with contemporary taste, and some of these are among the most delightful examples of garden *trompe l'oeil* painting still to be seen in Italy. Outstanding among them are the Sala dei Cariatidi with its caryatids that merge into a leafy pergola, depicted against a delightful landscape; the Camera dei Semibusti, with garlands resembling those of the Farnesina; and above all the Camera degli Amorini, whose entire decoration is framed in a setting of green garlands and branches, and includes a charming *trompe l'oeil* jasmine trellis. The aim of this type of painting was to emphasize the rural character of the villa by bringing the surrounding gardens and landscape right into the house – upon whose walls were thus depicted the bays, myrtles, and other greens for which the garden was famous.

While the redecoration of the old villa was in progress, the new one was being built in the contemporary Roman Renaissance style, and it is here that the influence of the Villa Madama is plainly evident. This new villa, which was attached to the old one by a bridge, repeated in its Ionic pilasters and the coffered vaulting of its garden porticos those of the house and garden of Villa Madama; but it was in the garden layout and its relation to the house that the Roman source of inspiration was most clearly demonstrated. As in Villa Madama, the whole building simply serves as a screen which surrounds a superb courtyard on three sides – the fourth being occupied by garden terraces cut into the hill in the same manner as the projected theatre of the Villa Madama shown in the Uffizi drawing.

All of this is clearly shown in Francisco d'Hollanda's drawing (pl. 132); here the villa is viewed from the top terrace that connects directly with the promenades laid out on its roof. In the foreground is the garden court, referred to in contemporary records as the '*sala scoverta*' or uncovered room, which is one of the most charming out-of-doors living-rooms in Italy. This is surrounded by cool grottoes and porticos – these last were apparently also designed to be used as the stage of a theatre – and shell-decorated rooms with fountains intended for use as dining- and ball-rooms in the summer heat (pls. 131, 133). Originally a classical bronze statue stood in its centre, but the court is now laid out with flower-beds.

131 VILLA IMPERIALE
The 'theatre' loggia in the garden court of the Villa Imperiale, Pesaro.

132 VILLA IMPERIALE
Francisco d'Hollanda's drawing of the Villa Imperiale near Pesaro from his sketchbook in the Escorial. The part of the villa seen here was built between 1522 and 1531 to the designs of Girolamo Genga, who had studied painting in Rome while the Farnesina and Villa Madama were being built, and the influence of the latter upon the garden design of the Villa Imperiale is plainly evident, especially in the loggias and the garden court. The villa belongs to Count Guglielmo Castelbarco. Vatican Library photo from a facsimile in the Library.

133 VILLA IMPERIALE
The garden court of the Villa Imperiale near Pesaro.

Spiral staircases provide access to the terraces above; the intermediate one on a level with the *piano nobile* was used as a lemon garden in the sixteenth century, while the upper one, connected with the promenades and belvederi, commands a wonderful view over the surrounding country.

This top terrace was laid out as a spacious walled garden, that originally had not only a gate, but also semicircular loggias at its two far corners, which led into the woods beyond. (pl. 134) The whole of the garden layout was evidently nearing completion in 1530, as in that year Francesco Maria Della Rovere ordered a fountain for it from Serlio; this was to have taken the form of a satyr milking a goat, but was never actually made. During the winter and spring of 1537-1538 a lively correspondence was carried on between the Duchess and her administrator about the planting of the gardens; from which it is evident that the poor man had to act as a peacemaker between the new gardener from Savona and Genga the architect – who had different views on the subject – as well as coping with the Duchess's and the gardener's demands and Genga's lamentations.

From these letters and other contemporary descriptions it emerges that the garden was a typically Renaissance one, not only in its enclosed and axial layout – so closely related to the house – but also in its planting. This appears to have been almost entirely of greens – Spanish myrtles, bays, many kinds of vines and a large variety of citrus trees. The walls of the lower terrace were covered with espaliers of bitter oranges and its sheltered parterres were planted with thirty-four citrons, two lemons and some of those curious and highly-prized hybrids known as '*bizzarie*', all of which were specially imported from Savona. It is likely that these plants were covered in winter and the potted ones removed to the greenhouses which are shown in early-seventeenth-century drawings of the villa; as both Genga and the gardener were understandably anxious about their survival in the colder winters of the Marche after the warm Riviera climate of Savona.

The walls of the upper garden were also covered with espaliered oranges and its paths shaded with vine pergolas and pleached alleys of bays. It was laid out as a topiary garden, with low hedges of roses and parterres of box, myrtle and rosemary, punctuated by citrus trees in pots and the topiary ornaments that were then so much admired – three ships in clipped myrtle or bays are described in all the records. Sadly no vestige of all this remains, as the villa was completely neglected during the last century, and the existing box parterres are of recent date. The garden fountains that Leandro Alberti saw in 1568 have also disappeared, including the surprise one that showered the unsuspecting visitor. Gone too are the *bosco* with its cypresses, and the oak woods of the game preserve, that covered the hill behind the upper garden. A path led through these to the now long-vanished Villa of the Vedetta on the top of the hill, built in 1583, and the Villa of the Duchess at its foot – the only Italian Renaissance one to have been built right on the sea.

For a hundred years Imperiale was one of the sights of Italy – Francisco d'Hollanda having included it in his sketch-book together with the greatest monuments of antiquity and the most famous Roman villas is a clear indication of this, which is confirmed by contemporary descriptions of the villa as the Farnesina of Pesaro and the long list of illustrious guests who went to see it. The Farnese Pope, Paul III, founder of the Orti Farnesiani and a well-known connoisseur of gardens, was there in 1543 and was much impressed, while that assiduous gardener, the humanist Cardinal Bembo, considered that Imperiale was 'constructed with more intelligence and true artistic science, as well as with more antique fashions and finely contrived conceits, than any modern building'.

By the middle of the seventeenth century the Della Rovere of Pesaro had become extinct in the male line and Vittoria, the last of them, had married one of the Medicis, leaving Imperiale to the beginning of the long decline, from which it was only rescued by its present owner Conte Guglielmo Castelbarco. At the time of writing he has just

134 VILLA IMPERIALE
The upper garden terrace and bosco of the Villa Imperiale, Pesaro.

embarked upon extensive restoration of the damage caused by fighting in the Gothic Line during the last war; it is to be hoped that the replanting of the gardens will be included in his plans.

The gardens of Imperiale, though strangely little known outside the province, are one of the most remarkable and complete survivals of the early sixteenth century that exist in Italy, and they set a pattern for garden design in the Marche whose influence lasted right up to the end of the eighteenth century. The gardens that followed were much simpler and lacked the architectural splendour of Imperiale; understandably so, because they were designed for families of well-to-do landowners but not for a ducal dynasty. But such was the conservatism of local taste in this remote province, and so well had Genga designed his garden layout to suit the rolling hilly landscape and windy climate of the Marche, that Imperiale's sheltered sunlit terraces and equally sheltered but quite separate and shady *bosco* continued to serve as models long after the villa itself had fallen into decay.

Villa Miralfiore - Pesaro

There is one exception to this rule, and strangely enough this is also a Della Rovere reconstruction of a Sforza villa, but here the difference in layout is due to the level site. The Villa Miralfiore which stands not far outside the old walls of Pesaro, was rebuilt about 1559 for Duke Guidobaldo II, son of Francesco Maria Della Rovere, by Filippo Terzi to the designs of Girolamo Genga's son Bartolomeo. Unlike Imperiale the villa has always been well kept, and the flat land round the house is laid out in three very fine parterre gardens, that still preserve their original late-sixteenth-century layout (pl. 135). The parterres are mainly outlined in box, and the robust simplicity of their geometrical layout is as striking as the fact of their survival. Some greenhouses and a neo-classical colonnade have been built at the end of the parterres behind the house, separating them from the *bosco*; but otherwise the gardens probably still look very much the same as they did in the sixteenth century; a most unusual occurrence in the rest of Italy, for which we have to thank *marchigiani* conservatism that has resulted in the preservation of this and other lovely old gardens in the Province. Miralfiore also belongs to a member of the Castelbarco family.

Villa Mosca - Pesaro

Closer to Imperiale, both geographically, as it also stands on the slopes of Monte di San Bartolo, and in the character of its garden layout, is the Villa Mosca or Caprile. This gay little house and garden, where Prinny's wife Caroline of Brunswick lived with Bartolomeo Pergami from 1817 to 1818, is much more typical of a Marche villa than Miralfiore. Although it was built about 1640, its simple layout is as well adapted to its site as the splendid one of Imperiale. The landscape round Pesaro is made up of rolling hills, terraced as vineyards, interspersed with clumps of trees; but as the sea is so near, the climate is windy. Thus the garden layout of Villa Mosca consists of a series of sunlit terraces, one of which is a large sheltered garden room, lying in the lee of the house; while for hot weather a shady *bosco* was planted some distance away (pl. 136). The garden was extended in 1780, when a green theatre was made in the *bosco*, and it is likely that the planting of the garden room also dates from this period, though its main lines are of the previous century. The garden of the Villa Mosca is kept in excellent condition by its present owners, the Agricultural Institute of Pesaro, and the mingled scents of flowers, lemon blossom and box greet one on descending from one terrace to the next. This can be something of a hazard, as fountains concealed in the steps can still be turned on to surprise the unwary, and it is delightful to find that all the naïve jokes and amusements that pleased the seventeenth-century travellers have been carefully repaired in this charming old-world garden. One of the seats, thoughtfully placed for those who wish to admire the view, can suddenly clamp the visitor in his place and give him a showerbath; while in one of the grottoes, little painted wooden automatons still perform their antics as they did in the 'pageants' that amused John Evelyn at Villa Aldobrandini. Only in the gardens of the Marche do these appealing little conceits still survive as a reminder of a gentler and more leisured age, and their discovery has something of the charm of the unexpected tinkle of an old musical-box.

135 VILLA MIRALFIORE
The garden of Miralfiore, Pesaro. The villa was rebuilt about 1559 and the well-kept gardens have retained the original design of their singularly fine parterres. The villa belongs to Count Alberto Castelbarco.

136 VILLA MOSCA
The garden of Villa Mosca, at Pesaro. Built around 1640, its terraced layout is typical of Marche gardens and ideally suited to the surrounding landscape. Caroline of Brunswick, wife of George IV, lived here from 1817 to 1818. It is now maintained in excellent condition by the Agricultural Institute of Pesaro.

Villa Montegallo - Ancona

The lovely green hill country of the Marche province of Ancona was also once a great villa and garden centre, but the last war took its toll here as in so many other places, and the once celebrated Centofinestre, among others, is now a wilderness. Fortunately, the even more interesting Villa Montegallo has survived, and its new owner intends to replant its neglected gardens according to the eighteenth-century plan which is still preserved in the house. A house of some kind already stood on the crest of the hill when Cardinal Antonio Maria Gallo bought the land in 1592; this he extended, and gave to the place the appropriate name of Montegallo. He also probably made the walled garden on top of the hill approaching the house, as the charming little garden casino there, frescoed by Pomarancio, undoubtedly dates from this period.

The house continued to be embellished by its owners, and early in the eighteenth century the Bibiena brothers were called in to decorate the *piano nobile*. But the great extension of the villa, and particularly of its gardens, was begun in 1760 by a local architect, Andrea Vici, who later became famous in Rome. It is interesting to note that even at this late date, the principles of Marche garden design were basically still the same as at Imperial

137 VILLA MONTEGALLO
A bird's-eye view of the garden of Villa Montegallo, near Ancona, from a drawing dated 1760 in the possession of the owner Count Buonaccorsi. Although the gardens are now in bad condition, except for a few details the layout is still the same and the owner intends to restore their original planting.

240

– consisting of a series of sheltered sunny terraces, designed to take full advantage of the wonderful view, while an extensive *bosco* was planted some way to the north. There was no question of the two intermingling, as they would have in a Roman garden even in the previous century, and this layout was not occasioned by any accident of site, as the same division of the two aspects of the garden occurs at Villa Mosca, Villa Centofinestre and in the Giardino Buonaccorsi. Thus even at the end of the eighteenth century the Marche clung sturdily to the old concept of the formal garden as an enclosed entity, well separated from what had originally been the barco or wooded hunting-preserve as at Imperiale; which in the eighteenth century was designed as a shady *bosco* for hot days. Just how conservative local gardening tradition can be, may be judged by the fact that at Montegallo some of the parterres are still surrounded by an edging of clipped thyme, as in the *Hypnerotomachia*, which I have never seen in any other villa garden during sixteen years in Italy.

The terraced gardens of Montegallo are still exactly the same as in the drawing of 1760, only the upper circular one is now planted with trees instead of being surrounded by a pergola, and the central gazebo is missing. (pl. 137) But all the rest, the turret aviaries, the Baroque stairs and fountains built in a beautifully mellowed rosy brick, still stand; though the parterres are sadly in need of replanting. The bottom terrace, which is only partly seen in the foreground of the drawing, was evidently used as an orangery; it is sunk deep in the shelter of its protecting walls, with no windows or other openings giving on to the wonderful panorama that surrounds it. The remains of old greenhouses cover one wall, and the provision of this large sheltered space serves as a reminder that the cool and windy climate of the Marche, which is only hot at the very height of summer, must also have played a decisive part in the design of these sunny terraced gardens, so unlike others in central Italy where the provision of shade was usually a first essential.

Although it is not strictly speaking an aspect of garden architecture, one other feature of Montegallo cannot be passed over because of its unique character – is is the *romitorio* or hermitage. Many drawings and plans of hermitages exist among collections of eighteenth-century architectural drawings in Italy, and in the Villa Chigi in Rome the ante-room to the chapel is painted in *trompe l'oeil* to represent a cave-hermitage inhabited by Franciscan friars. But here in the garden forecourt of Montegallo an entire cottage is decorated in *trompe l'oeil* with stucco and painting so that each room looks like a cavern. The little house contains several rooms and a fully-equipped kitchen, and is peopled with life-size figures of friars going about their household tasks. As far as the writer knows, this hermitage is unique in Italy, but whether it was really intended to be used as a retreat or was simply a picturesque folly, as it would have been in a romantic garden, is a mystery.

Giardino Buonaccorsi - Potenza Picena

Remote even from the small provincial capitals of the Marche, standing on the top of a green hill between Potenza Picena and the sea, is one of the most fascinating and least known to the outside world of all the gardens in Italy. Since its earliest origins the place must have been famous for its gardens, for it is called not Villa, but Giardino Buonaccorsi. Just to see this garden is an experience for any garden lover, and to spend a day in it is an event to be remembered. For here time has stood still and Giardino Buonaccorsi is that unique thing, an eighteenth-century Italian garden perfect in every detail, right down to the furniture of its grottoes and the stars and diamonds of its original parterres.

Unfortunately, practically nothing is known about the history of this enchanted place, although it is still in the possession of the same family that has owned it for several hundred years. Researches in the family archives have produced no documents referring to its creation or evolution and the only evidence with regard to its history is an old picture

that still hangs in the house (pl. 138). Judging from the dress of the figures seen in the foreground, this was painted about the middle of the eighteenth century, and the fascinating thing about it is that this picture shows practically the whole of the garden layout almost exactly as it is today. From the probable date of the picture and from the similarity of many of its features, such as the aviaries, promenades and grottoes to those of Centofinestre, Montegallo and Villa Mosca, it seems likely that these Buonaccorsi gardens were designed by Andrea Vici or some associate of his, though they were probably laid out on the site of an earlier garden, as part of the house dates from the seventeenth century.

Giardino Buonaccorsi is the perfect example of a Marche garden and, thanks to the loving care of its owners, it has survived in excellent condition to show us what the others must have been like (pl. XLI). The house stands on the crest of a small hill, with a delightful landscape of green hills and valleys extending between it and the sea. The hill behind the house and its southern slope have been laid out as a series of walled and sheltered terraces, open to the sun

XLI GIARDINO BUONACCORSI

242

and with a lovely view. There are five of them in all. The highest, which lies between the house and the chapel, has an open forecourt and a slightly raised *giardino segreto* that are still absolutely identical with the layout shown in the eighteenth-century view (pl. 140). Every detail of the garden furniture is the same as it was two hundred years ago, from the delightfully original obelisks to the statues, fountains, potted citrus trees, and even the magnificent espaliered lemons that cover the wall on the left. The most remarkable survival, however, unique in Italy, are the small stone-bordered divisions of the parterres, whose stars, diamonds and other geometrical shapes are the same as those of the original view. This layout is strongly reminiscent of those illustrated in Vredemann de Vries' books of the sixteenth century, yet another illustration of the conservatism of Marche garden design (pls. 138, 139). The moulded stone edgings are of the same type as some mentioned in the *Hypnerotomachia*.

The second garden terrace also is still today precisely the same as in the eighteenth-century view, though the growth of the planting makes this slightly less obvious (pl. 141). Not only are the parterres and garden furniture identical, but in the background the characteristically rounded trellis of a *berceau* can be observed, though today this is practically obscured by creepers. The robust and simple outline of the parterres on this terrace is reminiscent of those at Miralfiore, and it is possible that their design may have survived from the earlier seventeenth-century layout.

The third terrace, leading up to the statue of Flora (which can be seen on the right of pl. 141) is much narrower and was evidently intended as a sheltered walk for cold days. Here is the only change in the appearance of the garden since the eighteenth century – the statues of the Roman emperors that flank the walk are no longer enclosed in niches of clipped greens. It is interesting to observe that even in this gay eighteenth-century garden the more solemn aspect of humanist and Renaissance gardens has survived on this terrace, and the style of these Imperial statues is quite different from those of Pulcinella, Turks and other figures from the Italian comedies that people the rest. This leads to the supposition that the emperors are probably survivors from an earlier garden layout.

139 GIARDINO BUONACCORSI
*One of the parterres on the upper terrace of
Giardino Buonaccorsi, Potenza Picena, every
detail of which is identically the same as in the
bird's-eye view (plate 138), a circumstance which
is practically, if not wholly, unique in Italy.*

140 GIARDINO BUONACCORSI
*The chapel and upper terrace of the Giardino
Buonaccorsi at Potenza Picena as it is today.
With the exception of planting it is almost
identical to the view shown in the bird's-eye
view (plate 138).*

In the extreme right-hand and somewhat faded corner of the eighteenth-century view, two lower terraces can be faintly seen; these appear to have been laid out as simple grassy spaces at this date. Today, however, the fourth terrace is filled with parterres; though still simple and geometrical, their lighter design indicates a later date. The final terrace is now occupied by a series of shady walks, separated from each other by high clipped hedges, with here and there a fountain placed in an open space. This is the only example in this group of Marche gardens where anything resembling a *bosco* comes within the confines of the formal garden, and it is interesting to note that it is evidently of a very late date.

The orangery and walled orchard and vegetable gardens extend for some distance below this final terrace, but are separated from it by a high wall. In the centre of this wall, at the bottom of the stairs that link the succession of terraces, is a delightful little garden room,

guarded by the polychrome wooden figure of a watchman or huntsman (pl. 142). This also contains niches with automatons. These include a Harlequin and a Turk, who play musical instruments, and a miniature scene of a forge, and are the most complete examples of their kind to have survived among the hundreds that once peopled the gardens of Italy.

The whole of the Giardino Buonaccorsi constitutes an almost incredible survival from another age; a grotto near the house is peopled with Baroque figures of friars in attitudes of ecstasy, but even here the mischievous humour of the period is represented by a devil who suddenly emerges from a concealed niche. Much of the original planting has also survived; even on this exposed site the terrace walls are still covered with the superb espaliers of lemon trees, which were once the pride and scented joy of every Italian garden. In the cold winters of the Marche all these have to be carefully covered for months on end, involving, like the upkeep of the whole garden, infinite labour and pains. This, of course, is why garden art in general, and survivals like the Giardino Buonaccorsi in particular, are so rare and precious, for their beauty is much more ephemeral than that of any other kind and a generation of neglect can ruin all that has gone before. Most historic Italian gardens have survived largely owing to the fact that they are primarily architectural, for it is a sad fact that Italy which once led the world in gardens is no longer a country of garden lovers. But even an Italian garden also depends greatly for its effect upon its planting; when this has gone – as it has in so many cases – the whole atmosphere is changed; the scent, the colour and even the form is altered. For this reason garden history and garden lovers generally owe a great debt to Contessa Giuseppina Buonaccorsi who has preserved what is in fact the rarest of national treasures – a classical Italian garden of the eighteenth century in all its fascinating detail.

141 GIARDINO BUONACCORSI
The second terrace of the Giardino Buonaccorsi, Potenza Picena; except for the fact that the statues of the Roman emperors on the terrace are no longer framed by topiary niches, this is identical with the bird's-eye view (plate 138).

142 GIARDINO BUONACCORSI
The guardian or huntsman, a polychrome wooden figure in the grotto of the Giardino Buonaccorsi—his gun was stolen during the war. In the niches behind are the figures of Harlequin, a Turk, and a scene in a forge, all of which move and some play musical instruments, like the automatons in the Hellenistic gardens of Alexandria, copied by Italian Renaissance garden architects and described by Montaigne and Evelyn.

As in the Villa Mosca, Centofinestre and Montegallo, Giardino Buonaccorsi also has an extensive *bosco*, lying at some distance from the house and firmly separated from the formal garden by a high wall. This can be seen in the distance in the eighteenth-century view, behind the *berceau* and the statue of Flora, also in the background of the photographs of the garden today, where its growth now hides the distant view of the sea. This *bosco* was in all probability originally a *barco*, as in the eighteenth-century picture it already covered a good deal of the hill. Some time during the last century its layout must have been altered, as it is now a wooded landscape garden with an artificial lake and small knoll, from the top of which there is a charming view over the valley to the sea. Although the result is attractive and well suited to the site, one cannot help thanking providence — and the conservative taste of his patron — that the work of the local Capability Brown was limited to this portion of the garden, thus providing a pleasant postscript to the history of garden design in the Marche, without destroying its preceding chapters.

Although in general their sites and basic design are quite different from those of the Marche, the gardens of the Veneto share the same conservative preference for a well-established local style, though they have a longer and more complicated history. Petrarch, as we have seen, was the pioneer of gardens and country life, in the humanistic sense, in the area that subsequently belonged to the Most Serene Republic and later came to be known as the Veneto. When he built his little house at Arquà in 1371, the Euganean Hill district belonged to Padua, but within the first few years of the following century Padua was taken by Venice, whose hegemony then spread over the fertile valley of the Po to include such flourishing cities as Vicenza and Verona, reaching as far afield as Cremona by the end of the century. The political result of the Venetian conquests was to produce a settled government under the aegis of a great world Power, that brought peace and prosperity in its train and leisure, which is the friend of all the arts, particularly that of gardens.

In these favourable conditions it is not surprising to find that the humanist movement soon spread to the Veneto, and by 1460 nobles and well-to-do young men like Bartolomeo Pagello began to build villas in the smiling green countryside round Vicenza. Academies were founded on the model of the famous Platonic one of Florence, and their meetings were held in the members' gardens – among which Gian Giorgio Trissino's Cricoli was later to become one of the most famous. In 1490 the great Venetian diarist, Marin Sanudo, made a journey through the Veneto, and everywhere he noticed the old castles falling into ruin and the fine new villas with beautiful gardens that were replacing them. This happy state of things was interrupted by the outbreak of the War of the League of Cambrai, in 1509, when the whole of the Veneto was sacked. But as time passed life returned to the villas and in 1537 we find Trissino writing to thank Isabella d'Este, wife of Francesco Gonzaga of Mantua, for the loan of her gardener who had supervised the trimming of the box at Cricoli, 'and many other things the garden sadly needs'.

By the middle of the sixteenth century, villa building had become a passion with the Venetian patricians. Trissino's protégé, Andrea Palladio, was called in to design many for the greatest families; they were to be the prototypes of literally thousands that rose all over the Veneto in the next two hundred and fifty years. The simple country villas of the early-sixteenth-century humanists were replaced by grander and ever grander ones – the increasing decadence of the Republic seemed to act as a spur to the extravagance of the Venetian patricians, who spent their summer months in the elegant *passatempi in villa* that still live for us in the pictures of the school of Veronese, Guardi and the Tiepolos. The setting of many of these diversions were the gardens that by the end of the sixteenth century stretched almost from end to end of the Brenta canal, and fringed the famous *terraglio* leading to Treviso.

The mention of both of these famous places of *villeggiatura* serves as a reminder of the fact that the majority of Venetian villas were built on level sites that were not conducive to the evolution of gardens in the Tuscan, far less the Roman or even *marchigiani* style, whose common characteristic is the employment of terraces. As Luigi Dami pointed out, although Scamozzi – who has more to say about gardens than any other Venetian treatise writer – cites all the classic examples of outstanding Renaissance gardens, such as Villa Madama, Villa di Papa Giulio and Villa d'Este at Tivoli, when he actually gets down to the brass tacks of advising how to lay out a garden, a lawn, a paved court and a few parterres is about all that results. In France a similar type of site led to the evolution of a distinctive national style originating in the principles of classical Italian garden design.

Even where gardens were laid out on hillsides, and there were many of them, particularly in the later period in the Monti Euganei and Berici as well as the Alpine foothills, the ground was never exploited to provide the magnificently theatrical effect of terraces adorned with wall fountains and linked by stairs and ramps, as a similar site would have been used in Rome or any garden deriving from the Roman school.

The Venetian villas originally came into being as a result of the changing currents of world trade during the fifteenth and sixteenth centuries, when the discovery of America and the route to the East round the Cape of Good Hope had broken the Venetian near-monopoly of the Oriental trade. This turned a republic of merchant princes into a city of landowners – Marin Sanudo in his journey round the Veneto in 1490 also noted how many of the great Venetian families already owned land there. Shrewd businessmen, as they then were, the Venetian patricians realized the importance of overseeing the administration of their estates during the summer and autumn months, and originally their villas were built for this purpose, as well as to escape from the heart of the city; these practical considerations coincided with the humanist influence that envisaged a villa as a suitable setting for a cultured man of letters. As good farming land in the Veneto, like everywhere else, is usually flat, the early villas were mostly built on level sites.

The War of the League of Cambrai put an end to Venetian aspirations to hegemony over Italy and its end coincided with the beginning of Venetian decadence. Her patricians still possessed vast wealth, but the living force that had placed the city in the forefront of commerce and art was waning, and in such circumstances any society tends to become conservative. Thus, although the villas created by Palladio and his followers are as beautiful as any in Italy, their siting and the conservative psychology of their owners resulted in the gardens being retrograde in style and in fact not far removed from those of the Middle Ages.

The very large majority of gardens – from the sixteenth to the end of the eighteenth century – consisted of a flat or slightly sloping rectangular walled enclosure laid out in front of the house. The main feature was usually the central road or vista, leading from the gate to the portico of the house, which was often prolonged on the far side of the public road to enhance the effect of the vista when looked at from the house. The walled garden was laid out with parterres of increasingly elaborate design and a few fountains of the old cup or vase shape. *Berceaux* and, later, pleached alleys were almost always included in the layout, as they provided a shady walk in the damp heat of Venetian summers.

This aspect of Venetian gardens emerges clearly in contemporary documents and art; religious paintings often portray garden scenes and those painted in the Veneto in the sixteenth century show the simplest of enclosed gardens (pls. 143, 144). The love of gardens was evidently widespread among the Venetians and their letters provide plenty of evidence of their enthusiasm, which in this respect closely paralleled that of contemporary English country life. Titian, Navagero, Cardinal Bembo, Sansovino, Sanmichele and the members of the Aldine Academy met and entertained each other in their gardens; and what is far more remarkable, when compared with Italy today where no 'intellectual' would dream of wielding a spade, is that they actually worked in them. Titian's garden was on the lagoon behind the Church of Santi Giovanni and Paolo. Here he invited his friends to supper, and they lingered until midnight, talking and watching the boats on the lagoon and listening to music.

Navagero, who was a great scholar and public servant and frequently served the Republic as Ambassador, was also an ardent gardener, planting the apple trees in his Murano garden himself, and making use of his opportunities as Ambassador to collect new flowers and trees for his beloved garden. While on a mission to Spain in 1526, he wrote to his friend Ramusio saying: 'I care more for my gardens at Murano and the grove there than for anything else in the world.' He asked Ramusio to keep an eye on Frate Francesco who was in charge of the garden in his absence, adding: 'tell the friar that new trees must be planted in the grove at Murano, and let him take care to see that they are planted in formal rows and some distance one from the other and, above all, let him put plenty of roses between the grove and the boundary wall, and see that they are trained to grow on a trellis, after the fashion which I admire in Spain'.

Navagero went on to describe the interesting new plants that were arriving in Spain from overseas, the 'ladano' or *Cistus ladaniferus* with its white blossoms, 'caronba' trees and a curious root called 'batate, lately brought from the Indies and tasting like chestnuts'; also a new and delicious fruit that seems to have been a banana, and a flower like a 'bird of paradise' that might have been strelitzia. Some of the 'caronba' trees were dispatched to the garden at Murano and, according to Bembo, Navagero always returned from his voyages laden with seeds and plants. But for all this collection of exotics, it is evident that the garden itself was still of the old walled medieval type with roses growing over trellises, even if the trees were planted in imitation of the classical authors, in what Sir Thomas Browne called 'the quinquncal lozenge'.

Bembo, who had begun his meteoric career at the Court of Urbino with forty ducats in his pocket, but who rose to become one of the most famous scholars of his day and the intimate friend and counsellor of popes and princes, had two ruling passions – his love of letters and the joys of country life. In pursuance of these tastes, whose indulgence required, and still requires, a good deal of money, Bembo frequented courts and cultivated the great, from whose patronage he gained the wherewithal to retire in peace to the country estate that was his chief joy. This was at Santa Maria di Non on the Brenta, a few miles from the Padua – Citadella road, though no trace of the house and garden exists today. During the ten years between 1517 and 1527, Bembo lived in his villa from early spring until All Saints' day, spending the winters in Padua. Evidently his garden was also of the simple walled type with pergolas, flowers, vegetables and fruit trees all growing together. In a letter to Flavio Crisolino he writes: 'Your ivy has already covered a large pavilion at the other end of the garden, and I have made another pergola with ivy and larch poles . . . which in two or three years should be very beautiful.' Bembo's description of life in his villa reads rather like Pliny's, but even more like life in an English country village. He and his friends used to send each other presents of their garden produce, no doubt in friendly competition to see whose was best. A member of the famous Da' Porto family would send him a basket of his own strawberries and asparagus and once a young kid and a retriever. Countess Landi sent cheeses, salted tongues and lemons from her estate on Lake Garda, while from other friends he received preserved citrons, a book, a young tree and a jar of olives. In return Bembo would send poems accompanied by gifts of strawberries and vegetables from his garden, that he grew and picked himself, even pressing visiting Papal emissaries into service to help him.

Like so many of his Venetian contemporaries Bembo reveals his love of country life plainly in his letters and writings; here there is none of the artificial attitude that later

143 PAINTING BY L. TOEPUT
'Noli me Tangere', *school of Pozzoserrato (L. Toeput), showing simple geometrical sixteenth-century Venetian parterres.* Photo by kind permission of the Pinacoteca of Treviso.

144 PAINTING BY BENEDETTO
CALIARI
*Detail from 'Susanna and the Elders' by
Benedetto Caliari, showing a typical
Northern Italian garden of the sixteenth
century with its simple parterres and fountain.*
Photo by kind permission of the
Pinacoteca of Treviso.

transformed the Venetian villas into pleasure palaces whose inhabitants made the fashion-able migration from the town to the country at appropriate seasons. He writes: 'I hear nothing but the voice of nightingales warbling from every bush in joyous rivalry. I read, I write; when I choose I walk or ride. I spend much of my time in the grove at the end of a pleasant and fruitful garden, where I gather vegetables for the first course of our evening meal, and sometimes pick a basket of strawberries, which are not only delicious to the taste, but perfume the whole breakfast table with their fragrance. . . . The garden and house and the whole place are full of roses. . . . I spend the evenings, when it is more pleasant to be on water than land, in a small boat.'

We are also indebted to Cardinal Bembo for the description of a hill garden in the Veneto at the beginning of the sixteenth century. This was the garden of Asolo Castle where Queen Caterina Cornaro took up residence after she had relinquished her late husband's Kingdom of Cyprus to the Venetian Republic. Though these gardens were celebrated throughout the province, their description reads more like that of Boccaccio's *Decameron* than of a garden of a hundred and fifty years later. According to Bembo 'the garden was of rare and marvellous beauty. A wide and shady pergola of vines ran down the centre and the walls on either side were concealed by thick hedges of box and juniper; while bays arched overhead and afforded a most pleasant shade, and were so carefully cut that not a single leaf was out of place. None of the walls could be seen, only at the end of the pergola, above the garden gate, two windows of dazzling white marble let in a view of distant plains.' There was 'a little meadow at the end of the garden. Here the grass was as fine a colour as an emerald and all manner of bright flowers sprang in the fresh green sward, and just beyond was a shady grove of bays not clipped or trained like the others but allowed to wander at will. In the midst was a beautiful fountain . . . from which rills flowed all over the garden.'

This Asolo garden might, and probably did, serve as a model for countless others, as all the writers of the period, Alvise Cornaro, Bartolomeo Pagello and the rest, describe meetings of the academies and with their friends in just such settings. Here beautiful ladies sat on carpets, placed in the shade of bay trees, and sang songs to the lute or exchanged 'literary' conversations with humanist gentlemen, diversions that also seem to have provided an excellent opportunity for a good deal of flirtation. But with these humanist gardens of the Veneto it is the same story as those of the more practical *potager* type in the Siena area of the same period; lacking an architectural setting, their materials were just as perishable, and their groves, pergolas and lawns have long since disappeared.

Giardino dei Giusti - Verona

There is only one garden in the Veneto area whose origins date from this time, and probably a good deal earlier, that is still today one of the show gardens of Italy – as it has been for at least the last three and a half centuries. This is the Giardino dei Giusti at Verona. Considering that it is one of the most famous gardens in the country – a sight visited by every foreign traveller of note since Tom Coryat in 1608 – it is extraordinary how little is known about its origins and early layout. The Giusti, who were, significantly, of Tuscan origin, already enjoyed the full rights of citizenship in Verona in 1408, and, again significantly for garden history, their full name is Giusti del Giardino – the Giusti of the Garden. From this it appears likely that their garden was a very early one, possibly the first in the city, and was of so distinguished and unusual a type as to merit differentiation from the ordinary old-fashioned *orto* or vegetable garden. This hypothesis is borne out by the site – the Giusti palace backs on to the steeply rising hill of San Pietro, which is admirably adapted to a terraced pleasure garden in the style of Villa Medici at Fiesole.

Probably no other garden in Italy was so ill-adapted to the landscape style, but 'landscaped' the Giusti garden was in the last century; and with such zeal that, although an Italian-style garden has now been laid out on the level ground behind the house, it is exceedingly difficult to guess what the original layout was like. One of the most interesting survivals in the garden is a little pavilion, reconstructed probably in the last century, with fragments of what may well have been a portico or garden house of the fifteenth century, for its columns bear a strong resemblance to those found in the early villas of the neighbouring Valpolicella (pl. 145). It stands at the end of one of the terraces, that were formerly almost as famous a feature of the garden as the great avenue of cypresses that leads up to them (pl. XLII).

The earliest and most detailed description of the Giardino dei Giusti comes in Thomas Coryat's *Crudities* published in 1611, and from his enthusiasm it is evident how lovely these gardens must have been. After mentioning 'Count Augustus Justus's' picture gallery, he writes: 'Also the Italian showed me his garden, which is a second paradise, and a passing delectable place of solace, beautified with many curious knots, fruits of divers sorts and two rowes of lofty cypresse trees, three and thirty in ranke. Besides his walks at the toppe of the garden a little under St Peter's castle, are as pleasant as the heart of man could wish – being decked with excellent fruits, as figges, oranges, apricockes and with cypresse trees. In one of these walks is a delicate little refectory. In whereof there is a curious artificiale rocke, adorned with many fine devices as scallop shels, and a great variety of other prety shels of fishes brought from Cyprus, and mosse groweth upon the same as if it were a naturall rocke. This place is certainly contrived with as admirable curiosity as ever I saw, and moysened with delicate springs and fountains conveighed into the same by leaden pipes. I have seen in England one place something like this, even in one of the gardens of that most noble knight Sir Francis Carew of Middlesex; who hath one most excellent rocke there framed all by arte and beautiful with many elegant conceits, notwithstanding it is somewhat inferiour unto this.'

Judging from Coryat's description the Giardino dei Giusti was quite unlike any other garden of the Veneto but, with its terraces, fountains, and its 'artificiale rocke', it resembled

145 GIARDINO DEI GIUSTI
A pavilion in the Giardino dei Giusti at Verona. Apart from literary references little is known about the original layout of this famous garden, which has attracted visitors from all over the world since the seventeenth century. Landscaping completely changed its character in the nineteenth century, but a formal Italian garden has since been laid out near the house. The house and garden still belong to the Giusti family.

a Tuscan garden – a fact which would easily be explained by the family's origins. The shell decoration of the rock also helps to date the garden layout, as Venice lost Cyprus to the Turks in 1570; so this elaborate composition must certainly have been made before then. Nor need the transport of these shells so far, simply for garden decoration, occasion any great surprise; when the gardens of Caprarola were restored a few years ago, certain of the stones for the pebble mosaics had to be brought from a remote river in Piedmont, no other place in Italy being found to produce stones of a similar distinctive shape and colour. Coryat does not mention the great masks carved out of the natural rock of the hillside below the terraces, and one might be apt to date them to a subsequent period, were it not for the fact that very similar masks appear as fireplaces in the mid-sixteenth-century Villa Della Torre in the Valpolicella and in the Palazzo Thiene at Vicenza.

John Evelyn, Joseph Addison, Président de Brosses and Goethe all went to see the Giusti garden. Evelyn only commented upon the cypresses, describing the one near the gate as 'the goodliest cypresse I fancy in Europe'. Addison, whose addiction to landscape precluded a liking for formal gardens, simply says: 'I saw the terrace garden at Verona that

travellers usually mention.' To Président de Brosses, who was there in 1739, we are indebted for the information that the garden still preserved its original character, though there appear to have been a few additions. His description is very like Coryat's: 'the Giusti gardens gave me more pleasure; for they are full of rockeries and grottoes and endless terraces covered with little circular temples'; it is significant that these last were not mentioned by Coryat. After describing the cypresses, he continues: 'I got lost in a maze, and I was an hour wandering in the blazing sun, and would have still been there, had I not been taken out by one of the people of the place.'

Unfortunately Goethe gives no description of the garden except to say that it was well situated and had monstrous cypresses. He picked some of their twigs and made himself a posy with sprays of caper flowers, and was much amused to observe the astonished glances of the Veronese as he walked through the town afterwards with his little bunch of flowers. Goethe's omission of any factual description of the garden is a sad loss, as he was in Verona in September 1786 and was probably one of the last foreign travellers of note to see it in its original state. The mere fact that there were so many capers seems to indicate that the terrace walls on which they probably grew were still free of the mass of trees and bushes that now obscures their whole outline. It is sad that no plan of the original layout of the garden has ever come to light, as fountains and statues that evidently formed part of it still exist in the lower garden, and it might well be possible to restore this historic and unique garden of the Veneto to some semblance of its former being.

XLII GIARDINO DEI GIUSTI

Villa Brenzone - San Vigilio

Not far from Verona, on one of the most beautiful promontories of the lovely Lake Garda, at San Vigilio, there stands a charming villa and garden whose design is traditionally given to the great Veronese architect Michele Sanmicheli. Certainly the house was built about the middle of the sixteenth century for the well-known philosopher and lawyer Agostino Brenzone, who, appropriately enough for the owner of such a place, wrote a treatise on the joys of solitary life. Much of the garden is now laid out in lawns, but the wonderful avenue of cypresses that leads to the house through ancient olive groves and some other features of the old garden still survive. These include a fine pergola on a terrace overlooking the lake, and a charming little artificial mount, encircled by magnificent cypresses and curious little niches containing busts of Roman emperors (pl. 146). These might have provided the inspiration for Kent's British worthies at Stowe, and he was certainly in the Veneto in 1714. But it should be noted that this use of busts was common in Italy; the picture of the garden banquet in the Doria Gallery shows something of the same type, and the Roman emperors in Giardino Buonaccorsi were also originally framed in green niches.

The garden of Villa Brenzone was famous in the sixteenth century when its generous owner allowed the public to visit it. One of his contemporaries wrote of it that 'whoever in this new golden age, the sixteenth century, came from beyond Bythnia to see it, would be satisfied, as Catullus said of his Sirmione'. But for all that the villa can never have been a grand and showy place, and like Catullus' villa at Sirmione, not the ruined palace that is called after him, its fame probably rested more upon the exquisite beauty of the site and the literary reputation of its owner. Some clue to Brenzone's endearing character is afforded by an inscription that he set up in his garden inviting visitors to 'honour in this sanctuary the best and highest God, to drink the cup that will quench your thirst', and to 'fill your hands with boughs, flowers and fruit' before returning to 'the town and duty'.

146 VILLA BRENZONE
Busts of Roman emperors on the artificial 'mount' in the sixteenth-century garden of the Villa Brenzone at San Vigilio on Lake Garda. The villa belongs to Count Guarienti di Brenzone.

255

Orto Botanico - Padua

In Padua there still exists a garden that has changed even less since the sixteenth century. This is the famous Orto Botanico, made in 1545, and the earliest of its kind; this was attached to the school of botany at the University, where the first chair of that science had been created shortly before. The Orto Botanico is laid out as a circular walled enclosure, whose four gates are surmounted by exotic wrought-iron plants in urns (pl. 147). This is just the same as it was in the sixteenth century, so are the main divisions of the garden, though the actual layout of the beds has been altered somewhat during the centuries. The change is only one of detail not of general conception, as can be seen by comparing a plan in the Uffizi Collection with an early-nineteenth-century print. The print shows the garden exactly as it is today, with its geometrical stone-edged plots charmingly grouped round fountains (pls. XLIII, XLIV).

Fortunately the Orto Botanico has always been well kept, so much so that even some of the sixteenth-century plants still survive. The oldest of them all are the chaste tree or *Vitex agnus castus*, which was planted in 1550, and the famous palm, *Chamaerops humilis arborescens*, of 1585. It is said that the peculiar structure of this tree inspired Goethe in his studies of the morphology of plants, studies that resulted in his *Versuch, die Metamorphose der Pflanzen zu erklären*, published in 1790 after his Italian journey. John Evelyn was also very much interested in the garden, and noted in his diary: 'The next morning I saw the garden of simples, rarely furnished with plants, and gave order to the gardener to make me a collection of them for an *hortus hyemalis*, by kind permission of Cavalier Dr Veslingius, then Prefect and Botanic Professor as well as of Anatomy.'

147 ORTO BOTANICO
An early-nineteenth-century engraving of the Orto Botanico at Padua showing it as it still looks today. From the Uffizi. Photo by kind permission of the Soprintendenza alle Gallerie of Florence.

XLIII, XLIV ORTO BOTANICO - PADUA

Villa Barbaro · Maser

The most splendid sixteenth-century garden in the Veneto was undoubtedly the one that Andrea Palladio designed at Maser for his friends and patrons the 'Monsignor Reverendissimo Eletto di Aquileja, and the Magnifico Signor Marc' Antonio, fratelli Barbari', as he described them in his *Quattro Libri di Architettura*. Its magnificent Veronese frescoes and fine state of preservation single this Palladian villa out from many of its less fortunate sisters, but it is also remarkable for the fact that in his *Quattro Libri* its author described the garden in greater detail than that of any of his other villas. There was

148 VILLA BARBARO
The giardino segreto of the Villa Barbaro at Maser, designed by Palladio and probably dating from about 1560. In it the classical influence of Palladio's Roman journeys is plainly evident. The villa belongs to Countess Luling.

149 PAINTING FROM THE SCHOOL OF VERONESE

A picture of the school of Veronese from the Accademia Carrara, one of the earliest representing the passatempi in villa *that were so characteristic of Venetian country life. The waterside loggia and simple garden layout are typical of this type of villa. Photo Anderson.*

probably a very good reason for this, as Daniele Barbaro was a keen botanist who is said to have had a hand in the founding of the Orto Botanico at Padua.

Palladio's description of the garden at Maser reads as follows: 'The first floor is at ground level behind, where a fountain with an infinity of *stucchi* and painted ornaments is cut into the neighbouring hill. The fountain makes a little lake, that serves as a fish pond, and from here the water runs into the kitchen, then irrigates the gardens which are to the right and left of the road which rises slowly to the house. It makes two fish ponds with their drinking troughs above the public road, and from there it goes to water the orchard, that is very large and full of excellent fruit and many nut trees.' The Villa Barbaro belongs to Palladio's great 'middle period' in which his designs show most clearly the influence of his journey to Rome with Gian Giorgio Trissino in 1541, though the house was probably built some time afterwards – between 1560 and 1568.

It is noticeable, however, that both in Veronese's frescoes, which include pictures of Roman ruins and landscapes in the style of *topia*, and in the design of the *giardino segreto* behind the house, the Roman influence is the strongest, perhaps, of any Palladian villa. This is generally attributed to the fact that Daniele Barbaro was a most distinguished humanist, who had not only translated the works of Vitruvius and written a commentary on them, but was also interested in decoration in the classical style.

Whatever the reason, the *giardino segreto* at Maser is the most Roman, both in the classical and Renaissance sense, of any garden in the Veneto (pl. 148). In a small space – it is entirely enclosed by the house and hillside – it contrives to give an extraordinary feeling of grandeur, unequalled and not even approached by other gardens in the area. The whole effect is achieved by the semicircular fountain with its 'infinity of *stucchi*', whose richness is offset by the dark green of the wooded hillside and the clear waters of the pool that lies in front. Looking at this delightful composition, one is immediately reminded of the projected theatre of the Villa Madama and the hemisphere behind the Villa Aldobrandini at Frascati, so typically Roman is the scene.

The *giardino segreto* is the only part of Palladio's garden layout to have survived, though it is not precisely the same as it was in his day. His plan in the *Quattro Libri* does not give any indication as to the shape of the original fountain pool – his plans rarely do – but old photographs of the garden show a small round one, which it must be admitted was not nearly as effective as the existing large pool. It is likely from Palladio's description of the 'gardens which are to the right and left of the road which rises slowly to the house' that these were laid out in typically Venetian style, with a central vista and simple arbours and parterres like those shown in Pozzoserrato's paintings and frescoes of the Veronese school which decorate many villas of the area.

Another excellent portrayal of a riverside garden of this type appears in a picture of the school of Veronese in the Accademia of Carrara (pl. 149). For all the monumental style of the loggia or watergate – which was a common characteristic of these waterside villas – the garden itself is extremely simple, and it is noticeable that it also contains the same little rustic trellises surrounding the plots as were found in Roman gardens of the period. The picture is particularly interesting as being one of the earliest showing the famous '*passatempi in villa*'. The simplicity of the scene, with the table laid in the shade of the loggia, and the ladies peacefully fishing, contrasts strongly with the elaborate entertainments of later periods, such as those given in the gardens of the Villa Contarini on the Brenta where the fish ponds were used for miniature naval battles in imitation of the ancient Roman ones and plays and opera were constantly performed in the two garden theatres.

Villa Cuzzano - Verona

One of the very rare examples of the survival of a parterre garden in the Veneto is to be found at Cuzzano near Verona. Here the villa that was built for the Allegri family in the seventeenth century still preserves its original garden layout, though this probably dates from the end of that period. The plan of the garden is typically Venetian and strongly reminiscent of Maser; originally a straight road led from the gate on the main road up to the terrace before the house, providing a fine vista from both ends. Although this perspective still exists, unfortunately the drive now turns to the right, leading to a modern lodge and entrance. The

150 VILLA CUZZANO
The garden of Villa Cuzzano at Grezzano near Verona, built for the Allegri family in the seventeenth century. The garden layout with its superb parterre is a rare survival of its type. The villa now belongs to the Arvedi family.

main feature of the garden is a superb parterre laid out on the terrace before the house, where the fine clipped yews and cypresses frame a charming view at ground-level and provide a fascinating pattern when seen from the first floor of the house (pls. 150, XL).

The long lines of the Cuzzano terrace, which runs practically the full length of the house, blend admirably with the wonderful view over the Valpatena, whose landscape is dominated by the parallel lines of its famous vineyards. It is interesting to note that if the Veneto was highly conservative in its general conception of garden layout, here at Cuzzano at least the parterre design is strikingly advanced, its curving lines forming a continuous pattern that extends over the whole terrace. Thus it is much more closely related to French *broderies* than to Roman parterres, that were still divided up into separate rectangular compartments in the seventeenth-century gardens like Villa Pamphilj and Villa Muti. There is no doubt that the influence of French garden design made itself felt much earlier in Northern Italy and, geographical reasons apart, this is easily understandable, as Northern Italian garden sites resembled French ones rather than those of mountainous areas of Central Italy. The Cuzzano garden also contains some small architectural features – a charming little grotto in the midst of the double stairs leading to what was probably formerly a flower garden. There is also an extensive aviary and large dove-cots, that for centuries formed part of any Venetian villa layout.

Villa Donà dalle Rose - Valsanzibio

In a green valley of the Euganean Hills at Valsanzibio, not far removed from Petrarch's Arquà, is one of the great gardens of the Veneto. Laid out in 1669 for Procurator Antonio Barberigo, this garden is now usually called after its subsequent owners, another famous Venetian family, the Donà dalle Rose. For the Veneto today this garden is really remarkable, both for its extent and its elaborate layout. It is, with the exception of a few architectural features such as fish ponds, fountains and a rabbit island, now an entirely green garden, whose deciduous trees and evergreens mingle to provide an enchanting blend of formal and a freer type of planting. But in an early bird's-eye view, that used to hang in the Museo Civico of Padua, Valsanzibio looked very much more like other Veneto gardens represented in this type of painting. This is not surprising as, in spite of its large extent and hilly surroundings, it is still very definitely a Venetian type of garden, its whole design depending upon its vistas and the provision of shady walks. Although the former either lead, or direct the eye, up to the surrounding hills, no attempt has been made to turn these into terraces, as would have been the case in Tuscan or Roman Renaissance gardens; nor do these vistas ultimately merge with the landscape in the Baroque style. The garden itself remains a separate entity on the floor of the valley, no longer enclosed by walls it is true, but by the pleached alleys that provide an almost unbroken shady walk, and probably originally a continuous hedge as well.

Unfortunately the evolution of Valsanzibio, and other Venetian gardens, is not documented by prints and drawings of various periods like the great Roman ones; but natural growth and a little discreet landscaping have probably changed its appearance as much as that of the Villa d'Este at Tivoli for instance. Today we rightly regard the garden of Valsanzibio as a unique and lovely creation because it has survived, and, given the easily destructible character of the trees and shrubs of which it is made up, this is a miracle; but it is permissible to wonder if, had so many other large Venetian gardens of the period not fallen victim to the landscaper or sheer neglect they might not also today be almost as charming, and Valsanzibio not nearly such an isolated phenomenon as it now appears.

What probably saved the gardens of Valsanzibio is their remarkable site, and their perfect planning in relation to it (pl. 151). The house stands sideways in an amphitheatre of hills and stretching before and behind it, linking it firmly to the surrounding landscape, is the characteristic Veneto vista, carried to the summit of each wing of the hilly amphitheatre. In the days when the villa was built, the main means of transport in the area was the same as it had been in Petrarch's time, by boat through the numerous waterways that led across the plain to Battaglia and Padua. An imposing watergate was therefore just as much a necessity for the reception of guests at Valsanzibio as for any villa on the Brenta. This the architect provided, and linked it up with the secondary axis of the garden, that is formed by a superb series of fish ponds on slightly different levels. These lead the eye of the newly-arrived guest straight up from the entrance, over a glittering series of pools, cascades and fountains into the natural amphitheatre of the green hills beyond (pls. XLV, XLVI).

The rest of the garden was designed as a setting for these two wonderful vistas, providing, of course, the type of amenities and amusements which one would expect to find in a fine villa of the period – the shady walks, the fountains, the scented lemon trees in pots, the maze, and the *giochi d'acqua* concealed in the pebble mosaics of the terrace in front of the house, and so forth (pl. 152). There is one other amusing feature that has survived at Valsanzibio, though also for practical purposes it was once quite common in Italian as well as classical gardens; this is the rabbit island. Although it is practically unaltered today, Rossetti's charming print of this island, published together with others of the fountains in *Le Fabbriche e Giardini della Casa Barbarego* in Verona in 1702, gives a livelier picture of it than any photograph, as the rabbits who still live there resolutely refused to come out and pose for the photographer as they apparently obligingly did for the artist.

The last war served as a terrible reminder of many things, and among them the ephemeral character of gardens such as this. Many of the trees framing the vista, from where the general view of the garden was photographed, were cut down, and years of neglect nearly destroyed the maze. Both have been replanted, and the garden is again a peaceful oasis of shade, surrounding the rose-coloured villa that is so perfectly set among the green Euganean Hills. Here, as in the great Roman gardens, 'nature has in part resumed her rights', producing 'the most picturesque scenes' in the midst of which the gaiety and delicacy of seventeenth-century Venetian taste still live in such charming compositions as the fountain by the watergate, where four stone *putti* sit dangling their feet in the water while waiting to welcome the guests' arrival.

Corroborative evidence of changes having occurred in the evolution of the gardens of Valsanzibio comes in a famous Venetian gardening book of the early eighteenth century. This is Paolo Bartolomeo Clarici's *Istoria e Cultura delle Piante* published in Venice in 1726, after his death. Clarici says that Valsanzibio was famous for the cultivation of rare plants and for floriculture generally, its great speciality being the cultivation of double stocks which 'among the many rarities of this delightful garden grow to an extraordinary size and do not suffer from the cold, although they are left in the ground throughout the winter'. As Clarici's book is almost entirely devoted to floriculture, it is unlikely that the rarities he refers to were exotic trees, to whose growth the cold of Venetian winters is in any case not favourable, but it is probable that a large area near the house was laid out as a flower garden. Some flower-beds still exist on either side of the open space in front of the house but, judging from the regular layout of the paths round the grass plots that intervene between this area and the green garden proper, it seems likely that the whole of this sunny and sheltered space was once occupied by flower parterres of considerable importance. This is borne out by the fact that Clarici's reference to the flower gardens of Valsanzibio is one of the very rare topographical ones in his whole book, and they must have been celebrated in his day.

Clarici, who was born in Ancona in 1664 and died in Padua in 1725, spent most of his life in the Veneto, where his literary and scientific tastes brought him the friendship of many members of the great Venetian families. Prominent among these was Gerardo

151, 152 VILLA DONÀ DALLE ROSE
The gardens of Villa Donà dalle Rose at Valsanzibio. One of the great gardens of the Veneto, it was laid out in 1669, and is remarkable for its extent and elaborate design. It is now an entirely green garden of deciduous trees and evergreens. The villa belongs to Signora Pizzoni Ardemanni.

Sagredo, Procurator of St Mark's, for whom he laid out a splendid garden in the Venetian style for the family villa at Marocco. The place is only a few miles from Venice, practically on the shore of the lagoon opposite Burano, but no single trace of the house or garden exists today, except the name of a country road – the Via Sagredo. If any further reminder were necessary of the perishable quality of Venetian gardens surely it is this; in Rome and even Tuscany some trace of a former garden site – a terrace or an overgrown grotto – may survive for centuries, but of this garden, which was evidently a show-place in the eighteenth century, absolutely nothing remains.

XLV, XLVI VILLA DONÀ DALLE ROSE

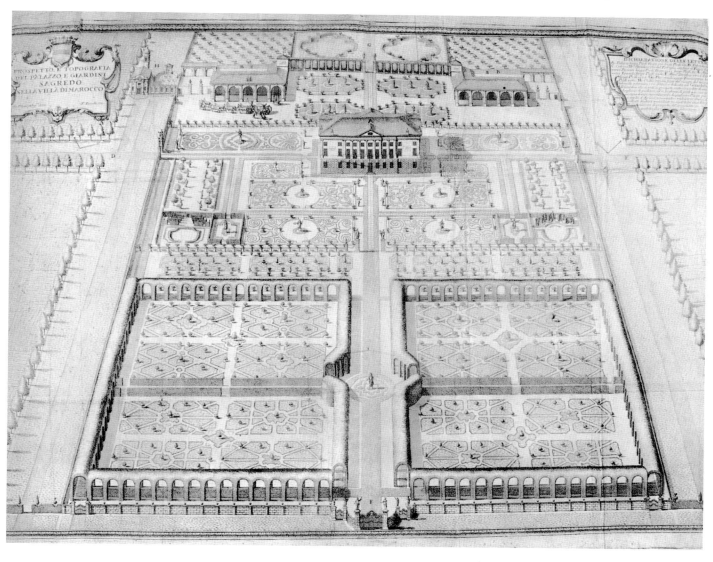

153 VILLA SAGREDO
The garden of the Villa Sagredo at Marocco near Treviso, used to illustrate a perfect Venetian garden design in P. B. Clarici's book on gardening, Istoria e Cultura delle Piante, *published posthumously in Venice in 1726. It will be noticed that even at this late date the garden conforms to the Venetian principle of a simple garden enclosure dominated by a central vista; the elaborate parterres were planted with flowers.*

Clarici used a print of a bird's-eye view of this Marocco garden in his book as an ideal example of layout (pl. 153). This is interesting for two reasons – even with all the complexities of eighteenth-century parterres, fountains, fish ponds and a green theatre, the garden still conforms to the basic Venetian layout of a rectangle dominated by a vista leading up to the house; also it was predominantly a flower garden. Although the parterre designs evidently reflect the latest French fashions, and this is not surprising as Clarici kept up a lively correspondence with gardeners outside Italy, in his choice of site and layout the author textually recommends the old Venetian principles of a gently sloping enclosure surrounded by a wall. In spite of the fact that his book appeared some time after Dezallier d'Argenville's *Théorie et pratique du Jardinage* (which John James translated into English in 1712), and his use of French parterre designs, Clarici sticks firmly to the old Venetian tradition of a formal garden, making no mention whatsoever of other current fashions such as *bosquets* and palisades, and his shady walks remain the old familiar pleached alleys.

What is particularly striking about Clarici's advice on the layout of parterres is that, although he agrees with the French principle that the most elaborate ones should be near the house, and strongly advocates the use of box in preference to brick or herb outlines, he makes absolutely no reference to the use of coloured earths for filling in the background. In direct contrast to d'Argenville and John James, who list the materials suitable for this purpose, Clarici gives detailed instructions for the planting of flowers in all his parterres, that he calls by the delightful name of *vanezze* or vanities. He writes: 'these vanities should be well measured and divided into beautiful designs, but it should be understood that the taller flowers should be planted in the furthest parts of the garden, so that they will not obscure the sight and enjoyment of the smaller ones, and these last should be placed in vanities whose design is in proportion to their stature, while the larger flowers should also be planted in [vanities] of proportionate size, but such as can be easily worked and irrigated'.

The garden of Marocco was very evidently laid out in conformance with these rules, even the sides of the pleached alleys being made 'opaque', as Clarici described their arches, so that the stroller could enjoy the sight of the flower-filled parterres uninterruptedly while he was making his promenade. From the rest of the book it is evident that floriculture was well advanced in the Veneto of the eighteenth century, as part of it is devoted to a practical gardener's calendar of what to do in the garden in each month of the year, while the other chapters are given over to detailed information about the history of the various flowers and their cultivation. This last part of the book is particularly valuable as a link between the early works of Mattioli, Aldino and Ferrari, and modern books on gardening for in the history of flowers he continually cites these authors, comparing their nomenclature with that of his own day, and from their various descriptions it is possible to identify many of the flowers that have been grown in Italian gardens through the centuries, also the date of the new importations. Thus it emerges that many of the exotics such as amaryllis, the red Cape tulip, and the ferraria or Cape starry iris were grown in Italian gardens well over a century before they were introduced into England.

Clarici's list of flowers and flowering plants is a long one and although, especially in the case of citrus trees, he is apt to list what were probably simply the products of grafting as different species, there is little doubt that Venetian gardens of his time were very far removed from the too prevalent conception of an Italian garden as a place from which flowers were practically banished. In support of this it is interesting to note that whereas in 1663 the famous French gardener Claude Mollet described only six kinds of roses, and another French book at the end of the century fourteen, Clarici lists no less than twenty-nine; though it is likely that here again he confused different colours with varieties; certainly as late as the eighteenth century, within a few years of the birth of Linnæus, he still tried to identify several of his roses with those of Pliny.

Villa Pisani - Stra

Many Veneto villas, especially those on the Brenta, stand right on a public road; traditionally the reason for this is ascribed to the fact that the ladies of the family got so bored by a life of rural seclusion that they insisted that the house should be built so that they could watch the carriages and boats going by, and at least they could know who was going to visit whom. As a result of this the gardens had to be laid out behind the house, and this inversion of the usual practice confronted architects with the problem of providing a suitable culmination to the central perspective or vista, that no self-respecting Venetian garden could be without. This they solved by the ingenious device of dressing up the stables and farm buildings – that were usually built on either side of the house – with a fine architectural façade, and placing them instead at the end of the inevitable vista. The best-known example of this type of layout occurs in the garden of the famous Villa Pisani at Stra, which was begun in 1735 by Girolamo Frigimelica for the Doge Alvise Pisani and completed by Francesco Preti. Here the vista, one of the most

XLVII   VILLA PISANI

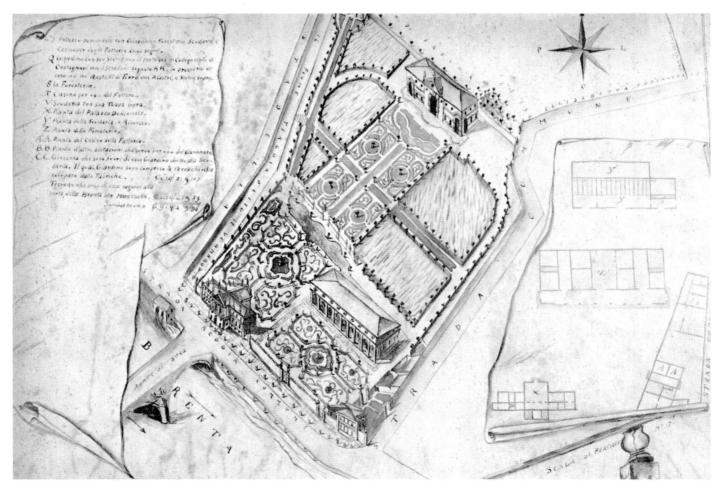

effective of its kind, takes the form of a long canal, in which the Palladian portico of the stables is reflected in a manner which recalls the famous Malcontenta (pl. 154). This villa was for a while one of the official residences of Eugène de Beauharnais, Napoleon's Viceroy in Italy, and it was probably in his time that the vast gardens were laid out as a park, for which for once their large area was really suited (pl. XLVII). However, the garden still contains some features that probably survived from an earlier layout, such as a maze, a garden pavilion, and some very fine wrought iron.

Villa Foscarini - Stra

A little farther up the canal, just opposite the Stra bridge, is the charming small Villa Foscarini, which was begun according to designs drawn up by Andrea Palladio but was only completed in the eighteenth century. In the house is still preserved an interesting plan of the whole layout, probably as it was at the end of the eighteenth century (pl. 155). Here again the main part of the garden had been laid out behind the house, and the central vista culminates in a decoratively designed stable building. Unfortunately nothing of this garden now survives, but in the plan it looks as if water was also introduced here, in a pool between the parterres immediately behind the house and the centre of the enclosed garden beyond. From the elaborate scroll-work in the parterres immediately behind the house and in front of the *foresteria*, or guest house, on the right, it is likely that the layout is of the second half of the eighteenth century, though Clarici's maxim of placing larger parterres farther from the house still holds good. The plan provides interesting documentary evidence of what many late-eighteenth-century Venetian gardens, including those of the Villa Pisani, probably looked like before they were landscaped during the next century.

Villa Rizzardi - Pojega

When so much has been swept away by changing fashions or neglect it is a relief to find that at least one Veneto garden of the eighteenth century has survived that is not only kept in perfect order but is one of the most fascinating of all Italy. This is the undeservedly little-known Villa Rizzardi at Pojega di Negrar in the Valpolicella, whose wonderful site, layout, condition and late date render it unique. It was designed by Luigi Trezza, some of whose plans fortunately still exist, notably that of the green theatre, which is signed and dated 1796. The garden was begun in 1783 and probably completed shortly after the theatre was laid out, so that it is certainly one of the latest to be designed in the Italian style, and it is indeed a worthy end to a great tradition.

A villa and garden had existed on the site in the seventeenth century but, judging from the closely-knit design, practically all that we see today must have been laid out by Trezza. The garden stretches along the side of a hill behind the house and is remarkable for the skill with which the changing levels are utilized in a variety of ways, as well as for the diverse settings provided for the wonderful views. Immediately beside the house a small piece of the hillside has been converted into an enchanting *giardino segreto*, which is directly connected to the first floor by a bridge, so that you can walk out of your bedroom to take the sun among its roses, arums and daturas. A little fountain trickles among the flowers, but the imposing waterfall in the central niche is an amusing piece of *trompe l'oeil*, as the cascade is really an enormous stalactite.

Although in general the design of the Villa Rizzardi garden is a complete departure from the normal Venetian style, with its individual interpretation of the use of changing levels that, in the Baroque manner, progress from the formal to the wild – represented here by an artificially planted *bosco* with a 'Roman ruin' – one of its main features is still a fine vista. This takes the form of a pleached alley of elms, stretching out from the small enclosed garden

154 VILLA PISANI
Gardens of the Villa Pisani at Stra, begun in 1735 for the Doge of Venice, Alvise Pisani. At one time the villa was the residence of Eugène de Beauharnais, Napoleon's Viceroy in Italy, and it was probably then that the vast gardens were largely converted to the landscape style, although retaining the superb central vista provided by a canal that reflects the fine façade of the farm buildings. The villa belongs to the State and is open to the public.

155 VILLA FOSCARINI
The gardens of the Villa Foscarini at Fossolovara near Stra on the Brenta as they were planted in the eighteenth century, from a plan in the possession of the present owners. The stables and farm buildings at the far end of the garden were provided with a fine architectural façade in order to provide a focus for the vista characteristic of Venetian gardens. The villa belongs to the Negrelli family.

156 VILLA RIZZARDI
The gardens of Villa Rizzardi at Pojega di Negrar in the Valpolicella. One of the most fascinating eighteenth-century gardens in Italy, which has survived in its original state, and is kept in perfect order. Designed by Luigi Trezza, it was begun in 1783. The villa belongs to Count Rizzardi.

157 VILLA RIZZARDI
The belvedere in the garden of the Villa Rizzardi at Pojega di Negrar.

behind the house to end in a leafy niche, where a statue stands backed by the tall spires of cypresses, thus providing a shady promenade at the lowest level of the garden. The next promenade is much less formal, consisting of an avenue of cypresses that leads across the open grassy hillside to where stone lions stand guard at the entrance to the theatre.

The third and highest promenade begins at some distance from the house; to reach it you first pass through an enchanting little circular lemon garden, whose green walls and terracotta pots are reflected in a central pond. Steps rise steeply from here to a statue framed by a cypress grove, affording a wonderful view over the vineyards of the Valpolicella (pl. 156). A path leads from the cypress shade into the 'wild' of the *bosco*, in whose depths lies concealed the charming little 'ruined' circular temple, designed as an *al fresco* dining-

room for hot days. The path leads on through the mysterious gloom of the *bosco*, where stone lions and other wild animals crouch half-concealed among the trees, recalling in this delightful eighteenth-century fantasy the game enclosures of ancient Roman villas and Pietro de Crescenzi's medieval wood for wild animals, that formed part of his garden designed for noblemen and kings.

Emerging from the wood at last one finds oneself at the top of a stately avenue of cypresses that links these three levels of the garden promenades at their far end. Here is one of the most beautiful belvederi imaginable, upon whose summit stand smiling stone *putti*, and before it stretches out a vast panorama of vine-clad hill and dale, framed in the dark spires of the cypresses (pl. 157). But the surprises of this enchanted garden are not finished yet; from the centre of the cypress avenue one enters the green theatre that, like those of ancient Greece, has an auditorium hollowed out of the side of the hill. This is the largest and finest of its kind in Italy; each tier of seats is edged with clipped box and, in imitation of the classical theatres, there is a grass-covered promenade at the top (pl. 158). This is enclosed by hedges, with statues framed in green niches on one side; on the other it is open to the wonderful view that serves as a backdrop to the stage.

The theatre plans are dated 1796, and it was certainly the last part of the garden to be laid out. One cannot help wondering if it was completed by the fatal 27th of October of the following year when, by the Treaty of Campoformio, the Venetian Republic that had lasted for a thousand years became extinct, and Verona and the Valpolicella Austrian territory. Created as a setting for the gay life of the last days of the Venetian Republic, the gardens of

158 VILLA RIZZARDI
The green theatre in the garden of the Villa Rizzardi at Pojega di Negrar, the finest of its kind in Italy; the original plan of the theatre, dated 1796, still exists.

the Villa Rizzardi are one of the few places that still retain their atmosphere as a living thing. It is not difficult to people its scented lemon garden or the gay little *giardino segreto* with brocaded and silk-clad figures, or to imagine them dancing minuets or organizing an impromptu concert on the lawn behind the house. How often its green alleys must have rung to laughter and music and been the scene of gatherings like the 'Concert in a Venetian Garden', that hangs in the Uffizi, before the grim days of war descended upon it.

Villa Emo - Battaglia

The years that followed were sad indeed for the Veneto, split as it was between the rival powers of France and Austria. With these new times came new fashions, also in gardens, and the mode for the *Giardino Inglese* swept the Veneto destroying all but a few of the beautiful Italian gardens that were the heritage of centuries of loving care. The Veneto was, however, fortunate in two things; as a result of cold wet winters and damp hot summers the landscape is naturally green, and much better adapted to the English type of park garden than most of the rest of Italy. Also in the first years of the nineteenth century the Veneto produced a really remarkable garden architect, Giuseppe Japelli, who can be considered as the last of the long line of Italian garden designers, for even if he was working with an alien medium his gardens are often suited to the landscape, and in some of them the classical associations, if not the traditional design, still survive. Although one cannot but regret his destruction of the previous gardens, his layout of the Villa Emo at Battaglia, for instance, is original. Here he created a 'Lake Avernus', formed by hot volcanic springs and set among gloomily romantic groves – but still with its characteristically Italian rabbit island – at the foot of the hill. His great staircase, leading up to the sunny terraces of the 'Elysian Fields' that surround the house on the hill-top, has a most dramatic effect. Even in the midst of his innovations in the romantic style, Japelli evidently did not have the heart to sweep away all traces of the preceding Italian garden, for here the terraces of the 'Elysian Fields' are still adorned with the delightful little stone baskets of fruit and flowers familiar in Italian gardens through the centuries, and particular favourites in the Veneto.

Venetian gardens have always been rich in what might be termed the minor arts of garden architecture such as this. Superb wrought-iron gates were the rule in all Venetian villas, and wrought-iron plants and flowers, like those which decorate the gates of the Orto Botanico at Padua were not unusual. The creation of garden sculpture is still a flourishing art in the Veneto, and this includes the making of delightful stone baskets of fruit and flowers like those of Villa Emo at Battaglia. In typically Italian fashion, these ornaments did not remain in the garden, but soon began to penetrate the house as well, as dinner-table ornaments; small white porcelain or pottery replicas of garden statues, urns and baskets of flowers and fruit have long been made in the Veneto. Often these represent the garden furniture of real gardens – an old family of Padua, for instance, has all the component parts for reproducing in miniature on their dinner-table the statues, obelisks and bridges that surround the famous public garden of Prato della Valle in their native town. Other family heirlooms may even be small replicas of the statues and fountains of their own gardens, whose whole layout could be reproduced for festive occasions, with lawns of chopped pine-needles and small parterres filled with flowers. Sometimes such fragile trifles are all that remain of the memory of a once prized garden, and until not long ago it looked as if much of that precious heritage of the Veneto – its famous villas, whose influence changed the face of the English countryside and spread as far afield as the plains of Russia and the cotton plantations of America – was destined also to disappear in ruins. The energy and national pride of a small group in the Veneto have awakened both Italian and international interest in their fate and legislation has been brought to their aid, but in restoring the villas it is to be hoped that some at least of the gardens of the Veneto will be remembered.

The Gardens of Northern Italy

Genoa was once a city of gardens; in 1561 when Jan Massys painted his 'Cytherian Venus' he portrayed her reclining upon a terrace from which the whole of the Gulf of Genoa could be seen stretching out into the far distance of dramatic cliffs and sunlit sea (pl. 159). In this wonderful setting, terraced gardens with marble fountains and pergolas sweep down to the water's edge, where porticoed palaces overlook galleys riding at anchor. This was no imaginary scene, but a faithful representation of gardens that were made by the great Genoese admiral and statesman Andrea Doria at the beginning of the sixteenth century, and which really existed for three hundred years.

Palazzo Doria Pamphilj - Genoa

The Genoese were, and are, a tight-fisted maritime people upon whom the Early Renaissance had exercised little influence. The merchant princes, who were better business men than patrons of the arts, still mostly lived in their grim medieval palaces in the narrow streets of the old town, when Andrea Doria decided to build his palace just outside the walls at Fassolo, which for the beauty of its site and luscious vegetation was called 'il paradiso'. Built between 1521 and 1529, this was the first real Renaissance palace in Genoa; open to the sun and air with a succession of terraced gardens that reached from the hill-top to the seashore and setting a fashion that was soon to be followed by the other great Genoese families.

The house itself probably incorporated some earlier buildings, and in order to redress its asymmetrical relation to the site the new palace was provided with loggias that artfully conceal this defect. The main building is the work of Caranca, the additional loggias stretching out into the garden and enclosing the *giardini segreti* are by Montorsoli, to whom the whole garden design is usually also attributed.

Perin del Vaga, who escaped from the Sack of Rome and came to Genoa in 1527, was responsible for the most important frescoes and stuccoed decoration in the palace which, especially in the loggia of the heroes, is strikingly Roman and reminiscent of Villa Madama on a smaller scale. On the whole, however, the palace and its garden have a definitely personal flavour, the main façade overlooking a level enclosed garden towards the sea is more Northern Italian than Roman, but the now vanished gardens stretching up the hill at the back of the house were an excellent example of the classic use of such a site in a terraced layout dominated by a central perspective of stairs linking the different levels. Andrea Doria was an outstanding personality – the dictator in all but name of Genoa at this period – also a man who applied naval discipline to the running of his own household, and there can be little doubt that when he built a palace his ideas on the subject were firmly imparted to his architects. This probably accounts for the individual character of this house that was more of a villa than a palace and something of a naval base as well. From the

terrace above the portico the owner could keep an eye on his galleys and arsenal as well as admiring his garden, which was enclosed by battlemented walls and laid out with fountains, parterres and pergolas in the Northern Italian style.

Along the seafront was a terrace supported by marble columns, under which was a grotto and a passage leading down to the wharf. It was on this splendid terrace that Andrea Doria received the Emperor Charles V and his son, the future Philip II of Spain, in 1533, and it was either there or on one of his galleys that the Admiral gave the legendary banquet at which the astonished Emperor saw the three services of silver plates off which they had eaten thrown into the sea; what he did not know was that fishermen were stationed with nets below to catch the plates as they fell. Today this lower garden is all that remains of the original enormous layout, and in its midst stands a sumptuous marble fountain made by the Carlone brothers in 1601, with Neptune reining in his prancing steeds, surrounded by the Doria eagles (pl. 160).

This fountain and the garden generally John Evelyn considered to be the finest in Genoa; he described it as follows: 'One of the greatest gardens here is that of Prince d'Orias which reaches from the sea to the summit of the mountaines . . . To this palace belongs three gardens, the first whereof is beautified with a terrace, supported by pillars of

159 DORIA GARDENS
Jan Massys' view of the Doria gardens overlooking the port of Genoa, a detail from the 'Cytherian Venus' painted in 1561 and now in the Stockholm National Museum. The gardens were made for the great statesman and admiral Andrea Doria at the beginning of the sixteenth century. Much of them was destroyed in the expansion of the city during the nineteenth century.

160 PALAZZO DORIA PAMPHILJ
The 'Neptune' fountain in the surviving part of the Doria gardens. It was much admired by John Evelyn, who visited Genoa in the year 1644. The palace and gardens still belong to the Doria Pamphilj family.

marble, there is a fountaine of eagles and one of Neptune with sea gods all of the purest marble; they stand in a most ample basin of the same stone. At the side of this garden is such an aviary as Sir Francis Bacon describes in his *Sermones fidelium* or Essays, wherein grow trees of more than two foote diameter, besides cypresses, myrtils, lentiscus and other rare shrubs, which serve to nestle and perch all kinds of birds who have ayre and place enough under their ayrie canopy, supported with huge iron worke tremendous for its fabrick and the charge. The other two gardens are full of orange trees, citrons and pomegranates, fountains, grottoes, and statues, one of the latter is a colossal Jupiter, under which is the sepulchre of a beloved dog, for the care of which one of his family received of the King of Spain 500 crowns a year during the life of the faithful animal.'

The description of the aviary reads remarkably like that of Varro, by which no doubt it was inspired, but it alas has vanished like the terraced gardens on the hill behind, where one of the large pools was used by the shrewd old Admiral to try out the sea-worthiness of the models of his galleys. Here the only thing that was not swept away by speculative building during the nineteenth century is the Gigante, Evelyn's 'colossal Jupiter', and Roland's tomb that is the source of many legends, including the one that Charles V gave Andrea Doria the Principality of Melfi to provide for the maintenance of this lordly hound.

By the time Président de Brosses came to Genoa a century later, its hanging gardens were famous, and they appear to have been not only terraces but actual roof gardens. He writes: 'The gardens in the air corresponding to the different floors are really curious . . . and in Genoa there are large numbers of them . . . the inequality of the terrain and the little there is, has given rise to these constructions made on the terraces that are built or specially arranged beside the apartments, which replace at great cost the lack of air that reigns in the town. Some of these roof gardens have beautiful fountains; and here the great apartments, that are always on the second floor, have kiosks *à la turque* so that one can walk in the open air.'

Palazzo Podestà - Genoa

Only one of these gardens survives in Genoa today. It is in the famous Via Garibaldi where formerly nearly every palace that backed on to the steeply rising hillside had a garden. This garden of Palazzo Podestà was begun in 1563 for Niccolò Lomellini, a member of the family who had originally owned the site of Andrea Doria's new palace, and later passed to the Podestà family in the nineteenth century. Perhaps it was to make up for the loss of a garden which had existed at Fassolo that Niccolò Lomellini decided to make such a charming one in his new town palace; be that as it may, his architect Giovanni Battista Castello, known as Il Bergamasco, laid out the narrow strip of land behind the palace as one of the most delightful gardens that it would be possible to imagine.

The architects who created these town palaces of Genoa seem positively to have welcomed the difficulties of the sites with which they had to contend, for probably in no other city have so many awkward hillsides been utilized to produce palatial effects of extraordinary grandeur and charm. In Palazzo Podestà a few steps across the entrance hall is sufficient to take one into another world, far from the bustle of traffic, where in a quiet courtyard fountains gush forth from two small terraces; above them green trees wave gently against the blue Mediterranean sky. The existing fountains were made by Filippo Parodi in the late seventeenth or early eighteenth century, but they must have been built on the site of earlier ones, as the terraces form an integral part of the design of the whole palace connecting, as Président de Brosses described them, with the different floors.

But this charming courtyard is simply a prelude, an ante-room as it were, to the garden proper, whose full extent — skilfully designed to appear much larger than it actually is — only becomes visible as one ascends the stairs. In actual fact the garden is no wider than the

161   PALAZZO PODESTÀ
The garden of Palazzo Podestà in Genoa, the only one of the old hillside palace gardens in the Via Garibaldi to survive. It was begun in 1563 and passed to the Podestà family in the nineteenth century, to whom it still belongs.

palace and only one and a half times its depth, but so artfully has it been laid out with fountains, tree-filled parterres, terraces and carefully-scaled sculpture, that it conveys an extraordinary impression of space (pl. 161). Two wings of the *piano nobile* extend backwards to join the garden, whose promenades stretch out directly from the tall french windows. These paths are carefully arranged to provide varying degrees of shade at different times of day; on the western side there is both an open sunny walk and one partly shaded by an old-fashioned rose pergola, which can be seen on the right-hand side of the photograph. While these are in the sun, the eastern promenade lies in the deep shade of palms, orange trees and a huge magnolia.

This main garden terrace lies on a gentle slope and is laid out in the traditional Italian fashion of four box-edged parterres divided up by paths with a fountain in the circular space at the crossing. Like all the sculpture in the garden, the statue of a boy struggling with a snake in the centre of the fountain is small, so that when viewed from the windows of the palace or from the topmost terrace the relative size of the rest of the garden appears to be increased.

A shallow grotto and wall fountain built against the retaining wall of the upper terrace culminate the central perspective of this delightful garden; here again the sculpture and stonework are carefully scaled to produce an effect out of all proportion to their size. A concealed spiral staircase leads to the upper terrace. This is laid out simply with four rectangular parterres, whose crossed paths are bordered by orange trees. More diminutive statues stand on the terrace wall, in the centre of which is a small balcony that affords a delightful view over the whole garden.

Villa Hanbury - La Mortola

Owing to its commercial importance as the first port in Italy, Genoa has changed in the last hundred years, more probably, than any other Italian city except Milan. It has become a world in which there is little room for what Alberti called the 'delicacy of gardens', and most of those that have survived are now public parks landscaped during the last century, very fine of their kind, but no longer forming part of the Italian garden tradition. Outside Genoa, practically on the French frontier, at La Mortola, there is a modern garden, interesting both for its site and acclimatization of semi-tropical plants. Like so many modern gardens in Italy, the Villa Hanbury has been made by foreigners, and owing to its style and date it does not come within the scope of this book, but it should not be missed by any garden lover who is visiting Italy.

Palazzo del Te - Mantua

As we have seen in a previous chapter, the Visconti and Sforza of Milan were among the pioneers of pleasure gardens in Northern Italy, that formed part of the hunting-enclosures of great castles such as Pavia, in the fourteenth century. In the following century both the Este and Gonzaga Courts of Ferrara and Mantua were famous for their gardens — Ferrara even boasting a public park, the first of its kind in Europe since classical times. The earliest Gonzaga garden, made in the middle of the fifteenth century, was at Marmirolo; the most famous was the sixteenth-century Bosco Fontana near by. As its name indicates, this was a forest in whose midst was a hunting-lodge with pleasure gardens and fountains. These and the gardens of the Palazzo del Te at Mantua must have been magnificent, as they were greatly admired by the Emperor Charles V when he was there in 1549; his Spanish courtiers who had seen the New World even compared them to the gardens of Montezuma in Mexico. The Gonzaga possessed many other gardens, notably at the Castle of Goito, for which the architect Traballese designed an even more alarming type of surprise than the usual fountains — a disappearing island. This, together with its connecting bridge, slowly submerged in the waters of an artificial lake, rising again after an interval during which the unwary visitors had got their feet soaked. Today the only relics of these famous Gonzaga gardens are the garden courts of the Ducal Palace and the Palazzo del Te at Mantua, where a few box-edged plots and beds of salvia remind us that they were once filled with the scent of jasmine and orange blossom, and provided a setting for one of the most cultured Courts of the Italian Renaissance.

From this sad world, peopled only by memories and ghosts, it is a relief to turn to the gardens of Lombardy and the lakes, one of the few areas in Italy today where the cult of gardens and flowers still survives. Apart from the world-famous Isola Bella, which is actually in the part of Lake Maggiore that belongs to Piedmont, these Northern Italian gardens have been surprisingly little studied. One of the difficulties is that they do not form a stylistic group of their own as do the gardens of the other Italian regions. The main reasons for this are probably geographical. The great waterway of the River Po, whose tributaries have created the lakes and valleys leading to the Alpine passes, has laid the area open to many influences, as well as providing very varied types of sites. Thus the gardens of Lombardy and Piedmont may be laid out on a mountain or lakeside site or in the plain, and their design may include anything from topiary to Roman terraces and water-stairs, or Venetian-style colonnades and French *broderies* and clipped palisades of deciduous trees.

Villa Cicogna - Bisuschio

One of the most interesting of these Northern Italian gardens is that of the Villa Cicogna at Bisuschio near Lake Lugano, which is one of the very rare villas in the area to have preserved its sixteenth-century character intact. Like so many other Lombard ones, Villa Cicogna was originally a hunting-box, where in the middle of the fifteenth century the Mozzoni family entertained the Sforza dukes of Milan to boar hunts. A hundred years later the heiress Angela Mozzoni, whose portrait still hangs in the house, married Ascanio Cicogna, and the whole house and garden was transformed into a villa in the Renaissance style. The eclecticism of Lombardy is well illustrated by this conversion; the house itself still resembles the old Northern Italian and Tuscan type of villa, with its porticoed court that leads into a delightful little sunken garden with fish ponds (pl. 162), but the Roman influence is very evident in the decoration of the loggias, where *trompe l'oeil* pergolas, like those of the Villa di Papa Giulio, adorn the ceiling. This garden type of decoration also penetrates the house itself, in swags of fruit, flowers and vegetables, which resemble Giovanni da Udine's garlands in the Farnesina; and in landscapes in the style of *topia*, painted by the Campi brothers of Cremona.

Much of the layout of the Villa Cicogna has also undoubtedly been inspired by Roman Renaissance gardens; its two outstanding features are a beautiful water-staircase, that provides a superb *coup d'oeil* for the principal rooms of the *piano nobile*, and a fine terrace that runs at right angles to it. Physically and visually the terrace provides the connecting link between the sunken garden, the water-staircase and the terraced garden that lies on the other side of the house, looking towards Lake Lugano. It also serves as a sheltered promenade, such an essential feature of all Renaissance gardens, from which the parterres of the lower gardens can be enjoyed, as well as fine views of the surrounding landscape.

Its arcaded retaining wall masks a subterranean gallery, one of two that are a uniquely classical feature of this Lombard garden, resembling as they do an ancient *cryptoporticus*. With their rustic stonework and graceful fronds of maidenhair, these cool retreats for summer days vividly recall the still surviving *'inferi'* of Hadrian's villa at Tivoli, and surpass even the nympheums of Roman villas as a revival of this aspect of classical garden architecture (pl. XLIX).

The tree-clad slopes of the hill above the water-staircase merge gradually into the surrounding woodland, in whose depths paths and occasional clearings have been cut, that afford fascinating glimpses of the blue waters of the distant Lake Lugano. The Villa Cicogna is now open to the public – one of the very few Italian private houses that are. Its superb collection of Renaissance furniture alone would make it well worth seeing, but its greatest attraction is undoubtedly the garden. In this the dramatic beauty of the site is combined with the mellow charm of a garden that has been in the possession of the same family for four hundred years.

162   VILLA CICOGNA
The sunken garden of the Villa Cicogna at Bisuschio near Lake Lugano, one of the very few villas in the north to have retained intact its sixteenth-century character. The villa still belongs to the Cicogna family who have owned it for the last four hundred years, and is open to the public.

XLIX   VILLA CICOGNA

Castello Balduino · Montalto di Pavia

Appropriately enough, for Lombardy is a land of garden contrasts, those of the Castello Balduino at Montalto di Pavia could not present a greater change from the gardens of the Villa Cicogna. Here a medieval castle, standing on the highest peak of the Apennines, has been surrounded by one of the finest topiary gardens in Italy. Unlike the terraces at Bisuschio, which merge gently into the hillside, those of Montalto stand out boldly from it, overlooking an almost unbelievable panorama of range after range of mountains, disappearing into the blue haze of the distance. To lay out a garden on such a site must have required quite considerable boldness, and this is exactly the quality that its designer evidently possessed; his terraces stand boldly and firmly outlined by four-square hedges, with the solid patterns of the topiary hewn – for that seems to be the only adequate word – out of sturdy yews (pl. 163).

Montalto might be cited as a textbook example of the Italian use of plants in architectural forms – even the flowers are treated like sculptural reliefs, solidly massed in various colours, and slightly raised in their evergreen setting from a background of gravel. Fountains and citrus trees look almost frivolous in this severely architectural setting, but as no Italian garden would be complete without them they too are integrated into the general pattern, on the terraces to the south of the castle, where the sunlight brings out the full effect of shining water and scented blossom (pl. 164). The potted lemon trees are ranged the whole length of a narrow walk – the only sheltered promenade in this exposed site. Their bright green

163   CASTELLO BALDUINO
The topiary gardens of the Castello Balduino at Montalto di Pavia. This medieval castle, standing on a high peak of the Apennines, has been surrounded by one of the finest topiary gardens in the whole of Italy. The garden terraces overlook range after range of mountains and are remarkable for their bold design on a very difficult site. The castle is the property of Count Balduino.

foliage stands out against the dark tones of a yew hedge that acts as a windbreak and prevents their delicate scent from being blown away by the four winds of heaven.

The oldest part of Castello Balduino is a tower that formed part of a stronghold of the historic Belcredi family of Pavia in the thirteenth century. Towards the end of the sixteenth century the Belcredi converted this into a less ferociously defensive residence; and thus it remained until 1735 when another member of the family called in Giovanni Antonio Veneroni, architect of the Palazzo Mezzabarba of Pavia, to make the castle into a villa and lay out the gardens. The area that had formerly been covered by walls and bulwarks was levelled to make way for the parterres and terraces of a formal garden, while the lower slopes of the hill were planted with trees. The property later passed into other hands and was for a long time neglected, until in 1909 it was bought by the Balduino family.

Fortunately the main outlines of the eighteenth-century layout, and Veneroni's original plans, still existed when the present owners of the castle commissioned the Piedmontese architect and art historian Giovanni Chevalley, to complete and restore Veneroni's work, early in this century. Chevalley had made a considerable study of villas and gardens and was well qualified for the task in hand and no doubt the garden today owes as much to him as it did to his predecessor, but it would be a captious critic indeed who did not succumb to the fascination of his bold treatment of this marvellous site. Especially in autumn when the bronze tones of the surrounding woods and hedges stand out against the blue haze of the distant hills, and the sculptured masses of flowers glow richly in the foreground, the garden of Castello Balduino appears as the setting of some fairy-tale or historical romance.

164   CASTELLO BALDUINO
The southern terraces of the gardens of Castello Balduino, where fountains and lemon trees provide a light relief to the sobriety of the solid forms and dark green of the topiary. On the left of the photograph the potted lemon trees can be seen ranged along a sheltered walk, one of the few places in the garden where their scent would not be blown away by the wind which blows constantly on this exposed but magnificent site. The loggia in the background was probably added to the old castle about the end of the sixteenth century.

Villa Arese - Lainate

L   VILLA ARESE

165   VILLA ARESE
Villa Arese at Lainate near Milan, the terrace in front of the extensive garden house, which like the rest of this fascinating garden is falling into ruin through neglect. It was originally a particularly fine example of a Lombard seventeenth- and eighteenth-century garden of the plain.

An even greater contrast, both in style and condition, is presented by the gardens of the Villa Arese at Lainate. Not only is Lainate situated in the midst of the vast Lombard plain but, whereas Castello Balduino and Villa Cicogna are kept to perfection, the gardens of Villa Arese are mouldering into a decay so profound that, if something is not rapidly done to rescue them, it will soon only be possible to refer to them in the past tense. This state of affairs is rendered even more tragic by the fact that Villa Arese represents, or represented, a particularly fine example of a seventeenth- and eighteenth-century garden of the plain. It is a rare survival of its kind, as this type of garden has in general been

particularly vulnerable to the inroads of landscaping, for, as Mrs Wharton pointed out, in the rich northern provinces, as around Florence, gardens have suffered from the affluence of their owners more than from neglect.

Originally this Lainate villa was evidently surrounded by a large formal garden, whose outlines are now somewhat difficult to trace among the undergrowth; but its outstanding feature was, and still is, the superb garden pavilion that surrounds three sides of a spacious terrace paved with pebble mosaics (pl. 165). In its long and gracious lines this building resembles the Venetian villas of the plain, while its many obelisks recall the chimney-stacks of the same form that, by some curious law, were reserved for the dwellings of the admirals of the Most Serene Republic. The function of this delightful building was, however, just the opposite – not to provide warmth, but a cool refuge from the humid heat of Lombard summers. It contains a remarkable series of saloons entirely decorated with pebble mosaics, each one of which is ornamented with different and fascinating designs carried out in the muted pastel tones of the natural stone (pl. 166). Hidden in the floors of these rooms were many tiny jets of water, that could be turned on to refresh the atmosphere as well as their inhabitants.

This charming pavilion, which is of a remarkable size, has also garden rooms open to the sky, probably intended for summer dining, with fountains and walls covered with rustic stonework. One of the largest of these is designed as an oval 'ruined' temple, lined with broken columns and statues of classical deities. The neglected remains of garden courts and shallow terraces stretch out on either side of this fascinating relic of the gaiety of other days, where sculptured fountain figures struggle with the invading weeds. On moonlight nights the scene must present a romantic spectacle beyond compare, but scarcely what one would expect to find within a few miles of Milan in the midst of a province so eminently conscious of the civic virtues as Lombardy.

Villa Il Bozzolo - Casalzuigno

As little known to the outside world as Villa Arese at Lainate, but for a very different reason, is one of the loveliest gardens of Lombardy, and indeed of all Italy. This belongs to the beautiful Della Porta villa of Il Bozzolo, which is hidden away in a verdant valley of the Alpine foothills near Laveno. The only explanation of the fact that this superb example of Italian garden design seems to have escaped the eye of students of garden architecture, lies in the isolation of its lovely site. Few strangers can ever drive along the country road that traverses the lonely Val Cúvia, and even fewer stop in the little village of Casalzuigno where the villa stands. If they do, they are at once rewarded by the sight of one of the most dramatically effective garden layouts in Italy, for Il Bozzolo is intended to be seen from the public road. The surrounding landscape is on the grandest scale, with forested hills rising precipitously from the floor of the valley, and to lay out a garden that would not be dwarfed by such surroundings might well be imagined to require a design on the scale of the Villa d'Este or the other great Roman villas. The inspiration of Il Bozzolo is indeed Roman in its grandeur, but the architect has achieved his superb effect with an extraordinary economy of means. The basic design of the garden is the classic one of a central perspective traversing a terraced hillside; the perspective begins on the floor of the valley and soars upwards to the crest of a forested hill, and the gradient and distance covered by it are truly spectacular. The ingenuity of the architect is displayed in the manner whereby he has succeeded in creating in the midst of this a garden of intimate character, adjacent to the house, and in relating it to the grand scale of the layout, with an exemplary balance of horizontal and vertical lines. The whole effect is achieved by five small stone-balustraded terraces and an octagonal grass enclosure.

In order not to interrupt the scenic effect, the house of Il Bozzolo has been placed out

166   VILLA ARESE
One of the rooms in the garden pavilion of the Villa Arese at Lainate, whose pebble mosaics are among the most elaborate and remarkable of their kind in Italy. If these also are not soon repaired they will be totally ruined. This superb pavilion was an outstanding feature of the garden and was filled with concealed fountains which added to its freshness in hot weather.

291

of sight on the left and, as a garden is a place to be lived in as well as looked at, a spacious terrace has been laid out before it at right angles to the central perspective (pl. 167). Above this rise the five small terraces, whose beautifully finished stone balustrades effectually emphasize their horizontal lines and provide a suitable setting for the fine flight of steps that forms part of the central perspective. Filled with the scent of lemon trees and the sound of fountains this part of the garden creates a charmingly intimate setting for the house and the shady walk that leads to the small chapel opposite.

The stroke of genius in this garden design is, however, provided by the next stage, where the architect has outlined an enormous slightly sunken octagonal grassy space on the steep hillside, enclosing it by a retaining wall. Cypresses stand out like exclamation marks around this, emphasizing its outline, and forming a barrier between it and the surrounding woods. The effect is inevitably foreshortened in a photograph, but to the eye it appears as a vast space soaring upwards to meet the forest trees. At the central point of contact attention is again concentrated upon the perspective by a monumental fountain flanked by staircases, which lead the eye upwards to the final cypress-lined avenue that traverses the forest to the crest of the hill.

The scale of the whole layout and its relation to the landscape is really only appreciated when viewed from this fountain and the small terrace above. From this vantage point, although the design is seen in reverse, one gains a far clearer conception of the distance covered and the steepness of the gradient than from the bottom of the garden, where the charm of the spectacle is such that it absorbs one's whole attention. The name of the architect of this remarkable garden is not even known, and very little about the history of the villa, except that it was built in the seventeenth century for a member of the Della Porta family, who still own it. Nevertheless, Il Bozzolo deserves to be ranked high among the great gardens of Italy, for few can rival the breadth of the imaginative conception that at one and the same time fitted it for such superb surroundings and, in the words of Tom Coryat, made such a 'passing delectable place of solace'.

Villa Sommi Picenardi · Olgiate

Another charming and little-known Lombard garden is that of the Villa Sommi Picenardi at Olgiate which stands a few miles off the main Milan-Lecco road. Dating from the eighteenth century, this garden affords another example of a hillside terraced layout, traversed by a central perspective of ramps and steps (pl. 168). But it is of a very different size and type from Il Bozzolo, scaled as it is to a landscape of small green hills and the position of a *giardino segreto* concealed behind the house. Here the house dominates, and the garden has been designed as an adjunct to it, spread out like an extraordinarily effective stage set to be viewed from the large 'picture' windows of the *piano nobile*. These are a most unusual feature for an Italian house of this period, where the interpenetration between house and garden is usually limited to porticos or loggias on the ground floor.

Although the layout and coloured mosaic decoration of the central staircase of Villa Sommi Picenardi are thoroughly Roman, and one of the very rare examples of their kind in Lombardy, the garden furniture already displays the delicacy of the eighteenth century. Stone garlands hang from the balustrades and ornamental urns, and the motif is repeated in festoons of real roses that are suspended between the pedestals of the upper terrace. Miniature bronze sea-horses prance in the central fountain, and the sculpture generally conveys the impression of drawing-room ornaments rather than the robust stone figures of an earlier age. The garden was restored at the end of the last century, and it is likely that the present layout of grass and fountains in the flat space behind the house was made at this time, but it has been skilfully done, preserving the general atmosphere intact and

167   IL BOZZOLO

The gardens of Il Bozzolo, Casalzuigno, near Varese. Owing to the isolation of its site in a valley of the Alpine foothills near Laveno this superb example of Italian seventeenth-century garden design is relatively little known. The villa was built for a member of the Della Porta family, who still own it.

utilizing the charming old garden ornaments to advantage. Villa Sommi Picenardi is one of the houses where on festive occasions this part of the garden layout was reproduced on the dining- table in miniature, with 'lawns' of chopped pine-needles and miniature beds of flowers.

Writing in 1568 in his *Description of all Italy* Leandro Alberti noted that 'almost opposite Stresa one sees Pallanza, and practically in the middle of the lake between them is an island on which Lancilotto Borromeo, a Milanese gentleman, has built a sumptuous palace and ornamented it with an agreeable garden'. This is one of the earliest references to the island gardens of Lake Maggiore for which the name of Borromeo – the modernized form of the original surname signifying good or frequent Roman pilgrim – has become famous wherever Italian gardens are known. The island referred to is, of course, Isola Madre, whose flat surface did not present such obstacles to garden layout as its now much better known sister Isola Bella.

168   VILLA SOMMI PICENARDI
The eighteenth-century gardens behind the Villa Sommi Picenardi at Olgiate Molgera near Como. Though little known outside Lombardy, the garden is one of the rare examples of a hillside terraced layout, ornamented with coloured mosaics, that are found in Northern Italy. The villa belongs to the Sommi Picenardi family.

Isola Bella - Lake Maggiore

169   ISOLA BELLA
An eighteenth-century bird's-eye view of Isola Bella in a print by Dal Re in the possession of Count and Countess Borromeo d'Adda. Until 1630 the island was a barren rock. Angelo Crivelli drew up the plans for its conversion into a fabulous pleasure palace and gardens for Count Carlo Borromeo. Both the architect and the owner died before the work was far advanced, but the garden layout was completed by 1670. The island belongs to Prince Borromeo and is open to the public.

At the beginning of the seventeenth century, Isola Bella was nothing more than an arid rock, and it was only about 1630 that Count Carlo Borromeo began levelling it, probably after the death of Angelo Crivelli, who had drawn up the plans of the original layout of what was to be called Isola Isabella after the owner's wife. He too died before the work was far advanced, but it was carried on by his son Vitaliano, who employed Francesco Castelli and Carlo Fontana among a host of other architects, artists and sculptors to complete it as far as it went; for after an interval of three hundred years the house is only now being finished according to the seventeenth-century plans, though the gardens were laid out by 1670.

Forty years seems a long time to make a garden, but the outcome was the conversion of an entire island into a vast pleasure galley, whose size and scope put to shame the efforts in this direction even of the Chinese and Roman emperors. The ten garden terraces of Isola Bella rise to some hundred feet above the lake, forming the poop of this fabulous 'craft' whose bows, shown in Dal Re's early-eighteenth-century print, have yet to be constructed (pl. 169). Although today the island looks very different from Dal Re's bird's-eye view, this gives a very much clearer idea of the basic lines of the layout than could any modern aerial photograph, owing to the growth of subsequent planting.

About one-third of the island is occupied by the palatial villa and the small village that grew up beside it; the whole of the rest is given over to the famous gardens. The first thing that strikes one on looking at Dal Re's print is the extraordinary bareness of the layout; practically the only trees are grouped around the north-eastern corner of the main garden, screening its terraces from the house. In actual fact these were planted to camouflage the asymmetrical position of the villa in relation to the gardens, whose main entrance is by way of a small court that intervenes between the long southern wing, in the centre of the print, and the main terraces. Here the thick growth effectively obscures the fact that the steps leading out of the court take a sharp turn to the right, and in walking through the garden one is unaware of the marked change of direction, which would have offended against the laws of symmetry that, in this aspect at least, still held good in Italian seventeenth-century garden design.

In direct contrast to this ingenious arrangement, it is noticeable that the other old Italian principle of increasingly dense planting as the garden recedes from the house, seems here to have been completely abandoned, the whole island being apparently laid out in elaborate parterres of *broderies*. This impression is so marked that it cannot entirely be explained by the simplification of a bird's-eye view and by 1726 when Dal Re's prints were published, there would have been time for natural growth to have softened the severity of the architectural layout. Other views of the period and Dal Re's own prints of details of the garden, such as the 'theatre' of grottoes and fountains that masks the northern face of the four highest garden terraces, portray the same somewhat arid type of composition (pl. 170).

As a matter of fact the representations of Isola Bella made by Dal Re and other eighteenth-century artists do not completely correspond to seventeenth- or eighteenth-century descriptions of the island, and their style is symptomatic of the artificial

170   ISOLA BELLA
The hemisphere or 'theatre' on the pen-ultimate terrace of Isola Bella, from a print by Dal Re in the possession of Count and Countess Borromeo d'Adda. Although it is probably exaggerated in order to give clarity to the drawing, the sparseness of the planting produces an arid effect.

LI   ISOLA BELLA

decadence that was soon to overwhelm Italian garden design. The mere fact that they represented planting as being so reduced as to be practically non-existent, giving the garden a lifeless appearance, is an indication of the current taste. Before the eighteenth century was far advanced in Italy, the rush to imitate the increasingly fashionable French garden had led to the adoption of its superficial elements, but rarely its beautifully integrated design. As a result the basic principles of symmetry, not just of the ground-plan, but of the balance of light and shade, and of a built-up or closely planted area with an open space, which for centuries had governed the layout of Italian gardens, were gradually undermined and forgotten.

Although no doubt something of this influence was beginning to make itself felt when Isola Bella was laid out, the process was not nearly as far advanced as it would appear from Dal Re's prints and Italy could still conjure up a garden scene that breathed enchantment. Of this fact we have two independent eye-witnesses, the English Bishop Burnet who visited the island in 1684, and Président de Brosses who was there fifty-five years later. As individuals and as representatives of two different worlds in the history of taste few men could have approached their subjects from more divergent standpoints.

171   ISOLA BELLA
The same view as shown in pl. 170 today, after freer planting and centuries of growth have provided a gentler setting for the fantastic Baroque 'theatre'.

172   ISOLA BELLA
View from the topmost terrace of Isola Bella, overlooking the Italian garden, which more than any other conveys the impression of standing upon some fantastic pleasure galley.

LII, LIII   ISOLA BELLA

But the naïve and somewhat breathless-sounding Bishop, continually anxious for the safety of his baggage train of 'portmangles laden upon mullets', and the ironically detached Frenchman, chauvinistically aware of Italian over-statement, agreed on one thing – that Isola Bella was unique, one of the 'loveliest spots of ground in the world' and a place 'worthy of fairies, who have transported here a portion of the ancient gardens of Hesperides'.

Bishop Burnet's description is particularly interesting as he was one of the earliest foreign travellers who have left a record of Isola Bella, and it is evident that architecturally at least the garden has changed little since his day. He writes: 'There lies here two islands called the Borromean Islands, that are certainly the loveliest spots of ground in the world . . . The ground rises so sweetly in them that nothing can be imagined like the terraces here . . . The whole island is a garden . . . and because the figure of the Island was not made regular by Nature they have built great vaults and porticas along the rock which are all made grotesque, and so they have brought it into a regular form by laying earth over these vaults. There is a first Garden to the East that rises up from the lake in five rows of Terraces, on the three sides of the garden that are watered by the Lake, the stairs are noble and the walls are all covered with Oranges and Citrons, and a more beautiful spot of a garden cannot be seen. There are two buildings in the two corners of this garden, the one is only a Mill for fetching up the water, and the other is a noble summer house, all wainscotted, if I may say so, with Alabaster and Marble of a fine colour inclining to red, from this garden one goes in a level to all the rest of the Alleys and Parterres, Herb gardens and Flower-Gardens, in which there are varieties of Fountains and Arbours, but the great Parterre is a surprizing thing, for as it is well furnished with Statues and Fountains and is of vast extent and justly situated to the Palace. So at the further end there is a great Mount, that face of it that looks to the Parterre is made like a Theatre all full of fountains and statues, and the height rising up in five several rows . . . and round the Mount answering to the five rows there goes as many Terraces of noble walks, the walls are all as close covered with Oranges and Citrons as any of our walls in England are with Laurel . . . The freshness of the air, it being both in a Lake and near the Mountains, the fragrant smell, the beautiful Prospect, and the delighting Variety that is here makes such a habitation for Summer that perhaps the whole world has nothing like it!'

As might be imagined, Président de Brosses, to whom the lack of 'order, design or sequence' of the Boboli gardens had appealed so much, was more interested in the site and planting of Isola Bella than the architectural features that had so impressed Bishop Burnet. He dismissed the layout briefly with the words: 'A quantity of arcades built in the lake uphold a pyramidal mountain, thirty-six terraces nine to each face.' But even he is carried away by the fantastic beauty of the scene . . . 'The back wall of each terrace is covered with a palissade, either of jasmine, pomegranates or oranges, and it is edged with a balustrade with pots of flowers . . . Certainly in France there are beauties of nature and art worth more than this, but none that I have seen that are so unusual or so unusually sited; it resembles nothing so much as a palace in a fairy tale.'

De Brosses' tour of the house was brief. The situation familiar to anyone travelling in company developed – his friends were in a hurry – and he was not allowed to look at the flower paintings which interested him, greatly to the chagrin of the accompanying footman who assured him that they had been done by a '*pittorissimo*'! A superlative that elicited the characteristically dry Gallic comment: 'an expression that was new to me'! At first sight de Brosses considered the main garden disappointing, but the wonderful luxuriance of its exotic trees and fruit enchanted him in the end . . . 'some parts of it are really exquisite, like the bosquets of pomegranates and oranges . . . and above all the great *berceaux* of lemon and citron trees covered with fruit; another place that is worthy of fairies, who have transported here a portion of the ancient gardens of Hesperides', and he concludes 'the Borromeo Islands are to my mind a stopping place worthy of Epicurus and Sardanapalus'.

For once, one can safely say that if Bishop Burnet or Président de Brosses were to return to Isola Bella today they would find it infinitely more beautiful than in their own time. Here perhaps, more than in any other Italian garden, 'the venerable impression of the hand of time' has brought a magic that before was lacking. Already early in the nineteenth century, if we may judge from contemporary prints, years of growth and freer planting had given the island the romantic loveliness we know today. Both at the water's edge and in the parterres of the great terrace, the mass of foliage and blossom of magnolias, camellias, roses, jasmine, pomegranates and citrus trees have added a range of colour and softness of outline that blend with the surrounding landscape of tranquil water and haze-covered mountains (pl. 172). This gentler setting increases the dreamlike fantasy of the great hemisphere or 'theatre' where the gods and goddesses, the *putti* and prancing unicorn and whole prides of white peacocks that are the 'crew' of this fantastic Baroque pleasure galley, stand or strut among the plume-crowned obelisks which are its masts (pls. 171, XLVIII, LI, LII, LIII). Even the ship's look-out is there upon the highest pinnacle, a toga-clad bay-crowned divinity, whose right arm is outstretched to welcome or to warn those who wish to embark that the ship itself is also the island of Cythera whose spell once experienced is not easily forgotten.

Indeed, since the days of Pliny, all the Italian lakes have exercised a spell as potent as any in Greek mythology; to Shelley's poetic imagination the hills surrounding Como resembled 'the abysses of Ida or Parnassus' and the lake itself exceeded 'any other I ever beheld in beauty except the arbutus islands of Killarny'. In April 1818 he tried to rent the Villa Pliniana but failed, a circumstance that prevented what might have proved a curious historical encounter, as his near neighbour would have been Prinny's rejected wife, Caroline of Brunswick, who was living just across the lake at Cernobbio, in the villa whose name she changed for some curious whim to that of d'Este. This villa has for long been a hotel, and only the water-staircase now survives of what must once have been one of the finest Renaissance gardens on the lake, made in 1570 for Cardinal Tolomeo Gallio by Pellegrino Pellegrini.

Villa Balbianello · Lake Como

The whole of this western shore of Lake Como is fringed with gardens, but one of the loveliest, whose peaceful and romantic site on a lonely promontory would also have delighted Shelley, is the Villa Balbianello. The headland is a mass of flowers, and embowered in their midst is the most enchanting casino, whose central loggia commands wonderful views over the lake (pl. 173). This has the same fairylike quality that delighted Président de Brosses at Isola Bella, and one would have imagined that it had been built as the setting of some young romance; but as a matter of sober fact it was made in 1790 for Cardinal Durini. The Cardinal certainly had an eye for beauty; few of the grandest gardens in Italy can equal the exquisite repose of Balbianello's lakeside terraces, where the gentle music of the fountains mingles with the flutter of leaves and the peaceful lapping of the lake (pl. 174). But the little *amorini* that play a game of see-saw on the stone balustrades and the beneficent stone saint that stands beside them have also witnessed dramatic events, for it was here that the Italian writer and patriot, Silvio Pellico, was arrested before he was imprisoned for nine years in the Austrian fortress of Spielburg.

173   VILLA BALBIANELLO
The casino of the Villa Balbianello at Lenno, on Lake Como, built about 1790 for Cardinal Durini on a flower-covered promontory enjoying superb views over the lake. The villa belongs to Mr Ames.

174   VILLA BALBIANELLO
The lakeside terrace of Villa Balbianello at Lenno whose exquisite repose is matched by few of the grandest gardens in Italy.

Villa Carlotta - Lake Como

Most famous of these lakeside gardens of Como are those of the Villa Carlotta, which was built in 1745 for the spendthrift Marshal Giorgio Clerici but owes its name to Carlotta Duchess of Saxe-Meiningen, whose mother gave it to her as a wedding-present in 1843. The romantic appeal of the site to the northerner of the nineteenth century is well illustrated by a picture by J. Bidault, which hangs in the Galleria di Arte Moderna in Milan (pl. 175). This also shows the charming eighteenth-century terraced garden, that would have pleased Pliny and Alberti, for it combines the spacious terraces of Pliny's Como villas with Alberti's 'places to walk' in sun and shade and wonderful views over the lake to 'familiar hills and mountains'.

In this delightful eighteenth-century garden the old Italian principles of symmetry still obtain in the simple *giardini segreti* that are laid out on either side of the house, and in the open lemon-scented terraces that lie just before it. For summer shade a small *bosco*, threaded by pleached alleys, has been planted at a lower level near the lake, to catch the cooling breezes that blow across its surface. In the nineteenth century a picturesque English garden was added to the layout. Here in spring massed banks of azaleas glow in the sunshine; a green dell has been converted into a fair imitation of a 'Douanier' jungle, where tree ferns and other exotics flourish in the mild lake climate, beside a woodland stream.

Villa San Remigio - Pallanza

Although it is of another age and cannot be considered as an Italian garden in the strictest sense, having been created during the nineteenth century by an Italo-Irish family, the Villa San Remigio near Pallanza on Lake Maggiore is in fact a fascinating by-product of the Italian garden tradition – the romantic conception of a classical garden. Its history begins early in the nineteenth century when a Mr Browne and his two daughters were delayed at Pallanza by an accident to their carriage. The damage was sufficiently serious to give the girls time to persuade their father to buy the hill-top where the romantic Chapel of San Remigio stands, commanding the most magnificent views over the lake. Later they built a house there and began to lay out a garden, to which succeeding generations of the family made additions. The result is the most fascinating interpretation of a formal Italian garden as seen through romantic northern eyes; for the fabulous beauty of the site it rivals the gardens of the Empress Elizabeth's Achilleion in Corfu. The whole garden is imbued with the same feeling: it is a dream world, Italy and the Mediterranean basin as the northerner imagines it, not as it really is (pls. 176). Thus classical goddesses drive their chariots through pools surrounded by romantic woodland, and lily ponds mirror the reflections of distant snowy peaks (pl. 177). The conception is neither wholly Italian nor wholly northern, but it provides a charming postscript to the history of the lakeside gardens of Italy.

By the middle of the eighteenth century, gardens of so characteristically Italian a style as those of Villa Carlotta were becoming rare, for the mode for French gardens had spread from Piedmont to Lombardy, carrying all before it. Like all foreign fashions the new style had its critics. They complained that the parterres were nothing but bizarre lines, plants had abandoned their natural shapes to appear as obelisks, tetragons and globes, and the old *boschi* were now trimmed to make the walls of mazes that led nowhere. This was very often true, but the fact remained that the formality of a French garden, with its carefully regulated open spaces surrounded by *bosquets*, whose depths were pierced by trim green alleys and shady garden rooms, was admirably suited to the villas of the Lombard plain. It was precisely for this type of site that generations of skilled French garden designers had evolved their national style, whose origins were based upon the classical Italian garden of

175   VILLA CARLOTTA
Villa Carlotta at Cadenabbia on Lake Como, a painting by J. Bidault now in the Galleria di Arte Moderna in Milan. Built in 1745 for Marshal Giorgio Clerici, the villa owes its name to Carlotta Duchess of Saxe-Meiningen, to whom it was given as a wedding-present by her mother in 1843. She later added a landscape garden to the formal terraces shown in the picture, which is today famous for its azaleas. The villa is now State property and open to the public.

the Renaissance, but which the French genius had adapted to the wider horizons and gentler landscape of their own country (pls. LIV, LV).

Thus the importation of the French garden into Italy did not really constitute such a break with tradition as its captious critics claimed. The trouble was that in Italy, even in the eighteenth century, gardens were much smaller than in France and local architects seized upon the superficial aspects of the French style, such as the parterres of *broderies*, whose proportions required such careful scaling to the site, and plumped them down in the place of the old hedged plots, destroying the harmony of the old layout without creating a proper setting for the new. Fortunately perhaps many of these 'French' gardens succumbed to the landscape fashion that succeeded them and their weakness and aridity is often now only a memory preserved in some old print, though a few of their straggly parterres still survive set in masses of unkept gravel.

176   VILLA SAN REMIGIO
The garden of the Villa San Remigio near Pallanza on Lake Maggiore. Laid out by an Italo-Irish family at the end of the last century and the beginning of this, it is a romantic interpretation of the classical Italian garden. The villa now belongs to Contessa Bonacossa.

177   VILLA SAN REMIGIO
The garden of the Villa San Remigio near Pallanza on Lake Maggiore.

LIV, LV VILLA SAN REMIGIO

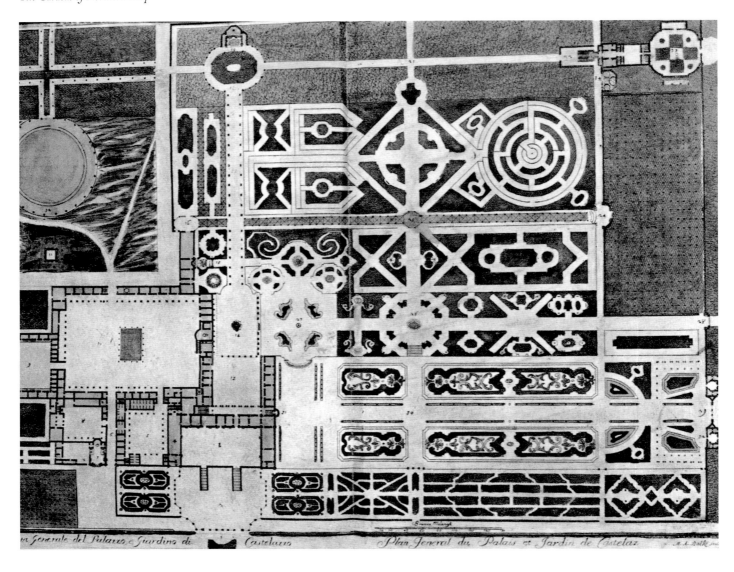

Villa Crivelli Sormani-Verri - Castellazzo

One interesting garden of this period does however still exist in Lombardy, and its extreme rarity makes it doubly valuable to the student of Italian garden history, as here it is not a question of a local adaptation of an existing garden, but a complete layout designed afresh on the site of a previous one by a Frenchman, Jean Gianda. The villa, now owned by Marchesa Crivelli Sormani-Verri, already existed at the beginning of the seventeenth century, having been built by the Arconati family on the site of an old castle, from which the locality takes its name of Castellazzo. In 1627 Count Galeazzo Arconati laid out a garden in the Italian style, even importing antique statues and fountains from Rome for the purpose. These were transported overland on wagons drawn by oxen, and a relation of this odyssey was preserved in the family archives until they were destroyed in the last war.

In the seventeenth century the gardens of Castellazzo were already famous as a meeting-place of all the wit and fashion of this part of Lombardy, and some idea of their style may be gathered from the fact that those of the Villa Arese at Lainate were made in

178 VILLA CRIVELLI SORMANI-VERRI Plan of the gardens of the Villa Crivelli Sormani-Verri, from the Delizie della Villa di Castellazzo. *The fact that the garden was designed by a Frenchman—Jean Gianda—is indicative of the changing fashions of a period when Italy, who had for so long led in garden design, now instead followed French, and in the nineteenth century, English fashions. The prints are of particular interest as the garden layout is still the same and the only one of its kind to have been preserved in Italy. The villa belongs to Marchesa Crivelli Sormani-Verri. By kind permission of the Archivio Civico of Milan.*

179, 180 VILLA CRIVELLI SORMANI-
VERRI
*Views of the gardens of Villa Crivelli Sormani-
Verri, at Castellazzo near Milan, from the
Delizie della Villa di Castellazzo by D.
Lucchese, published in Milan 1743.* By kind
permission of the Archivio Civico of
Milan.

LVI, LVII   VILLA CRIVELLI
SORMANI-VERRI

imitation of them. However, no trace today remains of anything so characteristically Italian as the garden pavilion at Lainate, as early in the eighteenth century the last of the Arconati Visconti commissioned Giovanni Ruggeri to enlarge and transform the house and Jean Gianda to redesign the garden.

This new garden of Castellazzo became even more famous than its predecessor, so much so that a book describing it, profusely illustrated with prints by Marcantonio Dal Re, was published in Milan in 1743. From these it is possible to establish, not only that the gardens were laid out exactly according to the original design, but that, except for the

181, 182 VILLA CRIVELLI SORMANI-VERRI
The fountains, steps and statues in a topiary setting, seen in the centre of the view (see pl. 180) of the Villa Crivelli Sormani-Verri, as they are today.

parterres which are now replaced by a lawn, the garden design has been preserved in every detail, and is probably the only one of its kind in Italy. Dal Re's plan clearly reveals the characteristically French style of the layout, with elaborate parterres lying immediately in front of the main façade of the villa, though it should be noted that the open space they occupied took, as was so often also the case in native French gardens, the horse-shoe shape of the old Roman hippodrome (pl. 178). The whole of this area is still surrounded by green walls of tall hedges, and the central perspective is outlined by clipped trees.

But the most interesting and exotic aspect of the Castellazzo garden from the Italian point of view is the *bosquet*, with its *allées*, *cabinets* and *berceaux* of shaven greenery. The garden is small in comparison with the enormous area of French gardens, and the cabinets are simply hedged enclosures, resembling those shown in early prints of the Trianon, rather than the elaborate garden rooms set in the vast plantations of Versailles itself (pls. 179, 180). The great *berceau* runs the whole length of the *bosquet*, dividing it in two; there is an octagonal space at its centre where it crosses the broad *allée* of the fountains. Although the design is still identical, the hedges no longer resemble the shaven walls of the prints and, with its fountains and sculpture, this part of the garden is easier to recognize from photographs than the rest of the layout (pls. 181, 182, LVI, LVII; compare with pl. 180).

Two features of ancient Roman villas that had survived right through medieval times

into the Renaissance and later migrated to France were aviaries and enclosures for wild animals. Like the villas of the Roman emperors, the Versailles of the Sun King had its menagerie and in laying out the gardens of Castellazzo Jean Gianda did not omit this time-honoured adjunct of a classical garden. Dal Re's print shows bears, monkeys and comparatively gigantic parrots in the fascinatingly Rococo zoo that still exists at Castellazzo (pl. 183).

Palace of Stupinigi - Turin

Throughout the centuries Piedmont had always been more open to French influence than the rest of Italy; its geographical propinquity and the fact that its dukes often married daughters of the kings of France combined to make the Court of Turin a reflection of the manners and modes of Paris rather than of the other Italian capitals. During the seventeenth and eighteenth centuries hunting held a social significance in Piedmontese Court life that was only equalled by that of Versailles, and the huge villas of the House of Savoy were usually called hunting-boxes. Thus, when in 1729 Vittorio Amadeo II commissioned Filippo Juvara to build what was really an enormous palace within a few miles of Turin, it was called 'the little hunting palace'.

This superb Palace of Stupinigi, which is undeservedly little known to the outside world, is one of Juvara's masterpieces, upon which he lavished infinite pains, personally supervising the smallest details, during the six years of its construction before his departure to Spain in 1735. It is interesting to observe that, in his efforts to give even this splendid Baroque palace something of the rustic character of a hunting-lodge, the old Italian custom of introducing the out-of-doors into its decoration still survives in painted hunting scenes and huntsmen's trophies, and even in such small details as candle sconces, where wrought-iron oak branches are entwined around gilded stags' heads.

183 VILLA CRIVELLI SORMANI-VERRI
The Menagerie of the Villa Crivelli Sormani-Verri reproduced from the Delizie della Villa di Castellazzo. *This was another ancient Roman survival that was very popular in Italian gardens of the seventeenth and eighteenth centuries.* By kind permission of the Archivio Civico of Milan.

184 STUPINIGI
The gardens of Stupinigi near Turin, where the French influence is plainly evident. The superb Palace of Stupinigi was designed for Vittorio Amadeo II of Savoy by the Sicilian architect Juvara, begun in 1729 and completed by others after the architect's death in 1735. The garden was, however, the work of two Frenchmen—a father and son of the name of Bernard. It was begun in 1740 and not completed for many years. The villa belongs to the Order of San Maurizio and is open to the public.

It is an indication of the acknowledged leadership that France had acquired in garden design by the eighteenth century that, while he employed an Italian architect to build his palace, the Duke of Savoy called in a Frenchman — Bernard père — to lay out his garden. This work was begun in 1740 and lasted many years, and Duke Carlo Emmanuele later sent the original Bernard's son to study garden design and cultivation in Rome, Paris and, significantly, England. Even in such small details as the wooden boxes, which replace the traditional Italian terracotta pots, for orange and lemon trees, the gardens of Stupinigi are entirely French (pl. 184). The courtyards and a large area in front of the main façade of the palace are laid out as gravelled open spaces in the style of Le Nôtre, though the few parterres are simple designs of cut grass, which French garden authors call 'parterres à l'anglaise'.

The main feature of the Stupinigi gardens is the great circular *bosquet*, bisected by a wide grass *allée*, axially placed so as to afford a superb tree-framed vista of the main façade of the palace. Its large extent and the damp climate of Piedmont, which favours the growth of fine deciduous trees, have combined to give this garden the genuine atmosphere of its French prototypes; it does not feel like a foreign importation brought there by the whim of fashion. The rest of the *bosquet* is laid out with the customary walks, maze and an artificial lake, but in it the beginning of the end of the formal garden is also apparent; part of it is laid out with irregular paths in the picturesque style that had already penetrated into French gardens by the second half of the eighteenth century.

The signs of this coming revolution in garden art had been evident since the beginning of the century; even in his *Theory and Practice of Gardening* which was the handbook of the formal gardener, Dezallier had warned against excessive formality and artificial exaggeration, adding that 'a garden should be closer to nature than to art'. This idea would have appeared eccentric and ridiculous to the designers of Italian Renaissance gardens, who felt that man's function was to order nature not to imitate it. In fact, many of these landscape gardens, especially in France, were just as artificial as their formal predecessors. Tacitus would probably have found some even more biting phrase than his: 'With their cunning and impudent artificialities Nero's architects and contractors outbid nature' to describe Marie Antoinette and her ladies drinking milk, brought from the Hameau, out of Sèvres cups.

Castello of Agliè - Piedmont

But the wheel had come full circle, and the excessive artificiality of the eighteenth century that ended in the French Revolution, brought the inevitable reaction against formality in gardens as in other things. Although the destruction it wrought in many lovely old Italian gardens was irreparable, it also brought some good things in its train and, in Piedmont especially, it resulted in the creation of some beautiful parks. These are outside the scope of this book, but that of Agliè might legitimately be included, as although some of its parterres have been swept away by irregular beds and shrubberies, its fine terraces remain, in a setting of flowers and green lawns surrounded by majestic woods (pl. 185). The seventeenth-century house and garden that were largely transformed about the middle of the last century now belong to the Italian State and are preserved exactly as they were. It is strange that the place is so little visited, for to those who are interested in the period it is a unique survival. Its greatest charm however lies in the peace and tranquillity of its sunlit terraces and the acres of green shade that surround them, providing the balance and contrast that have always remained the basic elements of Italian garden design.

185   CASTELLO OF AGLIÈ
The gardens of the Castello of Agliè in Piedmont. Here the original seventeenth-century Italian formal garden has been partly converted in the English landscape style, and is surrounded by a romantic woodland setting. The villa belongs to the State and is open to the public.

Postscript

I t is appropriate that the old Neapolitan realm, where the Palermitan palaces of the Moslem emirs and Norman kings had been surrounded by the earliest pleasure gardens of modern times in Italy, should also provide the postscript to Italian garden design. Although according to Leandri's description sixteenth-century Palermo still boasted beautiful gardens, including the remains of those designed in the amoresque style for the Norman kings, Southern Italy in general lagged far behind the rest of the peninsula in the development of the Renaissance garden.

Gardens had evidently flourished in fifteenth-century Naples, for their beauty so captivated the French King Charles VIII during his Italian campaign that in 1495 he took home with him a Neapolitan gardener, Pacello da Mercogliano. But from what we know about the gardens that Pacello laid out for the kings of France at Amboise and Blois, which presumably reflected the contemporary Neapolitan style, it seems that these fifteenth-century gardens of southern Italy were simple walled enclosures surrounded by galleries, where the central space was laid out with beds of flowers and fountains.

Charles VIII had seen Naples at the end of its brief flowering under the sovereignty of the kings of Aragon, but his own expedition and the subsequent Franco-Spanish alliance ultimately resulted in the unfortunate realm being ruled by Spanish viceroys for over two hundred years. This period was one of the most disastrous in its whole history; the neglect and avarice of absentee foreign masters and internal disorders and brigandage reduced the country to a pitiable state in which the arts languished, like everything else, at a time when they reached their full flowering in the High Renaissance and Baroque periods in most of the rest of Italy.

In 1713 the Treaty of Utrecht had awarded the realm to Austria but, after some years' struggle, Charles III gained effective control of it in 1734 and was finally recognized by the Powers as its king in 1748. He was a grandson of Louis XIV, his father was the Bourbon King Philip V of Spain, his mother, Elizabeth, the last of the Farnese. Thus on both sides Charles was descended from families whose passion for building has bequeathed to posterity some of the most famous palaces, villas and gardens in the world, and it is not surprising to find that no sooner was he firmly seated on his throne than he prepared to emulate his ancestors.

Over two hundred years of rule by mere viceroys had left Naples sadly unprepared for the residence of a king; this and its vulnerability to attack from the sea, which had been amply demonstrated by the action of the British Fleet in 1742, decided Charles to build not only a new palace for himself but an entire new capital at Caserta. The two outstanding Neapolitan architects, Vaccaro and Sanfelice both died in 1750, forcing the King to look outside his realm for someone well qualified to carry out his plans. His choice fell on Luigi Vanvitelli, the Italianized son of the Dutch artist Gaspar van Vittel, and he was commissioned to draw up the plans in 1751.

LVIII   PALAZZO REALE

It was typical of the age that the first building to be begun in the new capital in the following year was the King's palace, and that it was intended to emulate and, if possible, outshine Versailles. In actual fact the palace has perhaps been best described as 'the overwhelmingly impressive swansong of the Italian Baroque'; but the gardens were laid out in the French style that in 1752 was still the accepted model for most of Europe.

Palazzo Reale - Caserta

The size of these gardens is enormous; their area had only previously been rivalled in Italy in modern times by the hunting-parks of Palermo and Northern Italy and by the great seventeenth-century Roman villas; but in none of these had an axial layout been imposed upon the whole, and this Caserta owed to the Versailles tradition. The palace stands some two miles from a range of hills and the intervening space is spanned by the vast central perspective, which begins as a carriage road traversing lawns (originally intended to be laid out as huge parterres of *broderies*), continues as a series of canals, cascades and fountains, and finally culminates in the stupendous water-staircase that gushes down from the summit of a small wooded hill fifty feet above (pls. 186, LVIII). The perspective is framed by palisades of clipped trees that enclose *bosquets* pierced by avenues and *cabinets* containing pools and fountains in the same style as Versailles.

Although the perspective does not lack a certain grandeur, especially when seen from the foot of the water-stairs, it must be admitted that Vanvitelli was no Le Nôtre and that in his striving for effect on so large a scale his sense of proportion failed him (pl. 187). The most attractive feature of the gardens is the water-staircase, especially in the autumn when the seasonal tints of its woodland setting provide a varied background for the silvery veil of water that falls from rock to rock down the hillside, and the rich bronze tones are reflected in the great pool at its foot, known as the 'Fountain of Diana.'

The probable explanation for the particular attraction of this part of the garden is that it owed its creation to a personal predilection of the King and was not, like the rest of the vast park, simply conceived by an architect as part of the grandeur that provided a proper setting for royalty. The inspiration for the water-staircase and fountain of Diana was derived from the gardens of La Granja at San Idelfonso in Spain, where the water garden known as the Carreras de Caballos is conceived on the same plan in a similar setting, though on a much smaller scale. Whereas at La Granja the water-stairs and pool are separated by a terrace from a lower ornamental garden, whose axis is marked by another pool, at Caserta this layout has been enormously enlarged and prolonged to form the great central perspective, and through lack of proper proportions has lost much of the charm of the original.

Charles III was attached to La Granja because it was a garden that he had known in childhood; it had been laid out by his mother and father as their interpretation of a French garden in the style of Versailles. So by this curiously circuitous means a water-staircase – a form of garden architecture that had been employed in the Canopus *triclinium*, of Hadrian's villa and had enlivened the gardens of many Italian Renaissance villas – provided the climax of Charles III's French gardens at Caserta, laid out, like his parents' La Granja, in emulation of Versailles. Perhaps nowhere else in the world is the diffusion of the basic principles of Italian gardens so curiously illustrated; within the space of two hundred and fifty years, Italian gardens had been introduced into France, developed and expanded until they represented a national style that became the model for Europe, and then via Spain returned to their point of departure, the Neapolitan Realm, as a foreign innovation.

The patronage of kings, the enthusiasm of ambassadors, scholars and antiquarians, the work of artists, architects and engravers and the travels of country gentlemen such as

186 PALAZZO REALE, CASERTA
The cascades and fountain of 'Diana' which terminate the great central perspective of the gardens of the Palazzo Reale of Caserta. Although their vast size and woodland setting render them more French than Italian in character, the cascades are the lineal descendants of those of Renaissance gardens like Caprarola and Bagnaia; the use of sculpture and rustic stonework in the fountain has an even more ancient origin, dating as it does from Roman times. Thus Caserta, which was the last great garden to be made in Italy, provides a fitting postscript to the history of Italian gardens, as it is at one and the same time a monument to the enduring classical and Renaissance garden design and to its influence upon the other countries of Europe.

Montaigne, had all played their part in the introduction of Italian garden art into France. Twenty-five years after Charles VIII had settled Pacello da Mercogliano and a group of his compatriots at Amboise – thus making it the cradle of the Renaissance in France – Francis I pursued the same policy at Fontainebleau. Here Primaticcio, Serlio and Il Rosso contributed to a more sophisticated type of garden, where such typically Renaissance features as a rustic portico adorned with figures of Atlas and painted 'histories' – possibly of the familiar classical type of incidents from the Odyssey, baths and rustic stone decoration were introduced. By the second half of the sixteenth century, as we know from the drawings and prints of Jacques Androuet du Cerceau and, later, Alexandre Francine (or Francini), the Italian High Renaissance type of terraced garden, with a central perspective and copious use of water, had been laid out at Verneuil-sur-Oise and Saint-Germain-en-Laye.

Du Cerceau had spent several years in Rome and on his return to France had published books on Italian grotesque decoration, architecture, country villas and above all, in 1576 and 1579, his famous *Les Plus Excellents Bastiments de France* in which his own garden designs and those of many of the great French chateaux appear. Verneuil-sur-Oise, begun in 1565, was Du Cerceau's first large garden plan – previously he had apparently only been responsible for additions to other gardens – and with its axial layout and use of different levels it is strikingly in advance of most of the gardens in his book laid out by other architects and gardeners.

Saint-Germain-en-Laye, which was converted to the Renaissance style in about 1595, provided an even more striking example of the influence of the Italian garden in France. The layout bore a strong resemblance to Villa d'Este at Tivoli, though the water-parterre at the lowest level was very like that of Villa Lante at Bagnaia. The garden was laid out for Henry IV and his Italian Queen Maria de' Medici. The chief royal architect

of the day was Du Pérac who in 1573 had executed the famous print of Villa d'Este, as well as others of Villa di Papa Giulio and the Cortile del Belvedere. In view of this it is generally assumed that Du Pérac was responsible for the design of Saint-Germain-en-Laye, though the planting was carried out by the royal gardener Claude Mollet. In his book *Théatre des Plans et Jardinages*, posthumously published in 1652, Claude Mollet states that Du Pérac, who returned to France after many years' residence in Italy in 1582, drew garden plans for his father Jacques Mollet who was then gardener to the King of France. Thus it was not only by his prints that Du Pérac contributed to the diffusion of the Italian style of garden in France.

Mollet's book, which was apparently written at the end of his life, provides the most interesting evidence, not only of the Italian influence on French gardens but also of how during the first half of the seventeenth century these were already beginning to be transformed by the French national genius to suit another style of landscape. In his description of the basic principles of garden layout, after discussing the planting of the avenue of trees leading up to the house, Mollet writes: ' . . . behind it should be laid out the parterres and *broderies* of the same, so that they can easily be seen and enjoyed from the windows, without any tall obstacle such as trees or palisades spoiling the view. After these parterres of *broderies* should follow those of turf, also *bosquets* and high and low palisades, suitably placed so that most of the *allées* begin and end where some statue or fountain is placed; and at the extremities of these *allées* fine perspectives painted on canvas should be placed, that can be removed to shelter from injury in time of bad weather. To complete the scheme statues on pedestals should stand in suitable places, also grottoes should be built. Where the site allows some *allées* should be placed on terraces, nor should aviaries, fountains, *jets d'eau*, canals and other such ornaments be forgotten, as each in its right place

187 PALAZZO REALE, CASERTA
The canal and gardens of the Palazzo Reale of Caserta; the palace is seen in the distance. Although laid out in Italy by Vanvitelli, who was of Dutch parentage, this late-eighteenth-century garden is almost completely French in its vast size and conception. But the French garden drew its original inspiration from Italy and the gardens of Caserta may thus be regarded as the last legitimate descendant of the Italian gardens of the Renaissance. The palace and gardens belong to the State and are open to the public.

contributes to the formation of the perfect pleasure garden.'

From Mollet's description it will be seen that the old Italian principles of proportion in garden design had already taken root in France: the open space filled with parterres coming next to the built-up area of the house, and the planting becoming thicker and more luxuriant as it receded from it. The directions for the planning of the *allées*, to begin and end at some fixed point accentuated by the stonework of fountains and sculpture, correspond exactly to the Italian Renaissance principle, and it will be recalled that a painted landscape-garden decoration already featured in Firenzuola's ideal Sienese garden of the sixteenth century. Grottoes, aviaries and fountains are significantly Italian in origin, but the changes imposed by the French landscape and taste have also become apparent. Canals are definitely more French than Italian; in Italy large bodies of water were usually employed in cascades or pools; and the *jets d'eau* – in the form of the jet of water rising from the surface of a pool – was a French innovation though it was also in use in the Orient. Both the canal and the *jets d'eau* bespeak a flatter type of site than do the Italian wall fountains and cascades; likewise the mention of *allées* to be placed on terraces 'where the site allows' – in mountainous Italy the hillside terraced site was the rule, not the exception. But most significantly French of all is the prominence given to the parterres, especially the *broderies*, which on a flat site assumed so much importance; this is the reason why they were adopted with alacrity in Northern Italy when French fashions first crossed the Alps. It took some time before the *broderie* parterres penetrated to Tuscany and Rome and, as Luigi Dami pointed out, the old Italian compartments of hedged beds had to be swept away in order to make way for them. But even so, the French garden was still a development of Italian principles, not a revolution like the English landscape garden that in the end killed both.

Another extremely important aspect of Mollet's book, as two great French garden authors Achille Duchêne and Marcel Fouquier have observed, is that already it outlines many of the principles of French garden design that were to be transformed and developed on an enormous scale, consonant with the riches and power of Louis XIV, by the genius of Le Nôtre, so that his masterpieces at Vaux, Saint-Cloud, Chantilly, Saint-Germain and above all Versailles, became the models for the rest of Europe.

Just as the open and less mountainous landscape of France had resulted in the evolution of the basic principles of Italian garden design, the more temperate climate also played its part. Whereas in the long hot summers of Italy Baccio Bandinelli's maxim '*Le cose che si murano debbono essere guidi e superiori a quelle che si piantono*' is a basic necessity, in the forest-land of France it could be largely dispensed with, and much of the stone garden architecture was replaced by the architectural treatment of greens, like clipped palisades of trees and *bosquets* pierced by *allées* and *cabinets*, which assumed a size and importance they had never had in Italy. But it should be recalled that this type of garden had been foreshadowed in the great Roman park villas like Villa Borghese, Villa Ludovisi and Villa Pamphilj.

This use of deciduous trees for garden architecture was much better suited to the landscape and flora of northern European countries like Germany, Holland, Sweden, Austria and even Russia, to which the French garden style now spread. Insular England, where the cult of gardens had always flourished, was less affected in many ways as she had been less influenced by the Italian gardens of the Renaissance. It is indicative of her independence in these matters that while adopting the Italian Palladian style of architecture in the first half of the eighteenth century, she evolved her own ideal landscape setting for it.

The influence of the Italian Renaissance garden had, however, by no means been limited to France; it was because it was later superseded to a large extent in many countries, including Italy, by the French garden which had evolved from it, that the introduction of the Italian garden style into France is of particular interest. Even in

England, where the Reformation afterwards led to a preference for Dutch and German models, as early as 1521 Giovanni da Maiano had made terracotta busts of Roman emperors and 'histories' of Hercules for Cardinal Wolsey's gardens at Hampton Court. The use of these classical motifs and names such as the 'Mount of Venus' for different parts of gardens was evidently established in sixteenth-century England, as were water-engines and surprise fountains, since Hentzner mentions them in his description of Lord Burleigh's garden at Theobalds in 1598.

However, as Sir Reginald Blomfield pointed out, although English gardens of the sixteenth century were becoming large and elaborate, Italian importations were really limited to balustraded terraces, large flights of steps, and the use of sculpture, topiary and classical names. Evidence of French influence is apparent in England early in the seventeenth century. Gervaise Markham's *Country Farm*, published in 1615, was largely drawn from Olivier de Serres, and James I already employed a French gardener, André Mollet, son of the famous Claude. After the Restoration this tendency was increased by the reputation of Le Nôtre and the close relationship between the Stuart and Bourbon Courts, while the successful publication, running into several editions, of John James' translation of Dezallier d'Argenville's *La Théorie et la Pratique du Jardinage* in the eighteenth century, shows that even in England the French formal garden did not go down without a struggle before it was eclipsed by the landscape style.

Spain, whose isolation and conservatism is as marked as that of England, had in spite of her own flourishing indigenous style been more strongly influenced by the Italian Renaissance garden. Perhaps the similarity of climate had something to do with it, but a more obvious agent was the Emperor Charles V, who had seen and admired many of the famous Italian gardens and was the first to introduce the style into Spain. His son Philip II imported classical statues from Italy – some of them the gift of Cardinal Ricci for whom the Roman Villa Medici was originally laid out – for his Italian gardens at the Escorial. The island garden at Aranjuez, laid out by Charles or Philip, was also evidently Italian in style, for there Velázquez painted the picture of the Triton fountain that recalls his canvases of the Villa Medici.

During the seventeenth century the Italian influence was still paramount in Spain. Philip IV employed Cosimo Lotti, who had worked in the Boboli, both at Aranjuez and the Pardo, where he created a hemisphere and water-staircase that are reminiscent of Villa Aldobrandini at Frascati. Buen Retiro, now the park of Madrid, was laid out on a scale as vast as Villa Borghese, and here the Italian influence extended to floriculture. In 1633 Cardinal Pio di Savoia sent his Roman gardener on loan to the King of Spain to plant there his gift of bulbs, valued at 10,000 ducats. But, as we have seen, with the accession of the Bourbon King Philip V in 1701, garden art in Spain also passed into the French sphere of influence.

The Emperor Charles V did not limit his interest in gardens to the Spanish part of his domains; the garden he made at Vienna was filled with rare plants brought from all over his vast Empire. His brother Ferdinand was evidently also a garden enthusiast, and one of the most famous Austrian gardens of the sixteenth century was laid out around his Tyrolese Castle of Ambras. The family tradition was continued by Maximilian II in the gardens he created in 1569 at Neugebaude near Vienna, where the Italian influence was evident in the terraced layout.

Owing partly no doubt to geographical propinquity, the Italian influence was marked in early seventeenth-century gardens in Austria. Sometimes it was augmented by family ties, as was the case in the beautiful and markedly Italianate gardens of Hellbrun near Salzburg, laid out between 1613 and 1619 by Bishop Marcus Sittich, who was connected to the Borromeos and the Altemps of Rome. As in most of the rest of Europe the French influence gained ground in Austria in the second half of the century, and the famous

Baroque gardens of the Belvedere in Vienna with their clipped hedges, laid out for Prince Eugène of Savoy in 1693, afford evidence of this. The Belvedere owes not only its name to Italy — the concept of separate palaces for living and entertaining had been anticipated in the Villa Pamphilj in Rome. But at Schönbrunn, to quote Geoffrey Jellicoe, 'the whole plan is based like Versailles on the contrast between open space and woodland excitements'.

In sixteenth-century Germany the botanical aspect of Italian Renaissance gardens predominated over the architectural influence. The studies of individual German savants at Italian universities led them to create their own gardens of rare plants, even before the institution of botanical gardens at Padua, Bologna and Pisa encouraged cities such as Leyden, Leipzig and Heidelberg to follow their example in the latter half of the century. Owing to the division of the country into so many small States and Principalities there was no unified development of a Renaissance style of garden art in Germany, as might have been fostered by the fashions set by a dominating Court. Nevertheless beautiful gardens existed, and in many of them the Italian influence was evident — like those of the Residenz at Munich, with their statues, grottoes, mosaics and marble-edged plots. Stuttgart Castle was famous for its orangery and Haimhausen had a fine terraced garden in the Italian style, containing tree houses like the one which Montaigne had admired in the Medici villa of Castello. One of the most famous gardens in Germany was laid out by Solomon de Caux for Elizabeth Stuart, wife of the Elector Palatine at Heidelberg. Here a terraced hillside site was laid out with labyrinths, pools and tree-filled plots in the Italian manner, though the overall plan of Italian Renaissance garden design was lacking.

With few exceptions the disastrous Thirty Years War brought a stop to garden development in Germany. When peace was finally established in 1648 the French influence was in the ascendant, and as the long reign of Louis XIV advanced Versailles came increasingly to be regarded as the model for the princely Courts. Thus in the second half of the seventeenth century garden art in Germany aspired to follow the Versailles model though, as might be expected, interpretations of it were influenced by local conditions and psychology, to say nothing of the smaller size of princely pockets which necessitated a reduction in scale. However, as late as 1700 the Landgrave of Hesse commissioned the Roman architect Guerrieri to design the fabulous water-staircase of his gardens at Cassel, which is the swansong of the direct influence of the Italian garden in Germany.

By the beginning of the eighteenth century the influence of the French garden had reached the remotest corners of Europe — from Spain in the south to Sweden in the north, where it had early been adopted by Queen Christina, who employed André Mollet after he had worked for James I of England. But now, just before the advent of the landscape style that signed its death-warrant, the influence of the French garden spread even further afield — to Russia, where garden art had been unknown until the days of Peter the Great. The gardens of his splendid palace of Peterhof, near the newly-founded city of St Petersburg, were laid out by Alexandre Le Blond in the French style, and on a scale that for once really did rival Versailles, though their splendours were perhaps more Oriental than Parisian. Even Russia was not the furthest limit to which the fame of the French garden spread; in 1730 a Saxon architect prepared the plans for one to be laid out for the Moghul Emperor of India at his capital of Delhi. Thus to the Orient, from which its original inspiration had come in the days of Xenophon, the classical pleasure garden returned as a new foreign fashion, after an interval of 2000 years during which Greeks, Romans, Renaissance Italians and Frenchmen of the *grand siècle* had all contributed something to its evolution.

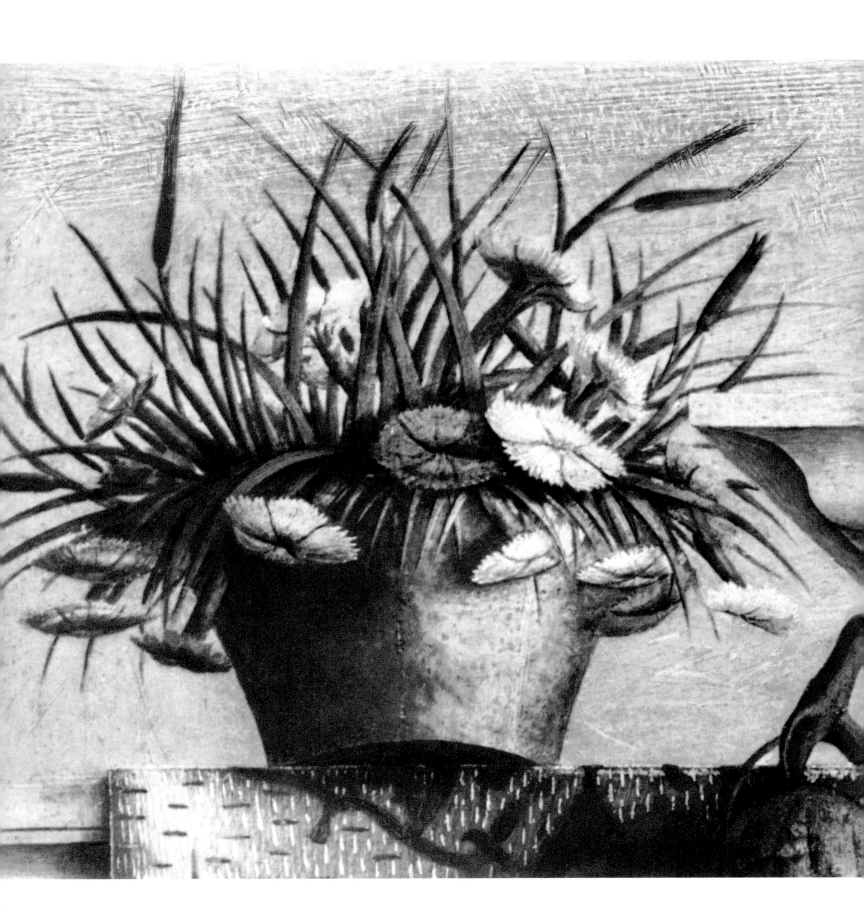

Flowers Grown in Italian Gardens

Strangely enough the only period for which a detailed study has been made of the flowers that grew in Italian gardens is the earliest one. From the works of archaeologists such as Dr Spinazzola, and particularly from the books of Monsieur Grimal and Lady Gabriel we have a fairly clear idea of what flowers and ornamental plants were cultivated in Roman gardens, especially in Pompeii. The list of Roman flowers, shrubs, creepers and ornamental trees which follows is drawn from these sources, and a few of the ornamental ones from the *Natural History* of Pliny.

As might be expected, in medieval times the number of purely ornamental plants decreased and those that were esteemed for their medicinal and culinary virtues held pride of place, though Pietro de' Crescenzi, in the part of his agricultural treatise devoted to garden layout, mentions such luxurious and ornamental plants as citrus trees and palms; however these were probably only within the means of a limited number of rich men in his day. The list of medieval flowers and herbs which follows was selected from the Agrarian Society of Bologna's study on Pietro's treatise.

What is really extraordinary, however, is that, apart from R. W. Kennedy's *The Renaissance Painter's Garden* and Monsieur Bazin's recent *A Gallery of Flowers*, practically no one appears to have investigated what kinds of flowers were grown in Italian gardens at later periods. Most books on Italian gardens either ignore the question altogether or state briefly that flowers were relegated to the *giardini segreti* in spite of the fact that sixteenth- and seventeenth-century garden prints provide evidence to the contrary. There are three probable reasons for this—firstly Italian gardens were distinguished for their wonderful architectural treatment of the site, and stones and mortar endure better than plants; secondly, in the eighteenth century, in the Roman area particularly, the flower gardens which had previously existed were swept away and often replaced by green parterres of box; this was largely the result of a curious fashionable dislike of scented flowers; finally, even in Renaissance times, Italians seem as a rule to have been strangely ignorant of the names of flowers—as M. L. Gothein has pointed out, even the humanists' descriptions of their much-prized gardens give purely generic references to the plants and flowers that grew there.

Nevertheless, a study of Renaissance works of art and contemporary letters provides evidence that flowers played quite a considerable part in Italian gardens of the fifteenth and sixteenth centuries. Most precious among these sources is the *Hypnerotomachia* of Poliphilus, the curious late-fifteenth-century romance that was really a peg upon which the author hung his theories about architectural and garden design. The *Hypnerotomachia* is quoted by almost every author who has written about Italian gardens in an architectural context, but few indeed have ever examined the author's detailed descriptions of the planting in the dream gardens that he describes. Whole lists of flowers are given, and the minutest details of the design and planting of the parterres. Owing to the curious mixture of Greek, Latin, and traditional country names given, identification of these plants is exceedingly difficult and the writer has only dealt with

188 PAINTING BY CRIVELLI
Pinks Dianthus plumarius, an old garden favourite, detail from a painting by Crivelli in the National Gallery, London. Anderson photo.

the few it seemed possible to identify with a fair degree of certainty by comparison with Bauhin's edition of Mattioli and G. B. Ferrari and P. B. Clarici's seventeenth- and eighteenth-century books on Italian gardening. Many of the flowers listed as grown in the fifteenth and sixteenth century are drawn from the *Hypnerotomachia*, others are from Girolamo Firenzuola's sixteenth-century agricultural treatise and from contemporary letters and paintings.

The strangest omission of all is the absolute lack of interest displayed by garden authors in the planting of Italian gardens during the seventeenth century, in spite of the fact that this is really very well documented by the pictures of the *fioranti* such as Mario Nuzzi, or Mario de' Fiori as he was generally known. Many of the great Roman palaces have pictures, painted mirrors and other floral decorations executed by him, in which many of the flowers are almost as easily distinguishable as in those of the Flemish flower painters. His work in Palazzo Colonna in Rome is outstanding in this respect, and one of the painted mirrors in the picture gallery has what is probably the earliest portrayal of an amaryllis.

It is evident that the work of the *fioranti* reflected a current fashion among the Roman cardinals and princes for growing the new exotic plants from the East and West Indies, the Americas and South Africa, which were beginning to arrive in Europe during the first half of the seventeenth century. The bulb craze was by no means limited to Holland, and in the warmer climate of Italy these exotics flourished and often flowered earlier than in northern Europe. Ample evidence of this appears in two contemporary books on horticulture— T. Aldino's *Horti Farnesiani Rariores plantae Exactissime descriptae* published in Rome in 1625, and G. B. Ferrari's *Flora overo Cultura de Fiori*, published in 1638. Both authors were in charge of the gardens of great Roman families and give most interesting information not only of what was grown in them, but also about the arrival and progress of rare exotics in all the other well-known gardens. Most famous among them were the gardens of Francesco Caetani, Duke of Sermoneta and Prince of Caserta, of which a unique manuscript list of the planting of the parterres in the year 1625 still survives in the family archive. Although much easier than for those of the fifteenth century, identification of these flowers still presents many difficulties, as the bulbs and tubers were usually all classified as hyacinths, narcissus, and sometimes colchicum, though many of the exotics are described as lilion-narcissus. Comparison between these earlier books and lists with P. B. Clarici's *Istoria e Cultura delle Piante*, published in Venice in 1726, and Thomas Mauve's *The Complete Gardener*, London, 1827, however, solves some of these problems, and the following list of seventeenth-century flowers has been compiled on this basis—but it is necessarily far from comprehensive.

Although floriculture appears to have lost popularity in Rome during the eighteenth century it was still flourishing in Northern Italy, and Clarici's book gives a long list of flowers, of which only the most interesting have been selected. To these have been added a few later arrivals among the exotics listed in Nicolao Martello's *Hortus Romanus*, Rome, 1778, which is a list of the plants cultivated in the Roman botanical gardens on the Janiculum at that time.

There is no doubt that detailed research into this almost totally unexplored field would be a fascinating study which might result in some horticultural surprises, and the writer hopes that the very brief and inadequate summary and lists given here may perhaps arouse sufficient curiosity in someone better equipped to undertake it.

Although in the text of the book the writer has used, wherever possible, the English traditional names for flowers, because in all countries these seem to have changed less than successive attempts at Latin classification (Cyclamen, for instance, has been Sowbread or Pan Porcino in England and Italy through the centuries), in the lists the Latin names are given first owing to the inclusion of the exotics in the later periods. In the medieval and fifteenth- and sixteenth-century lists the names of some plants are repeated to show what continued to be grown. In the seventeenth- and eighteenth-century lists only the names of additional plants are given.

Roman flowers

LATIN NAME	ENGLISH NAME	LATIN NAME	ENGLISH NAME
Acanthus mollis	Acanthus or Bear's Breech or Bear's Foot	*Lilium candidum*	Madonna Lily
Aconitum napellus	Aconite or Monkshood	*Lilium martagon*	Martagon Lily or Turk's Cap Lily
Adianthum capillus-veneris	Maidenhair Fern	*Lychnis Coronaria*	Red Campion
Adonis aestivalis	Pheasant's Eye or Ox-eye	*Melilotus officinalis*	Melilot
Anemone nemorosa	Anemone or Windflower	*Melissa officinalis*	Lemon Balm
Anthemis nobilis	Chamomile	*Narcissus poeticus*	Pheasant's Eye Narcissus or Poet's Daffodil
Artemisia abrotanum	Southernwood		
Calendula officinalis	Marigold	*Origanum marjorana*	Sweet or Knotted Marjoram
Celosia cristata	Cockscomb	*Paeonia officinalis*	Peony
Centaurea cyanus	Cornflower	*Papaver rhoeas*	Corn or Shirley Poppy
Cheiranthus cheiri	Wallflower	*Papaver somniferum*	Opium Poppy
Chrysanthemum coronarium	Annual Chrysanthemum	*Portulaca oleracea*	Green Purslane
Chrysanthemum segetum grandiflorum	Yellow Ox-Eye Daisy	*Rosa alba*	White Rose
		Rosa centifolia	Cabbage Rose
Convolvulus sepium	Bindweed	*Rosa damascena*	Damask Rose
Crocus sativus	Saffron Crocus	*Rosa gallica*	Provence Rose
Cyclamen europaeum	Cyclamen or Sowbread	*Rosa milesia*	Rose of Miletus
Cytisus scoparius	Common Broom	*Rosa praenestina*	Rose of Praeneste
Dianthus plumosus	Pink	*Rosmarinus officinalis*	Rosemary
Digitalis purpurea	Foxglove	*Ruscus aculeatus*	Butcher's Broom
Foeniculum officinale	Fennel	*Ruscus racemosus*	Alexandrian Laurel
Gladiolus segetum	Gladiolus or Corn Flag	*Senecio cineraria*	Dusty Miller
Helichrysum stoechas	Yellow Everlasting-flower	*Teucrium fruticans*	Shrubby Germander
Hesperis matronalis	Sweet Rocket	*Thymus serpyllum*	Wild Thyme
Iris Florentina	Florentine Iris	*Thymus vulgaris*	Common Thyme
Iris Germanica	Flag Iris	*Vinca minor*	Lesser Periwinkle
Iris pseud-acorus	Yellow Water Flag	*Viola odorata*	Scented Violet
Jasminum fruticans	Yellow Jasmine	*Viola sylvestris*	Wood Violet
Lavandula officinalis	Lavender	*Viola tricolor*	Pansy

Roman shrubs, creepers & ornamental trees

LATIN NAME	ENGLISH NAME	LATIN NAME	ENGLISH NAME
Acacia Vera	Mimosa	*Nerium oleander*	Oleander
Arbutus unedo	Arbutus or Strawberry Tree	*Phoenix dactylifera*	Date Palm
Buxus sempervirens	Box	*Platanus orientalis*	Plane Tree
Cornus Mas	Cornelian Cherry	*Punica granatum*	Pomegranate
Cupressus sempervirens	Cypress	*Prunus amygdalus*	Almond Tree
Cydonia oblonga	Quince Tree	*Prunus cerasus*	Cherry Tree
Hedera helix	Ivy	*Prunus persica*	Peach Tree
Laurus nobilis	Bay tree or Victor's or Poet's Laurel	*Pyrus communis*	Pear Tree
		Pyrus malus	Apple Tree
Myrtus communis	Myrtle	*Smilax aspera*	Prickly Ivy

Medieval flowers

LATIN NAME	ENGLISH NAME	LATIN NAME	ENGLISH NAME
Adianthum capillus veneris	Maidenhair	*Ocymum basilicum*	Sweet Basil
Anthemis nobilis	Chamomile	*Origanum dictamnus*	Dittany-of-Crete
Artemisia abrotanum	Southernwood	*Origanum marjorana*	Sweet or Knotted Majoram
Artemisia absinthium	Wormwood	*Papaver somniferum*	Opium Poppy
Arum italicum	Italian Arum	*Pistacia lentiscus*	Lentiscus or Pistachio
Borago officinalis	Borage	*Polypodium vulgare*	Polypod Fern
Brassica alba	Mustard	*Portulace oleracea*	Green Purslane
Clematis flammula	White Clematis	*Rosa centifolia*	Cabbage Rose
Crithmum maritimum	Samphire	*Rosa damascena*	Damask Rose
Crocus sativus	Saffron Crocus	*Rosmarinus officinalis*	Rosemary
Erythraea centaurium	Centaury	*Rumex patienta*	Herb Patience
Eupatorium cannabinum	Hemp Agrimony	*Ruta graveolens*	Rue
Gentiana lutea	Yellow Gentian or Butterwort	*Satureia hortensis*	Summer Savory
Glycyrrhiza glabra	Liquorice	*Scabiosa columbaria*	Scabious
Iris florentina	Florentine Iris	*Scilla maritima*	Squill
Iris germanica	Flag Iris	*Semperivivum tectorum*	Houseleek
Lilium candidum	Madonna Lily	*Symphytum officinale*	Comfrey
Lilium martagon	Martagon Lily or Turk's Cap Lily	*Thymus vulgaris*	Common Thyme
Nymphaea alba	Water-lily	*Viola odorata*	Scented Violet
Nymphaea lutea	Yellow Water-lily		

Flowers of the fifteenth and sixteenth centuries *

	LATIN NAME	ENGLISH NAME	HYPNEROTOMACHIA
H.	*Aceras antropophora*	Man Orchis	(Dilbulbo uomico Aequicoli); M. Testiculus; C. Antropofore degl Equicoli
H.	*Achillea rupestris? tanacetifolia?*	Yarrow	(Achilea)
H.	*Althaea rosea*	Hollyhock	(Malva)
H.	*Aquilegia alpina*	Aquilegia or Columbine	(Aquilegia)
H.	*Artemesia abrotanum*	Southernwood	(Aurotano); M. Abrotanum
	Asphodeline lutea	Yellow Asphodel	
	Bellis perennis	Daisy	
H.	*Caltha palustris*	Marsh Marigold	(Caltha)
H.	*Celosia plumosa*	Velvet Flower, Amaranth or Prince of Wales Feather	(Amarantho)
	Cistus Ladaniferus	Gum Cistus	
	Citrus aurantium	Sweet Orange Tree	
	Citrus aurantium bigardia	Seville Orange Tree	
	Citrus limonum	Lemon Tree	
	Citrus medica	Citron Tree	
H.	*Convallaria majalis*	Lily of the Valley	(Lilli convalli)
	Convulvulus sepium	Bind weed or Convolvulus	
	Cratae gus oxyacanthoides	Common Hawthorn	

	LATIN NAME	ENGLISH NAME	HYPNEROTOMACHIA
H.	*Cyclamen europaenum*	Cyclamen or Sowbread	(Cyclamino)
	Cytisus scoparius	Broom	
	Dianthus caryophyllus	Carnation	
	Dianthus plumosus	Pink	
H.	*Gladiolus segetum*	Gladiolus or Corn Flag	(Xiphion segetale); M. Xiphion segetale
H.	*Helichrysum angustifolium?*	Yellow Everlasting or Curry Plant?	(Heliochrysso)
	Hemerocallis fulva	Red Day Lily	
	Hesperis matronalis	Sweet Rocket	
H.	*Hippuris vulgaris*	Mare's-tail	(Hippotesi)
H.	*Hyacinthus orientalis*	Hyacinth	(Hiacynthi albenti, cerulei, purpurei that do not flower in Gaul)
H.	*Hyssopus officinalis*	Hyssop	(Issope)
H.	*Inula helenium*	Elecampane	(Lachryme di Helena)
	Iris florentina	Florentine Iris	
	Iris germanica	Flag Iris	
	Jasminum grandiflorium	Large scented Jasmine of 'Catalonia', imported from Orient	
	Jasminum officinale	White Jasmine	
H.	*Lavandula officinalis*	Lavender	(Lavendula)
	Lilium candidum	Madonna Lily	
H.	*Lonicera periclymenum*	Honeysuckle	(Periclymeno); M. Periclymenum madraselva
H.	*Myostosis palustris* palustre	Forget-me-not	(Auricole fluvicole); M. Myosotis
H.	*Narcissus tazzetta?*	Polyanthus narcissus	(Floribundi narcissi)
H.	*Nigella damascena*	Love-in-a-mist	(Mellantio or Gyth); M. Gith or Niella
H.	*Origanum marjorana?*	Sweet Marjoram	(Origani)
	Ornithogalum umbellatum	Star of Bethlehem	
	Papaver somniferum	Opium poppy	
H.	*Primula auricula*	Auricula	(Senniculo); M. Sanicula or Auricula ursi
H.	*Primula vulgaris*	Primrose	(Primula verisflorida)
H.	*Ranunculus acris flore pleno? bulbosus flore pleno?*	Yellow Ranunculus	(Dilherba anemone or Dilherba Tora); M. Ranunculus Tora Giallo
	Rosa centifolia	Cabbage Rose	
	Rosa damascena	Damask Rose	
H.	*Ruta graveolens*	Rue	(Ruta)
	Sambucus nigra	Elderflower	
H.	*Santolina chamaecyparissus? rosmarinifolia?*	Lavender Cotton	(Chamaepitas); M. Chamaecyparissus Chamaepytis, Santolina Cypressus
H.	*Teucrium fruitcans?*	Germander	(Chamaedryos); M. Teucrim Chamaedry, Germandrée
H.	*Thalictrum minus adiantifolia*	Maidenhair Meadow Rue	(Adiantho aquilegie)
H.	*Thymus serpyllum*	Wild Thyme	(Serpillo montano)
	Thymus vulgaris	Common Thyme	
	Vibernum tinus	Laurustinus	
H.	*Viola sylvestris*	Purple Violet	(Viole amythystine)
H.	*Viola odorata*	Scented Violet	(Viole olorine)
H.	*Viola tricolor*	Pansy	(Viole Luteole); M. Viole arborescens or Jacea or Pensieri

* *Those marked H. are mentioned in the* Hypnerotomachia *of Poliphilus. After the Latin and English names, the name given in the* Hypnerotomachia *appears in brackets, followed by the name or names given in Bauhin's edition of Mattioli, indicated by the letter M., and sometimes by Clarici's nomenclature indicated by the letter C.*

Seventeenth-century flowers *

	LATIN NAME	ENGLISH NAME	OLD ITALIAN NAME
CAE.	*Allium moly*	Yellow Allium	(Moly giallo)
CAE. F.	*Amaryllis belladonna*	Belladonna Lily	(Narciso Indiano Donnabella)
F.	*Amaryllis blanda*	Amaryllis	(Narcisco Indiano Vergognosetto)
CAE. F.	*Anemone coronaria*	Anemone	(Anemone, many varieties, single, semi-double, double)
F.	*Brunsvigia* sp.	Candelabra-flower	(Narcisco Indiano Gigliato Sferico Fiore Liliaceo)
CAE.	*Colchicum autumnale*	Autumn Crocus	(Colchico, many varieties)
CAE.	*Crocus* spp.	Crocus	(Croco, many varieties)
F.	*Cyclamen* spp.	Cyclamen	(Ciclamino, Pan Porcino many varieties)
	Delphinium ajacis	Larkspur	(Consolida regalis, Sperone di Cavaliero)
F.	*Ferraria undulata*	Black or Cape Starry Iris	(Fiore Indiano, Violato scuro)
F.	*Fragaria virginiana*	Virginian Strawberry	(Fragole Canadiane)
CAE. F.	*Fritillaria imperialis*	Crown Imperial	(Corona Imperiale)
F.	*Fritillaria Persica*	Persian Lily	(Pennacchio Persiano)
CAE. F.	*Fritillaria Meleagris*	Snake's Head	(Fritellaria Meleagride and other varieties)
CAE. F.	*Haemanthus* sp.	Blood Flower or Red Cape Tulip	(Colchico Massimo Indiano or Narcisco Indiano Suertio)
A.	*Helianthus tuberosus?*	Jerusalem Artichoke?	(Tubera Indiana Soleo from the Virgin Islands, introduced into England, then France)
F.	*Iris paradoxa*	White blue and crimson Persian Cushion Iris	(Iride di Persia fiore bianco celeste paonazzo)
CAE.	*Iris susiana*	Mourning Iris	(Giglio Faraone)
F.	*Iris xiphium*	Spanish Iris	(Iride bulbosa d'Andalusia)
CAE.	*Leontice leontopetalum*	Lion's Leaf	(Leontopetalum di Candia)
CAE. F.	*Lilium chalcedonicum*	Crimson Turk's Cap Lily	(Riccio della Signora)
CAE. F.	*Lilium martagon album*	White Martagon Lily	(Martagone bianco)
F.	*Lobelia cardinalis*	Cardinal Flower	(Trachelio Americana or Pianta Cardinale)
F.	*Lychnis coeli-rosa*	Rose of Heaven	(Licnide di Constantinopoli)
	Matthiola spp.	Stock many varieties	(Violacciocca)
F.	*Muscari botryoides*	Grape hyacinth	(Jacinto Botriode)
F.	*Muscari moschatum*	Musk hyacinth	(Jacinto Botriode muscato)
	Narcissus spp.	Narcissus	(Narcisco, many varieties)
F.	*Narcissus pseudo-narcissus*	Daffodils	(Colli di Camello, many varieties)
F.	*Ornithogalum arabicum*	Star of Bethlehem	(Giglio d'Alessandria)
CAE.	*Paeonia albiflora?*	White Peony	(Peonia bianca)
F.	*Paradisia liliastrum*	St. Bruno's Lily	(Gigliastro or Giglio di S.Brunone)
CAE. F.	*Polianthes tuberosa*	Tuberose	(Jacinto Indiano bianco tuberosa or Asfodele Indiano)
CAE. F.	*Ranunculus asiaticus*	Ranunculus, many varieties	
F.	*Rosa* spp.	Cabbage, Damask, Dog, Italian, Dutch Roses etc	(Rosa centifoglia, damaschena, canina, Italiana, Olandese and six other varieties)
CAE. F.	*Scilla peruviana*	'Peruvian' Squill	(Giacinto del Perù or Giacinto stellare di Portogallo)
A.	*Sprekelia formosissima*	Jacobean Lily	(Lilionarcisso rubeo Indiano Jacobi)
	Tropaeolum majus and I. minus	Tall and Dwarf Nasturtiums	
CAE. F.	*Tulipa* spp.	Tulip	(Tulipano, many varieties)

* A. indicates flowers mentioned by Aldino, CAE. those appearing in the Caetani MSS lists, F. those mentioned by Ferrari. The name given by Aldino, Caetani or Ferrari follows in brackets.

Seventeenth-century shrubs, creepers and ornamental trees *

	LATIN NAME	ENGLISH NAME	OLD ITALIAN NAME
A.	*Acacia Farnesiana*	Mimosa (much grown in France for perfumery)	(Acacia Farnesiana)
F.	*Bignonia species?*	American Trumpet Flower	(Gelsiminum Indicum Flore Phoeniceo)
F.	*Cytisus albus*	White Spanish Broom	(Genista bianca di Spagna)
F.	*Hibiscus mutabilis*	Cotton Rose or Hibiscus	(Ketmia or Rosa Sinensis Foliosa Arbuscula)
F.	*Hibiscus rosa-sinensis*	Blacking Plant or Hibiscus	(Ketmia or Rosa Sinensis)
A.	*Ipomoa superba?*	Morning Glory	(Campanula esotica delle Isole Virgine)
F.	*Jasminum odoratissimum*	Yellow Scented Jasmine	(Gelsiminum Indicum Flavum odoratissimum)
F.	*Jasminum Sambac*	Large White Scented Jasmine	(Mogarino or Gelsomino sambac)
A.	*Passiflora edulis*	Passion Flower	(Maracoto Indiano or Grenadiglia)
F.	*Prunus cerasus flore-pleno*	Double Flowering Cherry	(Ciriege fior doppio)
F.	*Prunus persica flore-pleno*	Double Flowering Peach	(Persica fior doppio)
	Syringa vulgaris	Lilac	(Lilac)
	Viburnum opulus sterilis	Garden Guelder Rose or Snowball Tree	
A.	*Yucca gloriosa*	Adam's Needle	(Jucca Indiana)

* Also marked for source A., C.A.E., and F. as above, with old Italian names in brackets.

Eighteenth-century flowers *

	LATIN NAME	ENGLISH NAME	OLD ITALIAN NAME
CLA.	*Anastatica hierochuntica*	Rose of Jericho or Resurrection Plant	(Raspi or Rosa di Gierico)
CLA. H.R.	*Anemone angulosa*	Blue Anemone	(Ranunculus tridentatus or Erba della Trinita)
CLA.	*Antirrhinum majus*	Snapdragon	(Antirrino)
CLA.	*Aster* spp.	Michaelmas Daisy, etc.	(Astro, Asterisco, Asteroide)
CLA.	*Campanula pyramidalis Rapunculus, etc*	Chimney Bellflower, Rampion, etc.	(Campanelle Piramidale, Rapunculus Hortensis and ten other varieties)
CLA.	*Canarina campanulata*	Canary Island Bellflower	(Campanula Canariensis Regia colore flammeo)
CLA. H.R.	*Canna indica*	Canna or Indian Shot plant	(Cannacoro)
CLA.	*Celosia cristata*	Cockscomb	(Amaranto Cristato)
CLA.	*Celosia cristata pyramidalis*	Red and Yellow Cockscomb	(Amaranto Cristato variegato)
CLA.	*Centaurea cyanus moschata alba suaveolens*	Cornflower, White and Yellow Sweet Sultans	(Ciano or Giacea and other varieties)
CLA.	*Cephalanthera ensifolia?*	White Helleborine	(Elleborine fiore albo)
CLA.	*Dictamnus albus*	Dittany, Fraxinella, or Burning Bush	(Frassinella)
CLA.	*Digitalis* spp.	Foxglove	(Digitale and twenty-one varieties)
CLA. H.R.	*Dracocephalum moldavica*	Moldavian Balm	(Moldavica Americana or Digetalis Americana Purpurea)
CLA.	*Eranthis hyemalis*	Winter Aconite	(Aconito unifoglio giallo tuberoso, flowers midwinter)
H.R.	*Erythronium dens-canis*	Dog's-Tooth Violet	(Dens Canis)
CLA.	*Galanthus nivalis*	Snowdrop	(Narciso Leucojo or Viola bulbosa volgare)
H.R.	*Gentiana verna?*	Blue Gentian	(Gentiana Alpina)
CLA.	*Gladiolus*	Gladiolus	(Gladiolo, twelve varieties including African)

* CLA. indicates flowers mentioned by Clarici, H.R. those from the Hortus Romanus. Old Italian names from these sources are given at the end in brackets.

	LATIN NAME	ENGLISH NAME	OLD ITALIAN NAME
CLA.	*Helianthus annuus et tuberosus*	Sunflower and Jerusalem Artichoke	(Corona del Sole or Girasole and Artichioco sotteraneo)
H.R.	*Heliotropium peruvianum*	Heliotrope or Cherry Pie	(Heliotrope Majus or Americana)
CLA.	*Helleborus niger*	Hellebore, Christmas Rose	(Elleboro nero)
CLA.	*Hymenocallis speciosa?*		(Atamusco or Giglionarciso delle Isole Vergine)
CLA.	*Impatiens balsamina*	Balsam	(Balsamina Bell'uomo)
H.R.	*Leonotis leonorus*	Lion's Ear	(Leonuro)
CLA.	*Leucojum aestivum*	Summer Snowflake	(Narciso Leucojo or Viola bulbosa di Primavera)
CLA. H.R.	*Mirabilis jalapa*	Marvel of Peru	(Jalapa Gelsomino della Notte or Meraviglia di Peru)
H.R.	*Monarda didyma*	Sweet Bergamot	(Monarda puntata)
H.R.	*Nicotiniana tabacum?*	Tobacco Plant	(Nicotiniana)
CLA.	*Ophrys apifera, aranifera, muscifera*	Bee, Spider and Fly Orchis	(Ofride or Serapias vespa, ragno, mosca)
CLA.	*Orchidacea* spp.	Orchis including Man, Lady, Butterfly, etc	(Orchis Orchide, Satirione, Palma Christi, etc)
CLA. H.R.	*Pelargonium* spp.	Geraniums and Pelargoniums	(Geranio Africano many varieties)
CLA.	*Philadelphus coronarius* and *flore pleno*	Single and Double Syringa or Mock Orange	(Siringa semplice or doppio)
CLA. H.R.	*Polemonium caeruleum*	Jacob's Ladder or Greek Valerium	(Polemonio or Valeriana Greca or Cericaria Valerianoides)
CLA.	*Rosee* spp.	Cabbage, Italian, English, Variegated Eglantine and Damask Rose, etc.	(Rosa Centifoglia, Italiana d'Inghilterra, Variegata Eglantina Damascena and twenty-two other varieties)
CLA.	*Scabiosa* spp.	Scabious, Mournful Widow, Pincushion Flower	(Fiore della Vedova Scabiosa and other varieties)
CLA. H.R.	*Sisyrinchium* spp.	Satinflower or Rush Lily	(Sisyrinchiou)
CLA.	*Tagetes erecta*	African Marigold	(Garofoli d'India)
CLA.	*Xeranthemiem* spp.	Immortelle or Annual, Everlasting	(Xerantemo or Perpetuino colorito and other varieties)

* CLA. *indicates flowers mentioned by Clarici, H.R. those from the Hortus Romanus. Old Italian names from these sources are given at the end in brackets.*

Eighteenth-century shrubs, creepers and ornamental trees *

	LATIN NAME	ENGLISH NAME	OLD ITALIAN NAME
CLA.	*Citrus aurantium*	Orange	(Arancio, many varieties)
CLA.	*Citrus decumana*	Shaddock, Grapefruit, Pomelo	(Pompelmo occidentale or Saddoks)
CLA.	*Citrus* spp.	Lemon, Lime, Bergamot	(Limone Lumia Bergamotto and many varieties)
CLA.	*Convolvulus*	Convolvulus	(Convolvolo, many varieties)
CLA. H.R.	*Datura*	Thorn Apple or Trumpet Flower	(Stramonio or Datura)
CLA.	*Jasminum sambac flore pleno*	Large double white Jasmine Grand Duke of Tuscany	(Mugarino doppio, only in Garden of Grand Duke of Tuscany)

* *Also marked for source CLA. and H.R., and old Italain name given in brackets.*

Flowers of the Fifteenth and Sixteenth Centuries

189-203 WATERCOLOURS

The following flower paintings in watercolour were taken from an anonymous manuscript in the Corsini Library in Rome. Although the manuscript probably dates from the eighteenth century, the flowers shown in it are of very simple types, often the same as those grown in medieval and even ancient Roman gardens. All of the flowers reproduced here are, however, definitely mentioned in the *Hypnerotomachia* of Poliphilus at the end of the fifteenth century, either as growing in paterres or flowery meads. As few flower pictures of this period are available, it seems that the somewhat naïve rendering of the flowers in these pictures corresponds with those described in the *Hypnerotomachia*. In some cases the artist has taken considerable liberties with reality, for instance in the picture of a hyacinth it is shown with a lily bulb, the artist evidently having no idea of what a hyacinth bulb is like; the growth of the cyclamen from its bulb does not correspond to reality either.

189 Amaranth, also called velvet flower and Prince of Wales' Feather, *Celosia plumosa*

190 Anemone, or windflower, *Anemone coronaria*

191 Yellow asphodel, *Asphodeline lutea*

192 Lily of the Valley, *Convallaria majalis*

193 Cyclamen or sowbread, *Cyclamen europaeum*

194 Wild gladiolus or corn flag, *Gladiolus segetum*

L.at: *Hyssopus Satiuus vulgaris*

Lat: *Inula & Helenium*

195 Garden hyacinth, *Hyacinthus orientalis*

196 Hyssop, *Hyssopus officinalis*

197 Elecampane, *Inula helenium*

Lat *Pseudonardus femina* et *Lauendula*
Ital: *Spigo & Lauanda*
Gall *Lauande*

Narcisus iv Mathioli

Lat: *Melanthium* siue Git:

198 Lavender, *Lavendula spica*

199 Bunch-flowered narcissus, *Narcissus tazetta*

200 Love-in-the-Mist, *Nigella damascena*

Lat: *Abrotanum foemina*
Ital: *Abrotano femmina, Santolina et Cipres*

Primula ueris Siluarum Lobellij
Primula ueris : Herba Paralysis
Braves de cocu; Prime vere

201 Pyramidal orchid, *Orchis pyramidalis*

202 Lavender cotton, *Santolina chamaecyparissus*

203 Primrose, *Primula vulgaris*

204 Passion flower, *Passiflora edulis*

Flowers of the Seventeenth and Eighteenth Centuries

204-212 ENGRAVINGS

Two important books on horticulture were published in Rome during the first half of the seventeenth century. The first was Tobia Aldino's *Horti Farnesiani Rariores plantae Exactissime descriptae* of 1625, which was a list of the rare exotic plants grown in the Orti Farnesiani on the Palatine. The second was Padre G. B. Ferrari's *De Florum Cultura*, first published in 1633 in Latin, in 1638 in Italian. The first illustrations come from the first book, the rest are from Padre Ferrari's.

205 Cape starry iris, *Ferraria undulata*

206 Jersey Lily, *Amaryllis belladonna*

207 Hibiscus, *Hibiscus mutabilis*

208 Detail of hibiscus, *Hibiscus mutabilis*

209 American trumpet flower, *Bignonia species*

210 A yellow jasmine, *Jasminum odoratissimum*

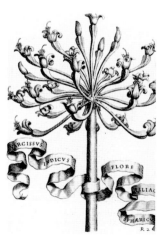

211 Probably Cape candelabra flower, *Brunsvigia species*

212 A posy of spring flowers, hyacinths, *Hyacinthus orientalis*, daffodils and jonquils, *Narcissus pseudo-narcissus* and *Narcissus jonquilla*, and double anemones, *Anemone coronaria pleno*

With the introduction of new exotic species, especially bulbs, flower painting became fashionable in Italy, especially groups of what can only be described as these 'collector's piece' type of flowers whose cultivation was much in vogue among the great Italian families in the first half of the seventeenth century. Foremost among Italian flower painters, or *fioranti*, as they were called, was Mario Nuzzi or Mario de' Fiori who lived between c. 1603 and 1673. Today nearly all the great Roman palaces contain pictures or mirrors painted with flowers by him.

213 MIRROR BY MARIO DE' FIORI
A painted mirror by Mario de' Fiori, in the picture gallery of Palazzo Colonna in Rome, showing climbing on the posts on the left blue morning glory (*Ipomoea*), nasturiums (*Tropaeolum*), in the top left-hand corner orange blossom, tulips and hyacinths as well as carnations and pheasant-eye narcissus (*Narcissus poeticus*), at the top hollyhocks (*Althaea*), just below this a garden iris (*Iris germanica*), a madonna lily (*Lilium candidum*), a scarlet turk's cap lily (*Lilium chalcedonium*), a spanish iris (*Iris xiphium*), larkspur (*Delphinium ajacis*), tuberose (*Polianthes tuberosa*), tulips, guelder rose (*Viburnum opulus sterile*). On the right centre an *Amaryllis belladonna*, and beside it on the left a red lily (either *Lilium tigrinum* or *L. speciosum*), below this anemones, a daffodil (*Narcissus pseudo-narcissus*), a yellow ranunculus, wallflower (*Cheiranthus cheiri*), periwinkle (*Vinca minor*), marigold (*Calendula officinalis*), more pink roses, anemones and narcissus, jasmine (*Jasminum officinale*), white roses, red and pink carnations and tuberose. In the extreme left-hand corner, the common daffodil, trumpet daffodil, double and semi-double anemones. Photo Gabinetto Nazionale Fotografico.

Bibliography

UNPUBLISHED SOURCES

CAETANI ARCHIVE I 105.488.106487 *Sanola di tutti i fiori in ordine Alfabetico che si Trovano nel Giardino l'anno* 1625. ANTONIO AVERLINO FILARETE *Trattato di Architettura*, Cod. Magliabecchianus Bib. Naz. Florence II, I, 140. P. LIGORIO *Sketchbook*, Vat. Lat. 3439. PALLADIUS *de Agricultura* (Petrarch's own copy) Va. 2193, fol. 156(1). RUSPOLI ARCHIVE Div. 1a. Armadio A. Prot 1. No. 2. Div. 2a. Armadio E. Prot 201. fasc 25. Armadio E. Prot 194. part 5.

SOURCES FOR ILLUSTRATIONS

T. ALDINO *Horti Farnesiani Rariores plantae Exactissime descriptae*, Rome, 1625. P. S. BARTOLI *Gli Antichi Sepolchri*, Rome, 1697. P. B. CLARICI *Istoria e Coltura delle Piante*, Venice, 1726. ANONYMOUS *Corsiniana Plantarium et Stirpium*. G. BOCCACCIO *Decamerone*, Venice, 1552. P. BRILL *Trophies of Marius*, Gabinetto Nazionale delle Stampe, Sc. R.I.128533. F. COLONNA *Hypnerotomachia Poliphili*, Venice, 1499. S. DU PÉRAC *Ninfeo della Vigna di Papa Giulio*, Gabinetto Nazionale delle Stampe, Sc. XXIV FN41135. G. B. FALDA *Li Giardini di Roma*, Rome, 1683? G. B. FERRARI *Flora overo Cultura di Fiori distinto in Quattro Libri*, Rome, 1638. J. LAURUS *Roma Vetus et Nuova*, Rome, 1614. P. LIGORIO *Forum Praenestinum*, Vat. Lat. 119A. D. LUCCHESE *Delizie della Villa di Castellazzo*, Milan, 1743. J. MORIN *Il ninfeo della Caffarella*, Gabinetto Nazionale delle Stampe, Sc. XXXV Inv. 43968. G. DE ROSSI Part I. *Le Fontane di Roma*. Disegnate e Intagliate da G. B. Falda. Part 2. *Le Fontane di Frascati*. Dis. e Int. G. B. Falda. Part 3. *Le Fontane ne' Giardini di Roma*. Dis. e Int. G. Venturini. Part 4. *Le Fontane del Giardino Estense in Tivoli*. Dis. e Int. G. Venturini, Rome, 1675-91. H. VAN SCHOEL *Giardini del Belvedere in Roma 1579*, Gabinetto Nazionale delle Stampe. B. PERUZZI *Pianta di un giardino con porticato*, Ufizzi Disegno 580A. E. TORMO *Los Disenos Antigualhasque vu Francisco de Hollanda*, Graz 1936.

SOURCES FOR PLANTS GROWN IN ITALIAN GARDENS

T. ALDINO *Horti Farnesiani Rariores plantae Exactissime descriptae*, Rome, 1625. ANONYMOUS *Corsiniana Plantarium et Stirpium*. C. BAUHIN *P. A. Matthioli Opera, Commentarii in VI Libros Pedacii Discorididis Anazarbei de Medica materia*, Basle, 1674. G. BAZIN *A Gallery of Flowers*, London, 1960. P. B. CLARICI, *Istoria e Cultura delle Piante*, Venice, 1726. O. COMES *Illustrazione delle piante rappresentate nei dipinti Pompeiani*, Naples, 1879. M. A. GABRIEL *Livia's Garden Room at Prima Porta*, New York, 1953. G. B. FERRARI *Flora overo Cultura di Fiori distinto in Quattro Libri*, Rome, 1638. P. GRIMAL *Les Jardins Romains à la Fin de la République et aux deux primiers siècles de l'Empire*, Paris, 1943. V. MANNUCCI *Trattato del Fiore e del Frutto*, Perugia, 1605. THOMAS MAUVE *The Complete Gardener*, London, 1827. N. MARTELLI *Hortus Romanus*, Rome, 1778. P. A. MATTIOLI *Il Discoride*, Venice, 1551. P. MISCIATELLI 'Antiche Ville Senese' (in *La Diana, Rassegna d'Arte e Vita Senese*), Siena. J. PITON, *Ortulus Praticus Botanicus*, Rome, 1737. SOCIETÀ AGRARIA DI BOLOGNA *Pier de' Crescenzi Studi e Documenti*, Bologna, 1933. V. SPINAZZOLA *Pompei alla Luce degli Scavi Nuovi*, Rome, 1953.

GENERAL ITALY

J. BURCKHARDT *La Civiltà del Rinascimento in Italia*, Florence, 1911. J. CARTWRIGHT *Italian Gardens of the Renaissance*, London, 1914. L. DAMI *Giardini d'Italia*, Milan, 1924. M. L. GOTHEIN *A History of Garden Art*, London, 1928. G. GROMORT *Jardins d'Italie*, Paris, 1931. C. LATHAM *Gardens of Italy*, London, 1905. R. W. KENNEDY *The Renaissance Painter's Garden*, New York, 1948. A. LE BLOND *The Gardens of Old Italy and How to Visit Them*, London, 1912. E. MARCH PHILLIPPS AND A. T. BOLTON *The Gardens of Italy*, London, 1919. R. STANDISH NICHOLS *Italian Pleasure Gardens*, New York, 1928. U. OJETTI *Catalogo della Mostra del Giardino Italiano*, Florence, 1931. L. PASTOR *The History of the Popes from the Close of the Middle Ages*, London, 1923-53. M. RECCHI 'La Villa e il Giardino nel concetto della

Bibliography

Rinascenza' in *Critica d'Arte*, Vol. 11, Florence, 1937. C. RICCI *Architettura Barocca in Italia*, Bergamo, 1912. J. C. SHEPHERD AND G. A. JELLICOE *Italian Gardens of the Renaissance*, London, 1925 and 1953. S. SITWELL *Cupid and the Jacaranda*, London, 1953. H. INIGO TRIGGS *The Art of Garden Design in Italy*, London, 1906. G. VASARI *Le Vite dei più eccellenti pittori, scultori e architetti*, Milan, 1807. E. WHARTON *Italian Villas and their Gardens*, New York, 1904. J. ADDINGTON SYMONDS *Renaissance in Italy*, London, 1904. G. TOFFANIN *Il Cinquecento*, Milan, 1929. L. VANVITELLI *Dichiarazione dei Disegni del Reale Palazzo de Caserta*, Naples, 1756.

GENERAL OUTSIDE ITALY

R. BLOMFIELD *The Formal Garden in England*, London, 1901. H. F. CLARK *The English Landscape Garden*, London, 1948. K. CLARK *Landscape into Art*, London, 1949. M. FOUQUIER *De l'Art des Jardins du XV au XX Siècle*, Paris, 1911. E. DE GANAY *Les Jardins de France*, Paris, 1949. G. GROMORT *L'Art des Jardins*, Paris, 1934. M. HADFIELD 'John James and the Formal Garden in England', in *The Connoisseur*, London, 1959. L. HAUTECOEUR *Les Jardins des Dieux et des Hommes*, Paris, 1959. M. JOURDAIN *The Work of William Kent*, London, 1948. E. LO GATTO *Gli Artisti Italiani in Russia*, Vol. 1. 'Gli architetti a Mosca e nelle province'. Vol. 2. 'Gli architetti del secolo XVIII a Pietroburgo e nelle tenute imperiale', Rome, 1934. J. LEES MILNE *Tudor Renaissance*, London, 1951. N. PEVSNER *An Outline of European Architecture*, London, 1953. F. PRIETO-MORENO *Los Jardines de Granada*, Madrid, 1952. G. QUARENGHI *Fabbriche e disegni di Giacomo Quarenghi illustrato dal Cavaliere Giulio suo figlio*, Mantua, 1844. E. SINGLETON *The Shakespear Garden*, New York, 1922. D. STROUD *Capability Brown*, London, 1950. M. TATSIU *Gardens of Japan*, Tokio, 1935. TETSURO YOSHIDA *Gardens of Japan*, New York, 1957. G. TAYLOR *Old London Gardens*, London, 1953. C. M. VILLIERS-STUART *Gardens of the great Mughals*, London, 1913. C. M. VILLIERS-STUART *Spanish Gardens*, London, 1929. VREDEMAN DE VRIES *Hortorium Viridariarumque elegantes et multiplices formae ad architectonicae artis normam*, Antwerp, 1583.

TRAVELLERS

J. ADDISON *Remarks on Several Parts of Italy etc. In the years of 1701, 1702, 1703*, London, 1726. LEANDRO ALBERTI *Descrittione di tutta Italia*, p. 265, Bologna, 1550. PRÉSIDENT DE BROSSES *Lettres familières sur l'Italie*, Paris, 1931. T. CORYAT *Crudities*, London, 1611. J. EVELYN *Diary*, ed. E. S. De Beer, Oxford, 1955. W. GOETHE *Goethe's travel in Italy, together with his second residence in Rome and fragments on Italy*, London, 1892. M. DE MONTAIGNE *Essais*, Paris, 1878. M. DE MONTAIGNE *Journal de Voyage*, Paris, 1909. P. B. SHELLEY *Letters and Essays*, London, 1887.

ROMAN GARDENS

G. CARRETONE 'Costruzioni sotto l'angolo sud occidentale della Domus Flavia', in *Notizie degli Scavi*, Rome, 1949. CATO *de Agri Cultura* or *De Re Rustica*, Ed. Loeb, London, 1934. CICERO *Letters to his Friends*, Ed. Loeb, London, 1927. O. COMES 'Illustrazione delle piante rappresentate nei dipinti Pompeiani', in *Pompei e la regione sotterrata del Vesuvio*, Naples, 1879. M. A. GABRIEL *Livia's Garden Room at Prima Porta*, New York, 1953. P. GRIMAL *Les Jardins Romains à la fin de la République et aux deux premiers siècles de l'Empire*, Paris, 1943. P. GRIMAL 'A Propos des "Bains de Livie" au Palatin', in *Mélanges d'Architecture et d'Histoire*, Paris, 1937. G. HIGHET *Poets in a Landscape*, London, 1959. G. JACOBI *I Ritrovamenti dell' Antro cosidetto 'di Tiberio' a Sperlonga*, Rome, 1958. G. JENNISON *Animals for Show and Pleasure in Ancient Rome*, Manchester, 1937. G. LUGLI 'L'Arte dei Giardini presso i Romani', *Boll. dell' Associazione d'architettura romana*, Rome, 1918. PALLADIUS *L'Agricultura*, Leipzig, 1898. PLINY *Letters*, Ed. Loeb, London, 1915. PLINY *Natural History*, Ed. Loeb, London, 1938. V. SPINAZZOLA, *Pompei alla Luce degli Scavi Nuovi*, Rome, 1953. SUETONIUS *The Twelve Caesars*, London, 1958. C. TACITUS *The Annals of Imperial Rome*, London, 1956. H. TANSER *The Villas of Pliny the Younger*, New York, 1924. VARRO *Rerum Rusticarum* or *De Re Rustica*, Ed. Loeb, London, 1934. VITRUVIUS *On Architecture*, Ed. Loeb, London, 1931. R. VIGHI *Villa Adriana e il Suo Canopo*, Rome, 1957.

MEDIEVAL AND EARLY HUMANIST GARDENS

G. AGNELLO *L'Architettura Sveva in Sicilia*, Rome, 1935. L. B. ALBERTI *Dell' Architettura*, Venice, 1565. M. AMARI *Storia dei Mussulmani in Sicilia*, Florence, 1872. G. BOCCACCIO *Decamerone*, Venice, 1552. G. BOCCACCIO *Visione Amorosa*, Florence, 1827. M. BORSA *La Caccia Nel Milanese*, Milan, 1924. F. COLONNA *Hypnerotomachia Poliphili*, Venice, 1499. PIETRO DE' CRESCENZII *Trattato dell' Agricultura*, Florence, 1605. C. DIEHL *Palerme et Syracuse*, Paris, 1901. FRANCESCO DI GIORGIO MARTINI *Trattato di Architettura Civile e Militare*, Ed. C. Promis, Turin, 1841. M.

LAZZARONE AND A MUNOZ *Filarete Scultore e Architetto*, Rome, 1908. C. MAGENTA *I Visconti e gli Sforza nel Castello di Pavia*, Milan, 1883. P. DE NOLHAC 'Petrarch et son Jardin' in *Giorn. Stor. Lett. Italiano*, Turin, 1887. W. VON OETTINGEN *Antonio Averlino Filaretes Tractat Uber die Baukunst*, Vienna, 1890. R. PAPINI *Francesco di Giorgio Architetto*, Florence, 1946. C. POPELIN *Le Songe de Poliphile*, Paris, 1892. G. V. SODERINI *Trattato della Cultura degli orti e dei giardini*, Bologna, 1892. F. MALAGUZZI VALERI *La Corte di Lodovico il Moro*, Milan, 1929. F. WITTGENS 'Un ciclo di affreschi Lombarde del Quattrocento' in *Dedalo*, Feb. 1933 Anno XIII fasc. II.

TUSCAN GARDENS

ARCHIVIO DI STATO DI FIRENZE, *Mostra Documentaria e Iconografica di Palazzo Pitti e Giardino di Boboli*, Florence, 1960. BACCIO BANDINELLI *Raccolta di Lettere sulla Pittura*, Ed. Bottari-Ticozzi, Rome, 1757. L. EINSTEIN *The Tuscan Garden*, London, 1927. G. GUICCIARDINI CORSI SALVIATI *La Villa Corsi a Sesto*, Florence, 1937. A. JAHN-RUSCONI *Le Ville Medicee*, Rome, 1938. C. G. LENSI ORLANDI CARDINI *Le Ville di Firenze*, Florence, 1954. Y. MCGUIRE *The Women of the Medici*, New York, 1928. P. MISCIA-TELLI 'Antiche Ville Senese', in *La Diana, Rassenga d'Arte e Vita Senese*, Siena. W. ROSCOE *Life of Lorenzo de' Medici*, London, 1902. G. F. YOUNG *The Medici*, London, 1924.

ROMAN RENAISSANCE GARDENS

J. S. ACKERMAN *The Cortile del Belvedere*, Vatican, 1954. V. ALDROVANDI *Di tutte le statue antiche per tutta Roma in diverse luoghi a case particolari si veggero*, Venice, 1558. T. ASHBY 'The Bodleian MS of Pirro Ligorio', in *Journal of Roman Studies*, Vol. IX, 1919. M. BAFILE *Il Giardino de Villa Madama*, Rome, 1942. C. BANDINI *Roma nel Settecento*, Rome, 1930. C. BANDINI *La Galanteria nel Gran Mondo di Roma nel settecento*, Rome, 1930. D. BARRIÈRE *Villa Pamphilia*, Rome, 1648. P. S. BARTOLI *Gli Antichi Sepolcri*, Rome, 1697. A. BRUSCHI, L. BENEVOTO, F. FASOLO, P PORTOGHESI, G. ZANDER 'Bomarzo' *Quaderni dell' Instituto di Storia di Architettura*, Rome, 1955. G. BRUSA CALUPI *Monografia Storica della Contea di Pitigliano*, Florence, 1906. L. CALLARI *Le Ville di Roma*, Rome, 1943. V. CIAN *Un Illustre Nunzio Ponteficio del Rinascimento B. Castiglione*, Vatican, 1951. C. D'ONOFRIO *Le Fontane di Roma*, Rome, 1957. G. FABRIZIANO *I Conti Aldobrandeschi e Orsini di Pitigliano*, Pitigliano, 1897. A. FERRUZZI *Soriano nel Cimino*, Viterbo, 1900. C. FRANCK *Die Barock-villen in Frascati*, Munich, 1956. D. GNOLI *Roma de Leo X*, Milan, 1938. U. GNOLI 'Ceramiche Romane del Cinquecento', in *Dedalus*, Rome, August 1921. R. LEFEVRE *Villa Madama in Rome*, Rome, 1951. G. K. LOUKOMSKI *Le Ville del Vignola nei dintorni di Roma (Vie d'Italia)*, Milan, 1935. T. MAGNUSON *Studies in Roman Quattrocento Architecture*, Figura Series 9. Ed. Institute of Art History, Uppsala University, Rome; Stockholm, 1958. G. MANILLI *Villa Borghese*, Rome, 1650. P. LIGORIO *Ichonographia Villae Tiburtinae Hadriani Caesario*, Rome, 1751. G. MARCHETTI LONGHI *I Boveschi e gli Orsini*, Rome, 1960. L. MONTALTO *Un mecenate in Roma barocca*, Florence, 1955. D. MONTELATICI *Villa Borghese*, Rome, 1700. P. DE NOLHAC *La Bibliothèque de Fulvio Orsini*, Paris, 1887. P. DE NOLHAC 'Pirro Ligorio', in *Mélanges Renier*, Paris, 1887. P. DE NOLHAC *Les Peintres Français en Italie*, Paris, 1934. F. PARISI *Istruzione per la gioventù* (for letter to Duke of Modena about Villa d'Este), Rome, 1781. A. DEL RE *Antichità Tiburtine*, Rome, 1611. A. SCHIAVO *Villa Doria Pamphilj*, Milan, 1942. S. SERLIO, *Tutte le Opere d'Architettura di Sebastiano Serlio Bolognese*, Venice, 1584.

GARDENS OF THE MARCHE AND THE VENETO

G. BONNARELLI 'I Giardini all' Italiana nelle Marche', in *Rassegna Marchigiana*, Ancona, 1931. J. DENNISTOUN *Memoirs of the Dukes of Urbino*, London, 1909. G. FASOLO *Le Ville del Vicentino*, Vicenza, 1929. GEORG GRONAU *Documenti artistici urbinati*, Florence, 1936? G. MAZZOTTI *Le Ville Venete*, Treviso, 1953. A. PALLADIO *I Quattro Libri di Architettura*, Venice, 1581. B. PAZAK *Die Villa Imperiale in Pesaro*, Leipzig, 1908. M. SANUDO *L'Itinerario per la Terraferma Veneziana nell' 1483*, Ed. Rawdon Brown, Padua, 1849. V. SCAMOZZI *L'Idea dell' Architettura Universale*, Venice, 1539. G. SILVESTRI *La Valpolicella*, Verona, 1950. Ed. Giulio Vaccai, *Pesaro*, Bergamo, 1909.

THE GARDENS OF NORTHERN ITALY

G. BASCAPÈ *Mostra Storica dei Giardini di Lombardia*, Milan, 1959. G. CHEVELLAY *Ville Piemontesi del XVII Secolo*, Turin, 1912. COMITATO PER LE ONORANZE A F. JUVARA, *F. Juvara*, Milan, 1937. S. DAVARI *I palazzi dei Gonzaga in Marmirolo*, Mantua, 1890. DIMORI GENOVESI, Ed. L. Alfieri, Milan, 1956. G. B. INTRA 'Il palazzo del Tè e il bosco della fontana presso Mantova', *Arch. Stor. Lom.*, 1887. G. PACCHIONI 'La Villa Favorita e l'architetto Niccolò Sebregondi', in *Arte*, Milan, 1917.

Plans

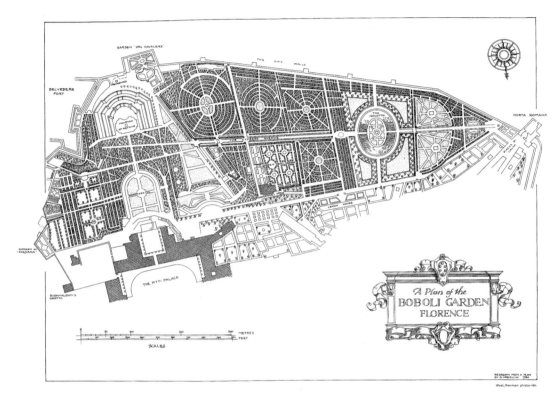

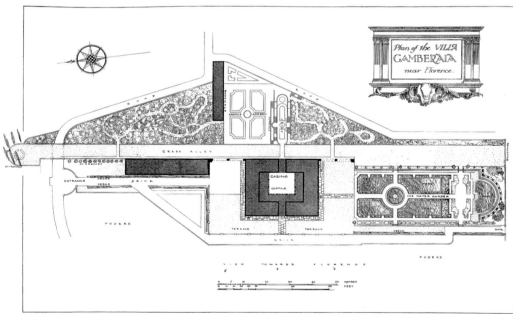

It has been considered useful to add a few images of the gardens' plans and sections, fundamental for a full comprehension of the gardens themselves, taken from books published in the first half of the 20th century and which were surely familiar to Georgina Masson. Drawn by architects for architects, they give the deserved relevance to the projections.

214 BOBOLI GARDEN, FLORENCE
Plan, from I. Triggs, The Art of Garden Design in Italy, London 1906, pl. 29.

215 VILLA GAMBERAIA, SETTIGNANO
Plan, from I. Triggs, The Art of Garden Design in Italy, London 1906, pl. 47.

216 VILLA PIA, VATICAN GARDEN
Plan and section, from I. Triggs, The Art of Garden Design in Italy, London 1906, pl. 68.

346

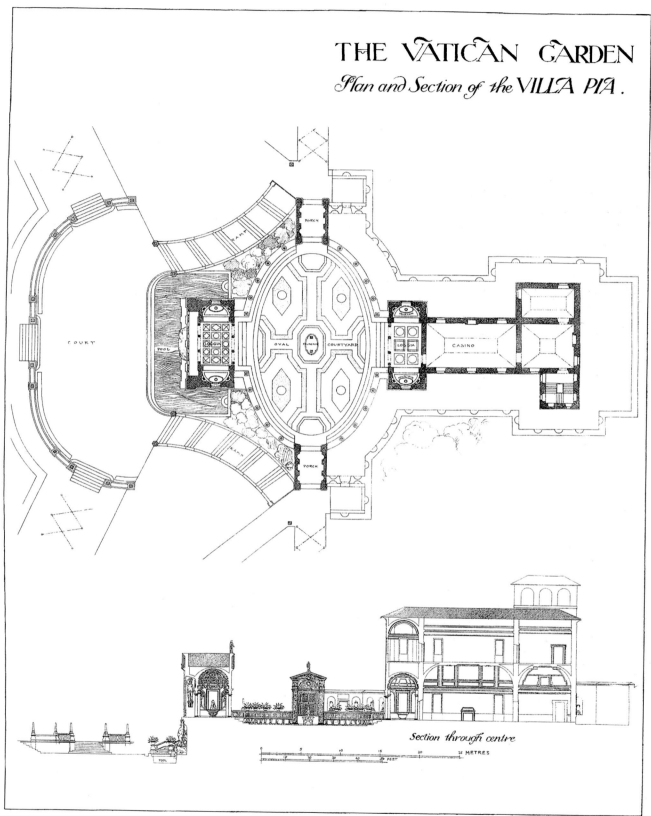

THE VATICAN GARDEN
Plan and Section of the VILLA PIA.

COURT

POOL

RAMP

PORCH

LOGGIA

OVAL FOUNTAIN COURTYARD

LOGGIA

CASINO

RAMP

PORCH

Section through centre

METRES

FEET

POOL

West, Newman photo-lith.

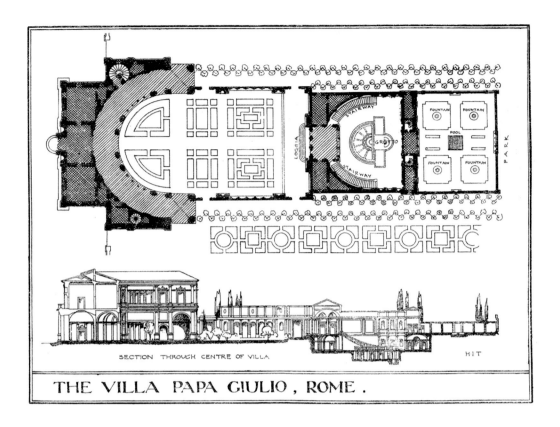

THE VILLA PAPA GIULIO, ROME.

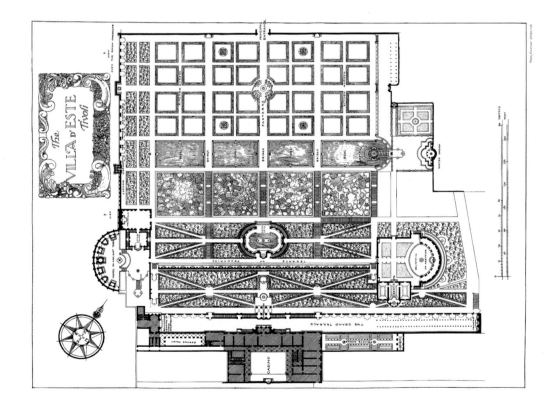

217 VILLA PAPA GIULIO, ROME
Plan and section, from I. Triggs, The Art
of Garden Design in Italy, *London 1906,
p. 32.*

218 VILLA D'ESTE, TIVOLI
Plan, from I. Triggs, The Art of Garden
Design in Italy, *London 1906, pl. 113.*

219 PALACE OF CAPRAROLA
Plan and section, from I. Triggs, The Art
of Garden Design in Italy, *London 1906,
p. 30.*

220 VILLA LANTE, BAGNAIA
Plan and section, from I. Triggs, The Art
of Garden Design in Italy, *London 1906,
pl. 118.*

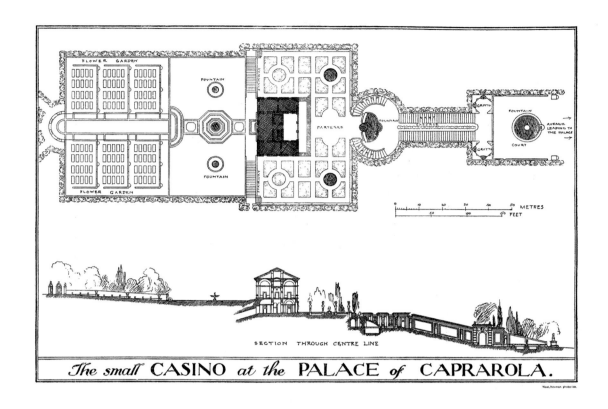

SECTION THROUGH CENTRE LINE

The small CASINO *at the* PALACE *of* CAPRAROLA.

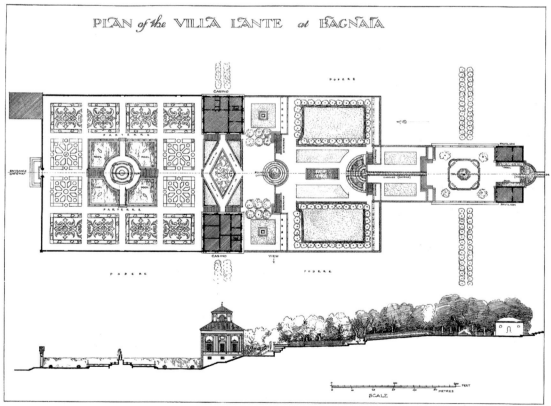

PLAN *of the* VILLA LANTE *at* BAGNAIA

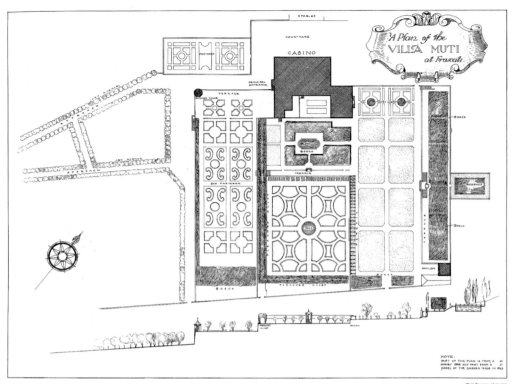

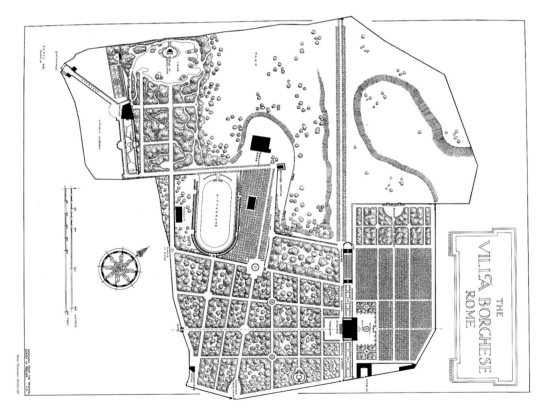

221 VILLA MUTI
Plan and section, from I. Triggs, The Art of
Garden Design in Italy, *London 1906, pl.
108.*

222 VILLA BORGHESE, ROME
Plan, from I. Triggs, The Art of Garden
Design in Italy, *London 1906, p. 75.*

223 VILLA PAMPHILJ, ROME
Plan, from I. Triggs, The Art of Garden
Design in Italy, *London 1906, pl. 80.*

224 PALAZZO DORIA, GENOA
Plan and section, from I. Triggs, The Art
of Garden Design in Italy, *London 1906,
p. 17.*

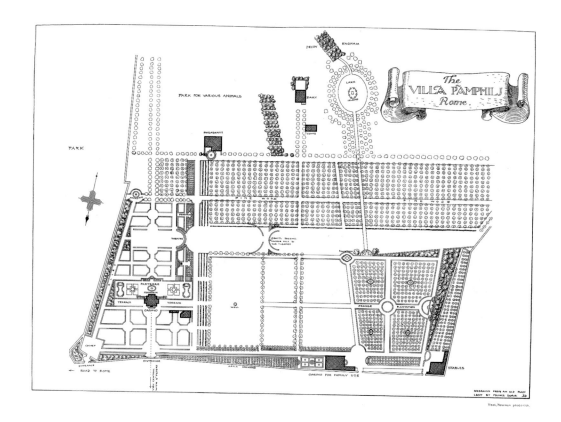

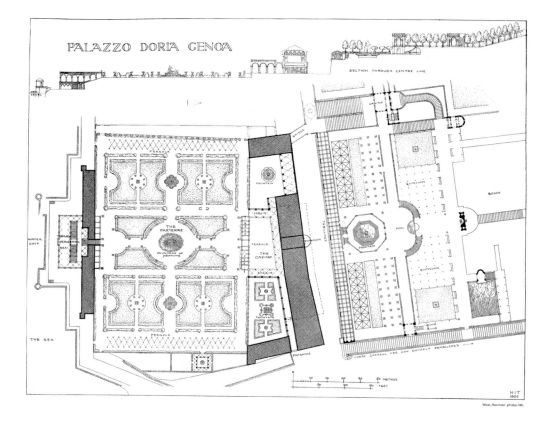

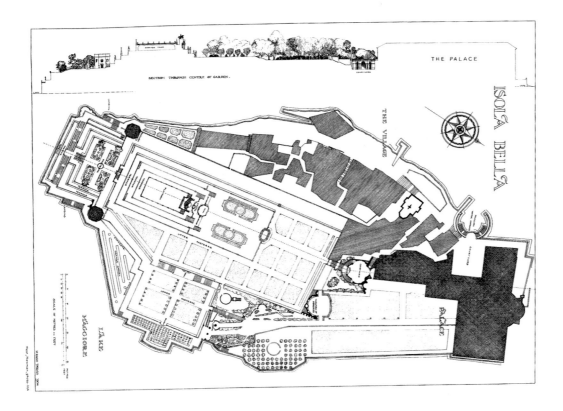

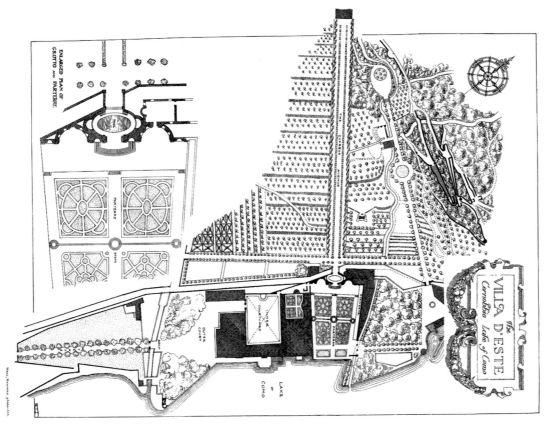

225 ISOLA BELLA, LAKE MAGGIORE
Plan and section, from I. Triggs, The Art
of Garden Design in Italy, *London
1906, pl.3.*

226 VILLA D'ESTE, CERNOBBIO
Plan, from I. Triggs, The Art of Garden
Design in Italy, *London 1906, pl. 8.*

227 VILLA CARLOTTA
Plan and section, from I. Triggs, The Art
of Garden Design in Italy, *London
1906, p. 11.*

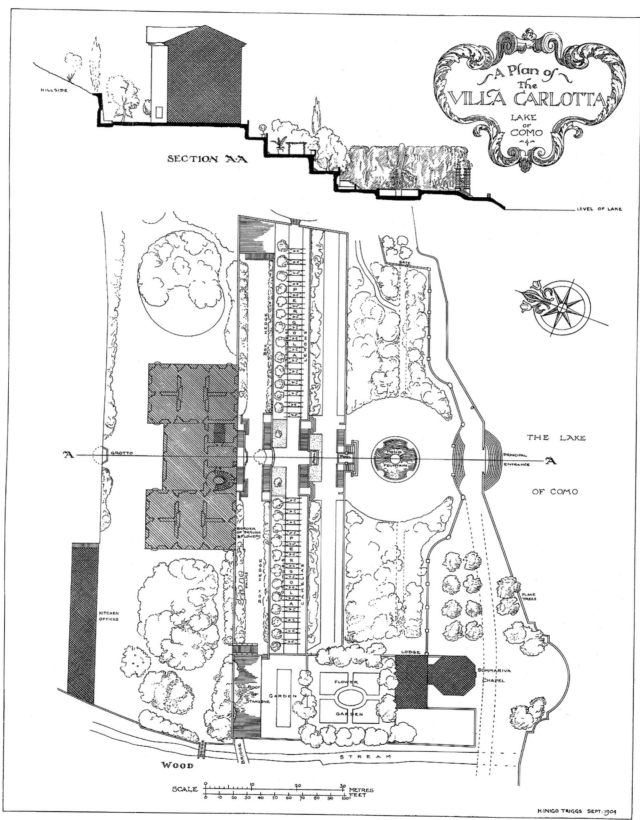

SECTION A·A

A Plan of
The
VILLA CARLOTTA
LAKE
OF
COMO
·4·

HILLSIDE

LEVEL OF LAKE

THE LAKE

OF COMO

GROTTO

PRINCIPAL
ENTRANCE

KITCHEN
OFFICES

BORDER OF SHRUBS & FLOWERS

BOX HEDGE

POND
FOUNTAIN

POOL

PLANE
TREES

LODGE

SOMMARIVA
CHAPEL

ROOF
STAIRCASE

FLOWER
GARDEN

GARDEN

GATE

WOOD

BRIDGE

STREAM

SCALE

METRES
FEET

H·INIGO TRIGGS SEPT: 1904

West, Newman photo-lith.

West, Newman photo-lith.

228 CASERTA, PALAZZO REALE
Plan, from I. Triggs, The Art of Garden
Design in Italy, *London 1906, pl. 132.*

Index of Places

Index of People

Page numbers in bold type refer to captions

Photo Credits

All black and white images are by Georgina Masson unless specified otherwise.

Francesca De Col Tana, pls. XXXVII, L, LIV, LV, LVI, LVII

Alex Ramsay, pls. III, IV, VIII, IX, X, XI, XXXIV, XXXV, XXXVI, XXXVIII, XXXVIX, XL, XLI, XLII, XLIII, XLIV, XLV, XLVI, XLVII, XLVIII, LII, LVIII

Agata Maja Zurkiewicz, pl. XLIX

All others colour plates courtesy of Antique Collectors' Club